AMERICAN
AND
JAPANESE
RELOCATION

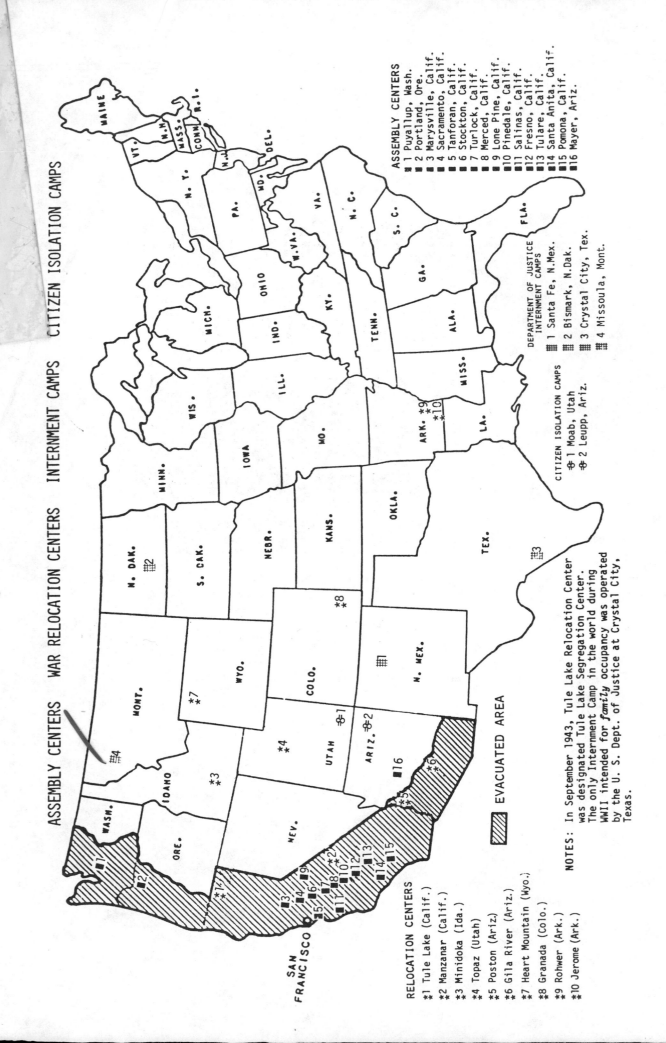

AMERICAN
AND
JAPANESE
RELOCATION
IN WORLD WAR II;
FACT, FICTION
& FALLACY

Introductory Remarks by Karl R. Bendetsen

LILLIAN BAKER

WEBB RESEARCH GROUP

Address all inquiries to the publisher: Webb Research Group
P.O. Box 314
Medford, OR 97501

Printed in the U.S.A.

Books on this subject by Lillian Baker:

The Concentration Camp Conspiracy: A Second Pearl Harbor 1981. (out-of-print) AFHA Publications

Redress & Reparations Demands by Japanese Americans 1984. Expanded ed. 1989. 0-936738-14-6 $9.95 (shipping $1.00)*

Dishonoring America; The Collective Guilt of American Japanese 1988. 0-936738-27-8 $8.95 (shipping $1.00)*

American and Japanese Relocation in World War II; Fact, Fiction and Fallacy 1990. 0-936738-34-0 $26.50 (shipping $3.00)*

*Published by Webb Research Group

Photographs credited to the National Archives were funded with a special grant to Lillian Baker from The Hoover Institution on War, Revolution and Peace, Standord University, and are a part of the Lillian Baker Collection in their Archives to be accessible to future historians and researchers.

Library of Congress Cataloging in Publication

Baker, Lillian.
   American and Japanese relocation in World War II : fact, fiction, and fallacy / Lillian Baker.
     p.   cm.
  Bibliography: p.
  Includes index.
  OSBM 0-936738-34-0
    1. Japanese-Americans—Evacuation and relocation, 1942-1945. I. Title.
D769.8.A6B39 1989
940.53′1503956073—dc20   89-8868
                                         CIP

Dedication

To my immigrant parents who gave me
the birthright of freedom,
and to the patriots of
World War II who fought and died
to preserve it.

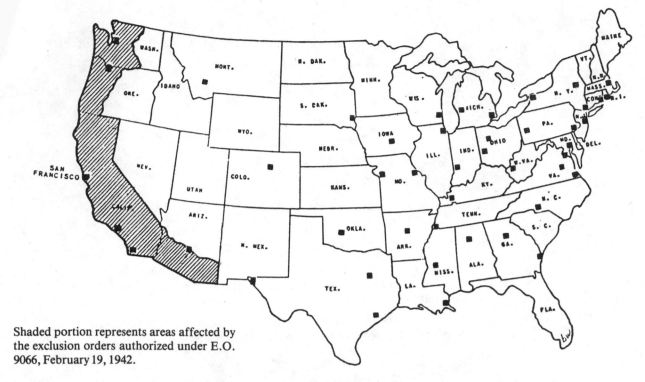

Shaded portion represents areas affected by
the exclusion orders authorized under E.O.
9066, February 19, 1942.

Alien Enemies Apprehended by February 18, 1942

(Before Executive Order 9066 Was Signed)

Identified by nationality and city and state where apprehended.

	Germans	Japanese	Italians	Totals		Germans	Japanese	Italians	Totals
Albany, NY	20	1	5	26	Memphis, Tenn.	8	0	1	9
Atlanta, GA.	7	1	0	8	Miami, Fla.	28	9	1	38
Baltimore, Md.	31	1	33	65	Milwaukee, Wisc.	83	0	1	84
Birmingham, Ala.	10	1	1	12	Newark, NJ	86	24	2	112
Boston, Mass.	30	4	7	41	New Haven, Conn.	26	9	1	36
Buffalo, NY	20	1	1	22	New Orleans, La.	18	8	4	30
Butte, Mont.	12	7	0	19	New York City, NY	212	275	86	573
Charlotte, NC	2	0	0	2	Norfolk, Va.	2	13	2	17
Chicago, Ill.	75	4	1	80	Oklahoma City, Okla.	7	0	1	8
Cincinnati, Ohio	21	0	12	33	Philadelphia, Penn.	62	2	9	73
Cleveland, Ohio	16	5	4	27	Phoenix, Ariz.	18	16	11	45
Dallas, Tex.	18	9	0	27	Pittsburgh, Penn.	10	0	3	13
Denver, Colo.	4	1	0	5	Portland, Oreg.	35	39	1	75
Des Moines, Iowa	12	0	0	12	Providence, R.I.	5	0	0	5
Detroit, Mich.	30	0	3	43	Richmond, Va.	11	18	4	33
El Paso, Tex.	30	0	0	15	St. Louis, Mo.	24	1	1	26
Grand Rapids, Mich.	11	0	0	11	San Diego, Calif.	21	92	2	115
Honolulu, Terr. Hawaii	79	389	11	479	San Francisco, Calif.	79	177	21	277
Houston, Tex.	27	9	2	38	San Juan, P.R.	11	1	2	14
Huntington, W.Va.	8	2	2	12	Savanah, Ga.	9	0	1	10
Indianapolis, Ind.	20	0	3	23	Seattle, Wa.	52	178	8	238
Jackson, Miss.	6	0	1	7	Sioux Falls, S.Dak.	3	0	0	3
Juneau, Terr. Alaska	2	7	0	9	Springfield, Ohio	4	0	0	4
Kansas City, Mo.	13	0	0	13	Washington, D.C.	12	8	4	24
Little Rock, Ark.	2	0	0	2					
Los Angeles, Calif.	78	890	15	983		1,396	2,209	267	3,872
Louisville, Ky.	10	1	0	11					

Table of Contents

KARL R. BENDETSEN
Photographed in his Washington, D.C.
office by Lillian Baker.

DILLON S. MYER
Photographed in his home near
Washington, D.C. by Lillian Baker.

KARL R. BENDETSEN (left) spent his adult life dedicated to serving the United States in times of war and peace. Former Under Secretary of the Army and Special Assistant to the Secretary of State, Colonel Bendetsen also helped organize the Provost Marshal's Office, the Military Police, and the School of Military Government. Colonel Bendetsen was also an Assistant Chief of Staff involved in the planning for the invasion of Normandy in 1944. In some circles, unfortunately, he has been mislabeled "the architect of the evacuation" when in reality he was *assigned* the duty during which time he worked closely with John J. McCloy, the highly respected Assistant Secretary of War. Colonel Bendetsen's activities and involvement with the relocation and with the assembly centers is covered in this book. Mr. Bendetsen died in May 1989. Mr. McCloy died in March 1989.

DILLON S. MYER (right) became Director of the War Relocation Authority when the WRA was just three months old. Myer had spent twenty-eight years of productive service in various agricultural fields. His choice for the WRA leadership had in mind that the relocation centers were all huge agricultural, food-growing enterprises. His leadership was demonstrated as he conquered turbulent episodes mixed with great achievements during his four year tenure. When the War Relocation Authority was eventually closed (1946) he was saluted for his "conscientious sense of trusteeship toward the evacuees" which had seen more than 50,000 evacuees leave the WRA centers for employment and settlement in the states away from the west coast. After the war Myer was Commissioner of the Federal Public Housing Administration, President of the Institute of Inter-American Affairs then as Commissioner of the Bureau of Indian Affairs. After leaving government service, Dillon S. Myer accepted appointments with the Group Health Association in Washington, D.C., a United Nations position in Venezuela and taught at University of Pittsburgh and was a consultant with the Brookings Institution. He died October 21, 1982.

Introductory Remarks
Karl R. Bendetsen

It gives me great pleasure and satisfaction to write this introduction to an excellently researched and honestly written publication involving the intelligence reports and its influence on the exclusion of persons of Japanese descent from the "red zones" of our Pacific West Coast States.

I first became acquainted with one of this book's co-authors, Mrs. Lillian Baker, by telephone when she called to urge me to give personal testimony before the Commission on Wartime Relocation holding hearings in Washington, D.C. during July 1981. I was informed that neither my *written testimony* nor that of former Assistant Secretary of War, Hon. John J. McCloy, had been included for distribution by the Commission in the *Press Packs*.

Acting upon this information, both Mr. McCloy and I requested personal appearances to give full, truthful accounting of what actually transpired during that historic period of World War II.

After telephone communication and letters, I eventually met Mrs. Baker who came to my office during one of her many visits to Washington, D.C., to continue her scholarly research into the National Archives and other files containing documentation relative to the War Relocation Authority.

On one of these visits, she also interviewed the late Dillon S. Myer, Director of the War Relocation Authority, who was gravely concerned about the usage of the inappropriate and historically inaccurate term "concentration camp" in lieu of "relocation centers." I, too, share that concern and for this reason alone believe it important to set the record straight by using declassified documents rather than downright deceit and colorful emotion.

Mrs. Baker and I, plus other witnesses of highest integrity such as the Hon. John J. McCloy, were greeted with hisses and unprofessional behavior by those charged with conducting democratic hearings about this misunderstood issue. The pressures brought upon any witnesses who felt duty-bound to testify on behalf of those in government, whose untarnished reputations were about to be darkened by outright revision of historical events and by political overtones, was at the outset unbecoming of those whose responsibilities were to carry out an edict of investigation into constitutional government actions.

However, in spite of uncontrollable heckling and demonstrations unheard of in our usual legislative procedures, Mrs. Baker stood by her guns fortified with ammunition gained by intensive research. This research provided solid documentation for the government's justification in concurring with the Commander in Chief, President Franklin D. Roosevelt, in issuance of E.O.9066, Feb. 19, 1942. Indeed, when tested for constitutional correctness during wartime, our Supreme Court upheld this action by affirming it 6-3, *(Korematsu v U.S.,* Oct. 1944 Term).

Strengthening the Court's decision and the President's action, are the recently released documents pertaining to MAGIC and its effect that brought about this most highly misunderstood and propagandized action of World War II.

Joining Mrs. Baker who has already proven her credentials with regard to the evacuation, is Mr. David D. Lowman, acknowledged expert on MAGIC—the papers released by President Harry S. Truman during the Pearl Harbor investigations in 1946. Much more recently, Mr. Lowman was called upon to testify on these Japanese decoded messages which clearly involve a network of espionage and sabotage units comprised of both first and second generation Japanese residing on our West Coast prior to and following that "day of infamy" at Pearl Harbor.

The documents used throughout this much-needed work have never been used by the multitude of writers who presumably were searching diligently "into the records" in an effort to tell the full historical facts about what brought about the exclusion and how MAGIC affected the ultimate decision made by President Roosevelt and with the full cooperation of his closest military advisors.

Good fortune has brought Baker and Lowman together, for their research and documentation definitely brings the puzzling pieces together into a forthright and full picture of the events as they really were. There's no conjecture here. There's no interpretation of events by revisionist historians. There are no political motives involved; rather a feeling of responsible patriotism rather refreshing at the time when we will soon be celebrating the Bicentennial of our United States Constitution.

Historical honesty but with human understanding seems to be the underlying basis for this much-needed work. Facts, not emotion, guide the course of this narrative which in many cases will seem stranger than fiction.

As one who participated in the beginnings of the 1942 happenings involving the assembly of persons of Japanese descent prior to relocation centers, I applaud the efforts of these two authors/researchers for their dedication to their task taken upon themselves at personal costs in time, effort, personal committment and financial drain.

From the beginning, I have urged Mrs. Baker to continue her efforts and am truly pleased that this monumental work is the combined pursuits of two conscientious historians intent upon sharing the truth and destroying the myths.

Americans need to be re-educated on this subject but based on documentation and not fabled emotion.

Karl R. Bendetsen
August 15, 1986
Washington, D.C.

Update to Mr. Bendetsen's Remarks

The INTRODUCTORY REMARKS by Karl R. Bendetsen were written prior to the decision by Baker and Lowman to author separate books on the RELOCATION—the evacuation of certain persons from the West Coast early in World War II—and MAGIC, the pre-war and wartime intelligence captured from the Japanese. It was also written before Mr. Bendetsen's death in May 1989.

Because of the wide range required in writing on each subject, it was mutually agreed between Lillian Baker and David D. Lowman to work separately.

David Lowman was a career intelligence officer with the National Security Agency where he received numerous commendations and honors, including the Agency's highest award—the Exceptional Civilian Service Medal. He holds a B.A. degree from Stanford University and J.D. degree from George Washington University. Mr. Lowman retired in 1976 as a Special Assistant to the Director of the National Security Agency. Later, he served as a consultant on the release of World War II intelligence, and is the author of a number of historical articles based on declassified intelligence from World War II, and was an expert witness in the Federal Courts on this subject for the United States Department of Justice.

No episode in World War II history can be accurately portrayed without some knowledge of MAGIC and World War II intelligence. This statement is extraordinarily appropriate in any book related to the relocation of persons of Japanese descent from the military sensitive areas located on the West Coast or "Western Sea Frontier" of the United States.

MAGIC and the intelligence reports dating from pre-Pearl Harbor and up to the issuance of the controversial Executive Order 9066, February 19, 1942, are facts bonded as closely as Siamese twins. Neither MAGIC nor the Executive Order under which the evacuation took place, can be separated one from the other by political opportunists or historical revisionists. Unfortunately, this separation is exactly what has transpired in the "official history" written forty years after the event. One of the major thesis of this book is to bring together the inter-dependency of MAGIC and the need for relocation thus providing a complete and honest portrayal of the role that intelligence played in miliatry decisions on the West Coast. This book offers a truthful discussion about what the evacuation was and how it affected those who had to move. The evacuees were both American citizens as well as resident aliens. The status of the aliens became, automatically, *alien enemies* following the declaration of war between the United States and Germany, Italy and Japan.

Try as one may, it is not possible to deny documents which are so absolutely germane to the subject of RELOCATION and the military necessity for such action. Persons who take the time to search out then carefully read declassified records and documents will find them sufficient to warrant our wartime government's actions. Members of the United States Supreme Court did exactly that when the Court upheld the constitutionality of the wartime measure—E.O.9066, February 19, 1942, the exclusion order under which relocation took place. □

Lieutenant General John L. DeWitt was responsible for the safety and defense of the western part of the United States and Alaska. When—on the basis of decoded Japanese diplomatic messages ("MAGIC") between Tokyo and the Japanese Embassy in Washington, D.C., and other cities—DeWitt delcared a "military area" from the Arizona-New Mexico border to the coast then along the coast to Canada, all Japanese, citizens and nationals as well as Germans and Italians were ordered to move. Photo from National Archives 208-N-4477.

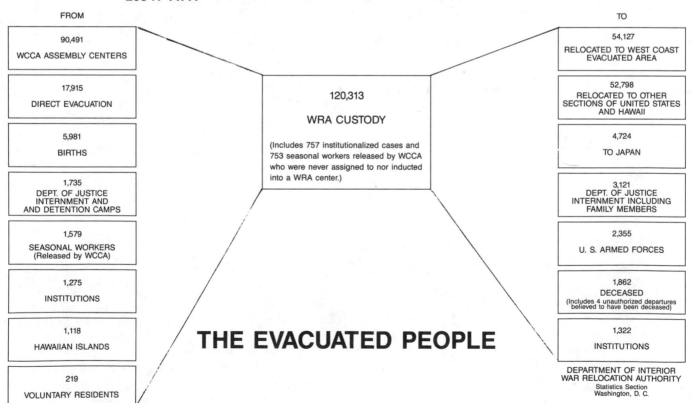

FROM

90,491
WCCA ASSEMBLY CENTERS

17,915
DIRECT EVACUATION

5,981
BIRTHS

1,735
DEPT. OF JUSTICE INTERNMENT AND AND DETENTION CAMPS

1,579
SEASONAL WORKERS (Released by WCCA)

1,275
INSTITUTIONS

1,118
HAWAIIAN ISLANDS

219
VOLUNTARY RESIDENTS

120,313

WRA CUSTODY

(Includes 757 institutionalized cases and 753 seasonal workers released by WCCA who were never assigned to nor inducted into a WRA center.)

TO

54,127
RELOCATED TO WEST COAST EVACUATED AREA

52,798
RELOCATED TO OTHER SECTIONS OF UNITED STATES AND HAWAII

4,724
TO JAPAN

3,121
DEPT. OF JUSTICE INTERNMENT INCLUDING FAMILY MEMBERS

2,355
U. S. ARMED FORCES

1,862
DECEASED
(Includes 4 unauthorized departures believed to have been deceased)

1,322
INSTITUTIONS

DEPARTMENT OF INTERIOR
WAR RELOCATION AUTHORITY
Statistics Section
Washington, D. C.

THE EVACUATED PEOPLE

Preface

On March 18, 1942, President Fr[anklin] Roosevelt created a new completely [agen]cy called the WAR RELOCATION A[UTHORI]TY. Its authority was strictly limited to form[ulat]ing a program which would carefully and humanely carry out an orderly relocation of persons of Japanese descent who were excluded from the military designated areas on the endangered West Coast.

The military designated areas were named under the separate authority given the Secretary of War, namely Roosevelt's Executive Order 9066, dated February 19, 1942. Under this executive order, the Secretary of War or his designated military commanders were able to prescribe specific military areas from which any or all persons may be excluded, or in which the movements of any or all persons may be legally restricted.

Until the 1977 broadened Freedom of Information Act, further broadened under President Carter's executive order, no *detailed* declassified documents were available to historians or researchers pertaining specifically to the *military necessity* of President Roosevelt's sweeping order that gave wartime powers to the military in whom the nation had placed its confidence in time of war—as inevitably it must. This fact was emphasized in the United States Supreme Court decisions upholding (6-3), Roosevelt's E.O. 9066, Feb. 19, 1942 "as nothing more than an exclusion order." (*Korematsu* v. *United States*, October 1944 Term).

Although President Roosevelt appointed Milton S. Eisenhower as the WRA's first Director, the long-term Director was Dillon S. Myer, who filled that post in June 1942 until the official termination of the WRA program, June 30, 1946.

In writing reports about the Relocation Program, Myer pointed out over and over again that the WRA had to deal with both citizens and aliens at every step in the WRA planning.

Dillon S. Myer, throughout the relocation program, assured the American people and the Japanese communities within the unaffected other 44 States, that resettlement was the main object of his Authority and that the term "relocation" was precisely what it meant. He stressed that it was because there were American citizens of Japanese descent in the relocation centers, that the WRA was particularly careful when denying any kind of indefinite leave or in transferring citizen evacuees to the segregation center at Tule Lake.

When Director Myer made public announcements regarding the War Relocation Authority—especially following the segregation of evacuees, "disloyal" from "loyal"—he stressed the fact that although a segregation program had begun in June 1943, the WRA and the Congress were awaiting the opinion on the constitutional validity of detaining American citizens of *questionable loyalty*.

The Department of Justice, the Executive and Legislative branches, agreed that detention of American citizens can be done in *wartime* on the basis of strong evidence of disloyalty or proof that such a detainee was a "potential threat to the national security."

"Consequently," wrote Myer in a talk before the American Legion in June 1943, "in developing our leave procedures we have had to walk a very narrow line between unconstitutional detention on the one hand and inadequate regard for national security on the other. I am confident that we have followed a sound middle course." (Stuart Library, MS27 1.8 File/Jacoby C-0721-P9-BU)

The United States Supreme Court is the final arbiter in deciding the constitutionality of any government action. It ruled that no "concededly loyal" evacuee could be detained against his/her will at a relocation center; but it also upheld the President's role as Commander-in-Chief to "wage war successfully," and for the Secretary of War and his military commanders to issue orders in the interest of public safety and national security.

There were thousands of adult Japanese nationals residing on the West Coast who had no security charges against them. Technically, they were alien enemies every bit as much as were German and Italian nationals designated as alien enemies. Under legal and long-standing law, *all alien enemies* were subject to internment in Department of Justice Internment Camps. *Only those alien enemies with valid security charges against them were interned in these camps.*

The *internment camps* had no connection with the civilian-run War Relocation Authority Centers. *Internment means deportation* and does *not*, and never has applied to *American citizens* of any race, creed or national origin.

Japanese aliens without charges against them were "allowed to be interned" at relocation centers providing they did not impede the war-effort against Japan. If they became "troublemakers," they were given a more restrictive confinement by being transferred to Department of Justice Internment Camps thereby being separated from their families who remained in WRA centers. With heads of household interned, the spouse and young children had little choice but to remain in the care and security of a relocation center. Some of these families, with American children, *voluntarily interned* themselves at Crystal City Internment Camp—the only *family* internment camp in the United States (indeed, anywhere in the world), which housed not just Japanese alien enemies but hundreds of *other* enemy aliens of varied nationalities as well.

The fact that the United States permitted *alien enemy Japanese nationals* in the relocation centers, was greatly misunderstood by other nations which never conceived of such a humane treatment of acknowledged "enemies" within their midst. Such wartime actions were unheard of in the Axis powers. Germany, Italy, and Japan each *interned* both innocent and guilty in internment camps for the duration of the war, regardless of term of residence, regardless whether civilian or military. History has told the stories of the treatment of such internees and POWs under the Nazi and Fascist regimes in Europe and in the Pacific.

An important implication of the United States relocation program in accepting alien Japanese into relocation centers, was that our wartime relations with Japan were greatly affected because there were a great many American civilians and American soldiers in the hands of the Japanese armed forces. Any repressive measures the United States might take against Japanese nationals in the WRA centers, would cause further awful retaliatory action by Japan. Aside from retaliation, Japan used the relocation program for *propaganda* purposes, broadcasting far and wide that the evacuation was "racist" against other oriental peoples, when *in fact*, these "other orientals" were our allies, i.e., Chinese, Koreans, Filipinos, etc. Japan wished to convince other Asian populations that the United States was conducting "a racial war."

Of course Japan neglected to mention that more than 25,000 persons of Japanese descent worked on war-jobs and remained in their homes throughout the 44 States which were unaffected by the exclusion order. The population of persons—both citizen and alien—who were of Japanese ancestry, was never "rounded up en masse" as were certain populations in Europe and as were all caucasians in the Pacific theatre of war.

The propaganda machine initiated by Japan during WWII, immediately following the initiation of the War Relocation program, did not concern itself with how the United States treated people. Rather Japan stressed that "American citizens" were "prisoners," proving the war in the Pacific by Japan was only "a crusade against the white man's racial oppression." Of course Japan, in its Far Eastern radio messages—some broadcast by "Tokyo Rose" and other American counterparts in Tokyo—deliberately refrained from making distinctions among the various kinds of detention in the United States during WWII.

Japan's falsification of the historical facts during World War II, has continued on an accelerated pace to the present day. Japan has rewritten its history books to represent WWII militarists and fascists as "protectors of Asians against foreigners." China, Korea and the Philippines threatened to break off diplomatic relations if Japan did not revise its textbooks to tell the truth about Japan's horrendous aggressive acts against other Orientals prior to and including World War II. Japan's Educational Minister backed down and the revised textbooks were removed from the shelves.

In the United States, Japan's influence in Washington D.C. has been felt through its powerful lobbyists. Falsifying United States history has become an obsession with certain dissident members of the Japanese communities throughout the United States. The Report, *Personal Justice Denied* is the prime example of the rewriting of WWII history relative to the exclusion of persons of Japanese descent in the United States.

Dr. Ken Masugi, son of alien evacuees, testified in Washington, D.C., before the Subcommittee on Administrative Practices and Procedures, that the Commission on Wartime Relocation's report, *Personal Justice Denied*, and the Commission's recommendations had three leading characteristics: "Intellectual dishonesty, moral posturing and political opportunism." Furthermore, stated Dr. Masugi, "...any legislation stemming from the report and recommendations will be far more likely to promote racism and bigotry than to dampen those evils."*

This book's purpose is to present for the first time *documented facts* that will enable a proper education of the American people and those legislators who were responsible for the passage of a public law based entirely on a *report* by a flawed and discredited Commission.

The unethical and irresponsible behavior of this politically appointed and politically motivated Commission must be exposed for what it was—a Commission with predetermined conclusions.

"The CWRIC overlooked evidence that could serve to contradict their conclusions."
—Dr. Ken Masugi
letter June 27, 1984

Scholarly research must not be discarded or replaced by emotional rhetoric, uneducated guesses and supposition, or by an ethnic clique who seem to have unlimited monetary resources and thereby political clout in Washington, D.C.

When the historical *facts* are presented, Americans will at long last shrug off a mantle of guilt which has hung all too heavily upon their shoulders for four decades. At long last, here is a book whose factual presentation of WWII events will expose the fiction and fallacies reported in other publications on this subject.

The author has summed up the courage to challenge the convictions held by other historians whose themes encourage and promote "America-bashing"—a recent and on-going political and journalistic sport.

I urge readers to read all about the "billion dollar fraud" spelled out in P.L.100-383, August 10, 1988, facetiously titled the *Civil Liberties Act of 1988*. (See Appendix B and C for Public Law 100-383.)

The Senate and House passed legislation and the President signed H.R.442/Conference Report into law *before it was ever printed and available for study*. It is entirely possible that the public, the members of the Congress as well as the Department of Justice, which is mandated to carry out the provisions of this Act *will read the law's provisions for the first time within the pages of this book!*

How can any serious historian do scholarly research without the cooperation and assistance of people in specialized fields covered herein?

---

*July 27, 1983, Hon. Sen. Chas. Grassley, Chair, Administrative Practice & Procedure, Committee on the Judiciary of the United States Senate.

Therefore, I wish to acknowledge with thanks the special friends and official personnel at the various institutions who worked directly with me or assisted with my work.

My heartfelt thanks to the late Dr. R. Coke Wood, the second person in California to be named "Mr. California" by the State Legislature (1976), who made available campus housing at the University of the Pacific (Stockton, CA), so that I could more easily research the important papers of WWII evacuees stored at the Stuart Library. (The Stuart Library was recently renamed Holt-Atherton Center for Western Studies.)

I owe Dr. Wood my gratitude for arranging interviews with individuals including Dr. Harold S. Jacoby, former Internal Security Officer, Tule Lake Relocation Center (California). Dr. Jacoby granted me an extensive interview (taped), which has become part of the historical record at the National Archives. He also made available his extensive personal files, including *confidential* files related to his activities at Tule Lake. All of these papers and documents will be available for future historians and researchers at the established *Lillian Baker Collection*, Hoover Institution at Stanford University.

Also helpful in locating materials relevant to the issue of the exclusion of persons of Japanese descent on the West Coast, were Dr. James Shebl and Dr. Ronald Limbaugh, Associate Directors at the Stuart Library who made available the extensive collection of *Guy W. Cook Papers (MS33) Nisei Collection 1942-46*.

Grateful thanks for the clerical assistance at the State Historical Resources Commission, California Parks and Recreation Department, in reproducing the hundreds of papers involving reports on the emplacement of the historical markers at Manzanar and Tule Lake. (Renamed California Landmarks Commission.)

Librarians at the Gardena Branch, Los Angeles County Library System, California, for assistance in the microfilming of the 1941-1945 newspapers and government reports. And a special thanks for the personal attention given by Linda Herman, Archivist, Fullerton University (CA), for guidance during my several visits to the vast reserve of materials and papers in the Japanese-American Oral History Project and related archival materials on the evacuation period.

The complete cooperation of John E. Taylor, National Director of the Nat'l Archives and Records Administration, Military Reference Branch, and of his able staff, for their unstinting service in assisting my research work of declassified documents under Mr. Taylor's supervision.

I was further assisted in researching individual evacuee cases by response to telephone inquiries and letters, by the staff under James B. Rhoads, Archivist of the United States, as well as by Frank G. Burke, Acting Archivist of the U.S. Nat'l Archives & Records Administration in the Capitol.

William H. Leary, Still Picture Branch, Audiovisual Archives Division, was most helpful in alerting me to the more than 15,000 official WRA photographs available for my perusal, and for the clerical assistance cheerfully given in Room 200B and Room 18N, at the National Archives.

An assistant, on my behalf and following my instructions, was given the opportunity of copying important documents at the Department of Justice, Federal Bureau of Investigation WWII files, which included alien enemy lists of apprehensions by the FBI from December 7, 1941, through November 1942.

Allen H. McCreight, Chief, Freedom of Information-Privacy Acts Branch (Records Management Division), was indeed helpful in alerting me to the pre-processed material pertaining to the Custodial Detention List (28,133 pages), concerning charges of sabotage or espionage against Japanese aliens. Such documents were available for viewing at FOIPA reading room, FBI Headquarters, Wash., D.C., and copies were obtainable and released for ten cents per page in accordance with Title 28, Code of Federal Regulations, Sections 16.9 and 16.46, which sets the fee.

Ferris Stovel, Director, and assistants at the WRA Research Office, Still Pictures Branch, Rm. 18N, National Archives, directed me in procedures of obtaining glossy prints which subsequently were published in my previous books on this subject, and appear in this volume as well.

Because no author rides "solo" into any project as extensive as is this investigation, there are those whose generosity of time, their sharing of knowledge and in some cases providing monetary support—travel and other costs have been high—have earned my highest esteem. Without them, this project could not have reached fruition. Therefore, heartfelt thanks to Bruce Bogue, Marke Brahe, Edith N. Carlson, Lt. Gen. Edgar C. Doleman, USA(Ret), Donald D. Ellenbaum, Dr. Howard D. Garber, Rear Admiral Robert M. Garrick, USNR(Ret), David D. Lowman,

H. Read McGrath, Maxine & Frank Moschetti, Mr. & Mrs. John Siegler, Mrs. Cherry Houston Smith, Robert A. Stewart, and Ralph Willis.

It would take a full volume to list the names of all who have earned my special tribute over the past decades. All have contributed in a unique way. Space precludes the names of many who deserve mention, and I hope I am forgiven for this omission.

In the forefront, of course, are members of my immediate family who have remained steadfast and patient and being generous with the hours, the days, and the years that separated me and my work from the role of wife and mother. Thanks for your love and for your understanding.

I have benefitted from the encouragement, understanding, advice and support and masterful assistance of my editor and friend, Bert Webber as well as for the wise and timely suggestions of his charming wife, Margie.

Lucile Nisen's clerical expertise facilitated the ongoing production of the mansucript; she is my loyal assistant over many years and a cherished friend.

I appreciate the establishment of *The Lillian Baker Collection* in the permanent archives of Hoover Institution on War, Revolution and Peace, Stanford University, by former archivist and now Associate Director Charles G. Palm. I am honored to be part of that prestigious Institution to which I have deeded all of my papers, research, books, etc., for future historians. My gratitude extends to Associate Director Richard T. Burress who made possible a monetary stipend awarded me by Hoover Institution for furtherance of my research on the subject matter of this book.

Special thanks to the competent and cooperative staff serving the Honorable United States Senator Jesse Helms: Andrew J. Hartsfield IV, Legislative Counsel, and Kay Kallum Ruocchio, Legislative Aide.

Several individuals now deceased, gave me unstinting encouragement on both a personal and professional level. Sadly missed is the personal contact and support of the late Col. Jack Adams, USA(Ret); Col. Karl R. Bendetsen, USA(RET); American Ex-POW James M. Scoggins, Sr.; and "the big guns" of Br. Gen. A. W. Beeman, USA (Ret). We have lost some in battle but we have not lost the war!

I'm obliged to and have been comforted by the support of Dr. S. I. Hayakawa who set an example of courage in the face of unfriendly dissident opposition as an honored member of the United States Senate. As Senator, Dr. Hayakawa often ran "interference" for me, thus enabling me to give oral and written testimony before the CWRIC and some Congressional committees. As campaign manager in the South Bay for Dr. Hayakawa's bid for a Senate seat, I came to appreciate his honesty and sincerity. His personal correspondence throughout these many years—so filled with words of encouragement, some praise; always with a touch of his inimitable humor—are a treasured legacy of two lives in accord when America's honor is at stake.

The value of correspondence from other members of the Japanese and American Japanese community in which I have resided for more than four decades, cannot be over-estimated. Although many of their names appear within the pages of this book, many others have requested anonymity because of intimidation from a dissident faction. I respect their wishes and understand their predicament.

From Tokyo, Japan, came personal correspondence from Kiyoaki Murata, former Editor, *The Japan Times*. He enclosed his writings and editorials denouncing the CWRIC's 1983 "findings" as a "falsification of history." Murata was a former evacuee who for awhile lived in the Poston Relocation Center. He was the last student from Japan to arrive just before December 7, 1941.

I recognize a debt of gratitude to the men and women of the organizations represented by:

Austin L. Andrews, Past Commander, American Defenders of Bataan & Corregidor; Arthur G. Beale, National Commander, American Defenders of Bataan & Corregidor; Mike Butrum, Commander, Southern California Chapter No. 1, American Ex-Prisoners of War; Hubert Campney, Commander, American Ex-POW, Iowa Great Lakes Chapter; Arthur Dinndorf, Past Commander, Southern California Chapter No. 1, American Ex-POW, and his activist wife, Mary Dinndorf.

Special kudos to the Washington, D.C. based National American Ex-Prisoners of War, Inc., and the California based American War Veterans Relief Association Legal Fund for instigating judicial review of P.L.100-383, filed March 9, 1989 in the Federal District Court for the District of Columbia. Supportive of this historic case are the filing attorneys represented by the Washington/Los Angeles firm of Coale, Kananack and Murgatroyd.

Deserving of my thanks for their support of my efforts are patriots of these organizations:

American Legion Post 192, Emmetsburg; Post 33, Ruthven; Veterans of Foreign Wars Post 2295, Emmetsburg, Iowa. VFW, Long Beach Gold Coast Chapter 279, California; 5th Marine Division Association, Phoenix, Arizona and Chickamaunga, California. 2nd Marine Division Veterans, Loganville, Georgia; Guadalcanal Campaign Veterans, Coloma, Michigan; Jewish War Veterans Post 175, Anaheim, California. Code Talkers Association, Window Rock, Arizona; Filipino-American Ex-POWs, Salinas, California; Arrowhead Ex-POWs, Leslie, Georgia; Western States Chapter, American Defenders of Bataan and Corregidor.

These Chapters of the American Ex-Prisoners of War, Inc. organization join the aforementioned and receive my thanks:

In California: Chapter 1, LaJolla; Veterans Adm. Branch, Los Angeles; Newark Chapter; Port Hueneme Chapter; Cecilia McKie Chapter, San Leandro; California Department, Westminster.

In Florida: SW Florida Chapter, Fort Myers; Suncoast Chapter, Loxahatchee; Collier Chapter, Naples; Manasota Chapter, Sarasota; Greater Tampa Bay Chapter, Wimauma.

Mile Hi Chapter, Aurora, Colorado; Leslie Chapter, Leslie, Georgia; Hibbing Chapter, New Mexico; Catawba Valley Chapter, Bethlehem; Metrolina Chapter, Charlotte, North Carolina; Northern New York Chapter, Potsdam, New York.

In Ohio: Department of Ohio, Cincinnati; Springfield Area, Springfield; North Central Ohio, Wooster. The Texas Panhandle Chapter, Amarillo, Texas; West Tennessee Chapter, Jackson, Tennessee; Northeastern Wisconsin Chapter, Cecil, and the Department of Wisconsin, Minocqua.

Individual members of the Pearl Harbor Survivors Association, across the country, rallied in memory of those who did not survive the December 7, 1941 day of infamy at Pearl Harbor.

For almost two decades, scores of men and women of all ages, races, creeds, religions and walk-of-life have sustained me with their constancy and faith in my ability and integrity. Most have met me only through letters, telephone communication, or through the broadcast media. For the latter opportunities, I'm indebted to: Ray Briem, (KABC, Los Angeles); Cecil E. Johnson, (KCKC, Riverside); George Putnam, (KIEV, Los Angeles); Lee Rodgers, (KGO, San Francisco); and Alan Stang (KCZN, Glendale, CA). Through the wide-reaching radio beams of these outlets, what I have had to say has been exposed to millions of listeners.

I again beseech forgiveness if a name is absent from this alphabetical list of recipients of well-earned kudos:

Gladys Adams, June Ahrens, Lee Allen, Virginia Archer, Dr. & Mrs. Paul L. Ashton, Robert Auchter, H. D. Austin; Shirley Babcock, Geraldine M. Ball, Don Barnier, Leona M. Baumgardner, Lee Bergee, Leora J. Bishop, John W. Braeutigam, Jr., Ruth M. Bragg, Frank Bryant, Eugene F. Burge, Randolph Buselmeier, Bev Butrum, Wayne Carringer, Robert A. Case, Tressa Cates, M. M. Chase, Mildred S. Combs, Ruth E. Cornelius, Lawrence Cranberg, Laura Cromwell, G. Thatcher Darwin, Mr. & Mrs. Harry Davis, Dolores DeLathouwer, Mr. & Mrs. Charles DeMarti, Mr. & Mrs. Dowlen, Gwen J. Duffy; Florence Edmunds, Margaret Ekstrom, Mr. & Mrs. J. Erchul, Emil Eusanio.

Brig. Gen Richard Fellows USA(Ret), Ruth N. Fickel, Mr. & Mrs. Rex Franz; John Gardner, M.D., Mr. & Mrs. V. Gaston, Ricki Goldstein, Hazel Grayson, Jerome Greenblatt, and Hazel Sample Guyol.

Mr. & Mrs. D. K. Hammell, Harley Hanan, Nancy J. Dickey Harding, Bryon E. Harshaw, Henry Harrison, Louis Hart, Rev. Msgr. William R. Harvey, Sybel Heller, Richard V. Hill, and Edna Horne.

Arthur and Viva D. Jacobs, Mimi Jaffe, Sonja Jason, Marie Johnson, Nancy Johnson, Eleanor C. Jones; Henry Kane, Francis X. Keefe, Mrs. John Knopp; Virginia Laird; Robert V. Larsen; Dora H. Lawhorn; Dr. Ruth Longshore; Mr. & Mrs. Jack Love; W. H. MacDonald, Mrs. Jerome Madans, Mr. & Mrs. Ralph O. Majors, Diane Malhmood, John Mancino, Barbara Marr, Mr. & Mrs. Brack J. Maupin, Lillian Mayer, W. J. Maynard, Sister Leona Michiels, June D. Moeser, Martha McAvoy, and Nona M. McClain.

Capt. David Nash, Veronica Newell, Ralph T. Nunn, and General J. & Edwanda R. Odum. Laura Orloff, Dr. Herbert I. Ott, F. D. Parsons, Bob Patrick, Marie E. Paul, Don

Peper, Dr. Alvin C. Poweleit, and Col. W. H. Powell, Jr. (Ret).

Also: Mrs. I. Rebert, Dr. & Mrs. Chris Reynolds, Mary Roach, Nat Rothstein, Mrs. G. M. Rydalch; E. D. Scamahorn, Herbert R. Schultz, Harold Schwartz, Judy Seneczyn, Larry Shepherd, Mortimer Simons, Frank M. Stall, Evelyn S. Straus and Stella Stubbe.

Lois Tausch, Henry Towne, Mr. & Mrs. O. J. Trover, Ben Wahrman, Lynn Warech, Polly Warfield, Charles Welbon, Col. Frederick B. Wiener, USA(Ret), Gil Wilson, Charles W. Winniger, Virginia Woodbury, Herbert D. Samms, Dr. R. P. Samuelson, and Victor W. Zeverino.

By the time this book has reached the market-place, many more names of concerned Americans will also have earned recognition for not standing idly by while America and Americans are denigrated by "America-bashing."

Inquiries regarding AfHA (Americans for Historical Accuracy) can be addressed to P.O. Box 372, Lawndale, California 90260. National distribution of this book, and my earlier books (except *The Concentration Camp Conspiracy: A Second Pearl Harbor*—out-of-print) is handled by Pacific Northwest Books Company, P.O. Box 314, Medford, Oregon 97501.

Lillian Baker
Gardena, California
November 20, 1989

Introduction

The book's thrust is solely for the purpose of presenting an historically correct narrative on this subject, based on recently unclassified and declassified documents ignored by those responsible for implementing legislation which adversely affects the citizens of the United States.

Specifically, the legislation referred to is the enactment of Public Law 100-383, August 10, 1988, known as "*The Civil Liberties Act of 1988*," and its enabling legislation which calls for payments of $20,000 each to persons of Japanese descent who were evacuated, relocated, or interned from December 7, 1941, through June 30, 1946. In addition, and in substance, the citizens of the United States are called upon to present a written apology to each and every person of Japanese descent affected by both the evacuation orders and December 7, 1941 military orders, the latter having absolutely nothing whatsoever to do with the exclusion of persons of Japanese descent under Roosevelt's Executive Order 9066, February 19, 1942.

Mr. Justice Oliver Wendell Holmes, Jr., stated:

**The first call of a theory of law is
that it should fit the facts.**

The historical data, documents, and exhibits presented within the text and in this book's Appendixes present *facts based on documentation*.

This book functions as an instrument to introduce new and vital information based on decades of scholarly research into this most widely propagandized and misunderstood action of World War II.

The United States Congress and the President enacted legislation in 1988 based *entirely* on a report titled *Personal Justice Denied*. This report representing the analysis of a nine-member Commission (CWRIC), is historically inaccurate and has been proven to be based on predetermined conclusions.

The composition of the Commission, of its staff, and the misconduct at the Commission's so-called "public hearings," are of itself a scandal. But the summation of the CWRIC's "findings and recommendations" of the Commission are fraudulent and constitute nothing less than a solemn public lie.

The CWRIC's Report, *Personal Justice Denied*, is boggled down with historical inaccuracies.

...the Commission's Report was tainted in its inception, sullied in its preparation, false in its assertions, and dishonest in its omissions. My materials support those conclusions with extensive and fully detailed reference.*

The Commission's selective sources of information were drawn from publications authored by historians with little or no recent declassified documents upon which to arrive at factual conclusions. A pointed example is the CWRIC's reference to Eugene Rostow as one who "wrote the seminal article" about the test cases for the exclusion and curfew in *1945*, and "dealt pointedly with the issue of factual proof of 'military necessity'." Eugene V. Rostow, Professor of law at Yale University and formerly with the State Department, called his article—referred to by the CWRIC on P.237-238, *Personal Justice Denies*—"The Japanese American Cases—A Disaster". The article first appeared in **June 1945** issue of *Yale Law Journal*; a few months later he titled the same article in what has now become more or less the catch-phrase of proponents for redress and reparations legislation: "Our Worst Wartime Mistake."

Rostow's 1945 article was reported to have been "improved by hindsight," inasmuch as it was rewritten after the war ended, September 1945. Since the declassification of MAGIC and other documents which would eventually prove the military necessity of the evacuation *did not come until more than three decades* after his "analysis" of the court cases and exclusion order was published, no credible historian or researcher could possibly place any value on such an outdated work.

Neither the CWRIC nor Eugene Rostow had heard the term "MAGIC," nor did they know what the code name covered. Hence the CWRIC, on the basis of one Yale University Law Professor (who quite obviously didn't advance his study by reading the 8-volume definitive publication: *The "MAGIC" Background of Pearl Harbor*), published in its Report *Personal Justice Denied* that:

> Today the decision in *Korematsu* lies overruled in the court of history. [p. 238 CWRIC Report]

*Personal letter to the author, 18 July 1987 from Frederick Bernays Wiener, Colonel AUS (Ret). See S.Hrg. 98-1304, August 16, 1984— Los Angeles, CA, U.S. Government Printing Office, Washington, 1986

When one examines the reference works relied upon by the CWRIC and its staff, one is justifiably dismayed to find that not one of the titles of these relied upon works was published after the broadened Freedom of Information Act (1977), and the release of WWII intelligence documents under President Carter's executive order in 1980. At that time, a vast flood of pertinent declassified documentation was made available to serious historians and researchers. All these were certainly available at the beck-and-call of the CWRIC staff.

These highly relevant documents clarify the issue of military necessity and the historical records reveal insight into the internment of alien enemies and the detention of American citizens of Japanese descent known to be disloyal to the United States.

The Commission's Report, *Personal Justice Denied* steadfastly claims there was:
1. No military necessity
2. Failure of political leadership
3. Outright racism

which resulted in the sad but necessary wartime actions taken by the United States Government in the interest of public safety and national security.

Research into these matters clearly establishes:
1. There *was* military necessity
2. Political leadership was at its highest
3. There was no racism as all German, Italian and Japanese aliens were treated alike

The United States Supreme Court tested the exclusion order even while our nation was struggling against superior forces, for we were ill-prepared for battle following the devastating blow at Pearl Harbor. The 6-3 affirmative decision of our Supreme Court upheld the constitutionality of Executive Order 9066, February 19, 1942, under which the exclusion took place.

EXECUTIVE ORDER No. 9066

WHEREAS the successful prosecution of the war required every possible protection against espionage and against sabotage to national-defense materials, national-defense premises, and national-defense utilities, as defined:

NOW, THEREFORE, by virtue of the authority vested in me as President of the United States, and Commander in Chief of the Army and Navy, I hereby authorize and direct the Secretary of War, and the Military commanders whom he may from time to time designate, whenever he or any designated Commander deems such action necessary or desirable, to prescribe military areas in such places and of such extent as he or the appropriate Military Commander may determine, from which any or all persons may be excluded, and with respect to which, the right of any persons to enter, remain in, or leave shall be subject to whatever restrictions the Secretary of War or the appropriate Military Commander may impose in his discretion. The Secretary of War is hereby authorized to provide for residents of any such area who are excluded therefrom, such transportation, food, shelter, and other accommodations as may be necessary, in the judgement of the Secretary of War, of the said Military Commander, and until other arrangements are made, to accomplish the purpose of this order. The designation of military areas in any region or locality shall supersede designations of prohibited and restricted areas by the Attorney General under the proclamations of December 7 and 8, 1941, and shall supersede the responsibility and authority of the Attorney General under the said Proclamations in respect of such prohibited and restricted areas.

I hereby further authorize and direct the Secretary of War and the said Military Commanders to take such other steps as he or the appropriate Military Commander may deem advisable to enforce compliance with the restrictions applicable to each Military area hereinabove authorized to be designated, including the use of Federal troops and other Federal Agencies, with authority to accept assistance of state and local agencies.

I hereby further authorize and direct all Executive commanders in carrying out this Executive Order, including the furnishing of medical aid, hospitalization, food, clothing, transportation, use of land, shelter, and other supplies, equipment, utilities, facilities, and services.

This order shall not be construed as modifying or limiting in any way the authority heretofore granted under Executive Order 8972, dated December 12, 1941, nor shall it be construed as limiting or modifying the duty and responsibility of the Federal Bureau of Investigation, with respect to the investigation of alleged acts of sabotage or the duty and responsibility of the Attorney General and the Department of Justice under the Proclamations of December 7, and 8, 1941, prescribing regulations for the conduct and control of alien enemeies, except as such duty and responsibility is superseded by the designation of military areas hereunder.

February 19, 1942

—Franklin D. Roosevelt

The opinion for the Court was written by Mr. Justice Hugo Black, who specifically addresses the questions raised by the Commission. However, the Commission's conclusions actually defy the Supreme Court's opinion, and in the CWRIC's Report proposes that the highest tribunal's opinion be dismissed and ignored in favor of the Commission's "official version" of the events surrounding the evacuation, relocation, and internment.

The Commission concluded that the exclusion was based on "racism." Mr. Justice Black, writing the opinion for the majority, answered the earlier charges of racism made in the JACL-ACLU briefs prepared on behalf of Fred Korematsu. Mr. Justice Black wrote:

To cast this case into outlines of racial prejudice, without reference to the real military dangers which were presented, merely confuses the issue. Korematsu was not excluded from the Military Area because of hostility to him or his race. He *was* excluded because we are at war with the Japanese Empire....

The Court recognized that "our properly constituted military authorities" had good reason to fear an invasion of our West Coast and in the interest of public safety and national security took actions deemed necessary to insure the welfare of both causes. Furthermore, the Court confirmed that the action was not only taken by the Commander-in-Chief, but *approved by Congress,* both reposing "its confidence in time of war in our military leaders, as inevitably it must."

Mr. Justice Felix Frankfurter, concurring, stated that the provisions of the Constitution confers on the Congress and the President powers to enable us to wage war successfully; that the validity of actions under the war power which were taken with regard to military actions on our West Coast, must be judged "wholly in the context of war." He emphasized that this action was "not to be stigmatized as lawless because like action in times of peace would be lawless."

For the Commission to simply ignore the Court's ruling and to conclude that the judgment of a military order, undertaken by those entrusted with the power to wage war successfully, is "unconstitutional," is to purposely suffuse a part of the Constitution with an atmosphere of *un*constitutionality. In time of war we must recognize that preemptive military action must be taken. To do otherwise is akin to providing weapons without ammunition to do battle against an enemy.

The CWRIC Report falsely claims there was not a single documented case of disloyalty, sabotage, or a case of espionage by Americans of Japanese descent or by those persons wrongly named by the Commission as "permanent resident aliens." According to regulations agreed upon under "The Gentlemen's Agreement" (1907-1908) between Japan and the United States, it was specifically agreed that the Japanese government would issue passports to continental United States "only to such of its subjects as are non-laborers or are laborers who, in coming to the continent would be designated as 'former residents, parents, wives, or children of residents,'

and/or 'settled agriculturists'."

The term, "permanent resident alien" did not come into existence until the United States Government granted "permanent legally admitted immigrants"—a special status—only to former *Peruvian Japanese* internees. (See Appendix.)

The Commission's *opinion* is not based on fact, but comes as another slap at our wartime government from the back of a hand seemingly determined to redden the face of our wartime leaders and government. Had the CWRIC been receptive to other viewpoints *based on documented facts*, it would have had at its fingertips documentation to discredit the "findings and recommendations" expressed in its flawed report *Personal Justice Denied.*

The Commission fails to question the reason why the government had to "sanitize" reports during the 1943-1944 court trials involving curfew and exclusion. It was impossible during the war to produce top-secret classified intelligence data which could have easily proven the military necessity of the exclusion orders. Yet today, the CWRIC, the JACL and the ACLU have charged our wartime government with unfair tactics such as withholding information, the altering of records, and racial discrimination. Such erroneous statements have eroded the whole cloth of our judicial system with illegal loopholes. With political opportunism, the Commission has seemingly broken the very backbone of democratic principles based upon our Bill of Rights.

The Commission's Report wrongly stresses violations of "civil rights" without considering for a moment that citizens from every walk of life, both in and out of uniform, have responsibilities as well as privileges in our free society, and in *wartime* all citizens are called upon to make sacrifices large or small for mutual survival.

The Commission has produced an emotionally-charged report and received testimony from Senators and Congressmen of Japanese descent who have followed the lead of Japan to rewrite and falsify World War II history.

There was no shame in the actions taken by our wartime government and its leaders; the real shame lies in the accusations by the CWRIC and the American Japanese legislators in both Houses of Congress who have maligned some of the finest leaders in United States history.

The Commission's Report *Personal Justice Denied* is so fraught with distortions of historical happenings as to be a "clear and present danger" to the foundation of our Republic. The Report represents a weapon of propaganda to our adversaries and lends credence to Japan's rewriting of the war in the Pacific Theatre.

Asian Report, 139 Vol. 16 No. 1, (1982), warns Americans about Japan's effort to falsify WWII history in an article titled:

What Meaneth This?

The nation of Japan has rewritten some of its history books. So what? Every country does it. But Japan's re-write job has raised a furor throughout Asia. Particularly troubled are the countries that felt the fury of Japan's unleashed militarism. The question is: what's behind the rewriting of Japanese history books? Is it, or isn't it, sinister?

For reasons, not fully understood, the Japanese occupation of Korea, China, Hong Kong, the Philippines, Singapore and other areas of Asia engendered some of the worst brutalities known in modern times. Several factors could be in part responsible.

The Japanese had just recently emerged from the violent and merciless Shogunate period. Historical accounts, as well as modern day depictions and novels of that period, emphasize the apparently normal brutality of the Shoguns. The deification of the Emperor could easily have been translated into justification, and even motive, for brutality against anyone that opposed the god-emperor. The Japanese soldier was a complete fanatic.

On top of all this was the obsession of the Japanese military to establish a "co-prosperity sphere," which simply meant the total domination of all Asia for the benefit of Japan. What seemed to make Japanese brutality worse than experienced in time of war was that it occurred face to face, not from the impersonal distance of say an aeroplane or an artillery piece.

Many Japanese of today are thoroughly ashamed of the past brutality. Does this seem to be a contradiction of a statement made by Jack Steward in his widely read book *The Japanese*, commenting on the Japanese attack on Pearl Harbor? Perhaps, but face to face brutality is very much a source of shame to those Japanese who know about it. This is where the textbook controversy becomes relevant.

Over 60 percent of today's population in Japan was born after the war and knows little about the 50 year rampage of the Japanese military machine. Japan's present ruling party,

which authorized the deletion of the blackest pages of history, may be trying to keep them from finding out. Many people, both in Japan and out, see a sinister motive behind the whitewash job.

They see it as a move to create a new mood of ultra-nationalism that would pave the way for a revival of Japanese militarism. They point to the fact that these same men are proposing amendments to the constitution that would, in effect, restore the Emperor's power and give the Prime Minister supreme authority to command the military, now known as the Self-defense Forces. In this regard, the Americans may be playing right into their hands by insisting on a significant strengthening of Japan's military capability.

It is the fear of a revival of Japanese militarism that has North and South Korea, China and Taiwan all saying the same thing. This is the first time in Asia's post-war history that the four have agreed on anything. There does appear to be reason for concern. In addition to the attempts to revise the Constitution, Prime Minister Suzuki has ignored the protests of opposition parties and religious groups and has paid official respect at the Shintoist Yasukuni Shrine—the symbol of Japanese militarism.

The Japanese are continuing to publicize the horrors of the atom bomb attacks and blatantly deleted Japanese atrocities in Asia from their history books. It is this double standard that has many Asians concerned.

An explanation to the reader is required with regard to the importance of the "official respect" being paid at the Yasukuni Shrine. On May 28, 1959, the late wartime Emperor Hirohito approved the inscription on the "sacred scrolls" at the shrine of the names of the war criminals who had been condemned to death because of wartime activities.

Acting on Emperor Hirohito's orders, Shinto priests placed the names of all dead Japanese war criminals on the sacred scrolls, and on that same day in May 1959, the Emperor and Empress prayed at a private shrine behind the main temple which is used only by bereaved relatives of soldiers who have died for their country. Then Hirohito addressed the White Chrysanthemums declaring:

I have a special appreciation for the families of our war criminals. I know what they have done for Japan. They are among our greatest leaders.*

When it comes to the Nazi Holocaust in Europe and the Fascist Holocaust in the Pacific, the United States government and particularly the major media, seems to have a double standard. The act of placing a mere wreath on the tomb of an unknown Nazi soldier at Bitburg, West Germany, by former President Ronald Reagan, *made headlines and protests* from not only the Jewish community but most of the liberal press. Yet not a word of protest or a word in print *against* the Emperor's actions, even though among the first names to be placed on the scrolls at Yasukuni Shrine—the supreme citadel of the Japanese national mystique—was that of Tomoyuki Yamashita, General of the Imperial Japanese Army during World War II.

Japan would like to rewrite its WWII history, including the atrocities, told in the October 1981 *Bulletin of the Atomic Scientists*, and an Associated Press news release based on a report in the *Washington Post*.

The Associated Press reported that American prisoners of war were among 3,000 human guinea pigs killed during germ warfare experiments by the Japanese during World War II. This was the infamous "731 Unit" in Manchuria which did its work under the cover title "Epidemic Prevention and Potable Water Unit." The AP release stated:

> The report in the October issue of the *Bulletin of the Atomic Scientists* says United States officials in exchange for information gathered in the tests, granted the Japanese involved immunity from prosecution as war criminals.
>
> Experiments also included infecting victims with various diseases, freezing portions of bodies and exposing prisoners to exploding fragmentation bombs, the report says. The prisoners included Chinese troops, Chinese civilians, Russian prisoners and the Americans.
>
> The report contains previously classified information kept at Fort Detrick, Md., a headquarters for military biological research...A confidential 1956 FBI memo confirmed captured Americans were used in tests...Its author, John Powell, was born in

China and served as an editor with the U.S. Office of War Information during World War II. Some information used in the report was obtained under the Freedom of Information Act...

> A secret cable from Tokyo to Washington on May 6, 1947, relayed (Lt. Gen.) Ishii Shiro's offer to supply full information about the experiments in return for guaranteed immunity against trial for war crimes. Powell said Ishii Shiro and many of his staff lived in Japan after the war and died of old age. A few are living in retirement in Japan.

The reader might well ask what these reports have to do with today's movement for "redress and reparations" and the enactment of Public Law 100-383, August 10, 1988, an Act which authorizes payments of $20,000 *for human suffering* to all persons of Japanese descent who were "evacuated, relocated, or interned" in the United States from December 7, 1941, to June 30, 1946.

The purpose of the foregoing narrative is to point out the stark contrast between the treatment in the U.S.A. of persons of Japanese descent—including known alien enemies—who were affected by the exclusion order or by internment in Department of Justice Internment Camps.

Of the estimated 120,000 persons affected by "evacuation, relocation or internment," there has *not been a single documented case of atrocity lodged against the WRA director or administrators, or against any person serving in the Immigration and Naturalization Service (INA), the FBI or the Department of Justice* during or immediately after the official closing of these facilities.

Yet forty-plus years later, we have American Japanese legislators in the House and Senate who have intimated that the United States had "concentration camps," with all the ugly connotations that term implies. Senator Matsunaga has made outrageous accusations regarding the treatment of evacuees, including the undocumented report about a grandfather who was killed by a guard while attempting to retrieve his grandson's ball.

Documented evidence tells of severe beatings by *pro-Japan* elements in the relocation centers, resulting in serious injury to Saburo Kido (Poston WRA Center); Thomas Yatabe (Jerome WRA Center); Professor Obata and Rev. Taro Goto (Topaz WRA Center), and Fred Tayama (Manzanar WRA Center).

During an uprising at Manzanar which coincidentally occurred on the first anniversary of the

---

*Potter, John Deane *The Life and Death of a Japanese General*, "The White Chrysanthemum" pp. 178-181, discusses "The Society of the White Chrysanthemum," an organization of widows and relatives of Japanese war criminals who were executed.

25

bombing of Pearl Harbor (December 6, 1942, Japan time), members of the terrorist pro-Japan Black Dragon Society attempted to run-down military police called in to quell the riots. Members of the Black Dragon Society accelerated a truck, leaped from it, and sent the driverless vehicle into the military police who had already tried to quell the disturbance with tear gas. In the confusion that followed, the military opened fire and caused two deaths and some injuries at the camp. Even these tragic deaths did not deter the pro-Japan agitators. They threatened the lives of a group of pro-American evacuees who were whisked away to hide in Death Valley, California, for their own safety; meanwhile, the agitators were sent to detention at Moab, Utah. The leader of the Black Dragons, who was one of the pro-Japan groups detained for questioning, is now called the "Manzanar Martyr" and hailed as a hero.

Another incident happened at Topaz Relocation Center when James Hatsuaki Wakasa, an Issei, was shot and killed by a young Military Police sentry when Wakasa refused to obey the MP's command to "halt." The sentry was given a trial and acquitted. In some circles it is reported that Wakasa was shot only because he "innocently walked too close to a barbed wire fence;" another report suggests that Wakasa was interested in creating an incident which would bring a negative report to the Spanish Consul representing Japanese interests of nationals of Japan who were residing in relocation centers, internment centers, or at Tule Lake Segregation Center.

On November 4, 1943, a riot at Tule Lake Segregation Center occurred following a truck accident wherein several evacuees were injured and one later died. The terrorists at Tule Lake took advantage of the unrest to provoke the Army which was called in following a declaration of martial law by the administrator of the segregation center.

For the sake of argument, the author will consider that a total of a dozen evacuees may have been killed or injured in the course of 3-4 years, involving approximately 120,000 in the War Relocation Centers, segregation center, and assembly centers. The 120,000 does not include the Japanese, German, Italian and other enemy nationals interned in the Department of Justice Internment Camps. (Incidentally, there has been not a single documented case of any evacuee or internee "trying to escape," therefore the charge that "some evacuees were killed trying to escape" is absurd!)

Can any other nation at war claim such a record of humane treatment of *alien enemies* and their families? In a two-letter word: NO! Why then should Americans permit their elected officials the right to enter false statements in the Congressional Record or to invent preposterous tales about events that never happened?

As we have seen, the Commission's Report, *Personal Justice Denied*, represents a propaganda weapon for those who would salve their own conscience or endeavor to erase the collective guilt of ethnic Japanese who have taken the sins of their fathers upon their shoulders.

The CWRIC's "findings and recommendations" have completely misled the President, the Congress, the media and the American public. The Report has abused the minds of future generations of American children by corrupting historical facts thus robbing them of pride in their national heritage. This same brainwashing tactic as used by the Nazi, Fascist and Communist dictatorships is being done under the guise of "education": *Repeat a lie often enough and it will be believed*.

The Report, *Personal Justice Denied*, offers nothing more than a collection of *uneducated* guesses on a subject only recently enlightened by declassified documents.

The Commission's Report is a *false* Report and can best be described by the legal maxim: *falsus in uno, falsus in omnibus. (Black's Law Dictionary*, rev. 4th ed. 727, contains a number of definitions with citations. The first definition given, after the maxim is: *False is one thing, false is everything.)*

The main purpose and thrust of this tome is to give the reader ample evidence to discredit the Report, *Personal Justice Denied*.

Secondly, the author urges Americans to demand a new investigation of the Commission itself; to demand that every single witness of all rank and favor, be placed *under oath* when giving testimony; and all testimony must be based on documentation—not emotion.

On July 7, 1989, the author submitted an *amicus* brief on behalf of the Plaintiff, Arthur D. Jacobs, and unnamed members of the Class (American citizens of German origin) who were similarly situated in Crystal City Internment Camp, Texas, with persons of Japanese ancestry.

This historic case (No. 89-607-JGP), is supported by a group of concerned Americans, a coalition of organizations, and many veterans groups. The *amicus curiae* was filed because it was necessary for me to act in realization of the obligation of all American citizens to uphold the honor of our Nation and Constitutional law.

This case will not be decided by the time this book is ready but perhaps this book's impact and its truthful revelations will result in a new surge of patriotism and support by those who would honor America.

August 1989
Gardena, California

Senator Spark Matsunaga (D-Hawaii) declared that evacuee children "lost educational opportunities." But the Honorable Senator must have been looking the other way. Picture in grammar school classroom at Tule Lake Relocation Center, 1943, made by photographer F. Stewart. (N.A.210-GA-633) For data on numbers of students and teachers, etc., in the relocation centers please see chart on page 72.

27

Testimony before Commission on Wartime Relocation and Internment of Civilians (CWRIC) stated that on trains carrying evacuees "windows were nailed shut and blacked out." Because of this "suffering" evacuees are to be paid $20,000 each. FACT: Windows were not nailed shut as seen in this National Archives picture (210-GH-376) where the "suffering" appears to be a smiling faced mother with her two children and her mother who are eating ice cream from Dixie Cups.

> Yesterday, December 7, 1941—a date which will live in infamy—the United States of America was suddenly and deliberately attacked by naval and air forces of the Empire of Japan.
> The United States was at peace with that Nation and, at the solicitation of Japan, was still in conversation with its Government and its Emperor looking toward the maintenance of peace in the Pacific
>
> • • •
>
> I ask that the Congress declare that since the unprovoked and dastardly attack by Japan on Sunday, December 7, 1941, a state of war has existed between the United States and the Japanese Empire.
>
> —President Franklin D. Roosevelt
> addressing the Congress December 8, 1941

Chapter 1

Facts versus Fallacies

As early as April 7, 1942, *resettlement* plans were discussed by Director Milton S. Eisenhower of the War Relocation Authority and Colonel Karl R. Bendetsen, of the Wartime Civil Control Authority. The purpose of the WRA was specifically to urge and assist evacuees to resettle in the unaffected regions of the United States. These regions included the 44 states away from the west coast, eastern Oregon, eastern Washington and southern Arizona.

Many evacuees left directly from assembly centers under the control of WCCA for seasonal work in the eastern portions of Oregon, well away from the coast. This included a group of 15 from the Portland Assembly Center for seasonal agricultural work in Malheur County. These evacuees were under no compulsion to return to the assembly center or to enter any relocation center.

The policy of leave clearances for loyal American-born Japanese and even some Japanese nationals who had arrived in the United States as students, was hastened under the leadership of the new Director of the WRA, Dillon S. Myer, who succeeded Milton S. Eisenhower who resigned to become Deputy Director of the Office of War Information.

Dr. Eisenhower wrote to me after he received a copy of my book, *The Concentration Camp Conspiracy: A Second Pearl Harbor* (1981):

> I am grateful to you for sending me a copy of your book [which] I am going to place in the Eisenhower Library in Abilene, Kansas, where all my other papers are held in perpetuity.

There they are available to research scholars. I have been able, by reading sketches here and there, over a period of several weeks, to realize that you have brought together original authentic documents which prove that I, as first Director of the War Relocation Authority, and certainly Mr. Dillon Myer, knew it was not the intention to create and maintain concentration camps.... I am happy that all relevant evidence has at last been brought together in a single volume.

The Commission on Wartime Relocation and Internment of Civilians (CWRIC) refused to accept or to utilize this volume in its research.

Dillon S. Myer took over the WRA on June 17, 1942, following his official appointment by President Roosevelt and *within three days* Myer adopted its first "leave policy." Under this policy, evacuees were able to accept private employment in the mid-west. The pamphlet, *They Work For Victory*, published by the Salt Lake City Chapter of the Japanese American Citizen's League (JACL), is reprinted herein for the first time since its April 1945 publication. That paper was not copyrighted and was distributed far and wide in an effort to assist in the task of bringing back residents from the relocation centers to the west coast.

On December 17, 1944 (effective January 2, 1945)—before war's end—the War Department announced the revocation of the west coast exclusion orders which had been in effect against persons of Japanese descent since Spring 1942. Immediately upon this announcement, Director Myer released a memo, December 18, 1944, that *all* relocation centers would be closed before the end of 1945.

The Japanese American Citizens League sent a delegation from the War Relocation Authority Centers to Washington, D.C., *begging the government not to close the relocation centers until after the war ended.* Delegates from the JACL explained that lands were leased for the duration of the war and evacuees would have no housing; besides, until the war ended in victory against Japan, the JACL insisted that a special program promoting the service of Nisei and other evacuees become an "educational" enterprise to prepare the west coast for the return of the people who had been evacuated under military necessity and the executive order.

President Gerald Ford's political move on the

34th Anniversary of Executive Order 9066, February 19, *1976*—year of our 200th birthday as a nation—to "revoke" E.O. 9066, February 19, 1942, was exactly that, a *political move*. Ford's action served no worthwhile purpose because wartime executive orders are effective only for the duration of a war and six months. Besides, as we have seen, the War Department had already announced the revocation of all exclusion orders effective January 2, 1945.

On Friday, Sept. 3, 1976, the Senate by voice vote repealed section 1383 of Title 18 of the United States Code. This action terminated certain emergency powers granted to the President in time of war. Section 1383 of Title 18 of the U.S. Code provided for criminal penalties for "Whoever, contrary to the restrictions applicable thereto, enters, remains in, leaves, or commits any act in any military area or military zone prescribed under the authority of an Executive Order of the President, or by the Secretary of the Army..." when it appears that the individual knew of the restriction or order and that his act was in violation thereof.

This section was originally enacted by Congress as a wartime measure on March 21, 1942.

Although President Ford, on Feb. 19, 1976, signed a Presidential Proclamation which terminated E.O. 9066, the legal authority still stood.

The House passed a similar bill, September 1975, and the Senate joined the action one year later. In essence, the United States Congress has tied the hands of future Presidents, in time of war, to take presumptive action against potential saboteurs, spies, or terrorists of any enemy nation.

In "Little Tokyo," Los Angeles, California, the entire locale was taken over by segments of the Black community, Filipinos, and other Orientals. With housing scarce, it would take a mass of carefully laid plans in order to peacefully remove the newly settled "strangers" in Little Tokyo. This was accomplished not only in Los Angeles, but in dozens of west coast communities, by the booklet *They Work For Victory*. This publication established the groundwork and groundswell proclaiming that *all* persons of Japanese descent were absolutely gung-ho *loyal* and patriotic Americans. Declassification of confidential and secret documents which could prove otherwise, were not available until the late 1970s; the majority being declassified under the broadened Freedom of Information Act of 1977-1978 and further de-classification under President Carter's 1980 Executive Order. There is little doubt in any serious scholar's mind that had these documents been made available *immediately* following the end of hostilities, the truth of Mike Masaoka's lines would ring true: If the Japanese-Americans did not cooperate with the military orders and there was an invasion by Japan, so that soldiers would have been needed to quell American Japanese uprisings instead of battling the enemy, "life in the United States for any Japanese would have been ended."

Masaoka was the representative of the JACL in Washington, D.C. Dillon Myer, in an interview with the author, stated that "nothing was done regarding the relocation centers without the approval of the JACL." Milton Eisenhower, in his testimony before the 77th Congress (when he was Director of WRA) made the same statement and extolled the JACL for its 100 percent "cooperation."

Even before the WRA centers were built, the Japanese American *National Student Council Relocation Program* was initiated. Under this program, 4,300 evacuee students were able to complete their educational pursuits in more than 500 colleges and universities throughout the United States (except on the West Coast), which had opened its doors and offered scholarships to these students. Yet the Commission on Wartime Relocation in its "findings" stated that evacuees lost "educational opportunities." The fact is that while many GIs, including loyal members of the 442nd, were fighting in faraway battlefields, *almost as many* were becoming professionals in their fields of endeavor, thus having a 4-year-jump on returning GIs, including members of the 442nd!

On August 13, 1942, the WRA held a conference in San Francisco to determine the best basic policies not only for the humane operation of the relocation centers as self-governing communities, but to lay plans for the quick resettlement of evacuees and the closing of WRA centers as quickly as possible.

By September 26, 1942, the WRA issued its basic leave regulations, effective October 1, 1942. Basically, leave was allowed any *loyal* citizen or for that matter any alien who would take an oath not to impede the war effort of the United States against the Axis powers. The second basic provision was that they should not become a "ward" of the community, but be self-supporting. To this end, the WRA set up agencies to find employment for willing evacuees.

Some of the mid-West states had already accepted hundreds of seasonal workers so on January 4, 1943, the WRA established a field office in Chicago to facilitate relocation and resettlement over a large area of the North Central States. As the JACL's pamphlet proves, the WRA's work was successful.

However, there were a great many anti-American agitators in the centers who, as history proves in hindsight, should have been separated from the loyal faction of evacuees. These troublemakers, and actual terrorists, caused some governmental agencies to question the ability of the WRA to function in the interest of national security. As early as 1943, it was even suggested by the Chairman of the Senate Committee on Military Affairs (Jan. 20, 1943), that an investigation be made into the feasibility of transferring the WRA to the War Department.

This plan was abandoned because of immediate action taken by Dillon S. Myer to decentralize the relocation program. Myer authorized the various directors to issue leave permits at once, providing such clearance was already given by the WRA Washington office. It should be remembered that the FBI and ONI had dossiers on evacuees who—as citizens—had to be detained in relocation centers because as citizens they could not be interned.

The first remedy for separating the loyal from the disloyal evacuees—especially the citizens—was suggested on April 8, 1943, in which Director Myer was urged by members of the United States Senate to separate "disloyal" evacuees. Further investigation and reports of the uprisings at Manzanar, Poston, and at Tule Lake, finally convinced Myer to initiate a segregation program. Myer's plans were laid out in a letter to Assistant Secretary of War John J. McCloy, on June 25, 1943. By October 11, 1943, the entire segregation program involving the movements in and out of Tule Lake were ended and Tule Lake was no longer a WRA center but a *segregation center*.

On July 1, 1944, with so many American Japanese requesting expatriation to Japan, and without a legal precedent for interning American citizens, President Roosevelt followed the suggestion of the 78th Congress by signing Public Law 405, permitting United States citizens to renounce their citizenship on American soil in time of war. This was not only approved by the Attorney

If the War Relocation Authority was truly operating clandestine "concentration camps," would it hold that the Bank of America would set up shop in the camp two days a week for the benefit of the "inmates"? If these were "concentration camps" would the government permit access to current newspapers and magazines at the news stand? If these were "concentration camps" then why would the government permit unlimited use of the U.S. mails for letters—*uncensored*—and why would the evacuees buy hundreds of thousands of dollars in U.S. War Bonds at these post offices? Photo from National Archives 210-GD-52. Postmarks from collections of Leonard Lukens and Nancy Sakuda.

General but it was the Department of Justice which instigated congressional action.

By October 1944, the United States Supreme Court upheld E.O. 9066, Feb. 19, 1942, as "nothing more than an exclusion order," and that it was untrue that evacuees had to report to an assembly center and relocation centers. Many thousands had voluntarily relocated; many hundreds more found a "new America" by resettling away from the West Coast.

Surely the JACL's pamphlet, *They Work For Victory*, is a more true and historical review of the place American Japanese held in American society and in the war effort. Far removed from the text and photographs is the "racism" which Americans are being accused of today.

Any historian or researcher anxious to have an historically clear picture of the Nisei during WWII, and of the evacuees in general, will find the following text and captions of photographs a refreshing and astonishing other side to this most highly propagandized and misunderstood action of WWII.

Legislators would do well to review these historical facts and based upon these facts then *rescind* as unacceptable and false, the "findings" of CWRIC and the terribly flawed Public Law 100-383, August 10, 1988, which is based upon this Commission's biased report, *Personal Justice Denied*.

Readers should question whether those evacuees described in the JACL's book; *They Work For Victory*, are deserving of monetary payments of $20,000 each as "damages for human suffering." Throughout the booklet, JACL recognizes the enemy as Japan and that the enemy included alien Japanese residing in Hawaii and those legitimately *interned* into Department of Justice Internment Camps—those with proven and valid security charges against them. Today's JACL does not object to a public law that has as its "eligibility date" *December 7, 1941*, the "day of infamy" at Pearl Harbor. Isn't it shocking that the JACL, in 1988, should sponsor a law to reward the terrorists and draft resisters in the WRA centers—those evacuees who did not join loyal Nisei in the wartime service of their country during WWII?

"...there are the Department of Justice camps, which hold 3,000 Japanese aliens considered potentially dangerous to the U.S. These and these alone are true internment camps." *Fortune* Magazine, "Issei, Nisei, Kibei", p. 8, April (1944)

Under P.L. 100-383, the government has authorized payments of $20,000 each to these 3,000 Japanese aliens because the flawed Commission on Wartime Relocation included the word "internment" and invented a new "legal definition" for Japanese aliens..."permanent resident aliens."

The historical fact is that German, Italian, and Japanese nationals were all considered nationals of countries with which the United States was at war. Therefore, under both national and international law, *all* Germans, Italians, and Japanese aliens (regardless of immigrant status), were subject to internment.

It is hoped that the publication of *They Work For Victory* will restore historical accuracy to textbooks and reports about the exclusion of persons of Japanese descent on the West Coast. Certainly the term "en masse" cannot be applied to persons of Japanese descent in the United States inasmuch as there were more than 25,000 persons of Japanese descent *unaffected* by E.O. 9066, Feb. 19, 1942.

The significance of the following will become quite obvious to readers, historians, researchers and legislators.

TRUE COPY with author's comments
shown in [brackets] or as footnotes

Text of
They Work For Victory

Edited and Published by
The Japanese American Citizens League
413-15 Beason Bldg., Salt Lake City, Utah

Respectfully Dedicated
to the Memory of
FRANKLIN DELANO ROOSEVELT

"The Story of Japanese Americans and the War Effort"
[Photo credits and captions appear at the end of the text]

WHO AND WHAT ARE THE NISEI?

NISEI: Second generation of Japanese in America or, American citizens of Japanese ancestry.

A decade ago the term "Nisei" was virtually unknown in the American vocabulary. Today it is coming into common usage and doubtless future

NOTE: Roosevelt died April 13, 1945.

editions of dictionaries will carry the word and its definition.

Though specifically it means "second generation" Japanese Americans, the term is more commonly applied to all persons of Japanese ancestry in this country, and it will probably be used to designate Americans of Japanese descent of the third and fourth generations, or so long as such a designation is needed. It is the hope of the Nisei themselves, however, that in the future such racial identification will become unnecessary and that they will be called simply "Americans."

[In late 1960, the term "Asian-Americans" came into popular usage by a group of young dissident American Japanese, most of whom were not born during WWII. The term "Nikkei" dubbed in for "Japanese community." Third generation American Japanese are called "Sansei"; fourth generation are called "Yonsei." Thus the Japanese community, itself, has perpetuated the hyphenated American Japanese.]

A cross section of the Nisei would reveal a representative American group.

There would be a few who have achieved national fame like Sono Osato, star of the ballet and the New York musical, *On Your Toes*, and Isamu Noguchi, sculptor-designer. There would be a group of young scientists and artists who have not yet achieved national reputation for their work but have in their fields performed creditably and often brilliantly. Among these would be Dr. Henry Tsuchiya who, at the University of Minnesota, has been directing experimental studies on sulfa drug research and has carried on chemo-therapeutic studies in work which must at the present time be regarded as confidential; Dr. Eben Takamine, doing important war work on a new process for the production of penicillin; Dr. William T. Takahashi, 1944 Guggenheim fellow, working in virus reproduction at Rochester University; Aiko Tashiro, pianist and teacher at Bennington College in Vermont; Dr. Edward Hashimoto, associate professor at the University of Utah; and Min Yamasaki, architect and designer.

But the great majority of the Nisei, like the great majority of Americans everywhere, are everyday people working at everyday jobs. They are farmers, domestics, small businessmen and workers. Some are professional men, others work with their hands. They are dentists, newspapermen, fieldhands and lawyers, and politically they are Democrats and Republicans in approximately the same ratio as the rest of the voting public.

Like all Americans, they lived normal, busy lives until Pearl Harbor broke suddenly and devastatingly on December 7, 1941.

Because the Nisei are racially identified with the enemy Japanese, they were subjected to a test of patriotism and loyalty never before demanded of Americans.

[A much harsher test of loyalty and patriotism was waged against all persons of German descent during World War I. Remembering such trials and tribulations, many German and Italian families anglicized their names during WWII to protect their schoolchildren and make life easier in the workplace. Although Americans of Japanese descent were not required to serve in combat duty in the Pacific, Americans of German and Italian descent were not given the choice of battleground in the European theatre of war.]

Within a few months of the start of war, all persons of Japanese ancestry were evacuated from the coastal areas of California, Washington and Oregon and parts of Arizona to relocation centers within the interior. One hundred and twelve thousand people were thus moved, and of these some seventy thousand were Nisei, or American citizens. The rest were their alien parents, most of whom had spent upwards of twenty years in these United States.

The centers were huge, sprawling camps in desert wastelands of the western and southern states. Barbed wire fences enclosed the living and working areas, and armed sentries patrolled by night and day.

Under a program of relocation the Nisei were allowed to move from these camps to any part of the United States save those areas from which they were evacuated. Despite the difficulties of making this new move, thirty thousand Nisei did manage by the end of 1944 to relocate to midwestern and eastern states, and large numbers of them went into farming and war work.

[Proponents of "redress and reparations" claim that evacuees were "prisoners" and "not allowed to leave the 'concentration camps'." In this report, 30,000 left to join 25,000 others in the 44 States who had been unaffected by the exclusion order. Thus, over 55,000 persons of Japanese descent were freely employed or resided in the USA *during* WWII.]

Thousands more were called directly into the Army, and blue service stars went up rapidly in the barrack windows of the relocation centers.

But even within the centers the work for an American victory continued. War bond drives, Red Cross work, the production of camouflage nets for the U.S. Army and the making of plane model for Navy training courses were some of the direct war contributions coming out of these desert camps. The Nisei were proving that despite the barbed wire and the armed sentries, they could and would prove their loyalty to the country in which they were born.

On December 17, 1944, that loyalty was vindicated. The Army on that day announced the reopening of the West Coast and the end of evacuation.

The Nisei had shown by loyal and courageous Army service overseas and by honest, earnest efforts at home that their loyalty was wholly American.

This is the story and a recounting of that loyalty.

JAPANESE AMERICANS IN KHAKI

All along the Western Front men talked of the "Lost Battalion."

For five days, 270 infantrymen of the 141st Regiment of the 36th Division had been trapped behind German lines near Bruyeres. They had not food, medical supplies or means of communication. Their water supply was a swampy mudhole, and when death came to the severely wounded, prayers were spoken over their bodies in whispers so that the enemy would not hear.

The whole surrounding countryside had been thoroughly mined, and the Germans held strong roadblocks all around.

On the sixth day American planes were able to drop food and supplies, but after dive-bombing, they flew off again into the sullen French skies.

It was the eighth day of isolation when one of their lookouts sighted a soldier in American uniform making his cautious way toward their slit trenches. The uniform was worn by a Japanese American, Pfc. Mutt Sakumoto.

The "Lost Battalion" had been saved, and the first men to reach it were members of the 442nd Regimental Combat Team, an all-Japanese American unit. For this action twenty-nine Nisei soldiers were decorated, and posthumous decorations were awarded eight others who died in affecting the rescue.

[In 1988, the media presented programs in which none others but members of the 442nd RCT are credited with this rescue. The *first men* to reach the "Lost Battalion" were Nisei, but they were members of a larger group of Americans who also fought.]

The story of Japanese American men in uniform has been a story of dramatic bravery. Eighteen thousand of them, proud of the uniforms they wear, are today proving to the world that they will live and fight—and if necessary, die—for the country of their birth.

[The 1988-1989 rewriting of history states that no less than 33,000 American Japanese served in WWII. This total, of necessity, would have to include those who served with the *post-war* occupation forces in Japan.]

They come from city and village, farm and factory, and thousands came from the relocation centers to which they were evacuated. Almost one thousand designate their home as the relocation center at Poston, Arizona, and the huge service billboard at the Minidoka center in Idaho has recently acquired two new wings to accommodate all the new names as their owners marched of to U.S. army camps.

THE PURPLE HEART BATTALION

The first all-Japanese American unit was the 100th Infantry Battalion, composed of Japanese American servicemen from the Hawaiian Islands. Former members of the territorial guard, they were sent in 1942 to Camp McCoy, Wisconsin, for training, and then Camp Shelby, Mississippi.

They trained like demons, these men of the 100th. They had lost friends and relatives in the attack on Pearl Harbor that fateful 7th of December, 1941. They had participated in the defense of their homeland that day, and some of them had died in that defense. One of their comrades, Private Torao Migita, had been one of the first American soldiers to fall at Schofield Barracks when the Japanese planes flew overhead. The first Japanese officer taken prisoner that day was captured by two of their men, and the first Japanese submarine was taken by a patrol of Japanese American soldiers led by Pfc. Thomas Higa.

So these Japanese Americans of the 100th Battalion went into action aching for revenge. Had they had their way, they would have faced the Japanese enemy, but the Army decreed otherwise.

They went into action in Italy on September 2, 1943, and within months their exploits became legends that spread through the American troops abroad, that were repeated on the continent and were caught up hungrily by the people at home in the Hawaiian Islands.

They landed at Salerno and then inch by inch they fought their way up the Italian boot. It was bloody fighting all the way. There were days of fast moving when objectives came into sight and defenses crumbled before them. But there were more days when the going was slow, tough and hard.

They crossed the Volturno—three times in all. Twice they fought their way over, twice they were beaten back. But the third time they stayed. They launched the first infantry attack against Cassino, spearheading the American move against this city. They participated in battles at Benevento and Santa Maria Oliveto, and they captured San Michele.

By the end of 1943, 96 of them had been killed, 221 wounded. The casualties marked a one-third loss in this unit of 1,000 fighting men.

[The 1988-1989 revised historical record is that there were over "300 percent casualties, the highest of any other unit in the armed forces."]

By July, 1944, they were well up the Italian boot. On July 19, led by Lieutenant General Mark W. Clark, they led the way into Livorno, and on the 27th of that month Gen. Clark bestowed upon them a distinguished unit citation. It was at this time that Gen. Clark said to the members of the 100th: "Your record in battle has been marked by one outstanding achievement after another. You are always thinking of your country before yourselves. You have never complained through your long periods in the line. You have written a brilliant chapter in the history of America's fighting men."

[The 442nd, consisted of about 1,200 Nisei volunteered from the relocation centers. The 442nd Combat Team went into training at Camp Shelby, Mississippi in

April 1943. The 100th Battalion from Hawaii arrived in Oran, North Africa, *September 2, 1943*. The 100th Battalion became the "first battalion of the 442nd Combat Team" in *May 1944*. The all-Nisei 442nd RCT from the States didn't land in Italy until *June 2, 1944*, when at that time the 100th became part of the 442nd RCT (much resented to this day since the 100th had seen many battles before the mainland volunteers and draftees arrived). *January 20, 1944*, the draft was reinstated through the regular Selective Service process and that's why the "Fair Play Committee" began its protest. Until the draft, these "draft resisters" had been content to sit the war out, having not volunteered with loyal Americans to serve in 442nd. In *April 1944* the draft resisters went into action against the draft and even the ACLU would not protect them. In April 1944, leaders of the Fair Play Committee (Heart Mountain Relocation Center), stated that if the U.S. Supreme Court ruled the exclusion was constitutional, then their "rights were not violated." The U.S. Supreme Court ruled E.O.9066 *constitutional*, but the draft resisters didn't bend to the law, but used even harsher tactics to coerce other American Japanese not to serve. The draft resisters were given trials; many of the leaders were segregated at Tule Lake before the October 1944 decision of the U.S. Supreme Court where the violators then joined other terrorists at Tule Lake. Because of this, many were then stripped of citizenship or renounced it, and were interned at Dept. of Justice Internment Camps. Others, asking for expatriation or repatriation, were at Tule Lake Segregation Center sitting out the war in relative comfort awaiting ship-out to Japan at war's end. In 1989 these disloyals, even those living in Japan, are eligible under P.L. 100-383 and the amended Act, making it an "entitlement" of $20,000 for "human suffering."]

The [442nd] unit had been awarded 900 Purple Hearts, four Distinguished Service Crosses, 36 Silver Stars and 21 Bronze Stars within its first six months in line. Its record had been written in blood, thus the 100th Infantry Battalion was thereafter known as "The Purple Heart Battalion."

Within the months following, the men of this single battalion added new honors to their star-studded record of battle. By March, 1945, this record included 1,547 Purple Hearts, 21 Distinguished Service Crosses, seven Soldier's Medals, six Legions of Merit, 73 Silver Stars, 96 Bronze Stars, 16 Division Citations, two awards from the Italian government and the War Department Distinguished Unit Citation.

The infantrymen of the 100th had come a long way from the sandy beaches of Hawaii and the West Coast.

"GO FOR BROKE"

If, early in 1943, there was still some doubt as to the loyalty of the Japanese American soldier, it was not shared by the War Department. In January it announced the recruiting of Japanese American volunteers for a new unit, the 442nd Combat Team.

The announcement brought a clearcut indication of the sympathies of young Nisei. In Hawaii local draft boards were swamped by 10,000 eager volunteers. "This is the chance I've been waiting for," said Christian Nakama as he volunteered. "As Americans we're entitled to get a crack at Tojo, Hitler and Mussolini."

Fifteen hundred young men from the relocation centers signed up with recruiting teams. Four brothers—Chet, Howard, Kenny and Ted Sakura volunteered at the Minidoka relocation center, and to their mother, Mrs. Misa Sakura, Secretary of War Henry Stimson wrote: "I am sure that you are proud of your sons who have willingly taken their places in the defense of their country."

The 442nd went into training in the lush pine growths of Mississippi and the swampy grounds of Louisiana. Volunteers all, they were imbued by a fighting faith and fervor that spurred them on, even during their early training days. They adopted as their slogan, "Go For Broke." They had put all their eggs in one basket.

[In the 1980s the "Go For Broke" organization propagandized the slogan stating it was "adopted by the 442nd during the 'Lost Battalion' episode." However, as herein documented, the slogan was adopted during state-side training long before this unit saw any overseas service. We recall that during this period in U.S. history, public facilities in southern states were clearly marked "white" or "colored." The American soldiers of Japanese descent always used the "white" facilities.]

They went overseas in June 1944, and at this time the 100th Infantry Battalion was officially made a part of the 442nd. Their first action was with the Fifth Army in its drive on Livorno. They went into battle with vigor, and in four days they charged fifty miles.

From the first they were subjected to the most intense front-line fighting in the Italian theater. In the first 29 days of fighting they lost 120 of their men. The 100th was attached to the 34th Infantry Division which had a record of more days on the line than any other American unit.

On October 15, they went on into the Seventh Army front in France, where they led the rescue of the "Lost Battalion," and they were on their way to Germany.

When Lieut. Col. Virgil R. Miller, executive officer of the 442nd was questioned regarding the unit, he said:

"What do you think of the Japanese Americans as fighters—that's what you want to know, is it? All right, then, you can quote me as follows: they're the best outfit in the United States Army." He paused, then he said: "You can go so far as to say that they're the best damn outfit in the United States Army!"

IN THE PACIFIC

Little news has come out of the Pacific area regarding Japanese American troops in that theater of war. But theirs is a striking and dramatic story. Several thousand of them are today proving that the Japanese American is as eager to fight the Japanese enemy as the German.

They have been at Bataan, in the Marshalls, Tarawa, New Georgia, Guadalcanal, Bougainville, Leyte and all those island points where American fighting men have struggled with the relentless Japanese enemy. In Burma, Sgt. Kenny Yasui, known as the "Baby Sergeant York," captured thirteen enemy Japanese on the Irrawaddy River. On Leyte, Sgt. Frank Hachiya, on a special and dangerous mission, was shot by a Japanese sniper. He was barely able to return to headquarters, but he accomplished his mission and then died of his injuries.

S/Sgt. Shigeo Ito was awarded the Bronze Star Medal and Ribbon in a ceremony on Leyte in the Philippines "for meritorious service in connection with the military operations against the enemy." Sgt. Ito fought in the Attu and Kiska campaigns in Alaska in 1943, served in Hawaii with the 28th Division, and then went on to join the 77th Infantry Division in the Philippines.

Many Nisei Americans served with Merrill's Marauders in that outfit's savage attacks upon the enemy. But all of the island outposts have known these Japanese American soldiers. A number of them have been decorated for bravery, some of them have died in action. And of them the radio commentator, H. V. Kaltenborn, has said: "American-born Japanese are doing one of the greatest services for our Pacific armies."

[The "services" referred to were mainly those of interpreters and translators of captured documents and diaries, and questioning Japanese prisoners of war. No American Japanese in the Pacific was ever used in translating intelligence messages.]

There was Sgt. Henry Gosho, called "Horizontal Hank" by his comrades in Merrill's Marauders, because "he's been pinned down so often by Jap machine-gun fire."

"One of our platoons owes their lives to Sgt. Henry G.," a fellow soldier once wrote. "Hank guided the machine-gun fire on our side which killed every Jap on that side. The boys who fought alongside of Hank agree that they have never seen a more calm, cool and collected man under fire. He was always so eager to be where he could be of the most use and effectiveness and that was always the hot spot."

Hank, who killed his share of the Japanese enemy, always brushed aside talk on that score. "Honorable ancestors much regret meeting Merrill's Marauders," he would say.

In December, 1943, a Nebraska farm boy came home from the wars. He was Sgt. Ben Kuroki, top turret gunner, who participated in 25 heavy bombing missions over Europe, North Africa and the Middle East, and then begged for more. He was granted another five missions with his Liberator crew, and then came home.

Ben Kuroki volunteered for Army service on the day after Pearl Harbor. Suspicion held up his enlistment until January 5 of the following year (1942), but immediately following his enlistment he begged for duty in the Pacific area. He had a tough time getting onto a crew and into active duty. During his training period he was called "Keep 'em Peeling," because he peeled so many potatoes waiting for an assignment.

He went finally to Europe, though he said, "I didn't join the Army with the intention of fighting in Europe. I joined to avenge Pearl Harbor."

This spring it was reported that Sgt. Kuroki had finally achieved his ultimate wish. He was reported in the Pacific theatre, and he wrote home to a friend, "I must concentrate on dropping some 'roses' on Tokyo Rose."

[Sgt. Ben Kuroki was a much-decorated and recognized hero in the Japanese communities during WWII. He was also a government witness in the trial of the "draft resisters" tried at Cheyenne, Wyoming, as The Fair Play Committee. Following the conviction of these "draft resisters," Kuroki told reporters that the members of The Fair Play Committee were "nothing more than fascists" and that he hoped Americans would not judge Japanese-Americans by these "draft dodgers." Yet in 1989, Frank Emi (who had been a leader of The Fair Play Committee), is being hailed as a hero of the "resistance movement" and has falsified his record of the WWII position of the Heart Mountain Relocation Center's Fair Play Committee, whose main leaders were finally segregated at Tule Lake Segregation Center. Even Roger Baldwin, Director of the WWII American Civil Liberties Union, condemned members of The Fair Play Committee and in a public letter stated that these men deserved the "harshest of punishment." As for "Tokyo Rose," President Ford pardoned Iva Toguri d'Aquino on January 19, 1977. In 1989, the former "Tokyo Rose" operates a family oriental gift shop in Chicago and she receives full Social Security and Medicare benefits even though she had been convicted of aiding and abetting the enemy—Japan—against the United States in World War II.]

On February 21, 1945, a large audience at Poston relocation center watched quietly as Brigadier General J. H. Wilson pinned the Distinguished Service Cross upon Mrs. Matsu Madokoro.

The award was a posthumous award to her only son, Pfc. Harry Madokoro, who was killed on the Italian front.

During the final assault on an enemy-held field near Molina A Ventoabbao, Italy, Pfc. Madokoro advanced ahead of his squad to a strategic position from which he could deliver effective automatic rifle fire. He dispersed a nest of snipers, neutralized another enemy nest and enabled his platoon to take a strategic hill. At Luciana, Madokoro occupied an advance position and proceeded to fire on the enemy entrenched on the outskirts of the town. With heavy fire directed at him, he held his position and provided covering fire when his squad was forced to withdraw. The following day, when his squad became separated from the remainder of the company within the town, he provided flank protection against enemy attacks. The enemy entered a nearby draw and threw hand grenades at him, but Madokoro crawled toward the draw, tossed a hand grenade into the enemy position and neutralized it.

He died in the line of duty on August 25, 1944. His citation noted that his Distinguished Service Cross was awarded "for extraordinary heroism in action" on two separate occasions.

● ● ●

War Department notifications of death or wounds received in action have gone to hundreds of Japanese American families throughout the nation.

Many families have sent two, three and more sons into the service of their country. Mrs. Haruye Masaoka, mother of six sons, has seen five of them replace civilian clothing for the khaki of the U.S. Army. By the end of 1944 one, Pvt. Ben Masaoka, was missing in action, and two more, Sgt. Ike and Pfc. Tad, were severely wounded in action. One other, Cpl. Mike Masaoka, still remained overseas.

They are good fighting men, these Japanese Americans.

And on January 21, 1944, the War Department announced that the Selective Service procedures for the Nisei, temporarily suspended after the start of the war, would be resumed. Further, it announced in December, 1944, that aliens of Japanese ancestry would also be eligible for military service.

Both of these rights had taken proof of loyalty and ability, and Japanese Americans in combat had provided that proof.

WAR PRODUCTION

Many people ask, "When will this war end?" There is one answer to that. It will end just as soon as we make it end, by our combined efforts, our combined strength, our combined determination to fight through and work until the end—and the end of militarism in Germany and Italy and Japan. Most certainly we shall not settle for less. (—President Franklin Delano Roosevelt)

LIKE THE WAR RELOCATION centers of the west the Tooele Ordnance Depot at Tooele, Utah, rose overnight from scrubland and waste. Within a few weeks the twenty-seven thousand acres comprising the project became one of the great munition centers of the nation. Here in the warehouses, shops, office and administration buildings, in the rounded igloos and on the fields, men and women are working to keep ammunition on the move to the fighting fronts. They load ammunition, they maintain combat equipment in top form, and they reclaim artillery cases. Tooele, Utah, is a war city dedicated to the defense of the nation, and among its hundreds of residents and workers are many persons of Japanese ancestry.

Close to one hundred Nisei are already employed here as mechanics, munitions handlers, loaders, clerks, stenographers, and typists. Most of them live with their families on the project, and they are a part of the city's life, as well as part of the working personnel.

First Japanese American on the project was Tom Okamura, medically discharged veteran of World War II. Since he registered, ten more Japanese American War veterans have taken their place on the Tooele production line, taking on the clothes of the war worker for the khaki of the American soldier.

PRODUCTION FOR VICTORY

Charles Nishikawa of Tooele produces for three brothers in Army uniform—for Pvt. Harry Nishikawa of Fort Snelling, Minn.; for Pfc. Masato Nishikawa, who was twice injured overseas; and for Pvt. Shigeo Nishikawa. Another Tooele resident is four-month-old Sandra Gail Okusu, whose father is a Tooele war worker. Sandra Gail's stake in World War II is a big one; seven uncles in the U.S. Army. They are T/3 Cosma Sakamoto, overseas in the Philippines; Sgt. Masa Sakamoto, with the 442nd in France; Cpl. Walter Sakamoto, with the 442nd in France, wounded in action; Pvt. Calvin Sakamoto, Fort Snelling, Minn.; Pvt. Ben Okusu, Fort Sill, Oklahoma; Sgt. Masaharu Hata, with the 442nd in France; and Pvt. James Fujioka, Presidio, San Francisco..

With such Army-record families, it is no wonder that the Tooele Nisei have run up amazing production records at this munitions depot, that their officers have pointed with pride to the cooperation, spirit and laudable good will of these Japanese Americans.

The Sioux Ordnance Depot near Sidney, Nebraska, too, has a large number of Japanese Americans working for victory. Some eighty Nisei are employed here, adding their manpower to the greatest war effort in the history of the world.. Thus at home and abroad, these young Americans work and fight and produce for the inevitable Allied victory.

BUT NISEI AMERICANS ARE NOT ONLY IN ORDNANCE WORK, for their contributions to the war effort are many and varied. In small industries and large, in city and country, they are producing directly for the war effort.

The green Hawaiian Islands, Paradise of the Pacific, were, after the treacherous Pearl Harbor attack, weak and defenseless. Great hulking ships lay useless in the harbor. Hickam Field was torn by bombs and shells.

The harbor was laid waste. Twelve men in a rowboat, it was said, could take the islands at any time.

But today the Hawaiian Islands have emerged as one of the strongest military posts in the world. The islands have been re-strengthened, rebuilt, refortified.

Ninety percent of the carpenters, as well as most of the mechanics repairing construction equipment and a large proportion of equipment operators, plumbers, electricians and other workers were of Japanese ancestry. According to Remington Stone, civilian assistant to the army depot engineer for the central Pacific area, "This preparation would have been virtually impossible without the aid of the many thousands of craftsmen and other workers of Japanese ancestry," he said.

CAMOUFLAGE NETS

THE MAJOR WAR PRODUCTION CONTRIBUTION of the war relocation centers has been the weaving of camouflage nets for the U.S. Army. The development of aviation reconnaissance and the accuracy of aerial bombardment in present day military operations has made imperative the masking of troop positions from enemy observation.

The idea that nets for this use could be produced by the Japanese Americans apparently originated at the Santa Anita reception center, one of the centers operated by the Army to which the evacuees were sent prior to going to war relocation centers farther inland.

Certain loyal citizens of Santa Anita, anxious to translate idle hours into positive production for victory, proposed the camouflage net program to the Wartime Civilian Control Authority, the Army authority under which the camp was run.

[*Disloyal* evacuees tried several times to disrupt the work of loyal citizens who were intent on working and producing goods for the U.S. war effort.]

The offer was accepted, and operations began under the Santa Anita racetrack grandstand, which gave the height necessary for the suspension of the nets while work was in progress.

From five hundred to twelve thousand evacuees have been employed on this project during its existence. Army engineers were sufficiently impressed by the performance at Santa Anita to proceed with the construction of net garnishing plants at Manzanar, Gila River and Poston, Arizona, relocation centers.

Each project included five garnishing sheds with 10 rigs in each, a cutting shed with 20 motor-driven reels, a warehouse, office space and other necessary space. Each rig could accommodate from eight to sixteen workers, depending on the size of the net being garnished. [All work at the relocation centers was voluntary. The workers were paid. *There was no forced labor.*]

Three blends of nets were produced—winter, summer and desert. Different shades of burlap were used for each at ratios established by Army specifications.

Nets of different sizes were in production at different times, with sizes ranging from nets of 144 square feet to 2,160 square feet.

Completed nets were spread in the yard and inspected by the U.S. Engineering personnel for workmanship and adherence to specifications. When accepted, they were reeled into company sizes and transported to the warehouse, compressed into bales, wrapped in watertight paper, strapped with steel bands, stenciled and shipped.

As this was a war contract and items produced are vital to the security of the armed forces, figures on production and information regarding disposition are secret. But it has been recognized that this production of camouflage nets was of vital importance as a wartime project. The net workers, all Japanese Americans confined to barbed-wire enclosed centers, set high records for rate of production. This was a war job that could be done within the camps, and it was done with a will.

DEFENSE PROJECTS

Late in 1943 the R. J. Ederer Company plant in Chicago was awarded the Army-Navy "E" for excellence in production for the armed forces. A plant engaged 100 percent in war work, it manufactured camouflage nets, commercial fish nets, air cargo nets and sports nets for the armed forces. At that time 33 Japanese-Americans, most of them women, were proud of their firm's record, participating as loyal employees in the company's war award.

Thus in Chicago, in Detroit, in Buffalo and elsewhere, such Japanese Americans are contributing their share to the nation's war effort.

The Electronic Mechanics Corporation of Clifton, New Jersey, has been engaged in secret work for the Navy, and numbers among its workers seven Japanese Americans. Ringe Shima, once of Stockton, California, is an engineer in charge of production at one of the company's plants. At the Rutherford, New Jersey, plant, another Nisei, Toshi Hirata, is in charge of research on spark plugs. Another Nisei, Al Funabashi, also of this plant, is president of his local union.

There are many names of Nisei Americans that might be cited for individual contributions to the civilian war effort. There is Min Yamasaki, architect and designer who planned the information room for *Time* Magazine at the *Time and Life* Building at Rockefeller Plaza.

Yamasaki helped design and construct army bases in Newfoundland just before the Pearl Harbor attack. After a year on the Newfoundland job, he aided in constructing and designing the site of the Sampson Naval Training base at Geneva, New York. He was one of the first persons there when the site was opened, and one of the last to leave when the job was finished. Nor is his war work finished. He has planned model housing projects for war workers and he is at present drawing plans for airplane test cells.

There was the father-and-son team, Shiro Ebihara and his son Hank, both aliens, both working in Cleveland at Johnston and Jennings Co. Ebihara worked on tank, truck and plane parts, while Hank was engaged mainly in boring gun parts.

Two years ago a letter directed to President Roosevelt and Secretary of War Stimson was given wide publicity. It came from Hank Ebihara, and it declared in part:

"I know you are a very busy man and I hate to bother you like this when you are so busy in more important matters...I was very happy when Secretary of War Henry Stimson announced that Nisei Americans would be given a chance to volunteer for active combat duty. But at the same time I was sad—sad because under your present laws I am an enemy alien. I am a 22-year-old boy, American in thought, American in act, as American as any other citizen. My parents brought me to America when I was only two years old. Since coming to America as an infant my whole life was spent in New Mexico.

"At Pearl Harbor my pal, Curly Moppins, was killed outright without a chance to fight back when the Japanese planes swooped down in a treacherous attack. And Dickie Harrell and other boys from my home town came back maimed for life. Then more of my classmates volunteered—Bud Henderson, Bob and Jack Aldridge, etc. They were last heard of as missing in the Philippines. It tears my heart out to think that I could not avenge their deaths.

"The laws of this country bar me from citizenship—because I am an Oriental—because my skin is yellow. This is not a good law and bad laws could be changed.

[In 1952, the Oriental Exclusion Order was repealed. However, as of 1989, *Japan* still excludes all persons who are not 100 percent Japanese (including other Orientals) from becoming citizens of Japan with the rights of Japanese citizens. This includes Koreans born in Japan to Korean parents captured by Japan and forced into slave-labor in Japan during WWII.]

"But this is not what I want to bring up at this time. As you well know, this is a people's war. The fate of the free people all over the world hangs in the balance. I only ask that I be given a chance to fight to preserve the principles that I have been brought up on and which I will not sacrifice at any cost. Please give me a chance to serve in your armed forces." [In 1942, any Oriental excluded from citizenship could gain naturalization rights by *volunteering* to serve the United States war effort.]

Nothing came of his letter at that time, and because Henry Ebihara, 22, could not serve in the Army, he applied immediately for defense work, and he and his father became a father-and-son for defense duo.

Then on November 25, 1944, the War Department announced that aliens of Japanese ancestry might volunteer for military service. Henry Ebihara was the first to volunteer under this new ruling. He was accepted, and in February, 1945, he was inducted into the U.S. Army, Pvt. Henry Ebihara.

In Detroit, Michigan, the wheels of industry are spinning fast, turning out the tanks and guns of war as fast as man and mind can work. The plants that yesterday sent sleek, shiny new cars down the assembly lines are today turning out sleek and deadly ammunition, ammunition that will one day find the enemy in the Pacific outposts and in Hitler's Germany.

Detroit is a city geared to the war program. Here almost all employment is considered essential or semiessential. The huge steel mills and the tremendous automobile plants are today converted to war production.

And here hundreds of Japanese Americans have found their place in the war effort. By January 1, 1945, approximately 23,000 Japanese Americans had settled in the teeming Detroit district, which includes all of Michigan's lower peninsula and Northern Ohio.

Of these 23,000, approximately 80 percent went directly into war work. They found jobs in the huge steel mills like the Copko, the McLouth, and the Ryerson plants; they went to the Chrysler, Cadillac and Ford industries and other war-production plants like the Guardian Glass Co., U.S. Rubber and Garwood Industries. And they found war jobs to be done at many of the smaller plants.

They were welders, they were mechanics, they were electricians. They worked over draughting boards, and they worked on assembly lines. They riveted, they repaired, they designed.

They were part of America's war effort. In New Jersey there was Jack Sumida, electrical engineer, working in electronics research; there was Kenneth Funabakoshi, machinist in an electrical plant. There was Kiyoshi Nishikawa, chemist in plastics; there was James Akiyama, junior electrical engineer. There was Ichiro Watanabe, designing vital parts, and there was Frank Terasaki, Minoru Kanagaki, Robert Okada— war workers all.

There was Barney Sato in Denver, working at the huge moulds of a vast plant which turns out products for railroads.

There were John Fujita and Milton Kanatani in Kansas City, industrial designing draftsmen. There was Bill Saito, radio engineer in radar work. There was Don Kozeni, metallurgist, and Harry Yanaga, mechanic.

There were men and women in the aircraft industry, designers and draughtsmen and mechanics. There was Riyo Sato, petite Japanese American artist who turned her talents to war work in a New York plane plant following Pearl Harbor.

In Hammond, Indiana, there were a large number of Japanese Americans at the Metals Refining Company plant. The plant produces copper, ore and lead powders, copper and lead oxides, lead and type metals—all items used directly in the production of implements of war. Despite severe labor shortages, this company has won the coveted Army-Navy "E" for excellence in war production, as well as an additional star to mark continued excellence. A great deal of credit for this record was given to the hard-working Nisei employed at the plant. Most of the Nisei were formerly farmers, students and businessmen. They had no direct contact with industrial work, but they were anxious to do their part.

Their names are Japanese, but they are Americans all.

FOOD FOR FREEDOM

EARLY IN 1942 a small caravan of cars and farm trucks made its slow way from California, across the bleak deserts of Nevada on into Utah. The passengers were all Japanese Americans, men and women and children.

They stopped, finally, at Keetley, Utah, and immediately they erected a huge billboard on the highway. "Food For Freedom," it said.

The ground behind the billboard stretched out rocky, hard with frost and covered with sagebrush. Drifts of snow lay against the buildings, and the white tops of the surrounding mountain ranges sent down sharp blasts of winter wind.

But within a few weeks the sagebrush coat was gone, the boulders in the ground had been taken out, and the soil was turned and ready for planting. A handful of Japanese Americans led by Fred Wada had turned 3,000 acres of unwanted land into acreage ready to produce for victory. New seed went into the ground early that year, seed to produce lettuce, cabbage, peas and meadow hay. The men worked 16 hours a day and more. Keetley, Utah, 6,300 feet above sea level, has a short planting season, and the settlers felt the urgency of planting and harvesting before another winter covered the ground with snow.

Keetley, Utah, did produce food for freedom that year as it has produced in the seasons since 1942. What was done there is typical of what Japanese American farmers have done ever since the start of the war to help the nation's food supply.

Literally thousands of young men and women have labored in the fields throughout the midwest and the east, some on their own fields and others as farm workers.

The first major call to farm work for masses of Japanese Americans came in 1942, when they were called into the staple cotton fields of the southwest. Huge acreages of this vital war material were in desperate need of picking, and Japanese Americans came out from neighboring evacuee camps to help in this critical situation. From that time on they were called on again and again to provide manpower for the agricultural industry.

In 1942 the huge sugar beet industry, sorely tried by an acute labor shortage, asked for volunteer evacuee help. Eight thousand answered, one thousand coming from the Heart Mountain Relocation Center alone. The response from the Minidoka Center in Idaho was so tremendous that the center felt an acute labor shortage of its own and women were drafted to carry on with heavy duties around camp.

[When Americans of all creeds, races and national origins, were called into the Armed Forces during WWII, women worked in men's places in war plants on a full-time basis.]

But during the first season in sugar beet work the 8,000 volunteers harvested 915,000 tons of beets, enough to produce 265 million pounds of sugar. In September 1942, Selvoy J. Boyer, chairman of the Utah State Labor Committee, reported that evacuee labor had saved much of the vital beet crop in Utah and Idaho, major sugar-beet states. Had it not been for this help, said Boyer, a large part of the crop in both states would have had to be plowed under. This sentiment was echoed by the Twin Falls, Idaho, Chamber of Commerce, which noted on April 2, 1943, that "a great amount of corps would have gone unharvested in this area last fall if it had not been for the Japanese evacuee labor. You can be assured therefore that the public is grateful." And the Preston, Idaho, Chamber of Commerce reported: "It has been conceded by our people that had it not been for...the Japanese American boys, the beet harvest in Franklin County could not have been accomplished." [Japanese American evacuee labor was voluntary and each worker received wages.]

Throughout 1943 and 1944, the relocation centers continued to send out large numbers of workers as the country's farm labor situation became increasingly acute. In 1944 the relocation center at McGehee, Arkansas, provided 532 workers. Topaz, the central Utah camp, sent out 1,032 workers during the same year. Seven hundred and seven of these placements were made for the War Food Administration and three hundred and twenty-five for the War Manpower Commission for canning and poultry work.

[In 1989, revisionists insist that the evacuees were "prisoners" and could not leave the WRA centers.]

In industries allied to food production, too, the evacuees have been doing work of importance. Hundreds have been employed in canning and processing plants from Utah to the eastern coast. The major number of workers at a packing plant in Utah, which processes poultry for the U.S. armed forces, was said to be of Japanese ancestry in press reports in February, 1945. Large numbers of Nisei have been working at the Seabrook Farms in New Jersey, a community devoted to processing food for army troops. In other cities and towns where the farm's harvest is preserved for future use, Japanese Americans have been doing their share, and in Spanish Fork, Utah, when the California Packing Corporation received its 1943 Army-Navy "E" award, thirty Japanese American workers shared in the honor.

A dozen aliens of Japanese ancestry have been aiding in the war effort of the N.S. Koose & Co. of Kenosha, Wisconsin. Edward Koose, president of this firm which supplies agricultural needs, declared of his Japanese American workers: "Their being here makes it possible for us not only to supply the fertilizer needs of Midwestern farmers but to accept orders from the U.S. Army as well."

JAPANESE AMERICAN FARMERS

Prior to the war thousands of Japanese American farmers in California, Washington and Oregon had tilled the soil. They harvested crops in green Washington's farm country, they gave tender care to fruit orchards in central California, and they struggled with the wind and sun and desert in California's barren Imperial Valley, and they made the desert bloom.

[The WRA centers have been described as barren, desert wastelands—although the sites were hardly different than California's "barren Imperial Valley" desert with its wind and sun and its dust storms.]

They were farmers and they loved the soil. And when the war started, they wanted to keep on producing. Today there are Nisei farmers in the sunny fields of the midwest, in the truck garden farms of new Jersey and the broad ranches of Idaho. There are the Jack Itos and the Tom Miyoshis and the Jim Sagamis in Mazomanie, Wisconsin; the Kishidas in south central Utah, who produced 80 acres of vital sugar beets; the Takagis who planted near Omaha, Nebraska; and the Furutas of Milford Center, Ohio. They are one with all farmers in America in producing food for freedom.

[These Nisei farmers who were evacuated from the West Coast, began a new life in what they called "the new America." Yet under P.L. 100-383, August 10, 1988 ("Civil Liberties Act of 1988"), every one of these farmers and their families are eligible for $20,000 each plus a government apology as "damages for human suffering." These men were exempt from military duty by the Selective Service System on the basis that they were "farmers." None of them risked their lives on the battlefronts of war.]

The Nakadas of Azusa, California, living in the Gila River relocation center, sent their seven sons into the U.S. Army, and then went home to Azusa to raise crops for these khaki-clad sons of America.

[Because the sons left from a relocation center, each is eligible for $20,000 under P.L. 100-383. Any other American draftee or volunteer is not eligible for "damages for human suffering." A question is plausibly raised as to why only soldiers of Japanese descent should be singled out for special monetary compensation for service and duty in WWII which was the responsibility of all citizens.]

Large farmers and small, they are part of the American food production program.

FOOD FOR LEND-LEASE

Among the more spectacular farm ventures of Japanese Americans is the onion-seed project of the Tachikis who began operating 800 acres of farmland near Elberta, Utah, in the "dust bowl of Utah County." The land in Utah County is dry and flat, and powdery white dust covers the ground. The summers are hot and heavy, and the winters are hard. In this region, in 1943, the Tachiki brothers planned a new experimental project, a plan to raise vegetable seeds and to produce for Lend-Lease at the same time.

The experiment, new in the state of Utah, was watched with interest by surrounding farmers, agricultural experts and farm bureau officials of the state. Seventy-six acres of land went into onions, twenty acres into lettuce, and fifteen acres into radishes—all to be grown for seed. The rest of the acreage was put into sugar beets, a vital war crop.

The experiment with vegetable seeds proved successful, and an experimental station was established there by the Utah State Agricultural College.

And of major importance, the entire crop of vegetable seeds was sent overseas for America's Lend-Lease program.

IN THE RELOCATION CENTERS

It must not be forgotten that while outside farm activities were the main contribution of Japanese American farmers to the war effort, many persons in the relocation centers should be credited with turning thousands of acres of land into food-producing farms of great value. The centers were, without exception, set on undeveloped, uncultivated soil, but willing hands and long hours of toil made the land productive, and this year ten thousand acres of cultivated land at Topaz were put on public sale.

In addition, the centers produced their own farm needs, thus cutting down on the cost of food and sparing that part of the nation's food supply that would have been necessary for the center residents. The Topaz center, by way of example, planted in 1944 approximately 400 acres of vegetables, which produced food valued at more than $30,000. They planted 724 acres of grain—wheat, barley and oats. They supplied in addition all of the beef, pork, poultry and eggs necessary for the center's vast population, a worthy record for persons behind barbed wire.

[There were no "barbed wire" fences at Tule Lake until it became a segregation center for expatriates or repatriates and their families. Manzanar WRA center had boundary wires made of three strings of cattle guard to keep youngsters from roaming into the desert and becoming lost and to keep cattle from neighboring ranches from wandering into the residential areas of the WRA center. No *loyal* evacuee was ever prevented from leaving the so-called "barbed wire" settlements set up for persons of Japanese descent. There were only two requirements to leave and resettle in the other 44 states (or eastern Oregon or eastern Washington) which were unaffected by the exclusion order: 1) Loyalty to the United States; 2) Employment in any workplace so the evacuee would not become a burden on the community. With war-jobs so plentiful, and with agencies set up in major cities to assist in placing evacuees during man-power shortages, no loyal evacuee who wanted to serve the war-needs of the U.S.A. was "confined" or a "prisoner" in the relocation centers.]

GOVERNMENT SERVICE

When war came to these United States, the Japanese language—the language of the enemy—became a weapon in our own hands, and those Nisei Americans who were able to speak and write that language became frontline fighters in the world of secret warfare.

Their story has not been told, nor can it be told wholly until the victory is won and the time and need for secrecy are over. They must in the meantime toil in anonymity, receiving no public avowal of their important work. Their only reward lies in the inner knowledge that theirs is work that must be done and that is invaluable in the prosecution of the war.

In government offices throughout the land, these Nisei Americans are engaged in research studies, in monitoring, in translating and editing. They are teaching the Japanese language to thousands of young men in the Army and in the Navy. They make transcriptions for broadcast in the battle of psychological warfare. They make maps of enemy territory. They monitor broadcasts from Japan. Twenty-one translators and announcers in San Francisco send programs to Japan for nine hours every day. [These broadcasts were over KGEI, short-wave radio, which had studios on Treasure Island (Yerba Buena Island) in San Francisco Bay.]

[In the few months before Pearl Harbor, the American military took a look at the Japanese who were already in the armed forces—some 5,000 of them. The Army found, to its amazement, that only a pitifully small number could speak or write the language. Accordingly, recruiters were looking for volunteers to enter special language schools. General DeWitt, whom some termed a reactionary to circumstances in which he found himself, ordered a Japanese language school be established right under his nose—in the Presidio of San Francisco. This was in the fall of 1941. A few months later with the start of the war he was shouting that he wanted all Japanese off his real estate, the Western Defense Command (had he been told about MAGIC?)—except the language school.

There were *Kibei* already in the Regular U.S. Army. Others were recruited into the language school after clearing loyalty screening. And *Nisei*? While the majority had become so Americanized they knew little or no Japanese, a few did. The linguistic test given to *Nisei* already in uniform revealed less than 10 percent could read or write more than a few words of their parents' tongue. Of the thousands tested, only about 100 could be called fairly competent. Of the total screened, *only about 15 were competent in both languages!* These findings were an utter jolt to the War Department. And the Navy took its smarts too for neither the Navy nor the Marines had accepted Japanese recruits. After the war started they were suddenly sorry.—Webber, *SILENT SIEGE II; Japanese Attacks On North America in World War II.* (1988) p. 220.]

The war brought on a crying need for hundreds of men and women who could teach others the Japanese language. The Nisei took on this difficult task and are today secure in the knowledge that their students are making valuable use of their training. In February, 1945, after a long period of secrecy, the War Department announced that the University of Michigan has carried on such a training program under Dr. Joseph Yamagiwa.

When the Navy's Japanese Language School at Boulder, Colorado, graduated "the largest class of Caucasians ever to learn Japanese," it also singled out for honor its Japanese American instructors, who comprised 90 percent of the teachers. Each of the instructors was given an engraved certificate for "outstanding faithfulness and diligence."

[Revisionist historians referring to these graduates, neglect to mention that they were *Caucasians*, and that the *teachers* were Nisei.]

Later Captain F. H. Roberts, commanding officer of the school, wrote concerning these instructors: "Their work has been outstanding and a direct contribution of the highest importance toward winning of the war. The genuine endeavors of patriotic Nisei cannot be stressed too much during these trying days of war. The part being played by American citizens of Japanese descent in preserving freedom and opportunity in America will in time become known to and gain the grateful appreciation of all citizens of the United States of America."

Japanese Americans are also serving with the Office of War Information in Washington, Denver and San Francisco; with the Foreign Broadcast Intelligence Service; with the Office of Strategic Services; the War Production Board; the Federal Communications Commission; and the Office of Censorship.

Many of these offices have clamped a close censorship upon their activities. The Office of Strategic Services, for example, exerts an almost complete blackout on information concerning Nisei employees and the nature of their duties. This in itself is indicative of the vital and confidential character of the services rendered by the Nisei. However, of their work, Edwin M. Martin, acting chief of the Far East Division, has written: "The Far East Division of the Office of Strategic Services has employed several Japanese Americans as translators and their work has been of real value to us. Through their translating efforts a great deal of valuable material has been made available to the War Agencies in Washington."

"Based on Holmes' unique personal experience, it is a tribute to the courageous and brilliant men whose work was so secret that they could not be recognized and whose contribution was so vital that it is no exaggeration to say without it the Pacific conflict might have been waged on the coast of California."
—Senator Daniel K. Inouye in "Foreword" *Double-Edged Secrets,* W. J. Holmes (1979)

[Arthur T. Morimitsu, Past Commander of the American Legion, claimed that "over 5,000" American Japanese served in U.S. military intelligence services; "over 1,000" with forces at Brisbane, Australia; that there were "30,000 members of the famed 442nd RCT...over half from internment centers." Morimitsu, 1989 JACL Veterans Affairs chair, prevented anti-appropriation resolution No. 259 from reaching the floor for a membership vote at the 1989 National American Legion Convention, Baltimore, Md. Morimitsu's figures are in total conflict and disagreement with official documentation. (*Rafu Shimpo*, Sept. 5, 1989)]

In the Foreign Broadcast Intelligence Service are more Nisei, again vitally a part of the important war work of that organization. On January 8, 1945, Edwin Hullinger, Assistant Director, said of the Japanese American employees:

"Our Japanese translators have done an outstanding job. All have proved themselves efficient as language craftsmen and fine as human beings. Our Portland staffmen are veterans in the organization, most having been in FBIS almost since Pearl Harbor. One of them, _____ _____, helped organize our Hawaiian Listening Post and is now planning to return to Hawaii soon to serve as head of the translation staff there, now in process of recruitment. In the Washington office, our Romaji staff is rated at the top of our foreign language translation groups, and the members are liked as individuals. Originally trained by Dr. _____ _____, their group efficiency has been maintained at a high level. I think it is no exaggeration to say they are regarded as one of the finest, if not the finest, language

technician staffs in the Government."

It must be noted here that not only American citizens of Japanese ancestry but also Japanese aliens are today working for the American government in the interest of the Allied cause. No more striking example of patriotism exists than these Japanese aliens who exert their energies for the victory of America over Japan.

Among such men is Yasuo Kuniyoshi, nationally-known artist who turned his energies toward the war immediately after Pearl Harbor.

[Yasuo Kuniyoshi taught at the Art Students League (New York), and the author was one of his students. Japan showed disdain for Kuniyoshi's work, calling it "too Westernized." Today, modern Japan feverishly collects the work of this late artist.]

Aside from spearheading activities of Japanese Americans in New York to strengthen our all-out war program, Kuniyoshi has written radio scripts and broadcast over shortwave to Japan for the Coordinator of Information and the Office of War Information. His script entitled "Japan Against Japan," was broadcast on February 10, 1942, and repeated on March 12, 1942. He has also created war posters for the OWI and made sketches for a booklet, *This Is Japan.*

[Yasuo Kuniyoshi's four sketches titled, *After The Battle—Madness* appeared in *Fortune* Magazine. (April 1944, Volume XXIX, Number 4), an issue devoted to Japan: a) A Military Power We Must Defeat, and b) A Pacific Problem We Must Solve. Caption describing Kuniyoshi's sketches: "In these sketches the American artist Yasuo Kuniyoshi angrily reports what happens when the Japanese Army goes berserk." *Fortune* errs when it describes Kuniyoshi as an "American" artist.]

Another artist who has done important work for the war services is at present on civilian war duty overseas. He is Taro Yashima, Japanese-born artist who escaped to America in 1941, shortly before the war. Tortured and imprisoned nine times by the Tokyo police, Yashima has brought his full knowledge of Japanese brutality to his present work.

These men, along with hundreds of other Japanese aliens, have by their work renounced Japan and are putting their full energies into her defeat.

In a sense, with almost every Government bureau geared to the war program, every Nisei's service in federal employment is auxiliary to the war effort. Besides these strictly wartime agencies in which the Nisei work, they are employed also in almost every Government office. [The same wartime government that employed Nisei as well as Japanese alien enemies in vital war-work, is today called a "racist" government with a "failure of political leadership."]

A large number of Nisei girls, trim, courteous and efficient, are working as secretaries, stenographers and clerks, helping to alleviate an employment situation made inordinately acute by a high turnover and a dire labor shortage.

Well trained and responsible, these women have been employed in Civil Service in Washington and other cities as well as in the Sioux, Nebraska, and Tooele, Utah, ordnance depots. Many of these women have husbands or brothers in the armed services, particularly in the 442nd Regimental Combat Team and in the Pacific theater. By working in wartime agencies they feel they are matching to the degree they are able to the military feats of their husbands and brothers on America's far flung battlefronts.

No Japanese American has ever been discharged for dereliction of duty or for disloyalty. They are the only employees in government service who can boast a quintuple check on their loyalty, having passed the microscopic scrutiny of the Federal Bureau of Investigation, the Army and Navy Intelligence, the War Relocation Authority and the Civil Service Commission.

[This statement is not entirely true. Dual-citizen Japanese in civil service or employment with Los Angeles Water & Power refused to renounce dual citizenship and take unqualified allegiance to the United States. These alone were *fired*. This occurred *prior* to the exclusion. *In 1987, 354 dismissed during WWII, received $5,000 from Los Angeles because of "racism."*]

OTHER WORK ESSENTIAL TO THE WAR EFFORT

TODAY ALL AMERICA is geared to the war program. Not all the young men and women in the country can serve in the armed forces or in actual defense work. But men and women who have taken over jobs in semi-essential industry, youngsters who save their pennies for War Stamps, and the civilian army corps, millions strong, are, to the extent they can, helping to win the war.

In Detroit, in Cleveland, in Chicago, in Minneapolis, in Milwaukee, Japanese Americans are serving in important capacities. They maintain the nation's industrial equipment, they operate machines, they work mines.

In Cleveland, Nisei are employed as electricians and repairmen, as tool and die workers, as power machine operators and grinders. About half of the Nisei in the city are contributing directly to war work in defense plants.

In Detroit, nerve center of a vast war-producing area, Nisei have added their skills and energy to keep the city producing at top speed. The city needed skilled workers, engineers to run and maintain transportation equipment, nurses to care for the public health, and laborers to keep roads in condition. Approximately 250 Japanese Americans are today in Detroit as servants of the city. They are mechanics, drivers and conductors of the Detroit Street Railway; they are engineers and draftsmen in the Post War Planning Division; they are

dietitians, diet maids, pharmacists, nurses and physicians in Public Health; and they serve in many other essential capacities to keep Detroit producing in top form.

In Chicago, thousands are in every conceivable industry. There are 225 with the International Harvester Company, which manufactures tractors for both domestic and overseas use. There are thirty-two more at one of the major railroad equipment manufacturing plants. There are 45 mechanics with a transportation maintenance company and twenty-five other Nisei with a plant manufacturing LSTs [Landing Ship—Tanks].

Japanese Americans have gone out on railroad work, volunteering in large numbers for some of the hardest maintenance work. They have gone into mining as metallurgists and miners. One small company, the Hudson Coal Company at National, Utah, with a payroll of only thirty-seven employees during 1944, produced 50,000 tons of coal in that period. Of their workers, two-thirds were of Japanese ancestry, and despite the small number of employees, the company is justly proud of its service record. Of its workers, six Nisei employees have gone into the U.S. Army, all of them serving overseas. Red Cross and War Bond drives have been heartily endorsed, and Franklyn Sugiyama, fire boss, has received citations from the Treasury Department and the Utah War Fund testifying to the company's participation in these drives.

Even in the relocation centers war activity has been kept going at a fast rate. In addition to the all-important camouflage net project, other war contributions have included a guayule project at Manzanar, California; silk screen projects at Heart Mountain, Wyoming, and Amache, Colorado; a ship model factory at Rivers, Arizona; and civilian war work such as Red Cross and War Bond drives at every camp.

The guayule project began in April, 1942, at the Manzanar center under the direction of Dr. Ralph Emerson of the California School of Technology. Laboratories and seed plots were set out, and 190,000 seedlings representing nineteen varieties of guayule were planted. Three chemists, two propagators and seventeen skilled nurserymen began the experimental work.

The entire project has been watched with close interest by scientists from many of California's educational institutions. Experiments are being made on the extraction of rubber from guayule by a new, fast process.

On this project both aliens and citizens of Japanese ancestry have pooled their efforts, working together to the end that this country might have a substitute for rubber, critical war material.

MODEL SHIP FACTORY

On March 19, 1943, a new kind of assembly line went into production at the Gila River relocation center. On this assembly line Japanese Americans turned out hundreds of sub-chasers, PT boats, and belligerent and Allied ships.

They were all models, made with meticulous accuracy and measuring from two to eighteen inches in length, and they were used by U.S. Navy training classes to train aviators and naval cadets in ship identification.

The factory, established under Navy contract, opened in March 1943, and closed in May 1944. During these fourteen months the workers produced 710 belligerent warship models in addition to earlier production of many sub-chasers and submarines of which no actual count was made. The original order for production consisted principally of the Battleship German *von Tirpitz*, the cruiser *Prinz Eugen*, the destroyer *Koeln*, a quantity of submarine models, and an unlimited number of PT boats. Personnel in the shop at that time numbered about twelve young men.

When production was started on allied ships, the personnel was increased to 70 workers, 15 of whom were girls. Production of allied models included U.S. sub-chasers, U.S. light cruisers, the U.S. aircraft carrier *Wasp*, PT boats, the destroyer *Fletcher* and the destroyer *Sims*.

Filling orders which called for larger and varied models required more precision. One model of the *U.S.S. South Dakota* was eight inches in length, with all parts above water fully operative. Draftsmen who were trained in the shop designed this model from a very small plan, photographs, and other limited information. When this model, valued at $1,200, was shipped to Washington, high praise was received from the Navy.

A model of the cruiser, *St. Louis*, 7½ inches long and fully operative, is now on display in the Navy Office in New York City as an example of fine craftsmanship.

Silk screen shops, too, at the Granada, Colorado, and Heart Mountain, Wyoming, relocation centers did work for the Navy in producing hundreds of thousands of posters.

• • •

IN APRIL 1943, the shocking, electric news of the Tokyo executions broke upon the American public. Three thousand Japanese American soldiers in training at Camp Shelby, Mississippi, sent their reply to the Tokyo warlords: they purchased $100,000 in war bonds in two days.

And in Hawaii other Japanese Americans collected $10,340 and presented it to Lieutenant General Robert C. Richardson, commander of the Army's Hawaiian department.

"We hope this money will be used for bombs to give Premier Tojo and his cutthroats bloody hell," said their spokesman, Walter Mihata.

Not all the civilian contributions of Japanese Ameri-

cans have been so dramatic, but they have been steady and sincere. In all Red Cross, War Bond and blood bank drives, Nisei have responded heartily. Thirty-five Nisei registered in Denver on January 29 to donate to the blood bank, and in New York City sparkling-eyed Katherine Iseri was a regular blood bank contributor until the time she was inducted in the Women's Corps Army [*sic.*—Women's Army Corps].

Nor have Japanese Americans contributed only to U.S. blood banks. On the 18th of September 1943, twenty-five members of the Japanese American Committee for Democracy appeared at the Chinese Blood Bank at 154 Nassau Street in New York City and contributed blood for the fighting armies of Free China. Since then many Japanese Americans have made regular visits to the Chinese blood bank. They have also participated in China Relief drives, and they are striking examples of the fact that Nisei Americans work and fight and give for America and America's allies. From that day years ago when a Japanese American was arrested on the San Francisco waterfront for picketing oil and scrap metal shipments to Japan, the Nisei have proven their loyalty lies with America.

In Salt Lake City, Utah, members of the Japanese American Citizens League during the Fourth War Loan Drive set as their goal 16 jeeps for Army's use. They rang doorbells, they called up prospective purchasers, they pounded the pavements. And by the end of the drive, the small but active group of committeemen and women had sold $25,000 worth of bonds and stamps. During the same drive the Idaho Falls chapter of that same organization sold $15,000 worth of bonds.

In the centers the sale of bonds has been impressive, especially in view of the fact that the residents are allowed for their full-time, eight-hour-daily jobs a cash allowance averaging $16 monthly.

[Evacuees in the War Relocation Centers received free food, lodging, medical and dental care, clothing allowance, education, hospital care, and all basic necessities. No evacuee was forced to labor. Those who worked an 8-hour shift at the centers, received a monthly stipend equivalent to men in the armed forces. Evacuees who were loyal to the United States were not only free to leave the centers but were urged to do so and were assisted in resettlement. The government even paid travel expenses and assisted in cases of emergency relief.]

The residents of the Heart Mountain Relocation Center in Wyoming have, in two and one-half years, contributed $41,390.35 through their purchases of stamps and bonds. During the same period the Rohwer center purchased $18,000 worth of bonds.

OTHER WORK ESSENTIAL TO THE WAR EFFORT

Some bonds purchases are large, more are small. It was Eikichi Toshima, a vegetable farmer, who walked into the Gila River camp's post office, laid a check for $6,000 across the bond window, took his receipt, and walked out without a word.

And there are children at the Rohwer relocation center who own three Army jeeps, jeeps which, they hope, are still seeing service somewhere overseas.

"Jeep or Bust," was their slogan when the campaign started. Their goal was one single jeep to cost $1,165, which was a lot of pennies and nickels and dimes for the school-age youngsters. But within two weeks they had passed their goal with $2,507.95. When the campaign was over, they counted up their sales-$3,505.95. And somewhere men in khaki are riding three jeeps that are the special pride and joy of these children, who had, in their own way, contributed to America's war program.

WOMEN IN WHITE

As registered nurses, volunteer nurses aides and cadet nurses, Nisei women have played an important part in wartime America.

Even in the relocation centers, hard hit by an acute shortage of trained nurses, youngsters of sixteen and seventeen have donned white caps and gone about the serious business of tending the ill. Wide-eyed and solemn, they go about their business, carrying trays that seem too heavy for their slim shoulders, carefully tucking in bed sheets, trotting on tiny feet down the long hospital halls. Their striped pinafores are starched and clean, and their tiny caps sat neatly on their heads.

Many of them have gone into regular training as cadet nurses since it was first announced in August 1943, that Japanese American women were eligible to join the U.S. Cadet Nurses Corps. First from the Gila River center to join the Cadet Nurses Corps was Anne Watanabe, who immediately applied for training at the Hamline University in St. Paul. Others followed in rapid succession. Within three months thirty-one left the Minidoka Relocation Center to train as nurses in hospitals scattered through eight [nearby] states of the Union. Like Nisei WACs, they felt they were doing their utmost in serving the nation.

Today hundreds of Nisei are serving as nurses or are in training. Rochester, N.Y., counted ten Nisei cadets at the beginning of the year at the Genessee, St. Mary's and Rochester General Hospitals. Eight more were in Kansas City—Jayne Shimada, Helen Mukai, Chiyo Iwamoto, Tomi Kawakami, Sonoko Matsu, Fumi Matsumoto, Riyoko Kikuchi and Michiye Fujimoto.

Many are already with the Army, like Lieutenants Marguerite Ugai and Yaeko Suyama, both serving in England, and Lieutenant Yaye Togasaki of the Army Nurses Corps. Meanwhile, a woman doctor, Captain Yoshiye Tagasaki, is at present with the United Nations Relief and Rehabilitation Administration.

[The Cadet Nurse Corps was under the U.S. Public Health Service. Much of the money for paying the tuition, room and board as well as a small cash stipend, was provided by non-profit Foundations which included the Kellogg Foundation. Women who entered this professional training program spent two years on a university campus then three years at a training hospital which included rotations to tuberculosis sanatoriums, mental health hospitals, "Visiting Nurse Service" in cities as well as in rural areas, rotations to children's hospitals and so on. Nursing was basically a 5-year program but during the war, the work was compressed into 4 years with student nurses going to school or doing "duty" in hospitals straight through summer vacation. Those entering programs in 1943 and completing the work, became "Registered Nurses" in 1947-1948 on completion of examinations by the Health Department of the State in which they were located. Nurses who finished the program—there were thousands—agreed to work for the duration of the war in "essential nursing." This could be by joining the Nurses Corps in the Army, Air Force, Navy, U.S. Public Health Service, or in any civilian hospital (but not accept employment in a doctor's office, etc.). By the time the Nisei girls graduated, the war was over thus the employment stipulation did not hold. Each graduate had a college degree and a *guaranteed professional job as a Registered Nurse for the rest of her life.* By 1989, those who entered the program if age 18, are either retired or about to retire. Yet each, if they entered this free nurse training program from a relocation center, will receive $20,000 under the Civil Liberties Act of 1988, Public Law 100-383 for "damages for human suffering."]

WHO CAN SAY these days what services are essential, what are not? And how can one's participation in the war effort be measured?

There are women, aliens mostly, at Heart Mountain relocation center who spend their spare moments sewing for European refugee children. Even within the barbed-wire enclosures, the plight of these Hitler-ridden children has touched the hearts of the evacuees.

There are other women, young and old, who knit sweaters for the Red Cross. This volunteer work, too, measures up well in earnestness and sincerity with the work of any assembly-line worker on the swing shift. There is Ruby Yoshino, singer, who has entertained in Army hospital wards, dedicating her songs to her five brothers in the service of their county.

In Royal Oaks, Michigan, Jimmy Kajiwara, once of San Francisco, has become a familiar sight on the streets of the city. And his work is arresting, too, for he is a trainer of Doberman Pinschers, who will later lead the blind. Kajiwara and another Nisei, Thomas Imoto, are both employees of the Pathfinder Kennels.

And in Nebraska, Father Flanagan's Boys Town has become a symbol of wise, intelligent and sympathetic treatment of homeless boys. The great buildings and the wide fields of Boys Town have sent into the world young men of high caliber and faith.

Among Boys Town employees are twelve young men and women of Japanese ancestry.

They have become a part of a great institution, living in and for a great ideal. They line up as follows:

Patrick Okura, assistant director and psychologist in the welfare department. Formerly with the Los Angeles Civil Service, Mr. Okura and his wife, Lily, have become intimately associated with the problems of Boys Town.

James Takahashi, landscape gardener; Henry Kodama, in charge of the Boys Town victory garden; Jerry Hashii and Eddie Hotta, gardeners; J. Momoto Oku, father of two sons in the armed forces and of another, Private Susumu Babe Okura, killed in action in France; Kaz Ikebasu, clerk; George Takemoto, dairyman; Mrs. George Takemoto, typist; Paul Takhashi, barber; and Mike Oshima, carpenter.

Can the value of their work to the war effort be estimated correctly? There are many others, trained in the ways of children and adolescents, who are doing their part in making America's youth self-reliant and strong.

There is Peter Ida, track coach and high school teacher. There is Abe Hagiwara, counselor in the Cleveland YMCA; there is Pat Noda, high school instructor.

America's war effort is a mighty one, unexcelled in spirit, unsurpassed in production, limitless in scope.

• • •

[Photo Credits and Captions]

A word of explanation: The author was unable to find an original copy of the pamphlet *They Work For Victory*. The late Dr. R. Coke Wood, co-founder of the Conference of California Historical Societies and past Director of the Pacific Center for Western Studies, and Professor *Emeritus* at the University of the Pacific, made available to the author his xeroxed copy of *They Work For Victory*. The poor quality of the xeroxed photographs prevents reproduction of those pictures in this book. However, the captions and credits give further insight into the historical truths of how persons of Japanese descent were treated in America's WWII society. More important, it reports the activities in the relocation centers. Readers will note that in no instance are the relocation camps centers referred to as either internment camps or as concentration camps. Nor are the evacuees referred to as "prisoners." Aside from "barbed-wire enclosures," there's no reference to "machine guns and guard towers"— because only at Tule Lake Segregation Center was

the military ever in control, with the exception of incidents at Manzanar WRA Center and Poston WRA Center, when military assistance was called for short periods during anti-American riots.

At Tule Lake Segregation Center, there was a period from November 4, 1943 to January 14, 1944, when violence occurred and Tule Lake was then under martial law. It was at this time that the reports we see in 1989 of "machine guns pointing inward" and "searchlights" and "soldiers with bayonets" are accurate. We need to be reminded when under *Martial Law* all civil rights are *suspended*! Therefore, evacuees at Tule Lake Segregation Center cannot today, *in 1989*, charge any violation of their "constitutional rights." As for the alien enemies who asked for expatriation to Japan, although the U.S. Constitution protects both citizens and aliens alike *in time of peace*, no alien enemy is cloaked with the protection of the Bill of Rights or the U.S. Constitution *in time of war*.

Xeroxed copies of the pamphlet *They Work For Victory* were submitted to the Commission on Wartime Relocation and Internment of Civilians (established under Public Law 96-317, 96th Congress, July 31, 1980). The author presented each member of the Commission with a copy at the Washington, D.C. hearings on July 16, 1981. Other copies were submitted for inclusion in PRESS KITS. But the CWRIC and its Staff ignored the pamphlet and failed to include this JACL publication in the PRESS KITS. Nor is there a reference to this important historical document in the CWRIC's Report, *Personal Justice Denied*.

In the interest of completeness and historical accuracy, we reproduce the text of this publication which has been in the public domain since April 1945. Readers should be reminded that this booklet, *They Work For Victory*, was dedicated to President Franklin Delano Roosevelt, the author of Executive Order 9066, February 19, 1942—the exclusion order under which the evacuation of all persons of Japanese descent from the military designated areas on the West Coast took place.

Dr. R. Coke Wood's xerox copy, now in *The Lillian Baker Collection,* is a part of the documents which will soon be in the Baker collection at The Hoover Institution on War, Revolution and Peace housed at Stanford University.

Page	Photo Credit	Subject and/or Caption

1 Elisolola — Ballerina Sono Osato with sculptor Isamu Noguchi

4 Iwasaki (for WRA)

These Are the Faces of the Nisei

Teacher, draughtsman, soda jerk and scientist—these are the faces of the Nisei. They are of every walk of life, they are of every religion. They are rich, and poor, famous and unknown. They are the children of immigrants, but they are also the sons and daughters of Americans, and some of them are:

TEACHER MILDRED SASAKI, shown here working at the Day Care Nursery and School, conducted by the Board of Education in Cincinnati, Ohio. A specialist in nursery and kindergarten work, Miss Sasaki's help is invaluable in caring for the pre-school children of war workers.

NURSE HELEN MURAKAMI, general duty nurse employed at the Lutheran Hospital, Omaha, Nebraska. Twenty-five years of age, Miss Murakami is a graduate of the University of Washington in Seattle and trained for three years at the Providence Hospital in that city. She also served for three years as a general duty nurse at the Sutter Hospital, Sacramento, California.

5 Iwasaki (for WRA)

STUDENT YANAKO WANATABE, major in arts and sciences at Univ. of Buffalo, NY. She is shown here studying at the Buffalo YMCA residence.

SODA JERK VIRGINIA MATSUMOTO, daughter of a World War I veteran, goes on duty at the Gumbo Inn, Chesterfield, Mo.

5 Parker (for WRA)

ARTIST TOM INADA, animator in the New York City studios of a movie cartoon producer.

MECHANIC SHO TAKAHASHI, former student of mechanical engineering at the Univ. of California at Los Angeles, maintaining machinery in a Chicago greenhouse.

SCIENTIST DR. WILLIAM TAKASHI, Guggenheim fellow, 1944, working in a laboratory at the University of Rochester, Rochester, N.Y.

ENGINEER EUGENE E. KOMO, graduate of the University of California, checking machinery used to mark gun ammunition at the Superior Type Company, Chicago.

8 (uncredited)

The Minidoka Relocation Center proudly presents its Military Honor Roll. Standing is Masako Fujii, WAC volunteer from Minidoka.

9 (uncredited)

JAPANESE AMERICANS IN SERVICE: Top row, left to right, PFC. TAKESHI YATABE, wounded in action; MAJOR WALTER TSUKAMOTO; 2nd LIEUT. KEI TANASHASHI, killed in action. Lower, left to right: PFC. PRICILLA YASUDA; 2nd LIEUT. MOE YONEMURA.

(Note: Since the material in this pamphlet was prepared, the War Department has announced the death of Lt. Moe Yonemura.)

12	U.S. Army Signal Corps	JAPANESE AMERICANS IN ACTION on the Western Front. UPPER LEFT: A team of Nisei GIs throwing 105mm shells at Germans in support of an infantry attack. LOWER LEFT: A unit moving out of its old command post, which is holding a section of the front lines. ABOVE: Members of the 442nd moving up toward the front lines in France. LOWER: A Japanese American machine gunner keeps himself ready for the enemy.
14	U.S. Army Signal Corps	JAPANESE AMERICAN WAC Chito Isonaga, native of Koloa, Kauai, eats her New Year's dinner with 57 comrades who enlisted in the Women's Army Corps in the Territory of Hawaii.
15	U.S. Army Signal Corps	TOOELE ORDNANCE DEPOT, TOOELE, UTAH
16	U.S. Army Signal Corps	UPPER LEFT: Hugo Kazato, left, George Kudo load 2,000 lb. bombs at the Tooele Ordnance Depot. LOWER LEFT: Japanese Americans store howitzer shells in igloo at Tooele; left to right: Ed Nakano, Jack Chikami, Tony Kishi. UPPER RIGHT: The "spirit of Tooele" is typified by Captain Harley Kinney and Dickie Murakami, 4, whose father is a war worker at Tooele.
17	Mr. Aoyama (for WRA)	Japanese Americans at Sioux Ordnance Depot, Sidney, Nebraska, unload "prop" charges from box car. (Right) Proud and happy residents of the Sioux Ordnance Depot project are Japanese Americans Mrs. Taft Beppu and her two-year-old daughter, Penny.
18	Iwasaki (for WRA)	JAPANESE AMERICAN WOMEN WORK FOR DEMOCRACY: (Cover photo) Ruth Nishi, 21, operating a turret lathe making parts for gas valves in a Chicago manufacturing plant. BELOW: War Worker Jeri Tanaka, employee in the Modern Lighting and Manufacturing Company in Des Moines, Iowa, a company now working on war contracts.
19	Parker (for WRA)	Kenneth Sugioka, Nisei, at work on a precision lathe in the defense plant of the Hathaway Instrument Company in Denver, Colorado.
	Iwasaki (for WRA)	Thomas Oki, Japanese American war worker, shown operating a flame sprayer applying molten metal on a piston head for a P-47 *Thunderbolt* fighter at the Neo Mold Company, Cleveland.
24	Iwasaki (for WRA)	ABOVE: George Shoji, Japanese American, produces food for victory on a 120-acre farm near Elkhorn, Wisconsin.
25	S. R. Boswell	PRODUCTION FOR LEND LEASE: On the ranch above Roy Tachiki introduced a new industry, the raising of onions for seed to the State of Utah. His entire 1944 production went toward Lend-Lease.
26	Aoyama	Rose Yokomizo, native of Scottsbluff, Neb., takes dictation from Major William A. Kutzke, post engineer at the Sioux Ordnance Depot, Nebraska.
27	Van Tassel (for WRA)	ABOVE: Ray Hashitani, formerly of Oregon, an employee of the OPA in Washington. BELOW: Dillon Myer, director of the War Relocation Authority, reads a copy of the Heart Mountain Sentinel with Civil Service employees Eiko Narita, left, Joan Ishiyama and John Kitasako.

28	Van Tassel (for WRA)	Mrs. Yoshiye Abe, employee of the Flag and Decorating Company in Denver, hopes the flag she is working on will be carried someday by a victorious army into Tokyo or Berlin.
29	Acme News Service	JAPANESE AMERICANS REMEMBER PEARL HARBOR: Two Nisei instructors at Northwestern University give their blood to the Red Cross on the anniversary of Pearl Harbor. Left to right: Captain Albert A. Granitz, Japanese Americans Tsune Baba and G. Byron Honda, and Red Cross Nurse Jane East.
30	Van Tassel (for WRA)	Ruby Yoshino, Japanese American singer shown entertaining in a ward at the Walter Reed [Army] Hospital, Washington, D.C. With four brothers in the U.S. Army and another in the Merchant Marine, Miss Yoshino carries on at home with volunteer war work.
30	(no credit)	This silk screen shop at the Heart Mountain Relocation Center has produced thousands of important war posters for the Navy. Japanese Americans participate in a sewing project for European refugees with Americans of other ancestries. Left to right: Eunice Allen, Mary Shigeta, Leona Evans and Toshi Baba. LOWER RIGHT: Katherine Iseri, ofttime blood donor at the New York Red Cross, is congratulated upon joining the Women's Army Corps by a Red Cross Worker. Now Pvt. Iseri, she is at Camp Ritchie, Maryland.
31	(photo from WRA)	Sono Matsu and Tomi Kawakami, Cadet Nurses
32	Ansel Adams	JAPANESE AMERICAN citizens and aliens have cooperated in a new venture, the production of guayule in an extensive project at the Manzanar Relocation Center which may prove to be a highly important contribution to the country's rubber needs.

[*TIMES'* Books, 1988 publication, *MANZANAR*, shows photo #32 on Page 103. Frank Hirosama is identified as the scientist in the laboratory at Manzanar War Relocation Center. However, *TIMES'* chapter, "Professionals Without Professions," fails to caption that Frank Hirosama was in a special laboratory, experimenting with *guayule* as a substitute for rubber. Furthermore, the editors of *MANZANAR* claim that Ansel Adams and Toyo Miyatake took "secret" photographs. The historical fact is that Ansel Adam's photo of Hirosama was made "public" in JACL's *They Work For Victory*. As for Toyo Miyatake, his entire collection of photographs was sponsored by the WRA, and have been exhibited many times since the war's end.]

Several persons who testified before the Commission on Wartime Relocation said that the military was "ever present" and that there were searchlights everywhere so that the Tule Lake center was never completely dark or "restful." At the risk of seeming critical, here are the *facts:*

As early as June 4, 1942, only nine days after Tule Lake was occupied, Dr. Harold S. Jacoby, Chief, Internal Security at Tule Lake Relocation Center, received a memo from Morton Gaba, a Japanese American who was one of the "block managers" (security police). Subject: *Street Lights:*

Several block managers report that groups of boys are hanging around the women's restrooms after dark and that, accordingly, women and girls are hesitant and even afraid to go to the restrooms without male escort. It is suggested that if street lights are not available, a hanging light from the women's restrooms will be sufficient for the present."

This letter was followed regarding the subject of "Lights," from Dr. Jacoby to maintenance control:

June 5, 1942: "Will it be possible to have globes placed in the outlets over the entrance ways to the utility buildings in each block? Complaints have been made that this area is very dark. Many of the colonists are very timid about making use of this building at night."

T. Nagasawa, (signing his name as "Warden"), reported that because of "darkness," he had almost fallen over some boards in the middle of a road and "almost broke my neck."

It would appear that the installation of better lighting by the War Relocation Authority for the benefit, safety, and protection of evacuees against a "delinquent element" of Japanese persons within the center, has been reported unfairly and with inaccuracy in recent testimonies and in statements by proponents for "redress and reparations."

On November 13, 1943, Dillon Myer issued a statement about segregation of those "evacuees who have indicated by word or action that their loyalties lie with Japan".*

In testimonies presented before both Congress and the Commission on Wartime Relocation, the term "segregation center" is avoided "like the plague." Today's revisionists describe the actual *reign of terror* which took place at this segregation center, as merely a group of Americans who "questioned their constitutional rights."

Myer described the Tule Lake segregation center as having a "peculiar status" among WRA centers. Indeed it did.

The four major groups designated for *segregation* were:

1. Those who requested repatriation or expatriation to Japan.

2. *Citizens* who refused during registration to state unqualified allegiance to the United States; and *aliens* who refused to agree to abide by the laws of the United States.

3. Those with intelligence records or other records indicating that they might endanger the national security or interfere with the war effort.

4. Close relatives of persons in the above three groups who expressed a preference to remain with the segregants rather than disrupt

family ties.

The WRA and the Army worked jointly in moving approximately 9,000 evacuees *from other WRA centers* into Tule Lake, and removing approximately that number *from* Tule Lake to the other WRA centers. The only governmental agency capable of handling this large a move was the Army.

At Tule Lake, the Army took over the responsibility of full protection of pro-American evacuees against the pro-Japan terrorist groups in the center by increasing the number of troops assigned to guard duty there. Originally, there was a simple, ordinary wire fence erected when the Tule Lake center was established. Because of the type of people in Tule Lake, after the segregation program took place, it was necessary to install a man-proof fence around the external boundary at the same time additional military equipment was provided. None of these measures were taken *prior* to the anti-American demonstrations which occurred there.

Dillon Myer reported:

Immediately following the segregation movement, some of the evacuees at the Tule Lake Center began to create difficulties. All available evidence indicates that a small, well-organized group—composed chiefly of persons transferred to Tule Lake from the other centers—was attempting to gain control of the community and disrupt the orderly process of administration.

Myer's report, a matter of public record, tells of beatings, broken equipment, damage to facilities including the hospital, and demands made by pro-Japan forces to which Myer declared the "*WRA would not accede to demands*" and if the residents of the center could not "*deal peacefully with the WRA they would have to deal with someone else.*"

All of these documented statements and activities which took place at Tule Lake Segregation Center have been specifically covered-up by proponents for legislation who would characterize the segregants as "victims" and "prisoners" instead of the threat that they were to other evacuees and to the nation's security in time of war.

Lest any reader envision the faction of residents who were described as "disloyal" and "terrorists" merely as "victims," as proponents for

---

*Press Release, WRA, Nov. 13, 1943, Office of War Information, *To Be Held in STRICTEST CONFIDENCE and NOT to be Used by PRESS or RADIO BEFORE 8:p.m., EWT, Sat., Nov. 13, 1943.*

"redress and reparations" choose to call them, here is Myer's report.

On Thursday afternoon, November 4, work was started on a fence separating the evacuee community from the section of the center where the administrative buildings are located and WRA staff members are housed. That evening a crowd of about 400 evacuees, mainly young men—many of them armed with clubs—entered the administration area. Most of the crowd entered the warehouse area. A few entered the motor pool area and some surrounded the project director's residence. The advance of this crowd was resisted by several WRA internal security officers, one of whom tripped, struck his head on a stone, and was then *struck by evacuees with clubs*.... As the crowd closed in around Mr. Best's home, he telephoned Lt. Col. Verne Austin, commanding officer of the military unit outside the center, and asked the Army to assume full control of the project area. Troops entered the center at once.... Many of them (evacuees) are children under 17, and they, together with a very large number of adults, have no responsible part in the recent events.

In presenting this factual statement, the War Relocation Authority wants to emphasize that reports of the events at Tule Lake are being watched in Tokyo. Already some of the recent newspaper accounts have been used by the Japanese Government for propaganda purposes. There is every possibility that they may be used as a pretext for retaliatory action against American civilians and prisoners of war under Japanese control. Under these circumstances, it is imperative that the situation at Tule Lake be handled with a scrupulous regard for accuracy.

Tragically, historical accuracy has not been scrupulously entertained in recent rewritings about Tule Lake Segregation Center and its disloyal population by those seeking "redress and reparations."

The many "children under 17"—most of them grammar-school aged and babes in arms—have a distorted history of these events which has been relayed to them by relatives here and in Japan who are not so terribly proud of their participation in the uprisings that occurred at Tule Lake during its reported reign of terror. Many were guilt-ridden and try to cover-up the truth about their disloyalties. But the truth will out, eventual-

ly, when the 50-year-standing-rule is lifted and *all* of the "confidential," "secret" and *declassified dossiers* on the troublemakers will become *matters of public record*.

It is possible, with the current court case under judicial review, that much of the historical truth *covered-up* by American Japanese legislators in both houses of Congress, will come to light.

Meanwhile, this book will serve as a forerunner to that much desired response to "the day of infamy," in which both *first and second generation Japanese were counted on by Japan to aid Japan in her victory.*

● ● ●

Security *within* the perimeter of the relocation centers was maintained by the *evacuee* police forces upon whom the center residents depended wholly for concerns arising relative to community affairs.

Complying with the original agreement between the War Department and the War Relocation Authority, the Army maintained military guards at all the relocation centers, but *strictly on the outside* perimeters of the relocation center and with particular duties at the Security Post(s) maintained at the entrance.

The WRA centers, on the average, had a capacity of from 10,000-15,000 inhabitants with the exceptions of Tule Lake (16,000 capacity); Colorado River (20,000); Gila River (15,000). However, when Tule Lake WRA Center became the *segregation center* for expatriates and repatriates and their families, the population rose to approximately 18,000 persons considered to be "disloyal." At that time, from *January to June 1944*, figures will show that military personnel *increased* from the time *martial law* was declared until the transfer of the "troublemakers" to official Department of Justice Internment Camps.

The chart at the end of the Chapter, based on documented figures established in the final reports of the War Relocation Authority, shows that there was on the average only *one military personnel per one thousand evacuees at the 10 WRA centers*. Security was tighter at the segregation center. Segregants comprised of pro-Japan and anti-American militants (citizens and aliens), created a riot to celebrate the first anniversary of the Pearl Harbor bombing. Military Police had to be called in to take control from the self-governing evacuees who made up the interior police (wardens). ☐

MILITARY GUARDS
Security Command Units

(Jerome, Arkansas WRA Center was officially closed in June 1944. No record of military guard.)

(Figures shown are at the highest total.)

| CENTER | Jan-Jun 1944 | | Jul-Dec 1944 | | | Jul-Dec 1944 | |
	Officers	Men	Officers	Men	Acreage	Approx. No. Evacuee Residents	Security Posts Maintained
Central Utah	1	13	1	9	19,900	8,000	1
*Colorado River	4	64	1	29	72,000	17,000	3
*Gila River	3	64	1	29	16,467	14,000	2
Granada	2	17	2	17	10,000	7,000	2
*Heart Mountain	2	25	2	25	45,000	11,000	3
*Manzanar	2	64	2	40	6,000	10,000	2
*Minidoka	1	15	1	17	68,000	9,000	1
Rohwer	1	13	1	9	10,000	8,000	1
*Tule Lake	29	736	32	588	26,000	15,000	14

*WRA centers where disruption or rioting took place. Tule Lake *Segregation* Center required tight security because of terrorist acts by pro-Japan forces against passive Japanese or pro-Americans. A comparison of the proportion of the evacuee population and security guards, plus the large acreage, should convince any reasonable person that the WRA centers were hardly a "prison" environment.

Chapter 2

Evacuation: Fact versus Fallacy

With respect to enemy aliens residing within the Western Defense Command, the War Department had no jurisdiction or authority over any enemy aliens in the United States until after President Franklin D. Roosevelt issued Executive Order 9066, February 19, 1942. Until that date, all action taken against alien enemies was under the jurisdiction of the United States Department of Justice and the Immigration and Naturalization Service. Departments within these two federal organizations acted immediately to round up and intern known alien enemies with valid security charges against them. After individual hearings on such charges, enemy aliens were either released, placed on parole, or interned at a Department of Justice Internment Camp run by the Immigration and Naturalization Service.

On December 7, 1941, the Empire of Japan sent its forces to bomb Pearl Harbor even while their Ambassadors were talking "peace" at the White House.

On December 8, 1941, President Roosevelt in his address before the Congress and the American people, announced that a state of war existed between the United States and the Empire of Japan. Too many historians falsely report that it was the United States which declared war against Japan rather than the fact that, faced with a "day of infamy" at Pearl Harbor, it was Japan that initiated an undeclared war by its sneak attack.

Prior to December 7, 1941, and Japan's attack at Pearl Harbor, the United States government in its newly established office of The Provost Marshal General, provisions were made for housing aliens of hostile nations in certain facilities where the Geneva Convention was applicable to prisoners of war. These facilities were specifically established to house only such aliens who were regarded by the FBI, the Intelligence Community, and other agencies or authorities, as being dangerous to the United States security if war came.

All photographs depicting *searches of alien enemy* premises by authorized government agents

(Opposite) Photograph made at Topaz Relocation Center, Utah after disloyals had been separated and were being transferred to Segregation Center at Tule Lake, California. The Commission on Wartime Relocation and Internment of Civilians declares the evacuees "lost everything." FACT: While the government had the right to confiscate all properties belonging to alien enemies including those persons who were citizens but renounced American citizenship and requested to be sent to Japan, the U.S. government, at taxpayer expense, shipped all personal belongings from the relocation centers to Tule Lake Segregation Center free of charge to the evacuees. (National Archives 210-GG-175)

or the many arrests made by FBI agents of alien enemies with valid security charges against them, took place *prior* to President Roosevelt's Executive Order 9066, February 19, 1942. This executive order gave—for the first time—jurisdiction to the War Department over "any and all persons" considered dangerous to the national security or to the public safety of the United States and its citizens.

The months following December 7, 1941, were particularly harrowing for the United States because the tides of battles in the Pacific flowed against it. The devastating surprise attacks at Pearl Harbor, followed by Japan's military invasion of Hong Kong, Guam, Wake and the Philippines, all before Christmas, brought shock-waves of fear throughout the Pacific Rim. Singapore fell with little opposition partially due to an effective Fifth Column of resident Japanese. These people rose to aid the Japanese army as the invaders roared onto Singapore from the Malaya Peninsula merely one-half mile away. The United States and Great Britain were suffering one defeat after another in the Pacific while Japan was becoming dominant and dangerous. The United States was ill-prepared for war.

The intelligence community warned the President and his intimate staff that there existed on the West Coast a dangerous and potential "Trojan Horse" consisting of both first and second generation Japanese (Issei and Nisei). The first opportunity in Hawaii for an American Japanese to show loyalty, proved that some American citizens chose to aid Japan. Accordingly presumptive action on the West Coast was needed.

It was the Attorney General's Office which first issued an order, January 29, 1942, establishing prohibited and restricted zones *along the west coast* and regulating the movement of *enemy aliens* therein. Attorney General Francis Biddle took this presumptive action followed by subsequent orders issued by him on January 31, February 2, 4, and 7, 1942. Lieut. General John L. DeWitt, Commanding General of the Western Defense Command and the 4th Army, *had no jurisdiction or authority over any enemy aliens, regardless of their nationalities*, residing within his command until *after* February 19, 1942.

Assistant Attorney General James Henry Rowe, Jr., and the Special Representative of the Department of Justice on the West Coast in Los Angeles, joined in expressing concerns shared by General DeWitt, the War Department, the FBI and the Justice Department in Washington, D.C., about danger to national security and public safety on the west coat. This was due to the preponderance of persons of Japanese descent living there. The majority of these residents were in areas of strategic importance as many naval, military and war production factories were in the same area. The adults of these residents were, in the majority, Japanese nationals. Others were American citizens of military age who held *dual citizenship which required military service to Japan*—that is, males who were 17 years and older.

General DeWitt, after conferring with various advisors, informed his superior, General George C. Marshall, the Chief of Staff of the Army, that as Western Defense Commander, he could not be responsible to provide for the security of the west coast installations. These fixtures included all the manufacturing facilities and the harbors. In addition, at the same time he was to train military personnel of his newly organized 4th Army. DeWitt explained that civil violence against persons of Japanese ancestry would rise because of reports coming in daily from the Pacific war zone.

In 1940 and early 1941, units of the U.S. Marine Reserves and of Arizona's National Guard, plus the California, Oregon and Washington National Guard units had been deployed and stationed in the Philippines. These units were being decimated by Japan's military forces during its conquest of the Philippines. As prisoners of war, both military and civilian personnel, as well as thousands of Filipinos, were brutally treated. The Bataan Death March and stories of Japan's inhumanity toward its prisoners were reported in the press. Persons of Japanese descent residing in the Salinas, California, area fled as refugees into the southern portions of California, seeking safe haven from outraged Americans, but particularly from the large population of Filipinos seeking revenge against the onslaught by Japan in the Philippines. Towns and cities receiving hoards of Japanese families seeking refuge, passed Council resolutions and sent letters appealing for State or Federal assistance in giving suitable places for families of Japanese to reside in safety. The Japanese American Citizens League, on February 17, 1942—two days before President Roosevelt's Executive Order 9066—recognized the plight of the Issei and their families and offered to assist the government. The JACL further assured the government that it would be responsible for the Issei so that there would be no anti-United States actions taken by Japanese nationals or their American children.

Meanwhile, throughout December 1941, January and early February 1942, concerns of General DeWitt and his staff, of the FBI, Clark of the Justice Department, and Naval Commander (Admiral Greenslade), were conveyed by Colonel Karl R. Bendetsen, acting as liaison officer between the War Department in Washington, D.C., and General DeWitt and others in authority on the west coast. It was Bendetsen's duty to report the findings and conclusions of the civil and military authorities on the west coast with respect to national security and public safety.

It has been falsely reported that the War Department prepared the Executive Order 9066, February 19, 1942, for signature of the Commander-in-Chief (the President). But the fact is that this Executive Order was prepared by the Justice Department and presented to the President with the full approval of the Attorney General, Mr. Francis Biddle.

A factor which could well have influenced President Roosevelt in signing the controversial and unprecedented order, was a February 13, 1942, letter to the president from the Pacific Coast congressional delegation which recommended the evacuation from strategic areas of all persons of Japanese descent, *and others*, both aliens and citizens, whose presence might jeopardize or hinder the nation's war effort. Too many historians have attributed such influence as coming from *various organizations*. In fact, urgent action was recommended by duly elected legislators, which included Governors of western states who urged *internment of all Japanese nationals*. Legislators had the responsibility of securing their States against potential espionage and sabotage. There was no recommendation or even *thought* given to "relocation" on a major scale, or that such a government agency as the War Relocation Authority come into existence.

No orders had been issued against American citizens of Japanese descent because until E.O. 9066, February 19, 1942, emphasis was on the government's alien enemy program.

Former Japanese, German and Italian *nationals* residing everywhere in the United States prior to declaration of war between the United States and Japan, Germany and Italy, were "resident aliens." However, once at war, these same persons were automatically reclassed "alien enemies" who, under the terms of the Geneva Convention,

were legally subject to *internment and confiscation of all their properties*.

James Rowe, Jr., Assistant to the Attorney General, flatly admonished:

"A nation at war safeguards its internal security above all else. Nothing must be allowed to injure that security. To survive long enough to win its war, any State—including the strong democracy which is the United States—must resolve strong suspicions about any and all individuals in its own favor and against those persons.

"The use of the fifth column as a tactic of total warfare has infinitely complicated the question where civil liberties end and treason begins—for the alien as well as for the citizen. Even the most tolerant and watchful members of this community of States (and this includes the American Civil Liberties Union) are aware of a fifth column's menace. They have watched its operation in Norway and France; they have seen its brilliant technique only too recently in Malaya and Java. They are convinced it exists at home. Gilbert and Sullivan's "liberals" and "conservatives" are of one mind in their proper suspicions, though they are not agreed whom to suspect. Time-test and precedent-minded liberals are properly fearful of "witch hunts," governmental or vigilante; yet in each mind lurks a new and corroding doubt: 'This time these charges may well be true, not just excuse for witch hunting,' an unpleasant dichotomy for the liberal.

Only the very naive will expect to find this troublesome fifth column primarily centered among alien enemies. For one thing, they are to amenable of control: the Constitution is no protection to them in time of war.''*

The facts are that the Department of Justice began planning strong presumptive and preventive actions against possible warfare by quietly doing its undercover operations. At least a year before Pearl Harbor, the FBI and other intelligence agencies began a list of possible saboteurs and enemy agents among the German, Italian and Japanese alien populations. A comparatively un-

*The Alien Enemy Program—So Far, James Rowe, Jr., COMMON GROUND, Vol. II, Summer 1942. CWRIC's report, Personal Justice Denied, Pg. 375, Footnote 106, Rowe is quoted in an interview by the Earl Warren Oral History Project: "...the first requirement of the government was order. Law comes after order." Yet on Pg. 337, Footnote 130, CWRIC Report, Rowe testified in 1981 that he opposed the exclusion, stating that he had "never seen any military necessity for it."

known division of the Department of Justice, the "Special Defense Unit," worked in secrecy planning vigorous counter-measures in the event of war.

Because of these operations, the Department of Justice and its agents were not as unprepared as were the War and Navy Departments on that Sunday in Hawaii.

That very Sunday, Attorney General Biddle submitted to the President for his signature, a Proclamation providing that Japanese alien enemies deemed dangerous to the public peace or safety were subject to summary apprehension. Contrary to revisionist historians, similar Proclamations pertaining to German and Italian nationals were issued Monday. The statutory basis for these Proclamations rested on the Act of 1798 which provides that in time of war alien enemies are subject to immediate arrest.

The Act of 1798 defines an alien enemy as a person who is an alien, denizen, citizen, or subject of a nation at war with the United States. The term "alien enemy" does not mean an enemy who happens to be an alien, but rather an alien who happens to have enemy nationality. "Alien enemy" is a legal term which describes the nationality of a person whose country is at war with the United States.

Within 24 hours following the Pearl Harbor bombing, the FBI had arrested more than 1,000 Japanese aliens. By the end of the week, 3,000 German, Japanese, and Italian aliens had been apprehended.

Attorney General Biddle formed a new division in the Department of Justice called the Alien Enemy Control Unit, charged with the supervision of more than a million alien enemies. The Department of Justice determined that an "alien enemy" was every person 14 years or over who was a citizen or subject of Germany, Italy, or Japan at the outbreak of the war; or every person whose last allegiance was to one of these countries.

The Alien Enemy Control Unit was instructed to set up procedures for hearing and reviewing the cases of those apprehended by the FBI. It also put into effect regulations controlling the travel and other conduct of the alien enemy population. The Alien Enemy Control Unit actually coordinated the activities of the FBI, the Immigration and Naturalization Service, the United States Attorney's office and other government departments, all of which performed many functions relating to alien enemies.

Every Federal judicial district had civilian personnel who heard the cases of arrested alien enemies. These hearing boards considered the evidence gathered by the FBI and the Immigration Service, interviewed and cross-examined the alien enemy and then made its recommendation to the Department of Justice. The Department of Justice, and not the War Department, decided the ultimate fate of each alien enemy, i.e., release, parole, or internment for the duration of the war. The recommendations of the boards were forwarded to the Alien Enemy Control Unit where each case was carefully reviewed. But only the Attorney General could issue orders regarding the alien enemy and such order was dependent on the Attorney General's judgment of the facts in each case.

James Rowe wrote:

The single test involved is that no chances can be taken, that any substantive doubts must be resolved in favor of the government. The number of persons apprehended since the beginning of the war exceeds 8,000.... So far internments have run about 50 percent of the cases heard; 33 percent have been placed on parole, and 17 percent have been released...in the first few weeks, the government took absolutely no chances on anyone.

The FBI agents have been thoroughly trained for this work. While their training course insists on scrupulous avoidance of Gestapo tactics, they are also taught not to take chances adversely affecting this country's welfare, which might allow a spy to remain at large or a saboteur to complete his work. A short time spent in custody by a person who has been erroneously suspected—while a definite hardship on the individual—is a small price to pay when weighed against the lives of American workers or the continued operation of plants supplying American soldiers. The purpose of the civilian hearing boards is to weigh considerations of the internal security of the nation against evidence pointing to suspicious activities of individuals. If any injustices are done, the technique exists specifically to remedy them as soon as possible while at the same time temporary detention safeguards the nation...

...all alien enemies have been forced to surrender radio transmitters, short-wave radio receiving sets, cameras, firearms, and certain other dangerous articles. These regulations are rigorously enforced. The FBI has conducted thousands of searches and has arrested many alien enemies for possessing prohibited articles. The penalty for possessing these is severe, and includes internment for the duration of the war.*

According to the CWRIC's report, *Personal Justice Denied*, published in 1983 as its "findings and recommendations" to the United States Congress, (P.88):

By May 1942, the FBI had seized 2,592 guns of various kinds; 199,000 rounds of ammunition; 1,652 sticks of dynamite; 1,458 radio receivers; 2,014 cameras and numerous other items which the alien Japanese had been ordered to surrender in January (1942).

Yet CWRIC stated in its "findings and recommendations" that there were no disloyalties among the thousands of resident Japanese nationals (alien enemies), and recommended payments of punitive damages for so-called "human suffering" even to alien enemies of Japanese descent who were apprehended by the FBI with valid security charges against them. The "eligibility" date according to the public law is *December 7, 1941*. $20,000 was the sum settled upon as payment to any "permanent resident alien" who was "evacuated, relocated, or interned." Japanese nationals were *not* "permanent resident aliens" as of December 7, 1941. They were *alien enemies* subject to internment under recognized international and national law.

Following the issuance of Executive Order 9066, Feb. 19, 1942, by the President, Secretary of War Henry L. Stimson was thereby authorized to prescribe military orders from which any or all persons may be excluded or in which their movements may be restricted. Under the executive order, Stimson could also designate this power to military commanders which he did. DeWitt's headquarters were in the Presidio of San Francisco and there he and John J. McCloy, Assistant Secretary of War, and Chief of Staff of the Army General Marshall conferred as to what steps should be taken to evacuate all persons of Japanese descent from the endangered West Coast. It was decided that a period of voluntary relocation should take place.

General DeWitt created the Wartime Civil Control Administration (WCCA) and appointed Colonel Bendetsen as its commanding officer and Assistant Chief of Staff. Under DeWitt Bendetsen was given full power and authority to act on DeWitt's orders which were immediately issued to Bendetsen via dictation taken by a stenotypist. DeWitt's order to Bendetsen read:

I hereby delegate to you all and in full my powers and authority under Executive Order 9066, which in turn have been delegated by The President to the Secretary of War, by the Secretary of War to the Chief of Staff, and by the Chief of Staff to the Commanding General of the Western Defense Command and Fourth Army. All rules and regulations of the Fourth Army over which I have any control or authority, you have authority to suspend, as in your judgment may be necessary. You will take this action forthrightly, you will establish a separate headquarters, you will have full authority to call upon all Federal civilian agencies as provided in the Executive Order and to call for assistance and the cooperation of the State authorities as The President has in turn asked the Governors of the states concerned to provide. You will do this with a minimum of disruption of the logistics of military training, operations and preparedness, and with a minimum of military personnel, and with due regard for the protection, education, health and welfare of all of the Japanese persons concerned. You will, to the maximum, take measures to induce them to relocate voluntarily under your authority, in areas east of the Cascades, Sierra Nevadas, and north of the southern half of Arizona and New Mexico, so that the burden upon them will be at a minimum. You will make known that the Army has no wish to retain them at any time for more than temporary custody. It would be contrary to the philosophy and desires of the Army to do otherwise. These measures are for the protection of the nation in a cruel and bitter war, and for the protection of the Japanese people themselves. You will use all measures to protect the personal property of Japanese, including crops.*

Col. Bendetsen stated that there were 24 temporary assembly centers established and equipped along the West Coast to house the

*The Alien Enemy Program—So Far, James Rowe, Jr., COMMON GROUND, Vol. II, Summer 1942.

*Karl R. Bendetsen, Col. USA (Ret.), July 9, 1981 Statement to the CWRIC.

evacuees affected by the exclusion orders which described the specific "red zones" on the west coast. In fact, the areas were strictly strategic so that *eastern portions of the States of Oregon and Washington never experienced any evacuation of persons of Japanese descent whatsoever*. Bendetsen later selected the sites for the ten relocation centers to which those persons of Japanese descent who had not already relocated to the interior States could be moved. The resettlement program would, of course, also eventually move thousands from the WRA centers into the economies of the 44 States *unaffected* by the exclusion orders. March 14, 1942, was the exact date of the establishment of the WCCA as an agency of the Western Defense Command.

In the latter part of February 1942, Hearings of the House Committee on National Defense Migration were begun on the Pacific Coast with regard to problems involved in dealing with enemy aliens and other persons living in that area.

On February 23, 1942, while still in session, the House Committee (known as the Tolan Committee) telegraphed the President, cabinet members, and all Congressional leaders urging the establishment of a regional office on the West Coast of *Alien Property Custodian*.

Under Bendetsen's lead, all of the Federal Agencies came to the assistance of the evacuees, including the Federal Reserve and the banks in the Federal Reserve system. The evacuees were given the assistance of the Departments of Agriculture and Interior under whose jurisdiction crops were harvested, sold, and monies were deposited into the respective accounts of the evacuees.

"The Federal Reserve Banks took charge of property owned by the evacuees, while The Farm Security Administration took over the agricultural property. This was necessary because of the social and economic vultures preying upon unfortunates expectant to evacuate."

—Mine Okubo, author
Citizen 13660, 1946

The 24 interim family assembly centers which were established, housed the evacuees in temporary shelters until the relocation centers could be built. Families were never separated except for some heads of households who had been arrested earlier and interned in Department of Justice internment camps. Mothers left with small children were well taken care of with special arrangements aboard trains to take them to designated evacuation zones and into temporary assembly centers which had been prepared especially to house them.

Many families relocated from assembly centers to other areas away from the excluded areas on the West Coast. Those who had not voluntarily resettled themselves were eventually moved to relocation centers. Once this was done, the Army by Presidential order, turned over the relocation centers to the War Relocation Authority. It was E.O. 9102 that created the WRA, a non-military agency with authority to formulate and carry out a program for a planned and orderly relocation of persons evacuated from military areas. Milton S. Eisenhower was the first Director, followed by Dillon S. Myer on June 17, 1942.

It has been falsely reported that the Japanese residents on the west coast were given only 24 to 48 hours in which to evacuate military designated areas. The facts are:

There was no mass evacuation of any persons until the authority to evacuate was given by President Roosevelt when he issued his Executive Order No. 9066 on February 19, 1942.

The only persons who were "rounded up" were those alien enemies known to be a danger to the national security. The arrests of German, Italian, and Japanese alien enemies began on December 7, 1941, and continued throughout the months of December 1941 and January 1942.

The very first order issued by Attorney General Biddle establishing restricted zones along the West Coast and regulating the movement of enemy aliens therein, did not come until January 29, 1942. Up until February 19, 1942, there were no exclusion orders pertaining to any American of Japanese descent.

The period of voluntary evacuation of persons of Japanese descent, including Japanese nationals who had no charges against them, began on February 19, 1942, under E.O. 9066, later ruled by the United States Supreme Court as "nothing more than an exclusion order." This was in *Korematsu* v. *United States*, (October 1944 Term). In a 6-3 decision, the U.S. Supreme Court upheld and affirmed the constitutionality of E.O. 9066, February 19, 1942.

Although General DeWitt had the authorization to exclude "any and all persons" and restrict movements of any class of people residing on the West Coast, he did not issue his first Proclamation until March 2, 1942, thereby designating military areas in the States of Washington, Oregon, California, and the southern half of Arizona. General DeWitt issued the March 2, 1942, Proclamation in order to designate Military Area No. 1 which included only the *western portions* of Oregon, Washington, and all of California. Military Area No. 2 comprised the remaining portions of these States. The *exclusion* order applied to *Japanese, German,* or *Italian* aliens as well as certain other persons known to support the Axis powers with whom the United States was at war. Meanwhile, alien enemies residing elsewhere who had no charges against them, continued to reside in their homes and work on jobs. Every alien enemy was required to complete a detailed questionnaire as the basis for receiving a certificate of identification which showed his photograph and fingerprints. All alien enemies—not just those of Japanese descent—were required to carry this identifying certificate with them at all times. All alien enemies—not only those of Japanese descent—were restricted to the communities in which they lived, except if commuting to their work-place. If travel was necessitated for any reason, complete information about the nature and destination of his trip had to be filed with the proper authorities. Upon approval for such travel, the alien enemy was given a special form indicating that the United States Attorney had been notified and approved the trip. No alien enemy was permitted to travel by air. No alien enemy could change his place of residence without permission of the United States Attorney. None of these requirements infringed on "civil rights" inasmuch as *alien enemies have no protection* of the United States Constitution or its Bill of Rights.

This recognized rule of international law has been overlooked by the recent Congress which accepted the "findings and recommendations" of CWRIC, which consistently refers to Japanese nationals as "permanent resident aliens." In fact, Japanese nationals—whether short-term or long-time residents of the United States—became no longer *residents* but alien enemies subject to internment under established national and international law.

Longtime residents of Italian and German nationalities were not upgraded to "permanent resident alien" status by this same Commission but were properly designated as alien enemies. Naturalization laws of the United States differed when it came to Japanese nationals, but the Oriental Exclusion Order was in effect lifted when the wartime government extended naturalization rights to *all* persons who would volunteer to aid the United States war effort against the Axis.

During World War I, there were a few Japanese nationals who gained United States citizenship by serving the war effort against Germany. Japanese nationals who were alien enemies following the bombing of Pearl Harbor by the Empire of Japan, could have joined other Orientals who had been excluded from citizenship, i.e., the Chinese, Koreans, and the Filipinos, in an opportunity to take out citizenship papers by virtue of fighting against fascist Japan. Not only did the Issei refuse the offer of citizenship under such circumstances, but the Nisei of military age were not forced to wage war in the Pacific theatre against the Emperor. The 442nd Regimental Combat Team fought in Europe; there were no American Japanese combat troops in the Pacific. Those Americans who served in Burma and other Pacific war zones, did so only as interpreters of captured Japanese prisoners or for translating confiscated enemy papers or diaries. Each American Japanese soldier in the Pacific was protected 24 hours a day by a guard, lest the American Japanese be mistaken for the enemy, or worse yet, be captured and tortured by Japan's military regime.

Those American Japanese soldiers in Europe and those in Military Intelligence Service in the Pacific, served honorably and well. Nonetheless, it is an historical fact that draftees and volunteers from other classes of Americans were not given the option of fighting in any particular war zone. This meant that Americans of German and Italian descent were often faced with battling the forces in Europe which were comprised of their own ancestors and, indeed, possibly distant relatives and even the immediate families of their parents.

Many of today's historians and government officials seem to forget or chose to overlook the fact that the primary duty of the President and the Congress was to secure the national safety. The United States Supreme Court recognized this by upholding the war powers of the Commander in Chief and by placing its confidence in time of war in our military leaders.

The provisions of the Constitution which confer on the Congress and the President powers to enable this country to wage war are as much part of the Constitution as provisions looking to a nation at peace. And we have had recent occasion to quote approvingly the statement of former Chief Justice Hughes that the power of the Government is 'the power to wage war successfully'. Therefore, the validity of action under the war power must be judged wholly in the context of war. That action is not to be stigmatized as lawless because like action in times of peace would be lawless.*

The adequate protection of military installations and strategic areas on the endangered west coast was of primary importance as was the safety of Japanese residents. Adequate protection in wartime must include government actions taken against any and all persons who are a danger, and disregarding the nationality of those persons. In the final analysis, it matters not if the disloyal is an American citizen for he is just as dangerous as an alien enemy loyal to the Axis nations. It was therefore determined that the power to exclude from any strategic military area must apply against "any and all persons" irrespective of citizenship.

Because initially the Department off Justice could only take action against alien enemies under the immediate Presidential Proclamations of December 7th and 8th, 1941, the Secretary of War requested that the President transfer the authority to exercise such power to "exclude any and all persons" based wholly on military reasons, from the Department of Justice to the War Department. This was accomplished by Executive Order 9066, Feb. 19, 1942.

It was enforced on the West Coast by the March 2, 1942, Proclamation of Gen. DeWitt and was also extended on the East Coast where military areas were also prescribed at Brooklyn Navy Yard and Staten Island, New York, and all other harbors and seaports.

The War Department and the Department of Justice worked cooperatively in treatment of alien enemies, with the latter having the ability and responsibility of interning dangerous alien enemies into Department of Justice Internment Camps. These *internment camps* for the proven disloyals must never be confused with the assembly centers under the Wartime Civil Control Administration (WCCA) or the relocation centers under the War Relocation Authority (WRA). These were established on March 14, 1942 and March 18, 1942, respectively.

It has been argued in the past and as recently as the hearings held by the CWRIC in 1981, that the United States should have followed the example of England by giving every single alien enemy in the United States individual hearings and based upon such hearings determined the need of alien enemy exclusion on the West Coast.

Former Justice Mr. Arthur J. Goldberg, who served as Commissioner on the CWRIC, testified before Committees of Congress that if such a small nation as England could handle their alien enemy problem, so then could the United States. Mr. Goldberg stated that the United States should have followed the example of Great Britain in time of war. However, Mr. Justice Goldberg failed to include that England had only 80,000 alien enemies with which to contend whereas there were about 400,000 alien enemies in New York City alone!

Furthermore, the techniques of "loyalty hearings" were never satisfactory because any trained espionage agent or saboteur could skillfully manufacture evidence of his loyalty and thus delude those who had not been trained in skills such as required by FBI agents or other intelligence agencies.

Milton Silverman, writing in the San Francisco *Chronicle* (May 26, 1943) informed readers:

> You don't have to work at Tule Lake. No matter whether you are a loyal American, or a dangerous enemy alien but smart enough to fool the FBI, you don't have to lift a finger and you'll still be provided with three meals a day, a room (which you furnish and clean yourself), medical care, and an opportunity to participate in the colony's recreation and educational facilities.

"The barbed wire at Manzanar consisted of three strings of cattle-guard wire through which anyone could walk if he wanted to. But nobody wanted to."
—Toyo Miyatake, Photographer
Manzanar and Poston WRA centers

To exempt certain groups of alien enemies, such

*Mr. Justice Felix Frankfurter, concurring in upholding E.O. 9066, Feb. 19, 1942, "as of the time it was made." *Korematsu* v. *United States*, (Oct. Term 1944), (323 US 214-248).

as those who were longtime residents, would be dangerous to national security because as intelligence reports prior to December 7, 1941, and throughout the war showed, dangerous and disloyal individuals infiltrated such groups, especially within the closely-knit Japanese communities. Many of these individuals used organizations and other "fronts" as protective cloaks for their anti-American activities.

Recent reports in the media and television "docu-dramas" falsely portray evacuees as being "herded" into cattle-cars accompanied by commentary stating these evacuees had less than "24 hours notice" to leave their residences. No mention is made that the majority of the *adults were alien enemies subject to internment and deportation.*

On March 6, 1942, the Federal Reserve Bank acted as an agent of the Treasury Department to assist evacuees; the Farm Security Administration assisted in placing non-Japanese operators on farms and properties held in trust for evacuees. Before these two agencies were given those responsibilities, the Alien Property Custodian had the burden. The claim that evacuees "lost everything" is a false claim and the facts are clarified in testimony given by Milton S. Eisenhower, first Director of the WRA, at Hearings of the Subcommittee of the Committee on Appropriations, House of Representatives, 77th Congress, June 29, 1942:

Before the War Relocation Authority was established, the Treasury Department had accepted the responsibility for establishing, through the Federal Reserve Bank on the coast, a voluntary system to aid the Japanese in disposing of their property in the military zone by sale, lease, storage, or otherwise. A little later the President signed an Executive Order setting up an Alien Property Custodian. Rather than to have two agencies dealing with the property problem on the coast, the Alien Property Custodian delegated all of its authority to the Treasury and the Federal Reserve Bank.

When the War Relocation Authority was set up, the Executive Order contained a brief section to enable the Authority to cooperate in handling the property problem. Again to avoid duplication, I also delegated such authority as I had to the Treasury. So the Treasury, through the Federal Reserve Bank, has worked with the evacuees to the extent that the evacuees wished,

in giving them a voluntary service in disposing of their property. Those who owned land in most instances leased it. However, very serious problems were encountered, where there were verbal leases and complicated debtor-creditor situations. Some—in fact, a good portion—of the household furniture, was stored.

"At another desk I made the necessary arrangement to have my household property stored by the government."
—Mine Okubo, author
Citizen 13660, 1946

Except for the immediate round-ups of dangerous alien enemies by the FBI, and the internment of these alien enemies in internment camps, there is no truth in charges that the United States gave "no notice or warnings" of impending evacuation of either alien enemies or citizens of Japanese descent residing in Military Areas on the West Coast.

Civilian Exclusion Order No. 1, issued by Gen. DeWitt, affecting all persons of Japanese descent, came on March 23, 1942, following numerous "hell-raising" events by the Imperial Japanese Navy along and just off the coasts of California, Oregon and Washington.

December 10-23, 1941	Nine aircraft-carrier Imperial submarines patrolling within sight of land from Cape Flattery, Washington, to San Diego, California. Ships *Agwiworld,* attacked off Santa Cruz; *Absaroka* hit off Southern California put into pier at Long Beach with huge torpedo hole in hull; *Samoa, Larry Doheny, Montebello* hit, escaped. *S.S. Emidio,* torpedoed off Cape Mendocino broke in half, stern sank—people killed.
February 16-23	Imperial submarine *I-17* patrols in Santa Barbara Channel, attacks onshore oil wells with deck gun on 23rd. (American serviceman wounded—received Purple Heart.)

The Pacific War had indeed come to the shores of the mainland of the United States. The public was nervous. The military folks no longer slept at night. Would other coastal installations be attacked? What about the Naval Station at San Diego? What about Bremerton Navy Yard in Washington?

Intelligence reports involved activities of both first and second generation Japanese residents and required evacuation of Bainbridge Island, in Puget Sound across from Seattle and adjacent to the Bremerton Navy yard. Although the Civilian Exclusion Order was issued on March 23, Japanese on Bainbridge were ordered off "on or before March 30, 1942." As we have seen, the government assisted evacuees with every agency put at its disposal.

On March 27, 1942, a curfew order covered German and Italian aliens and all persons of Japanese descent in Military Area No. 1, requiring them to be in their places of residence between the hours of 8 p.m. and 6 a.m. This order also forbid German, Italian and Japanese aliens to possess firearms, explosives, cameras, transmitting sets or shortwave receiving sets, and barred travel more than five miles from home without a permit. The reasons for including the Nisei (American citizens of Japanese descent), was the fact that the majority of Nisei of military age held dual citizenship. Under Japanese laws these Americans were duty-bound to give military service, regardless of residence, to Japan! Secondly, intelligence reports were so closely guarded—MAGIC intercepts—that the breaking of the Japanese code was later adjudged to have been the best kept secret of the war. Many of these intercepts clearly involved second-generation residents of Japanese descent (*American citizens*) with participation in anti-American activities and belonging to an active network of fifth columnists up and down the West Coast. When the curfew order against all persons of Japanese descent was tested, it was upheld unanimously by the United States Supreme Court. Because the test cases for both exclusion and curfew were in the courts while the United States was still at war and MAGIC could not be shared with either the Courts or the American public, the reasons of military necessity were not specifically given during those 1943-1944 trials. In fact, many of the documents were "sanitized." These documents were kept classified until the broadened 1977 Freedom of Information Act and the subsequent executive orders releasing this information.

A case in point is the 1977-1978 Department of Defense 8-volume set of books *The "Magic" Background of Pearl Harbor*, available from the U.S. Government Printing Office (008-000-00233-9). Ironically, the CWRIC had access to this material but in fact the CWRIC and its staff claimed never to know of MAGIC or its significance. Therefore, no consideration was given by the CWRIC of the effect intelligence had on President Roosevelt and his decision to issue E.O. 9066, Feb. 19, 1942. Serious study of Volume One of this set of books will convince readers of the *military necessity* for the controversial exclusion order.

FBI searches in Military Areas on the West Coast revealed that long after the order to turn in prohibited contraband, large caches of arms and ammunitions were still being uncovered as late as May and June 1942.

Although there had been arrests of alien enemy Japanese on Terminal Island, California, as early as December 7, 1941, and for weeks afterwards, it was determined that all persons of Japanese descent be evacuated from the strategic area because of intelligence reports—MAGIC—of continuing danger to the national security. Thus, on March 30, 1942, the remaining families of Japanese ancestry were ordered to evacuate Terminal Island. But not "overnight," as is claimed. They were to evacuate the Terminal Island area in Los Angeles harbor by April 5th and move to the assembly center at Santa Anita. Government provided transportation. Evacuees could take what they could carry with them. Heavy items would follow in Army trucks or be stored at government expense as long as necessary. No evacuee was asked or required to sell anything at a loss.

The *voluntary evacuation* from Military Area No. 1 by persons of Japanese descent had been prohibited just the day before (March 29, 1942), and from then on there was a more orderly movement of evacuees to assembly centers, then followed the resettlement program worked out by the War Relocation Authority. During the latter part of February, and before March 29, 1942, approximately *8,000 families voluntarily moved from the Military Areas into eastern Oregon and eastern Washington and to neighboring states*. However, voluntary evacuation did not work as well as earlier envisioned. Milton Eisenhower described his observations before the House Appropriations Committee on June 15, 1942:

> There was wide-spread and bitter opposition in the inter-mountain States (Utah and Colorado)

for a number of reasons: First, the States did not wish the evacuees to acquire real property, as some did. Evacuees moved to localities where there had previously been a small Japanese population and difficulties arose there. Second, demands arose that the Government should guarantee that evacuees would be removed from the States to which they were going as soon as the war was over. Third, the demand was made that evacuees be permitted to move only under guard. Serious trouble was threatened. At one location in Oregon and at another in Nevada, Japanese were arrested. In Utah a stick of dynamite was set off in protest against the arrival of 25 evacuees. In Colorado and other places mass meetings were held in protest.

Practically every governor of the Western States protested the dispersal of the Japanese. I think their feeling was, as expressed publicly, that if a danger existed in the military zone, then a similar danger existed in the inter-mountain States where there are a number of strategic works.

It's important to emphasize that the voluntary movement of persons of Japanese descent into these inter-mountain States, was not cordially received because of other factors. The heads of households in the majority of cases were Issei alien enemies who spoke only Japanese. Here then was a unique phenomenon. Midwest state folks could not handle this language barrier. Historical records also show there was hostility against those with German and Italian surnames, and in the latter case were described by a generalized nickname, "WOP." This term was adopted decades earlier by the Immigration and Naturalization Service to describe Italian immigrants who were "Without Papers" needed in the naturalization process.

Prior to World War II, the term "JAP" had no derogatory meaning. It was internationally accepted as an abbreviation for the country, Japan, and/or for its people: "Japs." The term "Jap" was also a handy contraction in newspaper headlines as it took considerably less space than spelling out "Japanese." But when the war erupted and the Japanese Army was quickly observed to be brutal, the connotation of "Jap" became a "dirty, aggressive enemy." Efforts were made in the United States to stamp out the word "Jap" after the war, but in 1989 many Americans, now in retirement, who took part in the war, still often use "Jap" in its war-time

connection. Some steps have been made to change this to JPN and NIKKEI as identifiers.

To keep the historical record accurate, it should be pointed out that some of the same American Japanese who led the movement to get rid of the term "JAP," have been the ones to promote the use of terms "concentration camps" and "internment camps" to describe wartime temporary relocation centers under the WRA.

It takes no historian to recognize that the World War II connotation of "concentration camp" is "death camp." Contrary to recent rewritings of WWII history with reference to the evacuation and relocation programs, the term "relocation center" is in no way a euphemism for "concentration camps."

A relocation center was precisely what it implied: a temporary shelter until resettlement could be made. The War Relocation Authority was called upon to assume the responsibilities of assisting in the relocation of individual excludees on both the East and West Coasts, of persons in addition to those of Japanese descent. For these people, there were no wayside shelters as was provided for Japanese residents. No attempt was made to provide even temporary quarters such as the assembly centers.

Instead, the War Relocation Authority merely undertook to assist these individual evacuees in transferring out of the Military Areas designated on both the East and West Coasts. Once the excluded persons were settled outside the military areas, the responsibility for providing him and his dependents with any further public assistance rested with State welfare agencies and with the Bureau of Public Assistance of the Federal Security Agency.

We observe therefore that the WRA handled excludees of German and Italian descent in a completely different manner than what was provided for Japanese nationals and their families who were permitted to reside in safety for the duration of the war in the relocation centers.

The War Relocation Authority gave the following assistance to persons (other than Japanese residents):

1) Advice and information to the excludee regarding employment opportunities and desirable work localities in unrestricted regions; 2) transportation and subsistence during a temporary period of adjustment, usually not over four weeks; 3) assistance in connection with property matters; and 4) special guidance in connection

with family difficulties.

The War Relocation Authority did not seek out individual excludees who had to leave the military areas, but acted only when the agency was requested to help in cases of actual need, including some financial aid. However, when it came to Japanese evacuees (alien enemy and American Japanese), every agency at the disposal of the War Relocation Authority was put into immediate action at great expense to the wartime government.

On the West Coast, the individual cases of hardship suffered by German and Italian aliens excluded from military areas were handled by the War Relocation Authority's Division of Evacuee Property from its offices in San Francisco, Los Angeles, and Seattle. To handle the same needs on the Atlantic seaboard, special offices under the WRA were established at New York City, Baltimore, Boston, and Atlanta. Hardship suffered by German and Italian evacuees receives little or no attention in history books or in the press thus making it appear as if only persons of Japanese descent were affected by the exclusion orders undertaken for military necessity and public safety.

Although this book's main theme is the relocation of Japanese and American Japanese from the endangered West Coast, the author would be remiss if the individual exclusion program affecting the 16 states in the Eastern Defense Command went unreported.

On September 10, 1942, Lt. General Hugh A. Drum, who headed the Eastern Defense Command, and had responsibility equal to that of General DeWitt on the west coast, announced an exclusion program for 16 states—Maine to Florida—along the Eastern seaboard. This exclusion affected "any person whose presence in the Eastern military area is deemed dangerous to the national defense." The WRA was then authorized to assist these persons. In some cases, where a German national was head of household and had been interned by the Department of Justice, arrangements were made for his family to *voluntarily* intern themselves with him in a special family camp known as Crystal City Internment Camp in Texas. This book includes a chapter about Crystal City.

The responsibility for assisting evacuees of Japanese descent on the West Coast was first handled by the Treasury Department, the Federal Reserve Bank of San Francisco, and the Farm Security Administration at the time of actual evacuation. The care of the evacuees was finally under the direct supervision of WRA Division of Evacuee Property. This Division set up branches in San Francisco, Los Angeles and Seattle. Evacuation matters that could not be handled by an evacuee, could be cared for through his authorized agent. In the case of the Issei, the Japanese American Citizens League helped cross the language barrier. The principal services of the Division of Evacuee Property were:

1) To secure tenants or operators for both agricultural and commercial properties; 2) to negotiate new leases or renewals of existing leases; 3) to obtain buyers for real or personal property of all kinds; 4) to effect settlement of claims for or against an evacuee. (If an indigent evacuee required legal services, such services were provided without charge); 5) to adjust differences arising as a result of inequitable, hastily made or indefinite agreements; 6) to obtain an accounting for amounts owing and to facilitate collection thereof; 7) to ascertain whether property was being satisfactorily maintained; 8) to check inventories of goods and equipment, and recommend utilization of material for the best interests of the evacuee and the nation at war.

In this last instance, the WRA worked toward the conservation of property on behalf of the evacuee while at the same time promoting the use of that property in behalf of the nation's war effort.

Farmlands, for instance, were kept in production to provide food. To this end, the WRA sought competent tenants for an evacuee's farm if the evacuee had been unable to do so himself. Management of residential properties such as apartment buildings, hotels and homes were put into the hands of others who would thus serve not only on behalf of the evacuee owner, but for the community where war industries had created an acute housing shortage.

Lands were leased; properties were not lost. Monies in the Yokohama Specie Bank were frozen. Although these funds did not earn interest, the monies were never confiscated. The accounts were held in trust.

Most of the requests for property assistance in the Los Angeles area involved the liquidation of small shops or the disposal of store furnishings and fixtures. In *all* cases, bids were obtained and submitted to the owners. However, some evacuees made no requests for assistance and handled disposal on their own. In some cases there is little doubt that losses occurred where unscrupulous people took advantage of the evacuees' wartime plight. But considering the fact that the majority of the adults involved were alien enemy Japanese Nationals, subject to internment and confiscation of all properties, the United States government, through the War Relocation Authority, handled situations not only in a businesslike manner but with an attitude for being friendly and understanding. Certainly every other nation at war gave little thought or priority to its alien enemies and their families. The Empire of Japan disregarded all human rights of alien enemies, both civilian and military, and used little or none of its resources to give "comfort to the enemy."

In contrast, at the time of the evacuation on the West Coast, the War Department instructed the Federal Reserve Bank at San Francisco and its West Coast branches, to lease 19 warehouses (totaling 386,000 square feet of space), to store the household furnishings and personal properties of evacuee families. The warehouses were leased in the principal cities of the evacuated areas and were offered *at no cost to evacuees* to store their goods and properties as these people wanted to place there until these items could be shipped to new addresses in unaffected areas or to relocation centers. Although 2,867 families took advantage of this free service, hundreds of other families privately arranged to store their furnishings in community churches, stores, private warehouses and other facilities in widely scattered communities. For example:

In a few days many of us will be moving out of Alameda with the parents, thus leaving the dear friends behind. Let us not look upon this evacuation as a persecution. It is quite a natural step for the government to take in wartime. Most of us have lived here for many, many years under the kindness and friendship of Americans. Let us leave with the feeling of gratitude and friendliness toward them.—Rev. Shimada, Alameda Methodist Church *Bulletin*, Sunday, February 15, 1942, Alameda, California.

• • •

Piano or any piece of furniture which you do not wish to take with you, or have it stored, will be appreciated by the Red Cross or by the U.S.O. Please see Min Akamatsu.

• • •

More on Draftees. Best wishes to Haruo Hanamura, who left for the U.S. Army last Thursday morning. Corporal Eiichi Suzukawa was home on an emergency furlough to help his parents evacuate. From the way he looked and talked, he certainly must be treated A-1 in Cheyenne, Wyoming.

The Valentine Party which was planned... will be canceled on account of this unfortunate situation.

The *Bulletin* of this Alameda church is dated *before* issuance of Executive Order 9066, February 19, 1942, and pinpoints the *voluntary evacuation*. Until February 19, 1942, and only after subsequent civilian orders were issued by General DeWitt, *no American citizen of Japanese ancestry was required to leave the west coast military areas. Earlier Executive Orders were applicable only to German, Italian and Japanese aliens.* In the latter case, evacuation of Japanese nationals was strictly on a voluntary basis. Even when the evacuation order finally came, it was acknowledged as a "natural step for the government to take in wartime."

The Japanese American Citizens League representatives were in full accord with the need for exclusion and evacuation of all persons of Japanese descent on the West Coast where an invasion by forces of Japan seemed imminent.

A publication of the Japanese Chamber of Commerce of Southern California (1960), *Japanese in Southern California: A History of 70 Years* declared:

The alien Japanese would have to go as a matter of course. They did not even have the cloak of citizenship with which they might question the evacuation orders. Most of them were and are the parents of Japanese Americans. They were and are very old as a group, averaging close to 60 years.... The least their children, the Japanese American, could do was to volunteer to go along with them and to help them as best they could as one way of trying to repay their parents for all the sacrifices which they had made for them. The Japanese Americans were duty-bound to share the adversity and hardships of a cruel adventure with their parents in the twilight of their lives.

In view of the fact that histories relating to American Japanese in the U.S.A. during World War II are now being "sanitized," it is no wonder this publication has never been listed on any recommended reading list for Asian-American

Studies courses, even though the book explains in full detail why the Japanese American Citizens League's leaders agreed to the evacuation of all persons of Japanese descent. The quotation printed here is attributed to Mike Masaoka, wartime Secretary of the National JACL.

No action undertaken by the WRA in Washington, D.C., under the leadership of either Milton Eisenhower or Dillon Myer, occurred without the approval of Mike Masaoka.

"The unprecedented acceptance of Japanese Americans everywhere in the land in the 1960s is a living tribute to the correctness and vision of WRA policies and practices."
—Mike M. Masaoka, JACL in
"Foreword" *Uprooted Americans*
(1971)

Forty-seven years after the war, Masaoka testified before the CWRIC and in his written Statement for the Subcommittee on Administrative Law and Government Relations, Committee of the Judiciary, United States House of Representatives, April 28, 1986, that:

...neither the Jews nor we, for instance, want our bitter and brutal stories of World War II forgotten, forgiven or forsaken. Though only half-a-century has passed since the holocaust in Europe and the evacuation in America, there are a number of Americans who insist that there were no genocide camps in Hitler's Germany and no nightmarish detention prisons in Roosevelt's United States.

In March 1942, Japanese American Citizens League leaders agreed that Japan's legions were on the offensive with the successful, surprise and deadly raid on Hawaii still fresh in everyone's minds, people were truly afraid of a thrust against America's west coast.

Looking again at *Japanese in Southern California: A History of 70 Years:*

America was just beginning to organize for the great task confronting her. To many, a Japanese invasion in force of the Pacific Coast was imminent. If we Japanese Americans had refused to cooperate with the government and the Army was forced to divert large numbers of its troops from preparing defenses to forcibly eject us from what were named as prohibited zones, the American people would never have forgiven us for such action. In America's darkest hours, we could not force her to weaken her defenses and invite invasion. And if Japan had launched a landing, timed with the army's pre-occupation with the Japanese resistance to evacuation, the future would not be worth considering for Japanese Americans in the United States.

As pointed out, responsibility for the storage of evacuee personal property became that of the WRA. By September 20, 1942, seven of the nineteen warehouses had been cleared. By now, 84,000 square feet of space for such additional storage was ready. Shipments of personal belongings to relocation centers had now cleared much of the storage space in these government-leased facilities. Accordingly, today's cry, "We lost everything," should fall on deaf ears. Those Japanese who did sell their various goods, may have done so in order to keep food on the table. This was one of many challenges confronting Japanese communities along the west coast and provided another reason for the establishment of shelters for families unable to care for themselves. Some families suddenly indigent, became so as the breadwinner often was an alien enemy who had been arrested then interned in a Department of Justice Camp. This left mothers with half-a-dozen mouths to feed and no income. Even though hundreds of evacuees who wanted to do so and otherwise could have left the assembly centers for unaffected areas, those *chose* to spend war years in a relocation center. At least in the centers there was a roof over their heads and the food was free. (It may be worthwhile to remind that the American civilian population was forced to stand in lines to obtain many foods which were rationed and required ration "stamps" to obtain. The residents of the relocation centers had no rationing worries.)

This offer of free room and board did not go unnoticed. Japanese families, as well as single persons residing in areas not covered by the exclusion orders requested to come from unaffected States into the relocation centers. All who asked to come were accepted.

It hardly holds if the relocation centers were "concentration camps" no one not directly affected would have asked to be admitted! (*Silent Siege-II* p. 212)

Some of the evacuees who moved voluntarily from the assembly centers and relocation centers to other areas in which they were permitted to reside, found that they could not find suitable jobs so returned to the relocation centers *voluntarily*. Most of those who left the assembly centers joined the 25,000 other persons of Japanese descent who were *never affected* by any military orders to evacuate their areas located in 44 other States.

Because there was a substantial percentage of the voluntary evacuees wanting to return to the WRA facilities, the War Relocation Authority announced that as soon as all of the relocation centers are built, the voluntary evacuees "may come to the relocation centers and live there for the duration of the war," stated Milton Eisenhower before the Hearings for Appropriations for WRA for 1943 (Testimony, 77th Congress, June 29, 1942).

He was asked further about the attitude of the evacuees about the exclusion. He testified:

Remarkably cooperative. For example, the Japanese American citizens have an organization called the Japanese American Citizens League, and it has carried on a most vigorous educational program among the total population, urging 100 percent cooperation. In fact, I just cannot say things too favorable about the way they have cooperated under the most adverse circumstances.

Eisenhower was then asked if the War Relocation Authority was doing anything which could, "by the most liberal interpretation," be construed as a failure to comply with all the provisions of the Geneva Conference in reference to the evacuated people from the West Coast put into his charge.

Eisenhower emphatically replied that the Geneva Convention "does not apply to American citizens or to evacuees generally; it applies legally to prisoners of war and, by unilateral declaration of the United States, as I understand it, to internees. **The Relocation Centers are not concentration camps or internment camps. I wish to emphasize that the evacuees are not prisoners of war or internees.**"

A summary of how the evacuation and relocation of persons of Japanese descent on the West Coast was handled was summarized by the man best able to clarify this most misunderstood and highly propagandized action—the late Col. Karl R. Bendetsen. His account was submitted to the CWRIC on July 8, 1981, with the request that it be placed in the records of the Hearings July 14-16 to be held in Washington, D.C. Bendetsen's written Statement was not entered into the CWRIC records nor was his Statement made available to members of the media in the PRESS PACKS distributed for information purposes. Written statements of others were read at these hearings but not that of Colonel Bendetsen.

The author of this book was the only pro-government witness allowed to testify at the July 16, 1981 Hearing, and reported to both Col. Bendetsen and the Hon. John J. McCloy, Assistant Secretary of War during the World War II, if they wanted their Statements made part of the historical record, I urged they give *oral* testimony which the subsequently did.

Bendetsen's summary of his points include:

First, about their assets, their lands [Nisei could own land], their possessions, their bank accounts and other assets, their household goods, their growing crops—nothing was confiscated. Their accounts were left intact. Their household goods were inventoried and stored. Warehouse receipts were issued to the owners. Much of it was later shipped to them at government expense, particularly in cases of those families who relocated themselves in the interior, accepted employment and established new homes.

Lands were farmed, crops harvested, accounts kept of sales at market and proceeds deposited to the respective accounts of the owners.

Second, it was never intended by Executive Order 9066, and certainly not by the Army, that the Japanese themselves be held in relocation centers. The sole objective was to bring about relocation away from the Sea Frontier. Japanese were urged to relocate voluntarily on their own recognizance and extensive steps were taken to this end. The desire was to relocate them so that they could usefully and gainfully continue raising their families and educate their children while heads of families and young adults became gainfully employed. They were to be free to lease land, raise and harvest crops, go into businesses. They were not to be restricted so long as they did not seek to remain or seek to return to the war 'frontier' of the West Coast.

In furtherance, from the very beginning I

initiated diligent measures to urge the Japanese families to leave with the help and funding (whenever needed) of the WCCA [Wartime Civil Control Administration] on their own recognizance and resettle east of the mountains. To this end, I conferred with the governors of the seven contiguous states east of the mountains. I called a Governor's Conference at Salt Lake City. I invited them to urge attendance by members of their cabinets, by members of their legislatures and by the mayors of their communities. It was a large and successful conference. I advised them in full, sought their full cooperation, asked them to inform their citizens and to welcome and help the evacuees to feel welcome without restrictions, to become members of their inland communities and schools and to help them find employment and housing. I told them that these people would become a most constructive segment of their respective populations. Those who resettled certainly did. Where needed, I told them that the WCCA would provide financial support for a limited period.

It is obvious why Bendetsen's Statement was never made public for it was in bold contradiction to the "official version" of the event being concocted by the dissident factions within today's Japanese communities. This group was described by Senator S. I. Hayakawa as "a wolf-pack of young Japanese-American dissidents, most of whom weren't even born during World War II."

This "official version" was discredited by the Department of Justice which recommended to President Ronald Reagan that the "findings and recommendations" of the CWRIC, published in its report *Personal Justice Denied*, be dismissed as invalid, historically inaccurate and based on what was described as "political opportunism, intellectual dishonesty and moral posturing."—Dr. Ken Matsugi, son of WWII evacuees, Fellow, Claremont College, California, before Hearings, U.S. Senate Subcommittee on Democratic Practices and Procedures, July 7, 1983, 98th Congress, First Session on S.1520, Report on CWRIC.

Karl Bendetsen's Statement was sent to the author for archival purposes. It serves the reader, and in the interest of historical accuracy, to publish additional remarks from it.

Further to this end, I conferred with the elders of each major Japanese community along the Pacific Coast, wherever they were. I carefully explained all this to them. I expressed deep regret that this unfortunate situation had arisen. I urged them to persuade their fellow Japanese to leave *before* the evacuation to assembly centers began and while it was proceeding. I assured them that the WCCA would provide escort, if requested, for those who felt insecure. We organized convoys and shipped to those who had resettled, their stored possessions. I urged their cooperation. To their eternal credit, it was given.

This phase of resettlement from temporary assembly centers came to a regrettable and unnecessary halt. Hostility toward the Japanese in the interior, at first minimal, developed quite suddenly and intensively in the western states of the interior as word of the brutalities committed against U.S. military and civilian forces by the Japanese [military] became generally known.

The protection of the evacuees mandated that such a measure be instituted. I visited each assembly center and discussed the reasons for this with leaders among the evacuees. They fully understood. Assurances were given that unremitting efforts would be taken with state and city officials and with community leaders to deal with and to defuse these attitudes. Further assurances were given that resettlement from the ten relocation centers would resume in due course. Fortunately, within four to five months, these hostile feelings moderated due to the good offices of officials, community leaders and the press of these interior states. The process of relocation from the assembly centers to the relocation centers resumed. The WCCA resumed its actions to foster relocation or more properly 'resettlement' directly from the relocation centers.

Over four thousand took advantage of the opportunity to leave on their own recognizance with WCCA help in the first three to four months following March 1942.

In Senator Spark Matsunaga's testimony before the CWRIC, he emphasized his *false* statement that evacuees were "prisoners" and could not leave the relocation centers; that they were "detained" unlawfully and were brutally treated. Mr. Matsunaga declared that evacuees died due to lack of medical care. The fact is that the only evacuees detained and unable to resettle outside the WRA centers, were those who *refused to take a loyalty oath* and give unqualified allegiance to the United States.

The U.S. Supreme Court's opinion in *Korematsu* v. *United States*, written by Mr. Justice Hugo

Black, verifies Colonel Bendetsen's statement that thousands never went from the assembly centers to relocation centers. The Court acknowledged that had Korematsu (the Plaintiff) left the prohibited area and gone to an assembly center:

> ...we cannot say either as a matter of fact or law that his presence in that center would have resulted in his detention in a relocation center. Some who did report to the assembly centers were not sent to relocation centers, but were released under the condition that they remain outside the prohibited zone until the military orders were modified or lifted.

The Court emphasized in its landmark decision:

> To cast this case into outlines of racial prejudice without reference to the real military dangers which were presented, merely confuses the issue. **Korematsu was not excluded from the Military Area because of hostility to him or his race.** He *was* excluded because we are at war with the Japanese Empire, because the military authorities feared an invasion of our west coast and felt constrained to take proper security measures • • • because Congress, reposing its confidence in this time of war in our military leaders—as inevitably it must—determined that they should have the power to do just this.

...I had been led to think when the Japanese evacuation cases were argued in Washington, D.C. that the Japanese Army might land on the West Coast and if it did, there was nothing to stop it short of the Rockies.
—William O. Douglas, Justice of the U.S. Supreme Court, letter to Bert Webber 1972

There was evidence of disloyalty on the part of some, the military authorities considered the need for action was great and the time was short. We cannot—by availing ourselves of the calm perspective of hindsight—now say that at that time these actions were unjustified.

Thirty years after Justice Black wrote his opinion for the court, he stated that he still held that opinion and had he been President Roosevelt he would have declared Martial Law on the entire west coast!

As for Senator Matsunaga's erroneous and outrageous claim that evacuees died due to bad medical treatment, WRA records show that the lowest incidence of disease anywhere in the United States during WWII, was in the relocation centers, as was the highest live-birth rate.

Colonel Bendetsen, in his SUMMARY emphasized that *internment* was never intended for the evacuees without charges against them. The intention and purpose, he said, was to resettle these persons east of the mountain ranges and away from the Sea Frontier on the Pacific Coast and away from the open boundaries between Mexico and the states of Arizona and New Mexico. The latter restrictions were based upon intelligence community reports of wide-range networks of Japanese long established in Mexico prior to Pearl Harbor, who had been counted on by Japan to aid in the invasion by Japanese forces on the Pacific Rim. Recently declassified documents from the FBI, the Office of Naval Intelligence, and the 1977-1978 Department of Defense publication, *The "Magic" Background of Pearl Harbor*, provides proof positive of the *military necessity* for our government's actions. This fact needs repeating.

Bendetsen prepared an Official Report, June 5, 1943, for General DeWitt. The letter of transmittal of the "Report to the Chief of Staff of the Army," consists of 10 paragraphs, and is included in the June 5, 1943 Official Report. The Library of Congress card catalogue reference under the letter "U" is officially titled: United States Army, Western Defense Command and Fourth Army, Japanese Evacuation from the West Coast.

This nine-part Report, consisting of 28 chapters with extensive reference materials and special reports appended, was offered to the Commission on Wartime Relocation. The Commission was told by letter where and how this Report could be found and utilized. These reference materials included the reports of many Federal civilian agencies which had been placed under General DeWitt's direction by order of President Roosevelt. In addition, various primary source materials were selected and bound together by the Government Printing Office. Two of these special reports, for example, were from the Farm Security Administration of the Department of Agriculture and the Federal Reserve Bank of San Francisco, a part of the Federal Reserve system. The special reports numbered twelve in all, and the entire Official Report and supplemental materials was filed in the Library of Congress as well as with the

War Department's custodial Adjutant General.

All of these papers including General DeWitt's Report were published immediately. At DeWitt's request, distribution of the Report and its associated materials were made available to Federal and State agencies, public libraries, colleges and universities. DeWitt's recommendations were adopted.

The only matters not detailed were the yet *classified* documents pertaining to MAGIC messages, which therefore could not be included in DeWitt's Final Report. However, in Chapter Two of Bendetsen's Report, DeWitt discusses the need for military control and for evacuation as well as subsequent chapter discussion of the establishment of the WCCA under E.O. 9066.

The complete Report which provided considerable detail of the nature and characteristics of Japanese communities along the West Coast, were offered to CWRIC and its Staff as a useful study of the evacuation and relocation, particularly so because of its context and setting. The Report was *urged* upon the CWRIC in order for the Commission to evaluate these past events in the perspectives of today's investigation and what would result in the CWRIC's recommendations to the Congress.

Bendetsen's Report and DeWitt's complete logging of materials available at the Library of Congress were completely ignored by the CWRIC and its staff because *the CWRIC had predetermined its conclusions!* □

In the Television Docu-drama (PBS) titled *Super Chief: Life and Legacy of Earl Warren* (1989), revisionist writers stated that "children were separated from their parents." Further, Senator Spark Matsunaga declared that evacuees "lost educational opportunities." These statements lack validity. FACTS: Families were kept together at great cost to American taxpayers. There were no "educational opportunities" lost per this chart from War Relocation Authority File C-2401 P61 bu. Semi-annual Report July/December 1944.

TABLE IX - ENROLLMENT AND TEACHERS EMPLOYED BY CENTER (WRA), DECEMBER, 1944

CENTER	ENROLLMENT/1			TEACHERS APPOINTED AND CERTIFIED EVACUEES			ASSISTANT TEACHERS		
	Total	Elem.	H.S.	Total	Elem.	H.S.	Total	Elem.	H.S.
TOTAL	18,202	8,263	9,939	477	197	280	236	105	131
Central High	1,427	617	810	32	11	21	27	9	18
Colorado Riv.	3,217	1,454	1,763	82	36	46	46	28	18
Gila River	2,621	1,289	1,332	63	27	36	25	14	11
Granada	1,681	790	891	47	20	27	29	7	22
Heart Mt.	2,195	972	1,223	63	25	38	29	14	15
Manzanar	1,349	678	671	39	18	21	9	5	4
Minidoka	1,699	685	1,014	44	19	25	13	5	8
Rohwer	1,869	856	1,013	53	23	30	13	5	8
Tule Lake	2,144	922	1,222	54	18	36	45	18	27

1/ Nursery school enrollment 1,313; post high school, adult and vocational 7,168.

Chapter 3

The Family Camp at Crystal City, Texas

CRYSTAL CITY INTERNMENT CAMP

Prior to the autumn of 1942, the United States government had been considering the establishment of a family internment camp. In this regard, a Farm Security Administration migratory labor camp was inspected and established for male internees, at Kenedy (Texas), and its female counterpart was operated at the Federal Correctional Institute for Women at Seagonville, Texas. However, it was clearly a priority of the Immigration and Naturalization Service (INS) to establish a family camp for internee couples and their children.

On November 6th and 7th, 1942, a few officials of the INS laid plans for converting a migratory labor camp, under the Farm Security Administration, into a family internment camp at Crystal City, Texas.

Originally, the Crystal City camp was intended wholly for persons of Japanese descent and it was estimated that this group would total no more than 2,000 individuals. However, it developed there were considerably more internees than expected thus at maximum, 3,500 people of Japanese descent were at Crystal City Internment Camp by early 1945.

The additional numbers included American Japanese from the Tule Lake Segregation Center who had renounced their citizenship and were therefore treated as alien enemies. They swelled the ranks of the "hard-core" pro-Japan enemies already at Crystal City, which also included Japanese from Peru, Mexico, and Hawaii. All of these people had been charged as security risks.

American citizens of Japanese descent who were at Tule Lake Segregation Center and had requested expatriation and a return to Japan, were permitted to do so under Public Law No. 405, July 1, 1944, 78th Congress, Amendment to the National Act of 1940. The amended act enabled dual-citizen American Japanese to renounce their American citizenship (in time of war) thus legally permitting internment of disloyal evacuees. Those who were interned could then be detained during the war to assure against espionage.

The Crystal City location was chosen because there were already 41 three-room cottages and 118 one-room shelters with service buildings equipped with adequate utilities. Also, the exceptionally mild winter climate was considered advantageous for custodial care of women and children who

Crystal City Internment Camp, Texas (probably summer 1944). Large circle on left is swimming pool which the internees converted from an irrigation reservoir. Swimming pool was available to everyone—Japanese, German, Italian. (Jacobs collection)

would be *voluntarily* arriving to join the father or head of the household who had been picked up by the FBI with valid security charges against him.

The operation of a family camp for nationals of enemy countries was not met with official enthusiasm by all. Many officials considered anything that appeared to give physical comfort to the enemy was not to be desired. Understandably, a public, hostile to enemy aliens, would not readily accept wartime rationing when such rationing was not applicable to nationals of enemy countries. Nonetheless, while in government custody, alien enemies and their families were treated humanely in the hopes that Germany and Japan would follow America's lead.

Crystal City Internment Camp came into being and consisted of 290 acres of land which was divided into areas. One-hundred acres were within a fenced compound. The remaining acreage was devoted to farming, personnel residences, playgrounds for children, and areas for utilities. These services included a deep well, sewage system and electrical generators.

The historical records of Crystal City Internment Camp show under the caption "Maintenance of Grounds," that the landscaping and beautification projects were accomplished entirely by Japanese gardeners who converted many unsightly sections of the camp into beautiful scenery. Such beautification was especially noticeable around such public buildings as the hospital and the schools.

Although the intent was to house Japanese, the first internees to arrive, on December 12, 1942, were 35 families of German origin. These folks totaled 130 persons. These families were German nationals and their American-born children or were mixed origin—German and American. The

74

U.S. DEPARTMENT OF JUSTICE   IMMIGRATION AND NATURALIZATION SERVICE

Feb 29, 1944

Civilian Alien Enemies in Custody at CRYSTAL CITY INTERNMENT CAMP, Crystal City, Texas and their AMERICAN spouses and/or AMERICAN CHILDREN who voluntarily interned themselves in CRYSTAL CITY INTERNMENT CAMP for families of ALIEN ENEMIES.

German   (Similarly situated with Japanese Internees)

NAME (last, first)	SEX	AGE	INTERNMENT SERIAL NUMBER	ALIEN REGISTRATION
Abele, Ferdinard Joseph	M	44	3-31-G-587-CI	4751708
" Marie	F	42	Voluntary Internee	4864521
" Helene	F	10	"	American citizen
Albers, Peter Heinz	M	35	3-31-G-1265-CI	American citizen
" Magdalena	F	40	Voluntary Internment	1806534
" Gertrude	F	36	4-37-G-114-CI	2759810
" Peter Heinz, Jr.	M	10-mo	Voluntary Internment	American Citizen
Arend, Walter	M	42	1605--CR(G)-CI	(Costa Rica)
" Elena	F	29	1132-CR(GR)-CI	"
" Karl	M	8	96-CR(G)-CI	"
" Walter, Jr.	M	10	954-CR(G)-CI	"
" Anneliese	F	3	1117-CR(G)-CT	"
" Rosemary	F	7-mo	(Born in Crystal City)	American citi...
Backhofen, Willy	M	41	3-29-G-1455-CI	
" Gertrude	F	43		
" June				

Japanese   (Similarly situated with German Internees)

	SEX	AGE	INTERNMENT SERIAL NUMBER	ALIEN REGISTRATION
				5025788
				5025729
Akamura, Masami	M	40	25-4-J-535-CI	American citizen
" Saki	F	34	Voluntary Internment	American citizen
" Richard	M	13	"	American citizen
" Arthur	M	11	"	2138018
" Alice	F	9	24-4-J-498-CI	1982471
Aizawa, Kanemitsu	M	58	Voluntary Internment	American citizen
" Fusa	F	46	"	5978578
" Kashiwa	F	8	19-4-J-110-CI	3587616
Akimaya, Michiharu	M	49	Voluntary INternment	American citizen
" Onatsu	F	43	"	American citizen
" Ichiro	M	20	"	American citizen
" Ryoso	M	17	"	3138467
" Shiro	M	15	24-4-J-62-CI	5783619
Aoki, Kamenosuke	M	63	Voluntary Internment	
" Iku	F	61		

NAME	SEX	AGE	INTERNMENT SERIAL NUMBER	ALIEN REGISTRATION
			(Born in Crystal City)	American citizen
				American citizen
" August	M	52	Voluntary Internment	American citizen
" Lucie Elsa	F	46	Voluntary Internment	American citizen
Bauer, Albert	M	36	10-12-G-1-CI	2436681
" Eva	F	31	Voluntary Internment	2436682
" Eva Louise	F	11	"	American citizen
" Robert	M	2	"	American citizen
Bauer, Gustav Adolf	M	46	3-29-G-1038-CI	American citizen
" Ella	F	33	3-29-G-981-CI	2876957
Beck, Karl	M	49	3-31-G-1464-CI	4284467
" Rosa	F	36	3-31-G-1463-CI	4284464
" Manfred	M	3	Voluntary Internment	American citi...

German aliens, wives, children do not receive money under Civil Liberties Act 1988

Japanese aliens, wives, children do receive money under Civil Liberties Act 1988

first birth at the camp was on March 10, 1943. This was a German male who *because he was born on U.S. soil was an American citizen.*

On March 23, 1943, 94 Japanese males were transferred from Lordsburg Internment Camp, New Mexico, for the sole purpose of preparing facilities for their families who would be joining them. Their work consisted of construction and completion of quarters for family occupancy.

On April 28, 1943, the U.S. Department of Justice, Immigration and Naturalization Service, issued a "strictly confidential" *Circular To All Officers and Employees* at the *Alien Internment Camp, Crystal City, Texas.* The purpose of this circular was to acquaint each officer and employee serving the interest of the United States government with the importance of their work.

It is particularly important that officers and employees fully realize that our work is an *important* part of our national war effort and that a grave responsibility rests upon each of us because of the bid we constantly make for reciprocity in securing equally fair and humane treatment of *our* civil and military prisoners held in custody of enemy nations....

In connection with what constitutes such fair treatment of enemy prisoners, many questions arise. These questions usually involve basic policies on a national scale and are properly determined by higher authority; for example, whether or not German or Japanese nationals detained in our detention facilities shall be permitted to celebrate their national holidays and, in the privacy of meeting places provided for general activities, display their national emblems, with a view to *our* citizens held as prisoners of war in those enemy countries being permitted to celebrate *our* national holidays and to display *our* national emblem is one which must be decided by those in high positions of authority at our seat of Government. Once these policies are adopted, it is the duty of each officer and employee to accept such policies without question.... He should, under no circumstances, express his views in public, for such action is apt to bring about misunderstandings in the community and result in actions which may detrimentally affect the welfare of prisoners who are nationals of this country and who are held by enemy nations.*

By March 1943, the original idea that Crystal City would be reserved strictly for Japanese habitation was abandoned when within the month the Crystal City population of 523 consisted of 378 Germans and only 145 Japanese. Therefore, plans were quickly formulated to accept and plan for a mixed nationality group. This reasoning proved to be exceptionally sound because throughout March and until the summer of 1943, there were in fact more families of German nationals than either Japanese or Italians.

It was not until July 31, 1943, that the Japanese population exceeded that of the German group. However in August 1943, there was a Japanese repatriation (exchange of Japanese diplomats for American diplomats) which left those of German descent in the majority.

The *New York Times* for Friday, September 3, 1943, ran a story:

1,330 JAPANESE SAIL ON EXCHANGE LINER GRIPSHOLM LEAVES ON SECOND TRIP— TEIA MARU TO BRING AMERICANS BACK HOME

The exchange liner *Gripsholm*, painted white and carrying in huge letters on her side D-I-P-L-O-M-A-T sailed from her anchorage in New York Harbor early yesterday on her *second* mission to exchange Japanese civilians for Americans who have been interned in the Orient since December 1941.

Gaily painted like the cruise ship she was before the United States Government chartered her in the spring of 1942 from the Swedish-American Line, the big vessel carried the gold and blue marks of Sweden, painted flags and brilliant lighting arrangements to identify her through submarine-infested waters. In her cabins there were, according to announcements of the War and State Departments in Washington, 1,330 Japanese civilians who will be exchanged for Americans and nationals of other Western Hemisphere nations in the port of Mormugao, Portuguese India, on or about Oct. 15. The Americans and their fellow internees—1,500 of them, including 1,250 citizens of the United States—are to travel from the Orient on the Japanese-flag liner *Teia Maru.*

Although nothing in the Geneva Convention dictates that a "family camp" must be established

---

*U.S. Dept. of Justice, INA, Apr. 28, 1943, Declassified per E.O. 12356, Sec. 3.3., NND775033, released May 15, 1989.

for enemy aliens, the United States, in the interest of humane treatment and understanding, permitted Japanese nationals (enemy aliens) to be interned at the civilian War Relocation Authority centers of which there were originally ten. Tule Lake Relocation Center became the segregation center for those asking for expatriation or repatriation. This segregation center also housed known "troublemakers" among the American citizen Japanese who could be detained but not placed in an Alien Internment Camp until he or she renounced American citizenship. (Hundreds did.)

The alien Japanese who were not considered security risks were permitted to reside with their families in the various relocation centers for the duration of the war *providing they did nothing to interfere with the United States war effort against the Axis nations*. However, there were some Issei (alien enemies) who did disrupt the communities in the WRA centers. They were removed from these places and interned in the Dept. of Justice Internment Camps under the Immigration and Naturalization Service.

An example of such an alien enemy "troublemaker" among those Japanese nationals who were first allowed to be interned with their families at a WRA center was:

Bert Nakano and his family were relocated during World War II. Nakano's father was a prominent man in Hawaii, the owner of a contracting company that served the Hawaiian Japanese Chamber of Commerce and was the president of the Japanese language school in Hawaii.

Bert Nakano was only 13 when Pearl Harbor was bombed and his father was among all the local Japanese community leaders who were rounded up and sent to a Federal Detention Center on the Mainland. It must be mentioned once again that the only alien enemies actually brought over from Hawaii after the initial round-up by federal agents, were those who were *known* to be security risks and who had valid charges against them. Nakano's father was an alien enemy who by June 1, 1943, was included in the total of 1,315 Japanese who had been apprehended in Hawaii. Of this figure, 812 were aliens and 503 Americans. Of the 1,315 apprehended by the FBI in Hawaii, 87 aliens and 38 American citizens were either released or paroled. An additional seven aliens and 305 citizens had been released from internment by order of the Military Governor of Hawaii and evacuated to Mainland USA

relocation centers. Nonetheless, 718 aliens and 160 citizens, a total 0f 927, remained in custody. The American Japanese were held in detention in Hawaii, but 619 of the interned aliens were removed by June 1, 1943, to Department of Justice Internment Camps on mainland USA.*

In the *New York Times*, December 11, 1941, it was reported that in a matter of hours after the attack on Pearl Harbor the FBI had apprehended nearly 1,300 Japanese alien enemies. The report quoted Attorney General Biddle, regarding this decisive action:

> The arrests were made in accordance with a plan of action made months ago after investigation of the persons concerned.... Every one of those taken into custody had been under observation for more than a year.

Actually it was reported through the intelligence community that almost *before the attack on Pearl Harbor had ceased*, martial law was declared, and the writ of *habeas corpus* was suspended. On every island, agents of the Federal Bureau of Investigation, the Military Intelligence Division, the Fourteenth Naval District Intelligence Office, all aided by members of the local police forces, *began rounding up Japanese already classified as potentially dangerous*. Taken into custody were all *toritsuginin*, literally, Japanese for "go-between man" but loosely translated "Consular Agent."

Also, all known reserve officers in the Japanese army, as well as a large number of prominent advisors to the Japanese Consulate, Shinto priests, Buddhist ministers, Japanese language school principals, and other individuals whose past actions indicated either possible espionage activity or definite Japanese sympathies.

Since 55 percent of all Japanese in the United States resided in the Territory of Hawaii prior to Pearl Harbor's "day of infamy," those thousands immediately picked up as dangerous would have had to have been under scrutiny by the intelligence community, and were so-called "handpicked" out of the vast population of Japanese nationals and American Japanese residing there. Among them was Bert Nakano's father. Here is

---

*Confidential report, "Japanese Activities in the Hawaiian Islands: As an Internal Security Problem," Prepared by the Counter-Intelligence Section, B-7-J District Intelligence Office, Fourteenth Naval District, Honolulu, T.H., June 30, 1943. Approved: H. S. Burr, Lt. Commander, USNR, District Intelligence Officer.

the wartime history of the Nakano family:

Nakano's father was brought over from Hawaii and transferred from detention at Lordsburg and Santa Fe, New Mexico, internment camps, into Crystal City Internment Camp. He was finally released on a parole basis to join his family at the Jerome Relocation Center in Arkansas.

Despite a declaration of martial law in Hawaii, there was a need to detain both Japanese nationals and American Japanese who were considered by the appropriate authority in the Hawaiian Islands to constitute a source of danger to our national security. There were no family relocation centers in Hawaii. Therefore, a *secret presidential authorization* of Hawaii evacuation to the mainland WRA centers was issued. The Commanding General, Hawaiian Department, was authorized by President Roosevelt, upon recommendation of Admiral Ernest J. King, Commander-in-Chief, U.S. Fleet and General George C. Marshall, Chief of Staff, to evacuate to the United States for resettlement in areas to be established by the War Relocation Authority, "up to fifteen thousands persons, in family groups, from among the United States citizens of Japanese ancestry who may be considered as potentially dangerous to national security."

This secret document was the *Revised Presidential Authorization of Hawaii Evacuation to Mainland* of July 15, 1942. This was declassified, GAS, NARS, Franklin D. Roosevelt Library, Hyde Park, New York file 5200.9 (9-27-58) and can also be located in Department of Justice Archives, Washington, D.C., where it was declassified on April 3, 1959.

Many of the family groups from Hawaii were resettled in the two Arkansas WRA centers (Rohwer and Jerome) or scattered within the other family groups in the other relocation centers. The Nakano family was kept together at Jerome until the segregation program began.

When the segregation program was undertaken—the separation of loyal from disloyal, and those requesting expatriation or repatriation to Japan—the Nakano family was moved to Tule Lake Segregation Center (1943).

On July 6, 1943, the United States Senate adopted Resolution 166 which related to the program for relocating persons of Japanese ancestry evacuated from west coast military areas. The Resolution asked the President to issue an Executive Order to accomplish two things: (1) to direct the WRA to segregate the disloyal persons, and the persons whose loyalty is questionable, from those whose loyalty to the United States has been established, and (2) to direct the appropriate agency of the Government to issue a full and complete authoritative statement on conditions in relocation centers and plans for future operations.

President Roosevelt responded to the Senate's Resolution 166, July 6, 1943.*

The President informed the Congress and the American people that the segregation had already been accomplished and therefore no Executive Order was necessary. A preliminary statement from Dillon S. Myer had already been issued on the subject of segregation on July 17, 1943. It was clearly stated by Director Myer that both steps called for in the Senate Resolution 166 had already been taken. Myer explained in his full report that the segregation program of the War Relocation Authority provided for transferring to a single center, Tule Lake Center in northeastern California near the Oregon border, those persons of Japanese ancestry residing in the relocation centers who have indicated that their loyalties lie with Japan. Furthermore, Myer informed the President:

> All persons among the evacuees who had expressed a wish to return to Japan for permanent residence have been included among the segregants, along with those among the citizen evacuees who have answered in the negative, or have refused to answer, a direct question as to their willingness to declare their loyalty to the United States and to renounce any allegiance to any foreign government. In addition, those evacuees who are found, after investigation and hearing, to be ineligible to secure indefinite leave from a relocation center, under the leave regulations of the War Relocation Authority, are to be included among the segregants....
>
> Arrangements are being completed for the adequate guarding and supervision of the segregated evacuees. They will be adequately fed and housed and their treatment will in all respects be fair and humane; they will not, however, be eligible to leave the Tule Lake Center while the war with Japan continues or so long as the military situation requires their residence there....

---

*Message to the Senate from the President of the United States, September 14, 1943, relating to the Segregation of Loyal and Disloyal Japanese in Relocation Centers, Congressional Record, Vol. 89, Part 6, 78th Congress, 1st Session, pp. 7521-7522.

With the segregation of the disloyal evacuees in a separate center, the War Relocation Authority proposes now to redouble its efforts to accomplish the relocation into normal homes and jobs in communities throughout the United States, but outside the evacuated areas, of those Americans of Japanese ancestry whose loyalty to this country remained unshaken through the hardships of the evacuation which military necessity made unavoidable.

President Roosevelt's message to the Senate (S. Doc. No. 96), concluded with words which could hardly be construed in the term of today's meaning of "racism," as charged by the Commission on Wartime Relocation and Internment of Civilians:

> We shall restore to the loyal evacuees the right to return to the evacuated areas as soon as the military situation will make such restoration feasible. Americans of Japanese ancestry, like those of many other ancestries, have shown that they can, and want to, accept our institutions and work loyally with the rest of us, making their own valuable contribution to the national wealth and well-being. In vindication of the very ideals for which we are fighting this war, it is important to us to maintain a high standard of fair, considerate, and equal treatment for the people of this minority as of all other minorities.

Following the President's death on April 13, 1945, at Warm Springs, Georgia, the Salt Lake City Chapter of JACL edited then published the booklet *They Work For Victory: The Story of Japanese Americans and the War Effort*. The booklet begins: "Respectfully dedicated to the memory of Franklin Delano Roosevelt." Here was the Japanese American Citizens League dedicating a printed work, which was intended for wide circulation, to the very Commander-in-Chief who initiated the exclusion order, E.O.. 9066, February 19, 1942, under which all persons of Japanese ancestry were excluded from the military designated risk areas along the west coast. The JACL thought that highly of their late President.

A 1945 photograph released from Press Association, Inc., carried this caption:

Convalescent veterans of the 442nd Combat Team present a check to President Harry S. Truman for $3,300 contributed by Nisei veterans for a memorial to their former commander-in-chief, Franklin Delano Roosevelt. Not in uniform are Earl Finch (left), President Truman and Harold Ickes (center), and Dillon S. Myer (right).
This photo appears in *Uprooted Americans.*

When the Nakano family chose to be segregated and were moved to Tule Lake Segregation Center, Bert Nakano's father and eldest brother participated in un-American activities. Because of these activities, Bert's father and his brother were removed to continue their lives in the Crystal City Internment Center where they would await deportation, as alien enemies, to Japan.

• • •

Under the regulations established by the WCCA, persons under 18 years of age were governed by the decision of their parents and had no independent choice. Dr. Harold S. Jacoby, former Internal Security Officer at Tule Lake Relocation Center, stated in an interview conducted by the author at the Stuart Library, University of the Pacific, Stockton, CA, August 23, 1976, the differences between "relocation," "segregation" and "internment."

These quotations are from transcribed tapes of the interview.

> ...I was added to the staff of the Tule Lake Relocation Center, actually invited there a week before it opened in May of 1942, and remained there until the middle of October, 1943; then from the middle of November, 1943, I was on the staff of the Chicago Relocation Office, the Midwest Regional Office, until the first of August in 1944....
>
> At Tule Lake, my title was Chief of Internal Security with the responsibility of building and administering the program of internal security, making use of the Japanese-American evacuees. Initially, I had responsibility for the social work program and for the fire department in the camp.

Responding to Baker's questions: "Were you in a civilian or in a military capacity?" Jacoby replied:

> Completely civilian because all of the WRA staff were entirely civilian. There was a military police unit *outside* the grounds with which I had some contact, but they were *not on the grounds* except upon the occasion of an emergency.
>
> ...I worked there [at Tule Lake Relocation center] until it was determined that it would

become a segregation center. And then I agreed to stay on in my capacity as Chief of Internal Security until the completion—or virtual completion of the segregation movements. They began, I believe, sometime around September of 1943 and they were pretty much over by the middle of October when I left the camp.

Question posed by Baker: "Can you tell me if you can recollect noticing any difference in the caliber of the residents at the relocation center and those who came in after it became a segregation center?"
Jacoby:

I couldn't put my finger on anything, except in one particular respect, that sometime early in 1943, some branch of government (and I don't know which), screened out somewhere around 500 Kibei in the Hawaiian Islands and brought them to the Mainland and they were initially distributed to three of the other camps. At the time of the segregation movement, they were all moved into Tule Lake. And they came in as a somewhat organized group of young men, very much intent on establishing control of the camp if they could, and this was a new element in the picture as far as I was able to remember that situation...
...By the time they reached Tule Lake...they had by one reason or another come to identify themselves as being pro-Japan...they came to think of themselves as persons who were expert on the subject of contemporary Japan and in the best possible position to lead the others in the segregation center into being *good pro-Japanese people*.

Baker: "They were definitely pro-Japanese?"
Jacoby:

Oh, I think they gave a great deal of evidence of it, and of course, from familiarity with both the literature that developed out of that segregation camp and with talking to many of my friends who stayed on, I think it would be justified to say that there were among them, at least, some who played a pro-Japan role in the operation of the camp...many of them I suspect found themselves to be kind of misfits over here, coming back (from Japan) with less perfect English than others of their own age who hadn't been educated in Japan. Whether they would have been dangerous to the war effort, I have no way of knowing. I think after they had been detained and brought to this country [from Hawaii] and kept in the camps, to have readily released them without any supervision might probably have been a mistake.

Baker: "Would you ever refer to these places (WRA centers or the segregation center) as *concentration camps*?"
Jacoby:

I'm very much on record on this particular point. It's ridiculous to refer to them as 'concentration camps.' If one has read the little book on *The Theory and Practice of Hell* by Kogon which was published shortly after the war by an inmate of one of those camps, prepared largely for use at the Nurenburg trials, you get a completely different kind of social situation. Or if you read Solzhenitzen's *Gulag Archipelago*, or any of his books, *One Day in the Life of Ivan Denisovitch*, for instance, you get a vastly different kind of social situation than was characteristic of the war relocation centers...it would certainly be a distortion of the English language to refer to them (WRA centers) as 'concentration camps.' It's not even correct to refer to them as internment camps, but it would be I think, a less twisting of language to use that term than 'concentration camp.'

Baker: "Well, in reality wasn't there a difference between the internment camps and the relocation camps?"
Jacoby:

Oh, definitely. That's what I say. The internment camps had a very definitely different meaning. They were under a different agency, they existed for a different purpose, particularly to detain persons who were aliens, and against whom there was a certain amount of evidence or at least some considerable measure of suspicion; whereas the relocation centers were prepared for people who were moved because they lived in a particular location and were of a particular nationality background.... The ones who were in internment camps were entirely alien. There were no citizens in the internment camps except, I think, at Crystal City where families joined the Issei individuals, who were aliens.... Tule Lake would not be an internment camp, because it remained under the War Relocation Authority and, of course, was populated by people who were alien, Issei, American-born

Nisei, and Kibei. The internment camps were under the Department of Justice.

Baker: "Did you say Tule Lake was not an internment camp?"
Jacoby:

Not in the sense that Crystal City and Bismarck and Lincoln....

Baker: "The internment camps then, aside from Tule Lake, were those for *only aliens*? Is that correct?"
Jacoby:

Yes. Except for Crystal City that did open a family arrangement so that the alien who was living in Crystal City had the privilege, or certain of them at least, of bringing in their families and they had family facilities set up so that their children, at least, would have been citizens living in Crystal City. But I think that's the only place where in *strictly an internment camp that you would find any persons of citizenship.*

Baker: "From all the literature I have read, Tule Lake began as a relocation center and then became a segregation center. Now, was that the term we should be using—segregation center— rather than 'internment camp'?"
Jacoby:

'Segregation Center' would be much more accurate in view of the fact that the internment camps were under the Department of Justice, whereas Tule Lake, even though it became a segregation center...it remained under the War Relocation Authority administration. It was a specialized type of relocation center in that there had been some selection of the persons living there...An unfortunate thing, if they (dissidents) give impressions that life in the relocation centers was in any respect similar to life in these concentration camps (in Germany), and this is of course the real import of the whole thing. 'Concentration camp' carries with it a picture of treatment, a picture of a quality of life that is so vastly foreign to what actually took place in the relocation camps....
I've just finished reading Weglyn's book, *Years of Infamy: The Untold Story of America's Concentration Camps*...this is silly because first of all, it's not *untold*...she (Weglyn) introduces two elements that I think are
not present in most of the other books. But it gives very clear evidence that she starts out with her conclusions and right from the very first selects her material, works it around, her phrasing is all in the direction of supporting a particular point of view on this whole thing...out to prove a particular interpretation of history that can't be fully substantiated by the facts....
I think it's a burning issue to a very small handful of Japanese-American youngsters, probably they're sansei, who ridiculously feel that they're embarrassed by the fact that their grandparents didn't stand up to the American Government, weren't more militant in their objection to being removed. There's a whole romantic fantasy involved in this whole thing that betrays an unfamiliarity or an unwillingness to look at the facts in the particular case.

Baker: "...these new generations will really believe, especially since Watergate, that we are covering up something we don't need to cover up. I have challenged these people (dissidents) to put photographs of our relocation camps next to the Nazi concentration camps and let the world judge. That has been my argument. How do you feel about all this?"
Jacoby:

Well, obviously, while I might disagree with a point here and there and some other place, this whole turn of events with regard to the relocation centers doesn't make me particularly happy. This really goes back to a generalization that I've made many times. I think that the evacuation was extremely unfortunate...but that having done it, we did it as well as one could expect in considerable measure in keeping with the best of ideals in American society. Now, maybe I'm saying this a little on the defensive because I was a member of the organization that had charge of running the camps...but the camps were not brutalizing. The camps were not areas of restriction...I am fairly proud of the kind of work that the War Relocation Authority did. Now I think perhaps what needs to be done is a more balanced picture of what life was like in the camps. One of the things that disturbs me, and I put this in writing, is that this Weglyn person spends all her time (in picturing of life in the camps) based almost exclusively on the riot at Manzanar and the riot at Tule Lake...I raise the question...is it significant that there were riots at two of the centers, or three actually, or that there were no riots at seven of the other centers? Secondly, she spends all of her time dealing with the registration situation at Tule Lake and if I ever got around to reminiscing on that, I could supply her with some other evidences of some foolishness that the WRA got into. But she doesn't spend any time on what happened at the other nine centers where the registration went along rather smoothly. And to so totally focus in on that which is most dramatic and most, oh, exciting is perhaps understandable, but it certainly doesn't tell what life was like in the relocation centers. And a real story needs to be done on that particular quality of life."

Baker: "Now I want to ask you, were there rapings, were there killings, were there brutalities?"
Jacoby:

It would have been absolutely impossible for any American military personnel to have been inside the camps or to have had any contact (in the relocation centers)."

Baker: "Can you tell me what was the purpose of the armed guards and watch-towers and barbed wire?"
Jacoby:

Well, I think part of this was somewhat precautionary. They were going to set these areas up...and they weren't sure what they were getting into.... So what to do? You take it at the lowest possible, maybe the worst possible way. So, you have a Military Police Company there that *patrols the perimeter*; you build certain towers. Now, I do not believe there were any watch towers at Tule Lake. I cannot remember any of them being built. I may be wrong. They were never manned.... I can't remember there being any towers [when I was there]. Now, what they did *after segregation*, of course, I have only limited knowledge of. And they may have built some at that time. But the ridiculousness of the whole thing is that *in no camp was there any real threat of people trying to run away*. As a matter of fact, the Tule Lake center before it became a segregation center, people in a sense felt more secure with the Military Police company there because the **Tule Lake basin had been a reclamation project beginning in the twenties when it was settled by people who had veteran's preference...and nearly all of the settlers up there were American Legion, First World War veterans. And they weren't very happy about those 'damned Japs' down at Tule Lake. And this became fairly well known to the camp fairly early. And in a sense the presence of the Military Police company at Tule Lake was looked upon far more as protection of the camp against, oh, not any systematic things, but against some goof who planned to take things into his own hands.**

Baker: "Shonin Yamashita tells me that at Poston, he felt that the protection of the barbed wire was primarily because there were so many young children and the location of the centers were in remote sections that if they had no barriers these young children, toddlers, could very easily have gone off into the wilds and been lost...that it was really more of a protective barrier than one to keep them prisoners."
Jacoby:

Well, at Tule Lake, except for the front of the camp, the center [of the camp] along the [frontage of the State Highway No. 139 between Klamath Falls, Oregon, and Alturas], the barbed wire fences were so far away from the residence areas that no one was particularly aware of them. That they were out of sight; they were beyond the areas where people moved around to any extent.... One of the first things we did at Tule Lake within the first month, right across the highway was a large, tremendously high—I suppose it went up about 1,500 feet—Castle Rock we used to call it. Well, right from the very first, we worked out with the military police, with the administration, that this would be open to camp every Sunday. Saturday afternoon and Sunday. And they (evacuees) could go climbing up that place to hike, to go on picnics. They could do all this. And this meant going through the fence, across the highway, over into other property that doubled the size of the camp. The first Sunday we opened that up, we had 2,000 people on that rock. There was no real preoccupation by the Administration or with the military police with this kind of rigid, police-type control you'd have in a concentration camp or a prison.

Baker: "Michi Weglyn, the author, was a teenager at Gila Relocation Center, Arizona. According to newspaper releases, she was at a 'concentration camp' and was then 'released' in order to go to college.... There was no such

82

thing as being 'released' because there was nothing really to keep them there as far as their being American citizens. Is this correct?"
Jacoby:

We had a number of different kinds of leave: we had temporary leaves, some of these were individual such as when I escorted a young family up to Tacoma [Washington]— their sister had been left and had not been evacuated because she was in a hospital for tuberculosis. She died and so the family went up there for the funeral.

Then there were the temporary leaves for agricultural work. And the very first fall we must have had six to eight to ten thousand men go out for sugar beet work from Tule Lake, from Minidoka, from Heart Mountain, and most of the other places.

Then there was student leave which had to be certified by acceptance in a particular school.... I have in my file the report of Harvey Otano, a particularly brilliant student from the University of California. Student relocation leave started the very first summer that they were in the camp. I've got the date because Harvey Otano was the first student we released out of Tule Lake.

Then there was what we called indefinite leave and this was the kind of leave that people went out on to actually get settled and go to Chicago or Cleveland or St. Louis or Minneapolis or Denver or one of these other places.... WRA had no power to do any releasing because every person had to be released in accordance with the procedure that was acceptable to G-2 in the Army, Naval Intelligence, and the FBI. And this was the reason we got into the registration program in January and February 1942, to provide a basis so that a person could more readily and more easily be given the necessary okay for release.

Baker: "Would you say that the persons who were in the relocation centers were actually urged to leave; were they rather encouraged to stay, or were they actually urged to leave?"
Jacoby:

I think this can be said in a very confident fashion that the main effort of the whole staff of the War Relocation Authority was to *encourage these families to get out*. Now there may have been some exceptions to this...but *the whole thrust of the WRA program was to prepare these people to go out and giving them*

every possible kind of assistance...everybody was supposed to be encouraging them to make up their minds to go out.

Now there was a considerable amount of not resistance, but of hesitancy, and this figures in two different ways. One of course was the age make-up of many of these families. The fathers, most of them, had come over here before 1910. The mothers came over from beginning anywhere from 1910 down to early 1920s...picture brides. Now this meant that most of the men were over 60; most of the women were over 50. Most of the children were under 20. Now, many of the families said, 'Look. We came. We built up a farm. We built up a business. We're too old to go out and start this whole thing over again.' They were discouraged...'We're more comfortable here [in the relocation center]; we're more secure. We don't know what the world's like on the outside,' [they said].

Baker: "Could this be what was meant when I interviewed some of these older people who said that they never had it so good? Is that what they're really talking about?"
Jacoby:

Well, not entirely, although that's another dimension that some of the older people, particularly the rural people [felt]. The actual housing [at Tule Lake center] was no worse than what they had had, particularly a lot of the older bachelors, when they were in agricultural work. A lot of the women were released for the first time from the routines of cooking and keeping house and all the other things. No, there were many features of life there that can be pointed to as being pleasant, but I'm thinking of the other dimension simply feeling, 'Look. We don't want to get out into a world we don't know, we're not as young as we were. We'd rather just sit here.' So that it was only those families that had children who were in their late teens or in their twenties who would go out, get a job, find housing, and then send for the parents and assist them to come out.... When I was in the Chicago area, we had lots of calls for older couples to come and live in; the woman work in the house and the man work in the yard, gardener, this kind of thing....

About 18,000 were at Tule Lake [maximum], and we had 15,000 people out on leave at the time that the Supreme Court declared the evacuation [constitutional].... We white Caucasians have developed extreme guilt feelings over many things that were done by our grandparents and parents...I refuse to accept guilt, for instance, let's say the Alien Land Law in California....

Baker: "I do not believe that the story of the WRA and the persons involved in the project have actually been told correctly or fully or truthfully and I'm wondering what are your opinions as far as the types of books that are now on the market? What I am trying to get at is, do you agree that there is a book needed that will educate the American—by and large—not just the student but the older person and those who have lived through the war who knew nothing whatsoever about the evacuation program and the complexities involved in it? Do you agree that such a book is needed?"

Jacoby:

Well, I agree that such a book is needed. Whether it will ever sell as well as something which has some element of excitement, of accusation, of anti-establishment, and so on. I don't think the book-buying public is going to be as avid for a book that says, 'Look, the WRA did a very good job,' as it will be for a book that seeks to expose what was wrong with some of our practices of the past.... It's this recent spate of books that has been trying to raise consciousness and to develop strong guilt feelings, for what purpose I'm not absolutely certain, that has sort of cornered the market more recently. Kind of hoping we're moving into a period of reaction to that; and that we're now ready to go back and say, 'Well, we made some mistakes, but we did some pretty good things at the same time.'

Baker: "I would like you to give me permission on this tape to quote from the review which you have written about *Years of Infamy*, quoting for the purpose of using it as an introductory remark to the need for my book."

Jacoby:

No question that I'd be happy to have you make use of that particular material.... I made almost *exactly* the same statement [as in my review of Weglyn's book], that *we must not be allowed to forget the total evacuation era but we need a balanced, objective and fair statement of actually what did take place.*

• • •

Four years after the aforementioned taped interview of August 23, 1976, Dr. Jacoby responded to several questions raised by the author during her further research about the relocation, segregation, and internment periods during WWII.

Dr. Jacoby's March 1, 1980, letter responded to several issues which were raised during a television interview in which the author participated. Dr. Jacoby commented:

I feel your statement that those who went to the Assembly Centers did not necessarily have to go to relocation centers, needs qualification. They went to neither place of their own accord. For a time in January and February of 1942, those living in sensitive areas were encouraged and assisted by the Army to move inland on their own—and some 10,000 did. But this was not a successful procedure and in early March all movement was frozen. Thereafter, those persons [of Japanese ancestry] remaining were *required* to go to the assembly centers—and subsequently to the relocation centers.

The U.S. Supreme Court differed on this point which Dr. Jacoby made. In the *Korematsu* case, the opinion of the court specifically stated that Korematsu "*either in fact or by law*" [italics added] was not compelled to go from an assembly center to a relocation center. Many thousands did not, going directly from assembly centers to resettle in the other 44 states, or in eastern Oregon or in eastern Washington.

Dr. Jacoby continued:

I feel the chief difference between the concentration camps and the relocation centers was the emphasis placed in the latter on *leaving* the camps. **From the first, there were a series and a variety of leave programs; so if anyone wanted to leave, every possible assistance and encouragement to do so was forthcoming by the WRA.** Did that occur in the concentration camps?

Most of those who remained in the [WRA] "normal" camps did so by reason of his own decision. There were very few whose applications for leave were rejected. They had to have a job or promise of support—but even this was not left up to the evacuee. The WRA set up offices in a score of cities to find jobs and help with housing and so forth. I know. I was in the [WRA] Chicago office [doing just this] for a year.

Now to the [Charles] Kuralt interview. There

is much confusion and misunderstanding about Tule Lake. From May 1942 to August 1943, Tule Lake was just another relocation center. *Then*—on the basis of the registration and answers to the infamous questionnaire—some 7,000 "loyal" Japanese Americans were moved out of Tule Lake and into other centers (or released "on leave") and 8,000 to 10,000 "disloyal" persons were moved to Tule Lake from the other nine centers.

The evacuation was a cruel experience, psychologically devastating and economically costly to the evacuees. Nor was their enforced residence in the relocation centers a picnic. But within the framework of the decision that was made, and the resources available at the time—manpower, housing, medical services and so forth—I feel the enterprise was carried out in a most humane and creditable manner. Not that the WRA didn't make any mistakes; or that there were no "bad apples" among the WRA staff. **Considering the speed with which the program was set up, the staff assembled, and basic services mobilized, the job that was done was one of which the country might well be proud.**

Mrs. Eleanor Roosevelt wrote the "Foreword" to *Beauty Behind Barbed Wire* (by Allen H. Eaton [1952] Harper) and said almost the same thing, that all Americans should be proud of the way the government handled this most sensitive situation involving alien enemies and their citizen children.

Jacoby insists:

Quarrel with the original decision to evacuate the Japanese-American population if you will but not with the way it was implemented.

Now, if one is talking about Tule Lake as the "segregation center"—which it became after August 1943—then it is true: those in Tule Lake had no choice but to call this home. They were not eligible for any leave program as they were persons who had *elected* to be classified as "disloyal."

Now this statement needs to be qualified. Under the regulations, if *one* member of the family had answered the questions in a "disloyal" manner, all members of the family could stay (or be moved to Tule Lake). Many families *elected* to be classified as "disloyal" simply because they didn't want to move out of Tule Lake.

If Ben T_____ was 13 years old and was in Tule Lake when it was a segregation center,

it was because *his parents elected* to go to Tule Lake. They could just as readily have been in another camp, from which it would have been possible to go out on leave.

Regarding the shooting of a teenager, I know nothing or have heard nothing about that. Even Weglyn doesn't mention it. There was a shooting (and killing) at the Tule Lake gate, but it had nothing to do with someone trying to go beyond a fence. I would be inclined to reject the story. Had it occurred *anywhere* it would have gotten such attention that at least Weglyn would have cited it.

In view of the efforts to encourage and assist evacuees to leave (and some 25,000 did), it would seem ironic to reward those who rejected or avoided the opportunities to leave by paying them for the time they spent in camp.

I would reward those who got out—who expressed their faith in the USA by taking wartime jobs and taking themselves off the WRA rolls. True, there were many elderly people who could not easily manage the resettlement move but far more persons *could* have moved than did.

Many feared the outside world (and strongly opposed the closing of the camps at the end of the war for this reason). Many felt more economically secure in the camps than trying new situations on the outside. Most of those in the camps were not kept there by guns or barbed wire. With rare exceptions, anyone who wanted to leave—and go east—could do so—except for those in the segregation center.

How unfortunate that Dr. Jacoby was not called nor did he volunteer a Statement to the CWRIC prior to when its report, *Personal Justice Denied* was published. As a thirty-year-old staff member of the Tule Lake Relocation Center, Dr. Jacoby was an actual witness and participant in the evacuation and relocation program. His statements point out quite vividly the fallacies which have been promoted by the CWRIC's "findings and recommendations."

Based upon the CWRIC's report, the misinformed and misguided Executive and Legislative Branches of government passed into law probably the most scandalous piece of legislation in this century. P.L. 100-383 represents nothing less than a raid on the United States treasury.

Following Dr. Jacoby's narrative via his interview and personal letters to the author, one can more easily relate to the final accounting of the Nakano family and how segregation affected Bert

Nakano after his father and eldest brother were interned at Crystal City Internment Camp.

With the head of the household gone, Bert Nakano chose to remain at Tule Lake Segregation Center to care for his mother, an 11-year-old brother, and an infant sister. There they remained for the duration of the war. Because Bert Nakano was a *minor* at the time decisions were made for the Nakano family, he had neither voice nor choice in the decision whether to remain or leave the Tule Lake facilities. *When Bert Nakano became of age, he left!*

Forty-seven years after the fact, Bert Nakano represents the dissident faction in America who now blames the wartime government for *decisions and actions taken by his father. Bert Nakano is the National Director of the Japanese American Coalition for Redress and Reparations.*

After Japan's surrender on September 6, 1945, Nakano was of legal age and made the decision to join the U.S. Army in 1946. This seems hardly a move from one who was "a prisoner in America's concentration camps" as he claims in 1989.

When Bert Nakano joined the American Army, he was assigned to the Counter-Intelligence Corps, a non-combatant unit in post-war Japan. This unit interrogated Japanese soldiers who were then returning from Siberian duty. When his tour of duty ended, he married Lillian Sugita in 1949. He had met his future bride when the Nakano family was at Jerome Relocation Center.

For his activist work on "redress and reparations," Nakano received commendations from the California Democratic Party Asian-Pacific Caucus and from the San Francisco City & County Board of Supervisors in 1986.

Bert Nakano is, in 1989, the driving force behind continuing pursuit of monetary payments of $20,000 to *each* so-called "permanent resident alien" and American Japanese who "suffered" either evacuation, relocation, or internment because of E.O. 9066, Feb. 19, 1942, under which the exclusion order was authorized, and/or *any military order* which resulted in the "forced internment, evacuation or relocation" of persons of Japanese descent.

Ironically, the Nakano family was not affected by the exclusion order on the West Coast but rather by the military action in *Hawaii* which took place on December 7, 1941. This was before the declaration of war between the United States and Japan was officially declared.

Pearl Harbor's bombing in an unprovoked sneak attack by Japan, came without warning and without a declaration of war. President Roosevelt, addressing the Congress and the American people, formally declared war on December 8, 1941.

Until recently declassified documents, very little was known about the safeguards taken in Hawaii against future attacks by Japan and against acts of espionage or sabotage by persons of Japanese descent: alien enemy or American citizen residing in Hawaii. In fact, dissident members of the National Coalition for Redress and Reparations have falsely claimed that "nothing was done in Hawaii" where the danger of invasion was greatest. This claim by those unaware of what happened in Hawaii could be accepted; but Bert Nakano was well aware of what was done in Hawaii to protect our nation's security and has thus concealed information which would have changed the "findings and recommendations" of the Commission on Wartime Relocation. CWRIC relied on myths and false statements that the United States took no action in Hawaii where the majority of residents were of Japanese origin.

The foretold narrative about the Nakano family provides a good example of what took place in a family which was "separated" due to its own acts rather than as a deliberate policy of the United States government.

It has been stated for the record by Senator Spark Matsunaga (D-Hawaii) the most outspoken and vigorous leader for reparations, that one of the many major crimes of our wartime government was the "separation of families." Senator Matsunaga has never specified *which* families were separated or the cause(s) of such separation. Nor does he mention the historical fact that the United States established family camps in the WRA centers, established a segregation center at Tule Lake and the family camp at Crystal City Internment Center which was established for precisely the purpose of *uniting and keeping Japanese families together!*

Senator Matsunaga entered many false statements into the *Congressional Record* such as the story about a grandfather being shot while trying to retrieve a ball for his grandson. Although such a story has never been documented, it has made the rounds and was grabbed by the media. Of course the Senator from Hawaii has made these statements knowing he was not under oath and would not be challenged by his colleagues in the Senate. Matsunaga tried to discredit the United

States intelligence community by reporting that his "innocent" father was picked up by the FBI and interned in Hawaii just because his father "was a leader in the Japanese community."

Nobody questioned the Senator regarding the potential danger from the *leaders* in the Japanese community following the bombing of Pearl Harbor. In the Pacific theatre, without exception, the militarists of Japan interned every single leader in the Caucasian communities, whether they be military or civilian. Internment by Japan of these persons has never been called "racist"; instead, it was the normal procedure in time of war to intern one's potential enemies. This is called "presumptive action" against possible espionage and sabotage. Yet when the United States interns only the *leaders* of the Japanese community, and those with *security charges against them*, Senator Matsunaga cries, "foul!"

No other country at war ever provided facilities to unite families of known enemy aliens, except the United States. Every alien enemy interned at Crystal City Internment Camp was considered dangerous to the United States. Even so, and in keeping with the Geneva Convention, internees who were "formal internees" had their own representative appointed to voice complaints or give input to the Administration at Crystal City.

The term "formal internee" means any internee who had been interned *officially* by the Department of Justice. Among the Japanese, a *voluntary internee male* had no voice in the "formal internee" affairs even when the youth reached majority age. During World War II, as was the custom in Japan, woman suffrage was not recognized. So it was the Issei, the *Japanese National male,* who was the representative and spokesman for those of Japanese descent residing within Crystal City Internment Camp.

This was quite a departure from how the Empire of Japan and Nazi Germany treated both civilian and military American internees.

It must be emphasized again that the *internment camps* were a completely separate unit from the Prisoner-of-War camps (POW) or the War Relocation Authority centers (WRA) in the United States.

The objective of those responsible for establishing the Crystal City family camp was to provide as best as possible, under wartime conditions, a normal family life for civilian internees. In many cases the family members were the innocent victims of the father's actions which resulted in his classification as a dangerous alien enemy subject to interment and deportation for reasons of national security.

Oddly enough, the historical record shows that Japanese individuals in custody at Crystal City preferred the arrangement of internment and life in this camp as to that in a civilian-run relocation center. This, despite the fact that there was closer security, censorship of mail and numerous restrictions in effect at the Crystal City Internment Camp in contrast to the relative freedom and self-contained communities in the wartime relocation centers.

(About the mail in the relocation centers. There was never any censorship of First Class letter mail coming into or leaving the centers. In fact, each WRA center had its own post office. Does it hold that if these centers were "concentration camps" as some insist, that the American government would allow free entry and leaving of the mails? Not hardly!)

It appears that the reasons why Crystal City seemed to be preferred was that the camp there had been designed years earlier for families. Accordingly, there were cooking facilities in the individual living quarters. But in the relocation centers, mess halls were the only answer due to huge populations there.

In addition, the general work programs at Crystal City kept most of the internees and families occupied with constructive and useful projects. Because there was relatively little so-called free time, there was almost no unrest at Crystal City. Also, Crystal City was a "jail" camp which was heavily guarded. But in the relocation centers, one's time was largely his own. While there were some work opportunities in the centers, Manzanar had the only major war materials factory (for making camouflage nets). With time on their hands, some evacuees caused chaos and actual rioting and terrorism especially over the *tests of loyalty to the United States*.

Riots did take place in three centers but *there were no riots in the seven other WRA centers*. The registration program and its resistance at Tule Lake has been expounded by many writers but little question is raised or answers given as to why the same terrorist tactics at Tule Lake were not encountered in the other WRA centers.

Jacoby wrote:

From the standpoint of simple statistics, the vast majority of the 108,000 evacuees not only

MAIL SERVICE FOR INTERNEES

CRYSTAL CITY, Tex. (Special) Alien Enemy internees at this Dept. of Justice Internment Camp are permitted to have mail service on a regular basis.

Correspondence is large, according to officials, who point out that internees are permitted to write four letters and two postal cards per week per family. Two extra letters are permitted for each child over 16.

Letters can be in English, German, Japanese or Spanish languages.

There is no limit on numbers of incoming letters and packages. But all mail must pass through a strict censorship before leaving the camp and before incoming mail is delivered.

The censorship office averages about 1,000 pieces of mail each day but there is an influx during Christmas season when limitations on correspondence are relaxed.

Censorship officers say they encounter humerous as well as serious subjects in letters. All censors are obligated to not disclose what they read if the matter is not on a "not approved" subject list.

Officials say the fact that a third party is reading a person's mail does not seem to bother the writers. Family secrets are bared, promises are made and broken, anger and disgust portrayed, etc.

"The mail seems most ordinary just as though the writer or receiver were not in custody," added a spokesman for the Internment Camp manager.

The Justice Department pointed out that Crystal City Internment Camp is operated completely different from the War Relocation Centers. In the WRA camps, there is no censorship of first class (letter) mail but incoming packages are inspected for possible contraband.

were not involved in any of these dramatic events; they were not even in the camps where the events took place.... By the time the Supreme Court decision in the Korematsu and Endo cases had been handed down (1944), almost 25,000 evacuees were out of the centers on some type of leave, a detail Ms. Weglyn somehow fails to mention anywhere in her book.

Dr. Jacoby did the review of Weglyn's *Years of Infamy; The Untold Story of America's Concentration Camps* (1976).

Some of the basic policies adopted at Crystal City by the Department of Justice, were stated in an April 5, 1943 "Memorandum to German and Japanese Councils," issued and signed by N. D. Collaer, Supervisor of Alien Detention, Crystal City Internment Camp. This memo was made available per Executive Order 12356 (Sec. 3.3, NND775033, The National Archives, Washington, D.C.

The adopted policies are:

1. That ALL internees will be given a voice in internee affairs;
2. That the management of this facility will not frown upon constructive suggestions coming through proper internee channels but will give sympathetic consideration to all requests and suggestions formally submitted;
3. That the internees of each distinct racial group may maintain liaison with the Officer in Charge independently of other groups.

It was recommended that if at all possible, consideration be given to the proposition of separate camps for each nationality. The Japanese submitted a request in this connection. This is covered in *Mixed Nationalities at Family Camps* letter to Mr. W. F. Kelly, Assistant Commissioner for Alien Control, INS, Philadelphia, August 17, 1943, from INS, Alien Internment Camp, Crystal City, Texas, relative to subjects for discussion at the proposed conference on detention and internment. Signed by J. L. O'Rourke, Supervisor of Internment. Declassified per E.O. 12356, Sec. 3.3., National Archives NND775033.

4. That every activity having to do with the administration, operation and maintenance of the camp will be under the supervision and direction of a competent official of this Service, assisted, usually, by competent internees selected strictly on the basis of qualifications for the job by the facility employment section of the Liaison Division; that

such internees will look for guidance and direction to the Chief of the Division to which assigned.

5. That no internee councilman, executive committeeman or spokesman shall directly give instructions to such an assigned internee concerning his assigned duties except through the Officer in Charge or the Division Chief.

6. That no councilman, executive committeeman, or spokesman shall interest himself in the strictly personal and private affairs of any internee unless requested to do so by the individual concerned; that if it is felt that the private affairs of any internee should be examined into, such internee representatives may submit the matter formally to the Officer in Charge (or informally if the matter be urgent) and will take such action as is deemed by him appropriate.

7. That no officer or employee of this Service or internee of whatever position, shall, directly, or indirectly, influence or attempt to influence any internee in the full enjoyment of his religious or political convictions, nor shall any internee be discriminated against, or favored, because of such beliefs;

8. That all internees shall, without discrimination, enjoy the use of communal recreation and educational facilities, and that no groups shall be permitted exclusive use of such facilities to the detriment of others;

9. That in so far as possible, only such activities shall be permitted in communal recreational and educational facilities as all internees at the facility can conscientiously and wholeheartedly participate in;

10. That any effort on the part of any internee to slander, discriminate against, or to place blame upon internees assisting officials of this Service in carrying out official policies, shall be effectively discouraged;

11. That no internee, not definitely assigned to a functioning division, including councilmen, executive committeemen, or spokesmen, shall be permitted access to the records of any official division for any purpose whatsoever, except through formal request made to the Officer in Charge in the manner provided;

12. That the only official at the facility authorized to deny any formal request of the Internee Council shall be the Officer in Charge or Acting Officer in Charge and unless the Central Office has theretofore ruled in the matter, the Officer in Charge will usually submit the question to the Central Office before formally denying such request;

13. That activities having a political aspect, calculated to disrupt the harmony of the camp because of the diversity of convictions on this subject, shall be discouraged by official and internee personnel.

The above-quoted memorandum ended with the statement that it went without saying that the fighting of the war "should be left to the armed forces and that the inside of an interment camp or detention station is no proper place for activities which give rise to debate, acrimony, hatreds and discourse."

If hatreds between detainees were to develop, they themselves would suffer, and Collaer stated in his ending paragraph that it was the earnest desire that the children who were living with their parents at Crystal City Internment Camp be given as far as humanly possible "in time of war" a chance to enjoy normal lives.

"This wish," Collaer stated, "also extends to adults. In order to make this possible the cooperation of ALL is earnestly requested."

Rules were adopted by the INA's Alien Internment Camp at Crystal City with regard to those granted a parole. *It was recommended that any enemy alien who was granted parole privileges should not be given an opportunity to decide whether to take advantage of parole or to remain in detention, but should be required to leave the internment camp with his family.*

In most cases, the family members were "voluntary internees" and were permitted in Crystal City Internment Camp only in cases which involved extreme hardship for the family of an interned alien enemy national.

Incredible as it may seem, considering wartime conditions, the United States government worked out a scheme whereby these enemies of nations with which we were at war, were able to have a *personal choice* in purchasing food by "spending" a token type of money in exchange for commodities at a "central store."

Subsistence items were readily available. Milk and ice were actually delivered to the doors of internees' quarters. This delivery was a money-saving event for the government as this negated the need for huge expenditures for extensive refrigeration plants.

An initial allowance was given each family for cooking utensils, furniture, bedding, etc., by a department, the Internal Relations Division of the Alien Internment Camp. When an internee "turned in" any worn out items, replacements were given to him.

Some testimonies of evacuees given before Congressional Subcommittees on the subject of relocation and exclusion, during the study of recent 1986, 1987 and 1988 legislation, wrongly included statements that evacuees were "issued uniforms." There is absolutely no documentation to substantiate such reports. Instead, photographic evidence in the WRA centers and of the Internment Camps, show varied types of dress among evacuees and internees.

At Crystal City Internment Camp, a clothing allowance in the form of "Camp Money," rather than the actual issuance of clothing, was undertaken by August 17, 1943. This policy involved *the regular issuance of camp money to all aliens in detention for all clothing needs*. A clothing store was operated on the same basis as the food store thus wearing apparel was selected on an individual basis.

Within six months of their arrival, internee families had already made improvements on their living quarters by the additions of porches and extra rooms, landscaping and gardening.

Grocery carts were a common sight and were parked by the housewives doing their daily shopping. "Many mothers leave their small children in these carts while they are obtaining daily needs inside the store," reported one Administrator in his report about Crystal City Internment Camp. Volunteers even built a swimming pool, tennis courts, baseball diamonds, volleyball and basketball facilities which were scattered in all the vacant spaces throughout the 290 acres of the camp. These details are described in *Historical Narrative of The Crystal City Internment Camp*, National Archives, declassified per E.O. 12356, Section 3.3, NND775033.

By December 29, 1944, the peak population at Crystal City reached 2,371 Japanese, 997 Germans, 8 Italians. The U.S. Department of Justice, Immigration and Naturalization Service, published a list of all Civilian Alien Enemies in custody there. This list included American spouses and/or American children who *voluntarily interned themselves in Crystal City*.

Dozens upon dozens of pages in the official listing show the names of internees, and include some listings of American-born Japanese with internment serial numbers. In cases of German origin, some Americans with internment serial numbers represent Naturalized American Citizens of German origin who, upon interment, were *denaturalized* and subject to deportation. In each case, individuals are identified as to sex, age—and where applicable—an internment serial number or an Alien Registration number.

Under Public Law 100-383, August 10, 1988,

the "Civil Liberties Act of 1988," *only persons of Japanese descent are eligible for $20,000 each despite the fact that persons of German and Italian origin shared the same fate and facilities at Crystal City Internment Camp*. This Act, which discriminates on the basis of national origin, violates the Fifth Amendment of the United States Constitution. The Constitution specifically prohibits Congress from making any law which discriminates on the basis of "national origin." Unfortunately, there has been confusion in the minds of many between "race" and "national origin."

At Crystal City where there were American children sharing the same nationality, these children differed when it came to their "national origin," i.e., those of Japanese descent and those of German, Italian, or other national origins similarly situated at Crystal City. All other internees, voluntary or otherwise, who are *not of Japanese origin do not qualify for $20,000 each* as "punitive damages" for "human suffering."

All internees, including families of enemy aliens who voluntarily interned themselves to be with spouses, shared the following experiences at Crystal City—regardless of national origin:

A well-rounded recreational and entertainment program, including outdoor sports and indoor parties and games common in any average American town. During the heat of summer, an agreement was reached with internees whereby they were permitted to use the irrigation water storage reservoir as a swimming pool. This in return for performing the necessary labor to dredge the reservoir and line it with concrete. This agreement was happily met.

Boy and Girl Scout activities were participated in by the Japanese group. All internees, regardless of national origin, presented frequent recitals, dramas, musicals, and related cultural activities, and were allowed to enthusiastically celebrate holidays whenever the occasion arose. In the *Historical Narrative of the Crystal City Internment Camp,* there's a note that the Japanese families especially asked to be excused from work in order to celebrate practically every holiday, whether it be a Japanese or an American holiday. The major festive day for the Germans was May Day and the Japanese conducted their major celebration on New Year's Day. The annual doll festival by the Japanese was also a big event, while the Germans joined in the general spirit of Christmas and Easter evidenced by Americans.

(Left) Residents of Crystal City Internment Camp could participate in religious services if they wished. Shown is Children's Christmas Program, 1945, in the German community. (Jacobs collection)

(Right) Arthur D. Jacobs' class in German School, Crystal City Internment Center, Texas, 1945. White square is placed just above Jacobs' head. (Jacobs collection)

German Social Hall, Crystal City Internment Center. Many parties were held here including dances for the teenagers. Men in background are bartenders and waiters. Note freshly cut flowers on each table and white table cloths. The musicians, left to right, German adult (cello). The girls playing the piano and the violin are of Japanese and German origin respectively and are probably "voluntary internees." Under Public Law 100-383, the only person shown allowed to receive $20,000 is the girl of Japanese origin the payment being for "suffering." (Jacobs collection)

Student body and teachers of the German School at Crystal City Internment Camp, Texas in 1945. There are 90 pupils and 18 adults pictured. (Jacobs collection)

The government provided moving pictures for internees twice each week, using 16mm sound-on-film equipment showing Hollywood and other productions as good and as recent as were obtainable.

Several forms of religion were practiced by different groups of internees. The majority of Japanese preferred Buddhism, but there were a number of both Catholics and Protestants in the group. According to statistics at Crystal City, 78 percent of the Japanese were Buddhist; 14 percent Christian; 6 percent Shinto; 2 percent unexpressed.

Regular services were held by both Catholics and Lutherans among the German group in a chapel erected by the government for the use of all. But as the various schedules conflicted, the internees were permitted to use schools for religious observances if the chapel was overbooked.

Through contributions from the YMCA, National Catholic Welfare Conference and American Friends, hundreds of books were made available to all the various groups of internees and their families. In addition, the internees made use of the loan service (by mail) provided by the library of the University of Texas.

Besides the Legation of Switzerland and the Spanish Embassy acting as protecting powers for the Germans and Japanese, respectively, various organizations also contributed to the welfare of the internees and their families at Crystal City. Among these were the YMCA, YWCA, American Friends, Red Cross, War Prisoners' Aid, and the National Catholic Welfare Conference.

On February 4, 1944, while the United States was still at war, Thomas R. Bodine, Field Director, National Japanese American Student Relocation Council representative, was permitted to visit Crystal City Internment Camp for the purpose of discussing the concerns for higher education with Japanese students who were graduating from high school at the camp. Many of these students would be eligible through the works of the National Student Council to continue their education in the east or mid-west. Bodine had been doing this work in cooperation with the War Relocation Authority.

The Student Relocation Council successfully placed over 4,000 American Japanese and Japanese nationals into more than 500 higher institutions of learning beginning in early 1942. Some left directly from military areas on the west coast during the "voluntary" evacuation; others spent perhaps a day to a week in an assembly center before transferring to midwest and eastern colleges and universities. Graduates from the Tule Lake Segregation Center High School were also assisted.

No Student Relocation Program was instituted

for evacuated American citizens whose parents were German or Italian enemy aliens made to leave both the east and west coast military areas. Yet *under the Public Law 100-383, August 10, 1988, only those of Japanese descent are eligible, including the 4,000+ evacuees who spent most of the war years in colleges and universities. They are "eligible" for payments of $20,000 each, plus a public apology from the United States government for "injustices" and "human suffering."* Those who earned their college and university degrees had a four-year *jump* on all the service men and women who fought the war—including members of the All-Japanese 442nd Regimental Combat Team.

Proponents for "redress and reparations" have stated that one of the "great losses" suffered was the lack of educational facilities and opportunities. Any such claim is obviously absurd as documentation proves the very opposite. In the Appendix of this book we reproduce directly from an original, *Our World 1943-1944* the Year Book of Manzanar High School, Manzanar Relocation Center. In *Our World 1943-1944* readers will observe every activity, club, entertainment, class units, athletics, music classes, recreation, foreign language clubs, P.T.A. groups, individual portraits of graduating seniors and *whatall* that all high schools offer.

As we have seen, there were thousands of American Japanese who had the opportunity to attend college or university thanks to the Student Relocation Council. To show their appreciation, these students have established scholarships to fund needy students of today.

• • •

On January 19, 1945, Joseph L. O'Rourke, Officer in Charge at Crystal City Internment Camp, was asked permission to film as a motion picture, the facility of this unique family camp as a historical record. N. D. Collaer, Acting Assistant Commissioner for Alien Control, U.S. Department of Justice, INS, Philadelphia, expressed his views concerning the value of such a film:

> As you know, Crystal City from the point of view of internment camps, not only in this country but in any other country, now has the center of the stage. I believe that we can safely say that it is considered to be one of the best, if not the best, internment camp ever operated by any country and, because of the children of various races, there is a wealth of excellent

pictorial material available there.

> I fully appreciate how difficult it is to make at any one time a satisfactory film because the interesting occurrence cannot be staged especially for this purpose, but I think that it should be entirely practicable to shoot a small roll of film during the course of one month, another during the course of the succeeding month, etc., as the various celebrations are held and conditions appear favorable.

> ...As you know, Mr. Kelly is also very much interested in creating a proper historical record of our facilities, and your views concerning the foregoing will be appreciated.*

The film project didn't get off the ground for several more months because of other wartime priorities. (We must remember, during the war photographic equipment was requisitioned by the government for use by official cameramen within the armed services. For all others, including non-military governmental agencies, priorities were assigned by the War Production Board through the Office of Price Administration for equipment purchases.)

On April 21, 1945, the Officer in Charge at Crystal City was notified by Ivan Williams, Officer in Charge at Santa Fe, New Mexico, Internment Camp, that the movie camera requested for filming could not be "spared" because the Santa Fe Internment Camp was expecting "to receive some 500 additional internees within the next two weeks from Tule Lake who are, of course, termed trouble-makers and in my opinion, it would not be wise to send you the camera as there is a possibility we may need it after these internees arrive. As soon as we determine no trouble will arise, we will give your request consideration."

The "trouble-makers" referred to were the American Japanese and Japanese who were actually labeled "terrorists" who coerced loyal Americans into renouncing American citizenship and threatened the lives of anyone at Tule Lake Segregation Center who showed pro-American "tendencies." To show they meant business, troublemakers made an example of an Issei who tried to protest the pro-Japan activities, by slitting his throat.

This information is from a "Confidential Letter" of January 9, 1945, from John L. Burling

---

*U.S. Dept. of Justice, INA, Declassified per E.O. 12356, Section 3.3. National Archives NND775033, File 56125/88-E.

93

for the Attorney General, Department of Justice, to Masao Sakamoto, Chairman, *Sokuji Kikoku Hishi Dan* and to Tsutoum Higashi, Chairman, *Hokoku Seimen Dan*, Tule Lake Center, Newell [California] in which Burling states that these leaders and their followers among the young men at Tule Lake Center "glibly assert their loyalty to the Emperor of Japan and their desire to fight in the Japanese Army." Burling stated that some of the troublemakers were American citizens (Kibei) who had been in Japan and fled back to the United States in order to avoid the Japanese Army draft. "Not only are the leaders of *Hokoku Seimen Dan* traitors to the country of their birth but it is very doubtful whether they are truly loyal to Japan." Although Sakamoto and Higashi are American citizens, they "have throughout most of the war refused to fight in the American army, been unable to fight in the Japanese army, and have *sat in safety and even in relative comfort in a Government Camp*. Tule Lake may not be delightful place to live but there is little doubt that the foxholes are worse.... Yet in time of war those young men, who were born in this country, have betrayed it and have demonstrated their loyalty to the enemy. They are not patriots but [they are] *traitors*."

The full text of Burling's letter—a scorcher—appears in Baker's *The Concentration Camp Conspiracy: A Second Pearl Harbor* pages 73-76, and in Baker's *Dishonoring America: The Collective Guilt of American Japanese*, pages 106-109. Further documentation is in *Acheson* v. *Murakami*, (176 F.2nd 953).

In the public record is a letter, May 1, 1984, referring to the Tule Lake "incident" and a photograph of the pro-Japan element is reproduced on the front and back cover of *Dishonoring America: The Collective Guilt of American Japanese*.

The May 1, 1984, letter states:

Many of those who refused to declare loyalty to the United States were sent to the camp at Tule Lake. There, many pro-Japanese and anti-American individuals undertook a campaign of violence to force other Japanese-Americans to execute certificates renouncing their American citizenship. There were beatings, stabbings, and at least one homicide. In all, over 5,000 citizens, including more than 70 percent of the Tule Lake Japanese-Americans, renounced their American citizenship. But the Commission's account of the Tule Lake reign of terror (Rep. 206-212, 247-251 of CWRIC's report, *Personal Justice Denied*), falls far short of revealing the facts judicially found in *Acheson v. Murakami*, a decision which, characteristically, the Commission never cites.

Frederick Bernays Wiener, Assistant to Solicitor General, Department of Justice from 1945-1948 and Colonel (Army of the United States, Retired), wrote this letter to the Honorable William V. Roth, Jr., Chairman, Committee on Governmental Affairs, U.S. Senate, Washington, D.C. re: S. 2116, 98th Congress, 1st Session, reintroduced as S. 1009, 100th Congress, 1st Session:

These bills, pending before the Committee on Governmental Affairs would if passed in the present form, constitute a gross and indeed flagrant fraud against the American people.... In actual fact, the entire process under which the Commission [CWRIC] operated was irreparably flawed with the consequence that its report [*Personal Justice Denied*] adds up to a deplorable exercise in mendacious revisionism.

The motion pictures of the Crystal City Internment Camp were sent for review to W. F. Kelly, Assistant Commissioner for Alien Control, via Railway Express Agency, Government Bill of Lading No. J-401,603, on February 10, 1947. A synopsis was attached to the notice of shipment to explain the scenes in the order in which they appear on the film. There was to be a collaboration with regard to any suggestions for completion of the motion picture, its general arrangement and titling of the picture.

By October 1943, there were sufficient activities of interest to make a short motion picture of Crystal City. It had already been suggested that such film cover what would normally be expected at a facility which housed known alien enemies who were a threat to national security. These expectations would include a watchtower with mounted guards and guards in automobiles patrolling the fence; a front gate with guards examining cars entering or leaving the area. Crystal City Internment Camp *was* a place for what was identified as "hard core" pro-Axis sympathizers and potential saboteurs or agents bent on serving enemy nations in espionage assignments.

However, in stark contrast to the axis nations' internment camps were the following sequences:

1. Shots of new internees arriving by bus, of the welcome given them by other internees; views of internees lined up at the fence to greet them; of the band playing and a view of the figure of Siegfried painted on the stage drop behind the band.

2. A shot showing a family of new internees being taken to their living quarters and receiving the articles of clothing supplied to them by the camp management.

3. Shots of houses and streets within the area, with special emphasis on the flower and vegetable gardens around some of the houses.

4. Shots of the canteen and foodstore showing customers purchasing food and supplies; a shot showing a housewife preparing food in her own kitchen and another shot of the family gathered around their table for their meal.

5. Shots of the Central Mess Hall showing internees eating; also one of the kitchen and the cooks at work, and one of the bake-shop.

6. Shots of the shoe-shop, beauty parlor, and barber shop.

7. Shots of internees at work in the carpenter shop making tables, benches and toys; in the sewing project and mattress-making shop, at the swimming pool laying in the concrete lining; on the ice-truck; on the farm and in the area landscaping and growing vegetables.

8. Shots of internees at play; listening to their orchestras, watching Punch-and-Judy shows, attending motion picture shows, playing tennis, soccer, and basketball.

9. A shot of the first grade in the American elementary school showing the children doing one of their pantomime songs. Preceding this shot, a brief one of the school principal ringing the bell. Shots also of some of the other classrooms, including those in the American high school and of students playing under the supervision of an American teacher.

10. Shots of the Japanese school including one of the kindergarten children exercising and dancing under supervision of their teachers; another shot to show one of the classrooms (fifth or sixth grade) with the students standing and bowing their greetings to the teacher.

11. A shot of a German classroom showing students standing stiffly next to their chairs until their teacher has entered and given them permission to be seated; a shot of German students doing gymnastics under the supervision of one of their teachers; a photo of their glee club performing, and some shots showing German adult education program in action.

12. Shots of the hospital showing internees receiving dental treatment, clinical treatment, shots of children's and infants' wards, and of the hospital mess kitchen. Shots of sterilizing and surgical equipment of nurses looking after some newly-born infant or child patient.

In the face of all this evidence, Senator Spark Matsunaga stated in the *Congressional Record*, at media interviews and at public hearings, that evacuees died "of lack of medical attention"!

"Apology number one should be from the members of the prejudiced, self-judging Commission (CWRIC) for its mendacious orchestration of half-truths, untruths and attempting to foist it on the American people."
—Frederick Bernays Wiener,
Hearings 98th Congress,
June 20, 1984

At Crystal City Internment Camp, documentation in the National Archives proves the opposite to be true. The War Relocation Authority reports that at the relocation centers, there occurred the lowest incidence of disease anywhere in the United States, and the WRA centers experienced the highest live-birth rate anywhere in the nation.

At Crystal City Internment Camp, the record shows:

In general the health of the camp has been remarkably good. There have been mild epidemics of influenza, strep throat, and diarrhea which would be normal to any community, and several still births have occurred. The only violent deaths during the history of the camp claimed the lives of three children; a German boy crushed by a truck, and two Japanese girls who drowned in the swimming pool. Other than these, all deaths were due to natural causes, in most cases already present at the time of internment. This is obviously an unusual record for a camp of this size over a 2½ year period and is quite contrary to a lengthy prognostication compiled by an internee physician during the early days of our existence, in which he portrayed a bleak outlook for the health and welfare of the persons interned here, chiefly because of the excessive heat during a long summer.

One hundred and fifty-five children have been born of internee parents while in this camp.

Under Public Law 100-383, August 10, 1988, these new-born of *Japanese ancestry only*, are "eligible" for $20,000 each in punitive damages "for human suffering," because these infants were "interned."

Other statistical information pertaining to enemy alien nationals and their *voluntary* internee families, portray the activities of the Medical Division at Crystal City Internment Camp, such as:

   204 major operations
   881 minor operations
27,614 complaints considered involving 84,200 out-patient treatments
 1,770 patients hospitalized, representing 16,772 days at the hospital
 9,225 immunizations
11,107 house calls
 1,298 refractions

The records clearly establish that:

   ...patients have frequently been sent outside the camp for treatment or consultation, including trips to San Antonio, Texas; New Orleans, Louisiana; Lexington, Kentucky; and Baltimore, Maryland. No matter what the cost, no patient ever went without necessary treatment.

The Crystal City narrative continued to tell of the human interest stories regarding special medical cases. One such history involved a 21-year-old who had infantile paralysis at the age of two years and had been fitted with a hip length brace at Crystal City medical facilities. Prior to this type of therapy, his legs had been useless.

Another case involved a boy, 14 years old when voluntarily interned, who at age 3, had taken a fall and hurt his head in a way that resulted in total loss of hearing. He was also unable to speak because he had been unable to comprehend sound. The United States government fitted this child with a hearing aid and for the first time in his life he could not only appreciate sound, but soon learned to talk as well.

Inquiries have been made in an effort to locate this filmed documentary of Crystal City Internment Camp in the National Archives. It is not known at this writing whether or not the motion picture has been declassified. Photographic evidence of this kind would be invaluable to historians as well as for the Court's consideration of the Arthur D. Jacobs' case, filed on March 9, 1989, in the Federal District Court for the District of Columbia. The plaintiff in the case, Arthur D. Jacobs, and similarly situated individuals, would have visual evidence that they experienced wartime internment equally with persons of Japanese descent. The significance and statement of this historic case is the subject of the next chapter in this book. ☐

Editor's Note: Data on medical matters on this page relate only to the facilities of the Medical Division at Crystal City Internment Camp. All ten of the relocation centers, which included the segregation center at Tule Lake, had major hospital facilities since each center was in reality a "city." Readers are directed to page 170 of this book for pictures and remarks about the hospital at Manzanar Relocation Center.

Chapter 4

The Historic Case Testing the Constitutionality of P.L. 100-383 Civil Liberties Act of 1988

"My purpose in doing this research is to help set the record straight regarding internments. I seek neither an apology nor reparations. My goal is historical accuracy."
—*Arthur D. Jacobs*

On November 23, 1988, a letter reached the author's desk which would make possible a challenge to a public law fraught with constitutional, moral, historical and economic defects. The writer of the letter, Arthur D. Jacobs, provided the necessary *standing* to bring suit on behalf of him and "similarly situated persons" who had experienced the same type of internment as other American citizens, but the "others" were of *Japanese ancestry*. Jacobs was of *German ancestry*! (See chapter, Crystal City Internment Camp.)

Jacobs' letter addressed to Lillian Baker, c/o Americans for Historical Accuracy, P.O. Box 372, Lawndale, CA 90260, was a God-send:

Re: Your appearance on the Ray Briem Talk Show, on Thursday, August 11, 1988.

Believe it or not, on the same day of the cited show I wrote Mr. Briem and asked for your organization's address. Two weeks ago I finally received your address.

My reaction after having heard you on Mr. Briem's show was "finally a breath of fresh air." I was beginning to believe that I was a "voice in the wilderness." A brief background statement follows:

For almost two years I have been campaigning to get the truth out about internments and relocation during World War II. I am a natural-born citizen of German descent, who was interned at age 12, along with my brother, age 14, and my parents in Crystal City, Texas, from May 1945 through December 1945. In December 1945 we were transferred to Ellis Island, N.Y., where we were processed for repatriation to Germany. On or about January 16, 1946, we sailed for Bremerhaven, Germany, and arrived there on or about January 26, 1946. There we were greeted by members of the United States Army, *trucked* to Bremen, Germany, loaded in *boxcars* and transported under *armed U.S. Military guard* to Ludwigsburg (vicinity Stuttgart), Germany. Upon arrival, men and boys were confined in Hohen Asperg (a prison for German war criminals which was operated by the U.S. Military), and women were housed in Ludwigsburg.

My purpose for writing you is to determine what information, if any, your organization has on the repatriation and/or deportation of European permanent resident aliens and their American citizen children. For example, how many were returned to Europe under the auspices of the U.S. State Department or other U.S. government agency. Of those who were

Evacuee children playing at Tule Lake Relocation Center. Each of these children, if still living, are in their forties in 1989 and each is destined to receive $20,000 for "human suffering" under Civil Liberties Act of 1988. (Photo by Rev. Thomas C. Grubbs)

returned, how many were deported, repatriated; what number were Germans, Italians. How many children were returned? Of the children how many were American citizens, what were their ages? The papers of the Wartime Commission on Relocation [CWRIC] contains some statistics but my research to date indicated that only partial data regarding *Europeans* are available in these papers. Do you have any suggestions as to where complete and accurate information may be obtained?

I have several responses pending from both the Department of Justice and Department of State. Based upon what I have learned thus far, I anticipate having difficulties in determining the "chain of command," that is to say, who (which U.S. agency) was the office of record from the time we left the ship (*S.S. Aiken Victory*) at Bremerhaven until we were released from Hohen Asperg? Where are these records located? Any assistance that you may offer in this regard will also be appreciated.

My purpose in doing this research is to help set the record straight regarding internments. I seek neither an apology nor reparations. My goal is "historical accuracy."

Jacobs' letter came within the same Thanksgiving Day week that another timely event occurred.

John P. Coale, Esq., of *Coale, Kananack &*

Murgatroyd, with law offices in Washington, D.C., and Los Angeles, California, agreed to take legal action against the implementation of Public Law 100-383, signed by President Ronald Reagan on August 10, 1988. The American War Veterans Relief Association, Inc., Anaheim, California, issued a check for a retainer. Then funds for the legal action began to come in from various veterans organizations and other concerned Americans. But the first order of the day was to find someone in *standing*. Arthur D. Jacobs was contacted. He agreed to work with the law firm.

The National American Ex-Prisoners of War, Inc., adopted a *resolution* at its national convention in Las Vegas, Nevada, to provide monetary support of the court action. Its *press release* of October 4, 1988, was sent to all major news wire services but *not a single major media covered this story!*

When the National Capitol office of the American Ex-Prisoners of War issued a statement on April 28, 1988, *For Immediate Release* to the wire services, *it was also ignored*. In fact, the major media "boycotted" the news conference held that day with the exception of representatives of the ethnic press, *The Japan Times*.

Albert J. Bland, National Commander, issued the statement:

98

The American Ex-Prisoners of War are adamant in their rejection of any attempt to compensate those living Japanese-Americans and permanent resident aliens of Japanese descent who elected to be relocated to government operated facilities rather than move to any of the 44 States not on the West Coast.

America always has and will operate for the good of all citizens of this great country. What was done in 1942 was believed to be in the best interest of our country, and history shows that the action was correct. The Supreme Court found the action to be proper.

Both S.1009 and H.R.442 must be considered the greatest insult ever perpetrated on the American Veteran. First, the payment of $20,000 to individuals previously compensated for any financial loss; then an apology for actions that were and are deemed to have been proper; and finally the pardon of criminals who committed acts of civil disobedience. What else could be done to rub salt into the wounds of the veterans of this great country?

S.1009 was tabled in deference to relabeling it H.R.442. Number "442" was assigned to this legislation strictly for political reasons. The World War II all-Japanese-American Regimental Combat Team was numbered "442." Although the Conference Report was ordered to be printed on July 26, 1988, at *10 p.m.* on the 27th when this Bill was called to the floor, the Report was not ready and nobody had read it. Nevertheless, with fewer than one dozen Senators present, they agreed to the Report which then became Public Law 100-383, August 10, 1988. [102 Stat. 916]

Public Law 100-383 set a precedent for limiting the powers of the Commander-in-Chief and the Executive Branch of government to act in the interest of public safety and national security in time of national peril.

The United States Supreme Court, for over 200 years, has consistently ruled that the United States government is *not liable* and *cannot be sued* for losses, damages, injuries, or *human suffering*, sustained as a result of the U.S. government's action as may be required to *defend* the public safety or national defense. P.L. 100-383 specifically states that compensation in the amount of $20,000 is for "human suffering," but payable *only to persons of Japanese descent*.

Every President, every member of Congress, every member of the Judiciary and all State officials, are made to take a sworn *oath* to *defend this country against all enemies, foreign and domestic*. Nowhere in the study of America's WWII action taken against known alien enemies, is there mention that *other nations* in the Western hemisphere took similar actions to remove alien enemies from military areas. Canada, Mexico, and South American republics took immediate action against German, Italian, and Japanese alien enemies. The United States excluded those of Japanese descent from military designated areas on *the west coast only*, when danger of invasion by Japan's forces seemed imminent.

Financial responsibility by the United States government has been ruled unconstitutional by Federal Courts and on subsequent appeal to the United States Supreme Court, including recent claims by plaintiffs alleging injury or loss of life due to nuclear testing (Jackass Flats, Nevada), the Bikini Atoll tests, and the atom bombing of Hiroshima and Nagasaki which forced Japan's unconditional surrender.

In time of peril, national defense has always been given top priority and rightfully and lawfully so. It is the duty of responsible men in position of command to "wage war successfully."

Ironically, P.L. 100-383, Aug. 10, 1988, authorizes payments of only $12,000 to Aleut evacuees whom the U.S. Navy removed at great risk to the Navy, in the face of approaching Japanese forces. During the battles in the Aleutians against the Japanese, destruction occurred mainly by the Japanese. Under Public Law 100-383, August 10, 1988, American taxpayers are being billed for the "clean-up" of military equipment abandoned by Japan and additional funds are requested to "rebuild a church" which was part of wartime destruction. Because of the mentioned recent decisions of our highest Court, any authorization for such payments violates judicial rule which takes precedent over the Executive and Legislative branches of government when it comes to the constitutionality of any Acts.

Regarding that portion of P.L. 100-383, Aug. 10, 1988, related to the Aleut evacuees, here is unequal application of law which is forbidden in the United States Constitution. P.L. 100-383 awards $20,000 to those of *Japanese* ancestry while awarding only $12,000 to the *Aleuts* for the same reason, "human suffering." Therefore, the higher award, and unequal application of law, is based on ethnicity.

According to the Act, one must be of *Japanese ancestry* to receive full benefits of the Act.

Other flaws in Public Law 100-383, August 10,

1988, are:

1) The law sets aside a U.S. Supreme Court decision (*Korematsu* v. *United States*, Oct. 1944 Term), by imposing the "official history" as written by the Commission on Wartime Relocation and Internment of Civilians (CWRIC), in its report, *Personal Justice Denied*. The Public Law accepts the "findings and recommendations" of the CWRIC whose findings contradict the 6-3 affirmative decision of our highest tribunal. The U.S. Supreme Court ruled that E.O. 9066, Feb. 19, 1942, was: a) "nothing more than an exclusion order"; b) that it was constitutional "as of the time it was made," (Feb. 19, 1942); c) that Korematsu was not excluded "because of his race" but because we were at war with the Empire of Japan; d) that because of imminent invasion, there was no time to separate loyal from disloyal, especially American Japanese who held dual citizenship; e) that the action was taken for "public safety and national security"; f) that "we must place our confidence in time of war in our military leaders, as inevitably we must"; g) and that "either in fact or by law" was an evacuee, such as Korematsu, required to go from an assembly center to a relocation center, and many thousands did not but relocated to the other areas unaffected by the exclusion order.

The Court also pointed out that "there were disloyalties" on the part of American citizens of Japanese descent—which contradicts the findings of the Commission that there wasn't "a single case of disloyalty" by either Americans or Japanese aliens on the west coast.

The fact is: The *Court*, under judicial review, has the legal right to decide the constitutionality of government actions taken to defend the nation in time of war or peace. Our Constitution does not delegate a Commission, the Congress, or the President the responsibility of deciding the constitutionality of any government act.

Mr. Justice Felix Frankfurter, concurring in the Korematsu decision, wrote: "Those actions taken in time of war shall not be stigmatized as lawless because like action taken in time of peace would be lawless." The CWRIC has, indeed, stigmatized as "racist" the wartime action of the President and Congress under the present Public Law. The CWRIC's findings are repeated in the public law, i.e., the *Commission* could not find a single case of disloyalty, espionage or sabotage by American Japanese or Japanese aliens during WWII. *The CWRIC could not find this important evidence because the Commission did not seek any.*

The CWRIC admitted that it not only didn't know the term "MAGIC," or of decoded intelligence reports pin-pointing a rabid fifth-column activity up and down the west coast and in Hawaii by first and second generation Japanese (Issei and Nisei), but the Commission also admitted it didn't know "MAGIC" *existed*. Nowhere in its Report, *Personal Justice Denied*, is there reference to the Department of Defense publication (8-volume set), *The "MAGIC" Background of Pearl Harbor*. This publication is from the U.S. Government Printing Office (1977-1978) under the broadened Freedom of Information Act of 1977 and by executive order of President Jimmy Carter. It was also under Carter's presidency that the CWRIC was formed.

Declassified documents, particularly in Volume I, provide conclusive proof that there was "fifth column" activity on the West Coast of the United States, throughout the American republics, and in Canada and Hawaii. The armed forces of Japan landed in the western Aleutians of Alaska. There was a network of Japanese, some of whom were American citizens of Japanese ancestry in South America and in Mexico, ready to join the "Trojan Horse" of first and second generation Japanese who were in the United States, some even in uniform serving the armed forces of the United States.

Secretary of State Cordell Hull was reading intercepts of Tokyo's diplomatic messages to its Ambassadors Nomera and Kurusa in Washington, D.C., even as bombs were falling on Pearl Harbor. These messages were coded by the U.S. as "MAGIC."

Just as they arrived, Hull received Roosevelt's telephone call. In a steady, clipped voice, the President advised Hull to receive the envoys, look at their statement as though he had not already seen it, and bow them out. Hull kept the Japanese standing while he pretended to read their note. Was Nomura, he asked, presenting this document under instructions from his government? Nomura said he was. Hull fixed him in the eye. 'I must say that in all my conversations with you during the last nine months I have never uttered one word of untruth.... In all my fifty years of public service I have never seen a document that was more crowded with infamous falsehood and distortions—infamous falsehood and distortions on a scale so huge that I never imagined until today that any Government on this planet was capable of uttering them.

Burns, writing in *Roosevelt: The Soldier of Freedom 1940-1945*, did not have available the now declassified material concerning Japanese (Issei and Nisei) implicating them in fifth-column activities thus requiring their removal from military areas along the west coast. As Admiral Edwin Layton expressed in his book, *And I Was There: Pearl Harbor to Midway*, "Any history on the subject of World War II written prior to 1977 is *obsolete*."

Cordell Hull's words, "infamous falsehood and distortions on a scale so huge," could properly be attributed to the statements entered into the Congressional Record, Sept 17, 1987, and subsequent statements by Senator Spark M. Matsunaga (D-HI). Not a single statement condemning our wartime government officials and members of the military was substantiated by documentation. Matsunaga's accusations against the War Relocation Authority were not given under oath nor can they be documented. Matsunaga was joined in fabrications of the truth by Congressmen Norman Mineta and Robert Matsui, who were 9 years old and 9 months old respectively at the time of the evacuation. Senator Daniel Inouye made outrageous accusations against our wartime government and concealed his personal knowledge of the importance of intelligence activities. None of these Japanese-descended elected legislators have, as yet, been put on the "hot seat" of inquiry into the cover-up and deception which they used to lobby and propagandize the WWII action for their own personal gain.

A rule of ethics in both Houses of Congress is that no legislator participate in bills for which they or their families will profit monetarily or in any other way. Under the public law which was pushed for hard and strong by these American Japanese, Matsui and Mineta and families gain $20,000 *each*, totaling thousands of tax-dollars. Matsunaga and Inouye have family, friends, and constituents who will "earn" thousands of dollars and a written public apology. This is of great importance to Senator Matsunaga as his father was picked up and interned in Hawaii as a potential threat to national security.

It is to be hoped that all of these political machinations will be exposed during judicial review of P.L. 100-383.

Other flaws in P.L. 100-383 will be taken up within this chapter as specifics regarding the court case are reviewed.

Case No. 89-607-JGP, *filed March 9, 1989 United States District Court for the District of Columbia*

Public Law 100-383 has been challenged because it violates the Fifth Amendment of the United States Constitution which prohibits unequal application of law or any law which discriminates on the basis of "national origin."

The case was filed on behalf of Arthur D. Jacobs, Plaintiff, an American citizen of German descent who was similarly situated during World War II at Crystal City Internment Camp (Texas), with other Americans but of Japanese and Italian descent.

Jacobs, the minor-aged child of German nationals interned at Crystal City family internment camp, voluntarily joined his parents as they awaited deportation following the end of hostilities. In fact, since Jacobs (age 12) and his brother (age 14) were *minors*, they had no part in the decision making regarding internment. Americans of Japanese descent who were minor children of Japanese nationals interned at Crystal City, also *had no part in decision making*. However, under P.L. 100-383, only Americans of *Japanese ancestry* are considered "eligible" for $20,000 each and a written apology for their voluntary internment. Germans and Italians, confined at Crystal City for the identical reasons, get nothing.

Also included as "eligibles" are Japanese alien enemies and their minor children (American citizens) who were deported to Japan after World War II ended, as well as American Japanese who renounced allegiance to the United States and requested expatriation to Japan. In essence, taxpayers are rewarding known *enemies* of the United States.

In fact, although German, Italian and Japanese nationals who became alien enemies upon declaration of war with their nations, were excluded from military areas such as Terminal Island, and other military designated areas on both the east and west coasts, only those of Japanese descent are "eligible." The "eligibility date" of the public law is *December 7, 1941* and therefore under the public law, *known alien enemies with valid security charges against them will be paid $20,000 each, providing they are of Japanese ancestry.*

The United States Constitution clearly provides

a separation of powers. Only the *Judicial Branch* has the *legal* right to rule on challenges to law brought before the Court. Citizens are given the right of redress through the court system, and Arthur D. Jacobs on his own behalf and on behalf of similarly situated persons, has brought a test case of P.L. 100-383. His case is now before the court.

Redress was granted persons of Japanese descent, and test cases for curfew and exclusion were heard even while the United States was at war to preserve the right of redress. Yet the JACL/ACLU propagandize that American citizens lost their "civil rights."

The Judiciary is mandated to rule on the constitutionality of P.L. 100-383. It would seem ethical that both the Legislative and Executive branches should have a "hands off" policy regarding statements or any appropriations in the budget, for an Act which is a matter of judicial review.

Notification of filing of the case was mailed to each and every member of the United States Congress, May 3, 1989, by the law firm representing Arthur D. Jacobs. This letter was also sent to the major media and wire-services across the nation. Yet few, if any of the media, publicized this historic case.

When Congressman Norman Mineta heard of the filing, he called it a "frivolous action." Congressman Matsui considered it foolish and even inappropriate. Yet on April 5, 1989, both Congressmen pressed for "dire emergency funding" in the 1988 budget, hoping to begin monetary payments *prior* to a court's judgment. The author appeared as a pro-government witness at the hearings held about these "dire emergency funds," and *witnessed* the two Congressmen urging that Neal Smith, Chair of the Subcommittee on Appropriations, *disallow* any testimony by the author and five other opponents to this funding on the basis that such opposition had already been heard during House and Senate hearings on legislative bills which were now "the law." Yet Matsui and Mineta insisted that *they* be heard even when a challenge was made regarding the ethics of these two congressmen pushing for legislation for which they and their families would benefit by receiving thousands of tax-dollars.

The end result was that when "dire emergency funding" reached the House floor, expenditures for payments to persons of Japanese descent were *deleted* from any "emergency funding."

Defendants in the Arthur D. Jacobs suit are: Richard Thornburgh, Attorney General, and Nicholas Brady, Treasurer.

The Attorney General responded to Arthur D. Jacobs' suit by asking Judge John G. Penn of the Federal District Court, to *dismiss* Jacobs' case.

John P. Coale, attorney for Arthur D. Jacobs (Plaintiff), responded to the Attorney General's motion to dismiss by stating that the Civil Liberties Act of 1988 and the Aleutian and Pribilof Island Restitution Act, both violate the equal protection guarantees of the Fifth Amendment to the Constitution. These Acts, both included in P.L. 100-383 (102 STAT. 903—100th Congress), purport to compensate persons who were interned, relocated or subject to exclusion orders; yet the Acts do not propose to compensate the Plaintiff because he (Jacobs) is *neither of Japanese or Aleut descent*. In other words, the Acts propose to compensate one group of persons affected solely on the basis of national origin without compensating the Plaintiff or the members of the class whom he seeks to represent.

The Defendants, Attorney General Richard Thornburgh and Secretary of the Treasury Nicholas Brady, base their Motion for Dismissal entirely upon the Commission on Wartime Relocation and Internment [CWRIC's] Report, *Personal Justice Denied*. Attorney Coale has emphasized that this report—regardless of its many flaws—is simply and clearly outside "the pleadings of this case and should not be considered." Coale argues:

> At the outset it is important to note that this case has nothing to do with racial discrimination. All of the exclusion orders were based upon a person's national origin, not upon race."*

The military orders and every exclusion order given during World War II were based upon a person's *national origin* and not upon *race*. Specifically, there were no exclusion orders of other *orientals* such as Chinese, Korean, or other non-Japanese, or was there any exclusion of non-German and non-Italian caucasians. The exclusion order, E.O. 9066, Feb. 19, 1942, does, in fact, specify that "any and all persons" deemed a danger to national security could be excluded

---

*C.A. No. 89-607 JGP, July 3, 1989 filing, Federal District Court, by John P.Coale, Esq. on behalf of Arthur D. Jacobs, Plaintiff.

from military designated areas. Previous executive orders and military orders were directed equally at German, Italian, and Japanese nationals who were "alien enemies," and were citizens of the nations with whom we were at war. As such, and under international law, were subject to internment and confiscation of all properties.

Thus, any claim by the Defendants that the Acts were designed to cure race-based discrimination is totally inaccurate and represents an attempt to deflect the Court's attention away from the real issue which is whether the United States could take action against individuals whose origin was from countries with whom the United States was at war. We are dealing with nations, not races.

—John P. Coale

AFFIDAVIT OF ARTHUR D. JACOBS

Arthur D. Jacobs, being first duly sworn on oath states as follows:

1. He is the Plaintiff in this case and has personal knowledge of the facts contained herein.

2. He is an American citizen by birth. His father however, was born in Germany. His father emigrated to the United States in about 1928 and was a permanent resident alien during the entire time that he lived in the United States. [Arthur D. Jacobs was born in Brooklyn, New York.]

3. In February of 1944 his father was arrested and paroled. In November 1944 his father was interned at Ellis Island. Thereafter, he, along with his mother and brother, was sent to Ellis Island for internment. In May 1945, he and his family were sent to the Crystal City, Texas, internment camp. He remained there until December 1945.

4. Because he was twelve years old at the time, he had the opportunity to experience and can remember what life was like at the Crystal City camp. While there he attended school. Although he was offered the opportunity to attend the federal school, he chose to attend the German school because his family believed that they would be deported to Germany and, as a result, he needed to learn German.

[The National Japanese American Student Relocation Program extended to Americans of Japanese descent and/or children of Japanese enemy aliens who were also born in Japan. No such program, including the procurement of scholarships in over 500 institutions of higher learning, were established to aid any other persons except those of Japanese ancestry.]

5. At Crystal City, Mr. Jacobs met many people of Japanese descent. While there, he made friends with the other Japanese children and learned how to make various crafts such as sandals and kites from the children. Although the Japanese ate different food from him, the camp had cultural exchanges during which he learned to eat *sushi* and other Japanese dishes.

6. He was able to observe, first hand, the conditions of the camp. Based upon what he observed, everything at the camp was identical for all residents. The Japanese were treated no differently from anyone else.

Further affiant sayeth naught.

(notarized under the signature of Arthur D. Jacobs, 6/23/89)

During the appropriate evidentiary hearing, Arthur D. Jacobs is ready to present to the court evidence to demonstrate the historical inaccuracies and bias of the CWRIC's Report upon which the Attorney General (and the Office of Redress Administration, ORA, Department of Justice) relies so heavily in its counter-suit asking for dismissal.

Much of the above mentioned evidence will prove that the CWRIC failed to consider declassified MAGIC intelligence documents, evidence of the dangers of internal subversion, evidence of the actual treatment of individuals of German and Italian descent who are not considered "eligibles" although similarly situated with persons of Japanese descent, or similarly affected by exclusion orders which extended to *all* alien enemies, German, Italian, and Japanese.

Evidence by documentation (and not by hearsay or supposition), will show that there was, indeed, a military justification for the exclusion of individuals of Japanese descent. Newly released papers provide intelligence data which reveals that the Japanese government and numerous persons of Japanese descent residing in the United States and other American republics, were attempting to organize—and in fact had already emplaced a Trojan Horse within our midst—massive fifth-column activities. These actions by Japan were not "potential acts," but were actions clearly stated *in past tense*, that *first and second generation Japanese (Issei and Nisei) were organized long before Pearl Harbor's "day of infamy"* to aid Japan in its aggressive acts in the Pacific and in the Western hemisphere. Most of the anti-American activities were on the west coast "Pacific Rim," and in Hawaii.

The case under consideration involves the Acts heretofore mentioned, as passed by Congress, in which the Congress selects to compensate solely those of Japanese origin and the Aleuts for alleged damages and "punitive damages for human suffering," and in the case of Aleuts for "unreasonable hardship endured," "personal property taken or destroyed." No consideration is given in the Acts to whether or not *others* also suffered harm who were affected by internment, relocation, or subject to exclusion orders, including *American citizens*.

Although Arthur D. Jacobs is not of Japanese descent, he and others similarly situated, "suffered the same harm" or constitutional violations claimed by those of Japanese descent.

Jacobs, and many other individuals have no right to compensation under the present Acts, or are they given the same consideration of those of Japanese descent. Many numbers of individuals were affected by orders which also affected those of Japanese descent, yet they are excluded from not only compensation but will not receive a "formal written apology" granted other Americans who experienced internment.

The discrimination against Arthur D. Jacobs and others who were interned, has been broadened by the change in *Rules and Regulations*.*

The general public, by and large, are not familiar with the *Federal Register*. Unless one is politically oriented, and is devoted exclusively to reading and/or subscribing to the *Federal Register*, the chances are that government "happenings" do not become "public knowledge" through this means of reporting. Therefore, when the Civil Rights Division (Department of Justice) was "drafting the proposed regulations" for "eligibility" and invited comments by publishing a Notice in the *Federal Register* (53 FR 41252— October 20, 1988) responses and comments were directed to the Japanese communities.

At taxpayers' expense, the Office of Redress Administration established toll-free telephone lines in Tokyo, Japan, and its own toll-free line in the U.S. Capitol, to receive information from those of Japanese descent seeking "eligibility."

On June 14, 1989, the Department of Justice

published a *Notice of Proposed Rulemaking* (NPRM) for the implementation of the Civil Liberties Act of 1988. Japanese lobbyists in Washington, D.C., and the ethnic press, were made aware of the "Notice" but *none* of the previous pro-government, anti-redress individuals were notified. By the "close of comment period" (July 14, 1989), input received was based on individuals and organizations "representing the interests of Japanese Americans."

The Department of Justice admits that section 108(2) of the Civil Liberties Act of 1988:

> ...limits the definition of an 'eligible individual' specifically to 'any individual of Japanese ancestry.' Indeed, the focus throughout the Act is on those of Japanese Ancestry and the discrimination they suffered based on their *race*.

It is truly incredible that the Department of Justice cannot understand the difference between "race" and "national origin."

Under the final rule submitted in the *Federal Register*, the Department of Justice:

> ...will submit legislation to the Congress to amend the Civil Liberties Act of 1988 to render eligible those *non-Japanese* family members who suffered the effects of the government's policy by *accompanying* their spouses or children of *Japanese ancestry* through the evacuation and internment process. (Italics added by author in these two paragraphs.)

Compounding the discrimination shown Arthur D. Jacobs, and many other individuals who *voluntarily* joined their families in internment camps, comes the stunning amendment that will also pay *non-Japanese married only to Japanese* or related *only to Japanese*, the sum of $20,000 each as well as an "apology"!

The Department of Justice contends that these "non-Japanese spouses and parents were confronted by a horrifying choice. They could either 'elect' to stay with their spouses or children throughout the removal and internment process or choose to be separated from them." At least in the United States, there was a choice and those who went with their troublemaking spouses were provided living quarters largely in separated cabins, free food and other essentials, and even encouraged to prepare their own meals! Compare this with the Japanese government's policy of

---

Federal Register, Vol. 54, No. 159, Friday, August 18, 1989, Pgs. 84157-67, *Subject*: Redress Provisions for persons of Japanese Ancestry [Order No. 1359-89]; *Agency*: Department of Justice; *Action*: Final Rule

merely slapping all Americans into overcrowded, dirty camps with none of the polite amenities of life.

Millions of wives, parents and children of American draftees were not given that "horrifying choice"—whether to join spouses or children in the military basic training camps at taxpayers' expense. To pay $20,000 to *non-Japanese* on the basis that they were *merely related* to persons of Japanese descent is a bolder and more shocking discrimination in violation of the Constitution which prohibits unequal application of law. If non-Japanese spouses, parents, and children of *Japanese* internees are eligible, then why not non-Japanese spouses, parents, and children of *German* and *Italian* internees?

In this same *Federal Register*, Page 34160, the Department of Justice takes up the cause of *Peruvian Japanese* as "eligible" (including children born of Peruvian Japanese at Crystal City Internment Camp), and has decided that because the United States allowed a group of approximately 300 non-citizen Peruvian Japanese to reside as "legally admitted immigrants," we should treat this group "retroactively" as "permanent resident aliens"!

The CWRIC's Report, *Personal Justice Denied*, (P.314) states in its text that the Commission had not researched "the body of material" relating to the matter of Peruvian internees, nor had they "definitively reviewed" the subject of the Peruvian government's refusal to accept these Japanese back because they were still considered dangerous persons to the American republics in the Western hemisphere.

The United States could not repatriate them to Peru because these Japanese were not *citizens* of Peru. And these Japanese didn't want to be shipped to Japan, devastated as Japan was after the war. The Peruvian Japanese wished to remain in the United States. A full five years after the internment period ended, the United States government legally admitted them on a special "permanent resident immigrant basis"...*but not retroactively to the internment period*.

All during the battle to fight off deportation, these alien enemy Japanese were paroled to join almost a thousand evacuees from relocation centers who were given jobs at Seabrook Farms, New Jersey.

A story about Seabrook Farms appeared in the *Sunday Star-Ledger* (Newark) December 8, 1985, headlined: "Uprooted Japanese Flourish," by Joan Babbage:

> Despite losing his freedom, business and home, while spending two years in a World War II relocation center, California-born Charles Nagao has endured and even prospered during his new life in Cumberland County.
>
> He speaks with affection of his former boss, the late Charles F. Seabrook, who once employed thousands of Japanese-Americans at his 20,000-acre truck farm, then the world's largest, and its food processing plant in Upper Deerfield Township.
>
> Hardworking Seabrook had an affinity for the equally industrious Japanese-Americans, who were seeking a chance to work and also gain their release from 10 desolate and remote camps located in four western states. "I always liked Charlie Seabrook. He was friendly and a fairminded man," said 59-year-old Nagao, who worked at the food processing plant from 1944 to 1967, rising from labor to management level.

Referring to the article, it states that there were 10 camps "located in four western states." **False!** Two of these 10 camps were in Arkansas (not a western state). There was one each in Colorado, Wyoming and Utah—not generally known as "western" states. The others were in Idaho (1), California (2), Arizona (2).

According to the article, Nagao was one of 2,500 Japanese Americans who traveled from the various WRA centers to Seabrook Farms in New Jersey. Seabrook provided his workers with housing in his "Seabrook Farms Village." As Nagao prospered, he moved his family from small quarters to a larger company bungalow and then to a "spacious farmhouse."

Nagao was one of thousands of American Japanese known as "Kibei"—born in the United States but educated in Japan. Nagao, his wife and twin daughters, could have left Manzanar WRA center to work at Seabrook Farms long before 1944, when he finally elected to leave. All he had to do was to take unqualified allegiance to the United States and not become a burden to any community in which he was employed. He was never a "prisoner" as he now contends. The choice was his. Nagao's brother, Arthur, served with the 442nd Regimental Combat Team. There is no record that Charles Nagao ever served his country in time of war.

Under the present public law, Charles Nagao and his twin daughters (his wife is now deceased), will be eligible for $20,000 each, as well as a written public apology for their "human suffering."

Nagao is 1989 Chairman of the Redress Committee of the Seabrook Chapter of the Japanese American Citizens League. He is an activist seeking monetary payments for "human suffering" for himself, his family, and for those internees whom he knows were interned for valid security reasons at Crystal City Internment Camp and at the other Department of Justice Internment Camps in Hawaii and in the mainland United States.

Activists such as Nagao fail to mention that monetary reparations for lost property and personal possessions were paid on 27,000 *family claims*, in the amount of $38,000,000, under the 1948 Evacuation Claims Act No. 886. Besides the $20,000 in punitive damages, the "redress" activists want $3 million more in a trust fund to "re-educate" the American public. Like Japan the nation, these Kibei are dead-set on rewriting the history of the evacuation based on fallacies.

The term "permanent resident alien" is one latched onto by the Commission on Wartime Relocation. This term is never applied to those of German or Italian descent who were alien enemies in the same class as Japanese nationals.

Japanese nationals who were issued passports to the United States, under the *Gentlemen's Agreement* (1908), were designated by the Empire of Japan as "former residents," "parents, wives, or children of residents," and "settled agriculturists." In no instance, either on behalf of Japan or the United States, was there an "agreement" that Japanese immigration would result in "permanent resident alien" classification. The Commission shows its own bias by describing Japanese aliens as "permanent resident aliens" whereas German and Italian aliens are called "alien enemies."

In all of World War II official papers, including those in the archives of the Department of Justice and FBI, *all German, Italian, and Japanese aliens became alien enemies* during World War II. *All* German, Italian, and Japanese alien enemies were required to carry I.D. cards and to notify the INS of change of residence. Yet according to the "rules and regulations" of the Department of Justice, *all* persons of Japanese descent, including those who *voluntarily* left the west coast, are eligible for $20,000 on the basis

that they—*the Japanese only*—had to report a change of residence. The official order to carry an I.D. card and report a change of residence was required of the mother of Joe DiMaggio, the baseball great (Italian), who was evacuated from Terminal Island, California, along with *all* alien enemies; and so did noted author, Thomas Mann, a refugee from Germany but an "alien enemy" nevertheless. Why, then, should only persons of Japanese origin be singled out as having special rights worth $20,000 apiece, when this "handout" is denied other alien enemies?

During the First World War, approximately 100 Japanese nationals became citizens because they served the United States in its war against Germany. In early 1942, naturalization of *orientals* in the United States was extended to Chinese, Koreans, Filipinos *and Japanese*, providing they would serve in some capacity in the war against Nazi Germany and Fascist Japan and Italy. However in World War II, the United States was fighting Japan and it was not surprising that persons of Japanese descent would not take up arms or assist in the war effort against the Emperor of Japan. Nonetheless, in essence, the Oriental Exclusion Order was lifted which dismisses the recent arguments that Japanese nationals were "denied citizenship."

Coming back to the incidentals about the Arthur D. Jacobs case. Except for the identity of *nationality*, Jacobs falls precisely within the intended purpose of the Act which is to "acknowledge the fundamental injustice of the evacuation, relocation, and internment of United States citizens..." (Because the United States was at war, there is a question as to whether *any* persons subject to exclusion or internment actually suffered "damages," inasmuch as all citizens in and out of uniform are called upon to make sacrifices and accept responsibility of citizenship.)

In Case No. 89-607 JGP, Plaintiff's Response to Motion to Dismiss, filed July 3, 1989, Federal District Court for the District of Columbia:

A failure to declare the Act unconstitutional stigmatizes the plaintiff [Arthur D. Jacobs] as someone who has little value and thus there is no need to compensate him for identical hardship and deprivation.

Further flaws in Public Law 100-383, August 10, 1988, include these:
1. The law prohibits access to certain docu-

ments that "have been in existence for not less than thirty years." Except for documents withheld in the interest of national security, the United States Constitution clearly prohibits Congress "from making any laws" which abridge the right of freedom of the press and public access to documents involving the "evacuation, relocation, and internment of persons of Japanese ancestry during WWII." The public law therefore violates the First Amendment of the United States Constitution and "the public's right to know."

2. The law makes all persons of Japanese ancestry eligible to receive $20,000 each and a government apology, including former Japanese nationals who were interned in Department of Justice Internment Camps. These alien enemies had proven charges against them, documented by the FBI prior to December 7, 1941. Yet the eligibility date for payments of $20,000 begins with that "day of infamy," *December 7, 1941.* The Executive Order under which the exclusion took place was not in effect until after February 19, *1942.* Yet the public law defines the *period of eligibility as December 7th, 1941, up to and including June 30, 1946,* but the war with Japan ended *September 3, 1945.* Those who were *segregated* or *interned after that date were awaiting deportation on their own requests for repatriation or expatriation* to Japan (the latter being dual-citizens who renounced their allegiance to the United States) all qualify for payments of $20,000 each! Accordingly, the American taxpayers are being *forced* to reward *former enemy aliens* and *former American citizens who sat out the war in the safety of American camps, being provided three meals a day, bed, free medical attention all while awaiting deportation to Japan.*

In a commentary recently, it was stated that if Pearl Harbor happened today (August 1989), the United States would be apologizing to any downed Japanese pilot, pay him reparations, and apologize for our allies' intervention. The analogy was being made with regard to the appeasement of "terrorists" and "hostage taking" of Americans in Iran. But ironically the public law—now seeking judicial review by a coalition of Americans supportive of Arthur D. Jacobs case, does exactly that—authorizes payments to known alien enemies who supported Japan's bombing of Pearl Harbor and Japan's aggression against its Asian neighbors in the Pacific.

3. The law authorizes payments of $20,000 to each member of Japanese ancestry who served in the armed forces, for which he was paid, after volunteering to do so from the WRA centers. If a member of the 442nd Regimental Combat Team was among those who were "evacuated, relocated or excluded by military orders from the west coast," then that member of the armed forces will receive $20,000 "punitive damages for human suffering." Millions of other men who served, but were of other ethnic groups, will not receive this kind of "bonus." Yet members of other ethnic groups served in both the European and Pacific theatres of war whereas those of Japanese descent were *promised* they would not have to be in *combat* against *Japan.* Americans of German and Italian origin were not given the option of where they would serve in combat. It should be recalled that the members of the all-Japanese-American 442nd Regimental Combat Team did not go into active service in Europe until the latter part of 1944 as the war was closing down in Europe. The fighting there ended in May 1945. American Japanese who served in the 100th Infantry unit from Hawaii were in battle much longer yet none of them are "eligible" for $20,000.

Incredibly, another group considered "eligible" for $20,000 each are "eligible individuals" who were "confined, held in custody, relocated, or otherwise deprived of liberty" as a result of any "directive of the Armed Forces of the United States, or any other action taken by or on behalf of the United States or its agents...solely on the basis of Japanese ancestry."

In this category are Americans of Japanese descent who formed the *largest case of draft resistance in the United States history.* By including these persons of Japanese descent, the Department of Justice is encouraging civil disobedience in time of war.

One of these draft resisters who is "eligible" for $20,000 and a written apology, is Frank Emi, who "championed in 1943 [as a founder of the Fair Play Committee] an organized draft-resistance movement" among evacuees at the 10 WRA centers.

The members of the Fair Play Committee are now called "founders of the resistance movement in the camps" and "have emerged from historical obscurity to become 'spiritual leaders' for the third generation of Japanese-Americans who have spearheaded the latest fight for reparations." (*Los Angeles Times*, Monday, Sept. 14, 1987.)

When the government reinstated Selective Service for American Japanese and called for volunteers from the WRA centers, hundreds refused to register for the draft. At Heart Mountain WRA center in Wyoming, next to Yellowstone National Park, Emi helped form the Fair Play Committee which tried to defend 85 "draft resisters" on constitutional grounds. There was a trial, convictions, and sentencing to prison. After the war, President Harry S. Truman granted pardons in the spirit of "let bygones be bygones."

However, during the activities of the Heart Mountain Fair Play Committee, the *Heart Mountain Sentinel* (camp newspaper) published an *April 1, 1944* edition in which the leader of the dissident draft resisters stated:

> ...if the United States Supreme Court rules evacuation was constitutional, then we will not have been deprived of our rights.

That was in April. In October 1944, the United States Supreme Court *upheld* the evacuation as "nothing more than an exclusion order" and therefore constitutional and nobody's civil rights were taken from them.

The leader of the Fair Play Committee was Kiyoshi Okamoto, who was guilty of disloyalty. He was transferred to Tule Lake Segregation Center because he was disruptive and a danger to loyal Americans who wanted to serve. These disloyalty charges against Okamoto came from the Washington, D.C., intelligence community.

Continuing articles published in the *Heart Mountain Sentinel* bordered on sedition, therefore several more members were shipped off to the segregation center.

Kiyoshi Okamoto wrote to the American Civil Liberties Union asking that organization for help in "testing the constitutionality of drafting citizens who were behind barbed wire."

In a public letter, ACLU Director during WWII, Roger Baldwin, disassociated himself and the ACLU from the Fair Play Committee fight. Baldwin asserted that the Fair Play Committee dissidents had "no legal case at all," and admonished Okamoto:

> Men who counsel others to resist military service are not within their rights and must expect severe treatment.

On May 10, 1944, a federal grand jury in Cheyenne (Wyoming) indicted the draft resisters in the largest mass trial of draft resistance in United States history. The government contended that the Fair Play Committee was a conspiracy against the Selective Service System and its war effort against Fascist Japan.

After the Fair Play Committee members were sentenced (including Frank Emi), a government witness against Frank Emi and the Fair Play Committee, Ben Kuroki (442nd) told the press:

> These men are fascists in my estimation and no good to any country. They have torn down [what] the rest of us have tried to do. I hope that these members of the Fair Play Committee won't form the opinion of America concerning all Japanese-Americans. [*United States* v. *Okamoto* et al, case No. 4930, U.S. District Court, Cheyenne, Wyoming.]

Under the 1988 law, surviving members of the Fair Play Committee are eligible to receive $20,000 each and a public apology because they are of Japanese descent, and were "deprived of liberty" because of government action. Also eligible are a group of American Japanese who refused to take combat training for overseas duty in 1944 and were given *dishonorable discharges*. But their discharges were recently rewritten to show separation from the services "at the convenience of the government." Nonetheless, these men will also receive $20,000 each because of a "military action."

Thus far, few historical reportings in either broadcast media or in printed publications zero in to the fact that the United States was not the only nation to take presumptive action against potential enemies within. Our allied American republics immediately south of the border and in South America, rounded up every single Japanese and simply interned them. As we have seen, arrangements were made between the United States and Peru for Peruvian Japanese to be interned in the United States. Mexico was quick to round up all Japanese there because Mexico was a sparsely settled, fairly empty land and without a military force sufficient to fend off any invasion—should one occur. Mexico operated an internment center in the State of Morales near Temixco, about 8 miles from Cuernevaca. How the detainees were housed and treated in Mexico seems elusive.

In Canada where there were 22,000 Japanese, some Canadian citizens, in British Columbia, relocation centers were set up at Kaslo in a hastily reconditioned "ghost town" as well as a completely new facility called Tashme.—*Silent Siege—II* p. 221.

Conditions in Canada were essentially much harsher than in the U.S., and the higher latitude and high elevations meant colder winters. Most of the Canadian Japanese had been fishermen from the milder coast climates thus in the camps they were forced to spend much of their time just trying to survive the cold.

In several Canadian newspapers, such as the *Windsor Star* (Ontario), voices have been raised protesting payments of reparations to Canadian-Japanese made in 1988. The reparations movement in Canada was instigated by Gordon Hirabayashi. He was one of the individuals in the test case for curfew and exclusion—*Gordon Hirabayashi v. United States*—320 U.S. 81, 1943 at 96-98.

On March 30, 1942, Gordon Hirabayashi, an American citizen, born in Auburn, Washington, was arrested by federal authorities and was convicted of having violated both the curfew and evacuation military orders in the State of Washington. Hirabayashi was found guilty in violating the curfew order (August 1943). He spent a few months in prison for refusing to register for the draft during World War II, pleading "conscientious objector." However, conscientious objectors *registered and served in WWII* as non-combatant draftees. Hirabayashi refused to serve his country in *any* capacity.

After the war and upon completion of his education, Hirabayashi taught sociology at the University of Washington then went, as a "landed emigrant" to Canada where he joined the faculty at the University of Alberta.

Gordon Hirabayashi appeared as a witness before the Commission on Wartime Relocation and Internment (CWRIC) during the 1981 hearings in Washington, D.C. There he repeated a phrase he used during other public appearances on college campuses:

> The United States is a racist nation and World War II was its excuse to practice it.

Hirabayashi violated an Act of Congress, March 21, 1942, 56 Stat. 173, 18 U.S.C.A., which made it a misdemeanor knowingly to disregard restrictions made applicable by a military commander to persons in a military area, as prescribed by the commander and authorized by an executive order of the President.

On May 15, 1981, Dr. Hirabayashi, while a visiting professor at the University of Washington, became the Chairman for the Seattle JACL Redress Committee.

Hirabayashi was quoted in *Rafu Shimpo*, May 15, 1981, Los Angeles: "...if the Japanese Americans were less than prepared to confront injustice in 1942, we have a second chance in 1981 with the National Commission that is just getting underway. How are we going to respond this time?"

Before the Commission was even underway with its hearings, the *Rafu Shimpo* (February 26, 1980), told of Hirabayashi's early activities in its story: "Redress Workshops Offer Tips For Hearing Testimony."

> SEATTLE: Gordon Hirabayashi, chair of the community committee to assist potential witnesses by running a series of workshops on oral and written presentation, * * * five volunteers read their testimony and answered questions from a mock Commission panel. Seattle Buddhist church donated the use of a camera and video recorder so that tapes could be played back to illustrate points regarding tone and body language. The audience of about 45 people then commented on the presentations.

Gordon Hirabayashi was the leader of the "redress and reparations" movement in Canada. When Canada approved "reparations," it was never mentioned in the media that Canada had *never before paid monetary reparations for property losses or personal property confiscated*. As we have seen, the United States had already paid monetary reparations to 27,000 *families*. What the United States taxpayers are *now* required to pay under P.L. 100-383 is "punitive damages for human suffering" but only to persons of Japanese descent.

Included in those "eligible" for payment of $20,000 and a written apology, is none other than draft resister Gordon Hirabayashi, another citizen who never served his country but did receive the benefit of constitutional rights—even in time of war—by having redress through the lower courts all the way to the United States Supreme Court. No other citizen can receive redress higher than that. Yet Hirabayashi insists that his constitutional rights were "violated."

Grace Macaluso, writing for Canada's *Windsor Star*, observed:

While most people know of the wartime internment of 22,000 Japanese Canadians—and the federal government's recent apology and $300-million compensation package—few remember that Italians and Germans were also branded enemy aliens and interned during the First and Second World Wars.... Before the Second World War was won, the RCMP [Royal Canadian Mounted Police] had supervised the arrest and internment of about 800 German and 700 Italian-Canadians, although some sources say the number of Italians was closer to 2,000.... But unlike the Japanese internment, where whole families were rounded up and sent to camps in B.C. [British Columbia], only the breadwinners of Italian-, German- and Ukrainian-Canadian families were interned.... What happened to the wives and children of these internees apparently did not seem to concern the Canadian government. And, while the Japanese were kept in camps of their own, German- and Italian-Canadians were interned during the Second World War *with German and Italian prisoners of war* in camps across Canada. [Italics added]

Within Macaluso's article comes an enlightening statement which can be related to the case of Arthur D. Jacobs:

Lubomyr Luciuk, spokesman for the Ukrainian-Canadian Committee, says the Japanese redress program 'sets a legal and moral precedent.

'Justice can't be selective [says Luciuk, a professor at Queen's University in Kingston, Ont.]. You can't say Japanese-Canadians deserve redress.

'It's ludicrous to assume they suffered more than other groups,' he says, adding the federal Multiculturalism Minister Gerry Wiener was 'very sympathetic' during a recent meeting to discuss compensation for Ukrainian-Canadians.

Last October, Wiener also received letters from the National Congress of Italian-Canadians seeking redress for wartime internment.

Alarmingly, in the United States, the Civil Liberties Act of 1988 is so broadly drafted that it compensates supporters of Japan's war effort.

Congress surely did not intend to pay spies and proponents of Japan's military campaign against the United States, but that is exactly what this Act does [according to C.A. No. 89-607, JGP, Arthur D. Jacobs, Statement by John P. Coale, Attorney for American War Veterans Relief Association, and Arthur D. Jacobs, before the Subcommittee on Commerce, Justice, State and the Judiciary, April 5, 1989, Washington, D.C.]

Within the broad language of the Act, "eligibles" include the following persons:

1) 1,370 Japanese nationals (enemy aliens) who were interned by the FBI for valid security reasons in Department of Justice Internment Camps;

2) 3,500 American Japanese (citizens with dual-citizenship) who renounced their allegiance to the United States and requested expatriation to Japan;

3) 160 members of the Black Dragon Society, an anti-American pro-Japan organization;

4) 18,000 expatriates and repatriates and their families segregated at Tule Lake Segregation center, whose adult members declared allegiance to Japan and refused to take a loyalty oath to the United States, or promise to abide by this nation's laws. A summary of the fanatic, pro-Japan segregants at Tule Lake who terrorized the pro-American evacuees or neutral alien Japanese, appears in *Acheson v. Murakami* [(1949) 166 2 F2d 953, 961-966]. Members of the various pro-Japan groups, such as the "Young Men's Fatherland," engaged in murder, beatings, intimidation and riots to accomplish their avowed purpose to keep Tule Lake in a state of turmoil.

5) Members of the Black Dragon Society at Manzanar Relocation Center who celebrated the first anniversary of the surprise attack at Pearl Harbor (Dec. 7, 1942), and held demonstrations, shouting *Banzai*!

Under P.L. 100-383, all of these persons of Japanese descent are eligible for $20,000 each and a written public apology.

As John P. Coale stated in his Brief prepared on behalf of Arthur D. Jacobs, in response to the Department of Justice's *Motion for Dismissal*:

No amount of emotionalism can erase the fact that Germans and Italians and others sat side-by-side with the Japanese in the internment camps. Only the most absurd form of legal sophistry can make it bad for those of Japanese descent and good for everyone else there.

No doubt, the final outcome of this historic case will be decided long after this book goes to press.

After the first filing of the case on March 9, 1989 and when the Department of Justice filed a motion to dismiss, seventeen intervenors of Japanese descent filed on behalf of the Department of Justice. These American Japanese called the case "frivolous." Their filing was followed by an *amicus* brief submitted by the Japanese American Citizens League. Another *amicus* brief entered the case by the Japanese American Citizens League Legislative Education Chair (JACL/LEC). All of the American Japanese are represented by *eleven separate law firms*.

As a counter-measure, there have been four *amicus* briefs filed on behalf of Arthur D. Jacobs; in each case, filed as concerned citizens, and *without the assistance of attorneys*.

The author filed an *amicus* brief as an historian/researcher.

David D. Lowman, Honolulu, Hawaii, filed an *amicus* brief to provide the Court with the background of MAGIC, the deception of the CWRIC, and the court proceedings in which Lowman participated as a government witness. His *amicus* brief, consisting of more than 235 pages, contains documents which prove beyond doubt the *military necessity* for the exclusion of persons on the endangered west coast.

Bill Kubick, Seattle, filed a short brief related to his experience at the Hirabayashi recent hearings in Seattle in which Hirabayashi was able to convince the Voorhees Court to "vacate" his former convictions.

Francis O'Keefe, Jupiter, Florida, filed an *amicus* brief on behalf of former American Ex-Prisoners of War and Survivors of Bataan and Corregidor.

These are historic events. One would suppose the media would be right on top of all of this. Unfortunately, this is not the case. If ever it was journalistically necessary to uncover a cover-up, this case is it!

The media didn't do its job while the legislative bills were being considered. It will be interesting to note if the media will take advantage of a second chance to redeem itself.

If an investigative reporter wants to earn a Pulitzer Prize, it appears this story may be a winner. □

Appendix A

Author's Note: All of the copy photography of the Manzanar High School Yearbook, *Our World,* is through the professional courtesy of Award-winning photographer D. K. Hammell, San Marcos, California. Reproduced copies of this yearbook were sent to every member of CWRIC as well as to every member of the Senate and House Judiciary Committees as evidence presented in Doc. 1a, Apr. 5, 1989. The purpose of this distribution was to let people know what really happened at Manzanar Relocation Center which was not unlike all the other relocation centers in daily operations.

Published in *Pacific Citizen,* Friday, June 13, 1975 for 30th Class Reunion, Manzanar High School. Reprinted courtesy of *Pacific Citizen.*

On June 12, 1987, of my own free will, I gave to Lillian Baker the hard-cover yearbood titled *Our World —Manzanar, California*. I have given Mrs. Baker permission to copy this book and enter its contents for the record to be used by legislators and historians.

My purpose is to let the record show what life in a relocation center was really like for the majority of Americans of Japanese descent and the Issei (Japanese Nationals) residing there. I have stated that my years at Manzanar beginning with my 15th year of age through 18 years of age (when I graduated Manzanar High School), were some of the happiest of my life.

I am a member of the Japanese American Citizens League. The members of the JACL who are proponents for "redress and reparations" are of a small, young, but very vocal minority of Sansei or Nisei who were not born during WWII, or were very young when they experienced the evacuation.

I represent one of the majority of Americans of Japanese descent (average 15.6 years), whose experience is most honestly shown in the abovementioned publication.

This letter and that publication should be made part of any hearings on the subject of the evacuation/ relocation, and I respectfully request that this be done regarding the current bills pending, H.R.442, and S1009. [Finally, P.L. 100-383]

> Document 1A
> Lillian Baker, STATEMENT
> Hearings, PL100-383, April 5, 1989
> Subcommittee on Commerce, Justice, State
> & Judiciary, U.S. House of Representatives

Note: It is regretable that some of the type in the text in yearbook (Appendix A) is hard to read. The loss is due to the various steps necessary in copying the original so it could be reproduced here. We ask readers' understanding. —The Editor.

Our World

1943 · 1944

Manzanar High

This Souvenier Book
was not printed at
Government Expense

Manzanar War Relocation Authority
Manzanar, California

From a dusty wasteland to a lively community, Manzanar has progressed to become an exciting chapter developing from World War II. This part of the story depicts the temporary war time life of 10,000 tireless, self-sacrificing residents living in one square mile of barracks.

To those people with their simple pleasures....to those men and women with their green growing gardens of the spring and snow covered barracks of the winter, who have put aside temporarily the life of their sea and their own ....to the husband and his wife, to the son in the service, his children....to the grandparents, the aunts, the uncles, the cousins, the nephews, the ....to those who are unknowingly......to those who....... and their ....and our way of life, we hereby dedicate...

Our World

office workers

parent-teachers association

Anita Nicolaus—Handicraft, Commercial and General Art; Louis Frizzell—Music, Drama

Blanche Chester—English 11; Helen Ely—American Life and Institution

Oma Spivey Umhey—English 12; Clive Greenlee—Speech

Lucille Smith—Social Studies 10; Harriet Pusey—Counselor

Janet Goldberg—Journalism, Senior Problems; Mary Jean Kramer—Senior Problems, Latin

Marjorie Davalle—Geometry, Algebra; Chloe Zimmerman—Mathematics

Tadashi Kishi—Physics; Mas Nakagawa—Chemistry; Hideyu Uyeda—Chemistry

Harold Rogers—Spanish, French; Ruth Budd—Librarian, Library Science

Eldridge B. Dykes—Biology, General Science; Tatsuo Miyake—General Science; Albert Nagashima—Science 8

Wilhelmina McGavern, Mathematics, Social Studies 8; Doris Abel—Social Studies 9

Sarah Oltmans—English 10, Typing; Virginia Hayes—Social Studies 7

Ione Ingalls—Mathematics, Social Studies 8; Miss Thelma Kellesvig—Social Studies 8

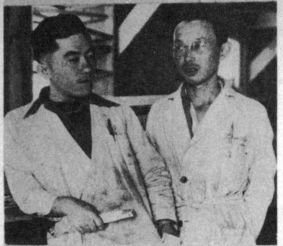

Brieuc Bouche—Woodshop, Drafting

Bertha Rude—Shorthand; Elizabeth Nail—Typing; Emi Maeda—Shorthand

Dorothy Rau—Clothing, Homemaking, Family Living; Beatrice White—Foods, Clothing

Mike Oshima—Shop; Frank Takimoto—Shop

Leland Abel—Farm Management

Forward

Since that first day when Manzanar High School was called in session, the students and faculty have been trying to approximate in all activities the life we knew "back home". With the publication of this yearbook, we feel that we have really come closer to our goal. To meet the deadline, the staff of the book has worked many a Saturday and Sunday in addition to the regular school day. As a result of their hard work Our World is a history book of Manzanar, with the school emphasized as the center of the community. In years to come, when people will ask with real curiosity "What was Manzanar?" we can show them this volume and say that Manzanar was a chapter in the life story of some 10,000 evacuees whose normal routine was upset for a few years. As the rest of the world rushed by on their busy road of destruction we in Manzanar, in Our World, were busy laying the foundation stones for a better world. The bridge leading to our new world is called relocation. Many who have crossed that bridge write back the same message. They have said, "Life in camp becomes something unreal in the past, once we reach the outside world. You just carry on as though that camp episode was a two-day rest in the country." And in retrospect we can see that life in camp was just that, an interlude in one's life that was not meant to be permanent. The new friends one made and the new work experiences one enjoyed stand out sharply against the realization that such a thing as evacuation could actually take place.

This book then merely becomes a record of a pleasant past for us to carry into the future.

contents

Ralph P. Merritt, Project Director

Adminis

GREETINGS TO THE STUDENTS OF THE MANZANAR HIGH SCHOOL

WHEN YOU READ THIS MESSAGE AT THE END OF THE SCHOOL YEAR YOU AND I WILL BOTH BE IN MANZANAR. BUT TODAY, MARCH 12, I AM WRITING THIS NOTE OF GREETING FROM WASHINGTON.

IT IS MANY, MANY MILES FROM WASHINGTON TO MANZANAR, BUT FOR THE PAST WEEK I HAVE BEEN WORKING HERE WITH A LARGE GROUP OF GOVERNMENT OFFICIALS WHOSE SOLE PURPOSE HAS BEEN TO PLAN FOR YOU AND THOUSANDS MORE LIKE YOU. WE HAVE WORKED OUT PLANS FOR GOING ON WITH SCHOOL AND PLAY, FOR HOUSING AND EATING AND WORK. BUT WE HAVE GIVEN THE MOST TIME TO THE STUDY OF HOW TO MAKE YOUR FUTURE AS AMERICAN CITIZENS SECURE AND HAPPY, SO THAT EACH OF YOU CAN FIND A PLACE IN THIS COUNTRY FOR NORMAL LIVING AS FREE CITIZENS. OF COURSE THIS ALSO DEPENDS ON YOUR CO-OPERATION AND COURAGE AND INITIATIVE. BUT THE DOORS ARE OPEN AND THAT PART OF AMERICA WHICH IS NOT SOLELY DEDICATED TO WAR PURPOSES IS INVITING YOU TO COME.

AS I LOOK OUT MY WINDOW HERE I CAN SEE THE WASHINGTON MONUMENT, THE WHITE HOUSE AND MANY, MANY GOVERNMENT BUILDINGS WHERE THOUSANDS AND THOUSANDS OF GOVERNMENT PEOPLE WORK. THESE PEOPLE ARE OF EVERY RACIAL ORIGIN; SOME OF THEM ARE OF JAPANESE ANCESTRY. THE GOVERNMENT OF AMERICA IS NOT ONE MAN OR ONE AUTHORITY; IT IS ALL THESE PEOPLE AND MANY THOUSANDS OF OTHERS WORKING TOGETHER TO GUIDE, PROTECT AND LEAD ALL OUR PEOPLE EVERY-WHERE INTO A BETTER WAY OF LIFE. YOU CAN AND SHOULD HAVE A PART IN THIS, EITHER AS A WORKER OR AS A VOTER, SO THAT GOVERNMENT MAY BE BY THE PEOPLE AND OF THE PEOPLE. NEVER WAS YOUR FUTURE SO BRIGHT AS NOW!

RALPH P. MERRITT, PROJECT DIRECTOR

trators

In its growth, Manzanar has become a combination of all the worthwhile elements of modern city life while maintaining its rural location. It is a composite of a hundred other cities, yet like no other one in the world. Manzanar is the expression of self sacrificing and determined people. It shows the marked influence of two generations in a program devoted to furthering the betterment of the community.

Manzanar's good fortune is to be found in its scenery. Located in the center of the Inyo Mono Valley, the lofty Sierras punctuated by Mt. Whitney lie to the West, the Inyo Range on the East and the world famous Death Valley to the Southeast.

Its foundations in an abandoned apple orchard, Manzanar has become one of the largest cities in the valley. Approximately 10,000 residents were housed in 36 blocks of barracks covering approximately one square mile, but now that relocation and segregation have claimed so many people the population has been cut to about 6,500.

With ambition of becoming a self-sustaining camp, Manzanar has its farm, industries, factories, repair shops and victory gardens. Although this ambition has not been fulfilled as yet, it is hoped that it will be accomplished soon.

Like many other cities, Manzanar has its government, newspaper, churches, recreation, welfare workers, hospital, orphanage, schools, libraries, stores, theatres and post office all working together to make the best of the temporary wartime pattern to which they have been transplanted.

Lucy W. Adams—Assistant Project Director in Charge of
Community Management

Robert L. Brown, Assistant Project Director in Charge of Operations

Edwin H. Hooper, Assistant Project Director in Charge of
Administration

Friends

Unique in that its students came from over 200 schools Manzanar High School at one time reached a peak enrollment of 1,000 pupils. For the first time the entire student body and faculty gathered together when school opened in September, 1942 with an assembly at the outdoor theatre. Under the guidance of Leon High, our first principal, classes met in the barracks of block seven. With no chairs, books, or customary classroom equipment, the students carried on. In the first student body election, Senior Tommy Ajisaka was unanimously chosen to lead as student body prexy.

During the first semester few activities outside of the Senior Class Christmas Dance were scheduled. With the advent of spring and warmer weather more of an extra curricular program was carried on. Second semester found the A Capella Choir organized and preparing for public performances.

"The Ballad for Americans" was the theme of the school concert put on in the latter part of June by the choir. On June 19, the "B's" gave the "A's" a fine time at the Senior Prom. Then—graduation and summer vacation!!!

In September Mr. Rollin C. Fox succeeded Mr. High as our principal and George Nishimura took over the job of student body president. At the same time the junior high elected Mamoru Ogi as their prexy.

With the formation of the Boys' and Girls' League in the late part of October, the girls of Manzanar Senior High scheduled their first dance, the successful Spinsters' Skip for the first month in the new year. Manzanar schools observed American Education Week with "Better World Understanding" as their theme. Supervised by Mr. Louis Frizzell, the Christmas Concert and the senior play "Growing Pains" were well attended and enjoyed by many.

At this time the long-awaited auditorium was begun. In a colorful ceremony on February 19, important documents were sealed in a cornerstone. "F.D.R." Nishimura was elected for a second term and Mary Horami took over the job of the junior high school student body prexy.

Although saddened by the departure of the Tule Lake segregees in February the students embarked upon a spring schedule of activities as the days grew warmer and longer.

Towards the end of the semester, the auditorium was finished and officially opened. One of the first programs to be held there was another Frizzell extravaganza, this time an operetta.

In years to come many an alumnae of Manzanar high school will be able to look back with fond memories at the days spent in Block 7 . . . those outdoor pep rallies, the after school dance practices, the bull sessions following seventh period. How many will think longingly of the dances held at Mess Hall two, the little theater in 7-15, and those last minute rushes peculiar to the journalism dept.? The first snow storm, the many dusty days, and the early signs of spring will all be a precious part of the memories of the graduating classes of Manzanar High School.

Dr. Genevieve W. Carter, Superintedent of Education

Rollin C. Fox, Principal

Marion E. Potts, Vice Principal

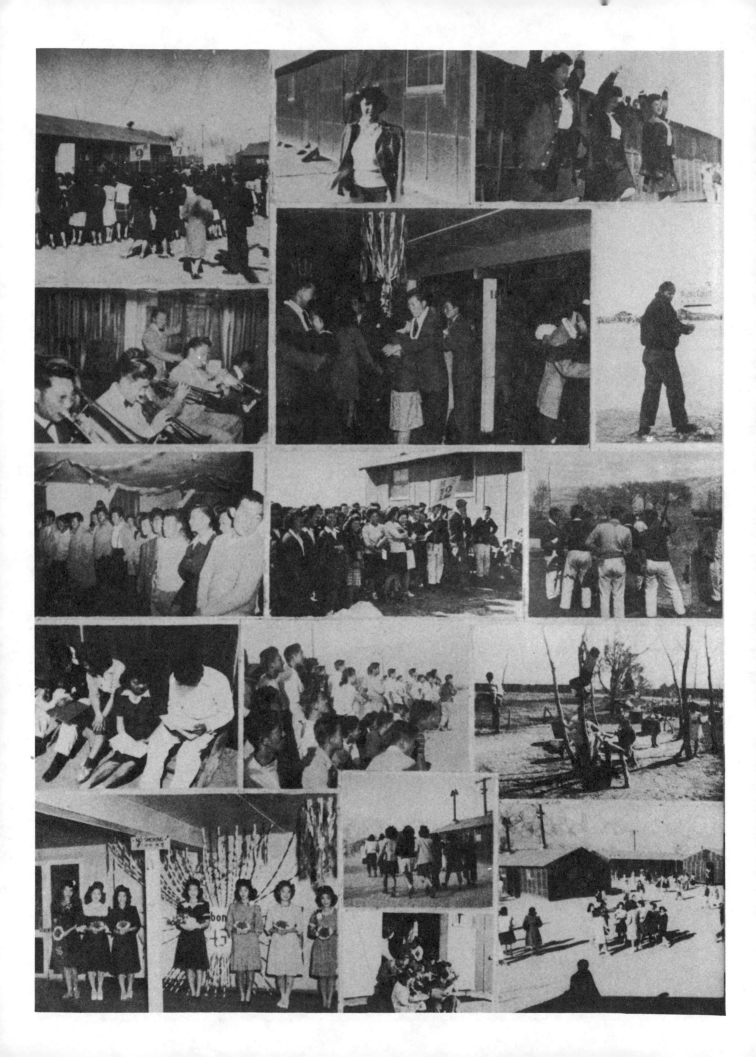

s' 44 officers

first semester

Mike Minato, President
Irene Morimoto, Vice President
Rosie Maruki, Secretary
Teiji Ohara, Treasurer
Ralph Lazo, Publicity Manager

senior calendar

With Janet Goldberg, Mary Jean Kramer and Clive Greenlee as advisors, the Senior Class rolled off an exciting year. Starting the term with lots of pep, the class had a hard fought game on the gridiron with the "Duces", the class of S'45, who held the Seniors to a 0-0 tie.

Sweater day gave the entire student body a chance to view the seniors in their navy blue sweaters with powder blue emblems. This was followed by a Senior talent show which was a big "hit". Dancing was provided by the well known orchestra, the "Jive Bombers". To close the first term, the Senior class presented the ever popular comedy "Growing Pains", to a packed house for one week.

The second semester started with the Installation dance when the officers of the new term were introduced. The term rolled by rapidly with the Senior Prom, Senior Banquet, Baccalaureate Service and the long awaited Graduation Ceremony.

For the Seniors who have now graduated, the colors navy blue and powder blue stand as the symbol of some of the best school days of their life.

second semester

Arnold Maeda, President
Yoshindo Shibuya, Vice President
Rosie Hanawa, Secretary
Maito Hori, Treasurer
Bruce Kaji, Publicity Manager
Kohei Nakaji, Historian

kahoshi, Chiyeko
Theodore Roosevelt

kashi, Thelma
University

kemoto, Sadaye
Thomas Jefferson

Ando, Takuko
Eastmont Jr.

Anzai, Suzanne
Catholic Girls'

Aoki, Lucy
Santa Monica

Araishi, Jean
University

Araki, Alice
University

Eto, Keiji
San Pedro

Fujii, Osamu
Herbert Hoover

Fukushima, Clara
Elk Grove

Fukushima, Taira
J.H.F. Polytechnic

Furuya, Sachiko
Belmont

Hanawa, Rosie
Reedley Joint Union

Hasegawa, Naruye
Theodore Roosevelt

Hatae, Mariko
Abraham Lincoln

Hayashikawa, Aiko
Thomas Jefferson

Hazama, Katsuji
San Fernando

Hirabara, Thomas
Elk Grove

Hirami, Soichiro
North Hollywood

Hiraoka, Chiyeko
James Garfield

Hiyoshi, Gertrude
Woodrow Wilson Jr.

Hohri, Willie
North Hollywood

Hori, Meito
Reedley Joint Union

Horii, Masako
John Marshall

Hoshizaki, Denise
Sacred Heart

Hoshizaki, Lois
Sacred Heart

Hoshizaki, Ritsuko
Thomas Jefferson

Ida, Agnes
Sacred Heart

Igasaki, Lillian
Theodore Roosevelt

Ikeda, Jack
Sawtelle Tech

Imai, Minoru
Thomas Jefferson

Inohara, Yukiye
Abraham Lincoln

Iriye, Hiroko
Phineas Banning

Ishino, Masanobu
San Pedro

Itatani, Harold
Galileo

…to, Alice
  Theodore Roosevelt
…wasaki, Isamu
  San Pedro
…aji, Bruce
  Theodore Roosevelt

Kamimura, Margaret
  Belmont
Katano, Yasunari
  Belmont
Katayama, Shoji
  San Fernando

Kato, Ayako
  Venice
Kato, Toshiko
  Theodore Roosevelt
Kawaguchi, Saeko
  San Pedro

Kawamoto, Tom
  Elk Grove
Kikuta, Harry
  Thomas Jefferson
Kimura, Masako
  Whittier

Kishi, Jim
  Herbert Hoover
Kitada, Kay
  John Marshall
Kitagawa, David
  University

Kitaoka, Emiko
  Theodore Roosevelt
Kodama, Umeko
  Theodore Roosevelt
Koga, Mary
  Alameda

Kosaka, Minoru
  Venice
Kunihiro, Luriye
  Van Nuys
Kuniyoshi, Tokuko
  Belmont

Kuramoto, Tomoyo
  San Pedro
Kurihara, Goro
  Herbert Hoover
Kuroyama, Noriyuki
  Belmont

Kusaba, Torao
  Venice
Kusayanagi, Irene
  Susan M. Dorsey
Kusunoki, Yoshiko
  Thomas Jefferson

Kuwata, Teruko
  Thomas Jefferson
Lazo, Ralph
  Belmont
Maeda, Arnold
  Santa Monica

Maeda, Kunio
  San Pedro
Maruki, Rosie
  Theodore Roosevelt
Maruyama, Shoji
  Santa Monica

Masuda, Setsumi
  San Pedro
Matsumoto, Hideo
  Santa Monica
Matsumura, Tsutomu
  Santa Monica

Matsuno, Hideko
  Herbert Hoover
Matsuno, Isao
  San Pedro
Matsuoka, Kiyoko
  Thomas Jefferson

Matsuoka, Lucille
  Thomas Jefferson
Matsuzawa, Fumika
  Theodore Roosevelt
Minato, Mike
  Los Angeles

Miyamoto, Frank
  Theodore Roosevelt
Miyatake, Atsufumi
  Theodore Roosevelt
Mizumoto, Michiko
  San Pedro

Morimoto, Irene
  University
Morita, James
  Elk Grove
Motoike, Sam
  Linden Union

Motooka, Sadao
  San Diego
Murata, Mamoru
  San Pedro
Nagai, Kazuko
  Venice

Nagano, Aiji
  Susan M. Dorsey
Nakaji, Kohei
  San Pedro
Nakamura, Mitsuru
  Theodore Roosevelt

Nakashima, June
  Glendale
Nakashima, Sumiko
  Theodore Roosevelt
Nakashima, Tadahiro
  Thomas Jefferson

Nakata, Kenneth
  Bainbridge
Nakayu, Yutaka
  Venice
Nenashi, George
  Elk Grove

Nishi, George
  San Fernando
Nishimura, George
  University
Niwa, Ujinobu
  University

Noda, Haruko
  San Fernando
Noda, Yasuko
  San Fernando
Nomura, Ayako
  North Hollywood

Nomura, Fujiko
  University
Odahara, Grace
  University
Ogawa, Chiyeko
  San Pedro

Ogawa, Ernest
  Theodore Roosev
Ogi, Haruko
  Gardena
Ohara Teiji
  San Pedro

Ohno, Peggie
Elk Grove
Oka, Tazuko
J.H.F. Polytechnic
Okada, Kiyoshi
Herbert Hoover

Okamoto, Mitsuo
San Pedro
Okamoto, Toru
Venice
Okamuro, Masayuki
Excelsior

Okimoto, Yoshiye
Herbert Hoover
Okumura, Nobuko
Venice
Ono, Sam
Venice

Osajima, Paul
Santa Paula Union
Ryono, Misuko
San Pedro
Sakaki, Michiko
Thomas Jefferson

Sakamoto, Shizuko
Santa Monica
Sakata, Florence
University
Sakata, Tsugimaro
Santa Monica

Sano, Miko
Belmont
Sato, Charles
Theodore Roosevelt
Sato, Gordon
San Pedro

Sato, Kiyoko
University
Sawamura, Shigeo
Elk Grove
Sedohara, Sachiko
San Fernando

Segimoto, Kiyomi
San Pedro
Seko, Saburo
San Pedro
Shibuya, George
J.H.F. Polytechnic

Shibuya, Yoshindo
Belmont
Shikami, Reggie
Santa Monica
Shimamura, Kazuko
Theodore Roosevelt

Shimizu, Miyeko
Belmont
Shimizu, Tatsuhiko
Santa Monica
Shimoda, Anne
Belmont

Shintani, Hanako
Narbonne
Shintani, Tadao
San Pedro
Suzuki, Joe
Loyola

Takachi, Ruth
Irving Jr.
Takeda, Kenichi
San Fernando
Tanaka, Miyoshi
University

Tani, Diane
  Venice
Tanioka, Hiroshi
  Theodore Roosevelt
Tatsui, Hanabusa
  John Marshall

Terada, Masako
  San Pedro
Tomita, Toshiyuki
  Venice
Torii, Seiichi
  Loyola

Ujiye, Tomiko
  Manual Arts
Umehara, Betty
  University
Uyeda, Haruko
  Gardena

Uyeda, Sumiko
  San Pedro
Uyeda, Tommy
  Gardena
Uyemori, Bob
  University

Uyemura, Lillian
  J.H.F. Polytechnic
Wada, George
  Lynwood Jr.
Watanabe, Takako
  Thomas Jefferson

Yamane, Jimmy
  North Hollywood
Yamane, Robert
  North Hollywood

Yamashina, Aiko
  Theodore Roosevelt
Yamashita, Kiyoko
  Girls

Yamashita, Mary
  Hollywood
Yokomizo, Hideo
  San Fernando

Yoshida, Kiyo
  J.H.F. Polytechnic
Yoshie, Shizuko
  John Marshall

Yoshimoto, Miyuki
  University
Yoshinaga, Seigo
  Cathedral

the classes

May luck ad alot of happiness te yours. Flo

s' 45 officers

Left to right: Seated, Girls' Vice-Pres. Yuki Shiba, Pres. Short Hashimoto, Recording Sec. Teddy Hayashi, Boys' Vice-Pre Tommy Hashimoto.

Standing, Corresponding Sec. Gladys Matsumoto, Yess Leade Seizo Tanibata, Historian Florence Kimura, Treas. Katsuyu Marumoto, Yell Leader Tosh Morishita, Boys' Ath. Mgr. Nobu yoshi Ishino,

Camera Shy Yell Leader George Takahashi, PUBLICITY MGR Gumpe Honda (Tule), Girls' Ath. Mgr. Mary Myose (Tule).

Best Wishes Kazy Kaito

junior calendar

With the Junior-Senior Football Game as a starter, the mighty "Duces" completed an activity laden year. Following the election of their officers for the first semester, an installation dance was held on October 23, 1943. Then the generous, thoughtful Juniors donated mirrors for the latrines on November 10, 1943 with Teddy Hayashi acting as chairman. A "Flunkers' Frolic" on December 10, this time with Yuki Shiba as chairman, was next on the list of their many activities. Under the supervision of Kats Marumoto, a "Christmas Seal Drive" was held with donations going to the Manzanar Hospital. For their first social of the new year, a Valentine Day Dance with "Be Careful It's My Heart" as the theme was held on February 7, 1944, with Tom Hashimoto as chairman. Bidding adieu to Miss Ely, on March 10, 1944, a "Farewell, Miss Ely" social was held with Yuki Shiba and Tommy Hashimoto directing the program. Next came the "Duces' Raffle and Dance" on April 21, 1944 with the chairmen Hisao Hashimoto and Teddy Hayashi. The highlight of the year, the Senior Prom, was given by the Juniors on May 27, 1944 with active Hisao Hashimoto, and Teddy Hayashi acting as chairmen. As the final fling of the year, the "Duces" enjoyed a picnic on June 7, 1944.

Left to right: Row 1, Florence Ito, Lily Ashizawa, Grace Hochi, Toshiko Kubota, Takeko Maeda, Martha Ban, Yoshimi Ido, Satomi Kuramoto, Chiyoko Mano, Sumiko Masuda, Sharlen Bannai, Sho Jeniye.
Row 2, Satoye Hikiji, Nagisa Kawaguchi, Mary Honda, Cecelia Higaga, Rose Honda, Florence Kimura, Teruko Hayashi, Virginia Kikuda, Haru Kodani, Kazuko Kadota, Naoko Kono,
Row 3, Kazuo Hoshiyama, Ray Chomori, Hiroshi Jujii, Thomas Amano, Jimmie Hoshiko, Hidekazu Akahoshi, Masamichi Kataoka, Joe Fudushima, Shig Kato, Susumu Ioki, Tom Hashimoto, Shorty Hashimoto, Sei Ikebuchi.
Row 4, Al Inouye, Yoshihiro Kawauchi, Katsuyuki Marumoto, Masaru Kusaba, Nobuyoshi Ishino, Susumu Iwasaki, Ikie Komatsu, Ray Kawahara, Lawrence Honda, Tamotsu Isozaki, Henry Harada, Rokuro Kurihara, Akira Hirami, Jiro Iwata.

Left to right: Row 1, Takashi Mukai, Joe Ozaki, Ujiaki Niwa, Yuzo Matsutsuyu, Kyosuke Ono, Yoshio Otsuka, Haruki Murakami, Kazuyoshi Nagashima, Kuniaki Sakamoto, Toshio Ogura, George Sakamoto.
Row 2, Nagatoshi Nojima, Togo Mikuriya, Tamotsu Nakahara, Henry Nakano, Kazuo Naruto, Isao Sakata, Roy Muto, Joe Shikami, Arata Ota, Mitsuo Natsume.
Row 3, Ruby Nakamura, Aiko Miyake, Grace Nishi, Velma Sato, Ellen Oshio, Satoye Okuji, Shizuko Sakihara, Tokiya Oto, Mary Matsuno, Fumi Miki, Himeko Nakashima, Kazue Shibuya, Sumiko Nemoto.
Row 4, Mary Mizumoto, Martha Mizumoto, Ikuyo Nanchi, Gladys Matsumoto, Judy Nakao, Kayoko Sato, Yuri Sanada, Masumi Ono, Tamaru Shijo, Haru Ogawa, Yuki Shiba, Matsue Nishimori, Toshiko Morishita.

Left to right; Row 1, Ruth Yoshida, Fumi Suzuki, Ryoko Yano, Kathlene Yoshizawa, Emiko Yato, Tayeko Shimizu, Kazie Yoshimura, Sumi Takeuchi, Chieko Tanaka, Toshiyo Watanabe, Junko Yoshimoto, Sumiko Tanaka, Yoshiko Yada.
Row 2, Marina Maeda, Grace Shinoda, Haruko Tasumi, Kyogo Uyeshima, Teruko Sugihara, Kyoko Shinden, Chimiyo Shioji, Yeiko Yamazaki, Marian Uyematsu, Rose Tamai, Mary Toguchida, Shirley Tani, Utako Toyama, Chizu Watanabe,
Row 3, Toshimichi Tomita, Ken Yamamoto, Bill Taketa, George Takahashi, Eddie Tanaka, Hiroshi Yamashita, Seizo Tanibata, Takaaki Shinto, Takashi Osumi, Victor Takamoto, Fred Yamada, Hideo Sugimoto, Ichio Shishido.
Row 4, Yoshio Shishido, Leo Uchida, Akira Toda, Katsumi Suzuki, Gene Suzuki, Taka Uyeno, Sachio Sotani, Yoshihiro Kawauchi, Harry Yamashina.

s'46 officers

first semester

sophomore calendar

Known to the Student Body as the "solid" class, the Sophomore flag bearers completed a year of successful activities. With their monthly socials, they really went to town. Clad in jeans and cotton for the "Barn Dance" on the eve of November 20, 1943, the "Prospectors" gathered for their first social of the year. On this occasion, Akira Kishishita and Masako Koni waltzed away with the Waltz contest prize. Sharing the prevalent Christmas spirit of the camp, the Sophs held their Christmas Dance on December 18, with New Year resolutions being read. With Shoji Hamachi's "Paper Doll" and Kei Ono's tap dance to keep them in the mood, the Prospectors started the year off with the "Follies of '44." In honor of the Tule-bound Sophs, a Pre-Valentine Dance was held on February 8, 1943, the hi-light of the event being Mas Yano and Rosie Shizumura's duet. Other activities of the year were the "Ides of March" on the fifteenth, and an "April Fools' Day Festival." This was followed by the "May Day Dance" with the graduating Seniors present as honored guests. Inter-homeroom football games were some of the other activities of the year.

second semester

Left to right: Row 1, Vonita Harada, Elsie Hatago, Meiko Kami, Mabel Ito, Miyeko Hata, Masako Hori, Seiko Furuya, Amy Araki, Elizabeth Kitagawa, Kyoko Kamo, Kimiko Hamane.
Row 2, Alice Kakoi, Kimiko Anzai, Clara Fukuda, Yukiko Hara, Mutsuko Ando, Julia Horimoto, Kumiko Bato.
Row 3, Mutsuo Kawagoye, Tsutomu Hori, Nobuo Hori, Teddy Ikeda, Shoyei Kitayama, Nobuo Kitaoka, Hajime Fukumoto, Akio Itamura, Susumu Hiraike, Tadashi Arita.
Row 4, Masaji Hataa, Shigeru Honda, Billy Akira, Tsuneo Ida, Willy Fukuhara, Akira Isozaki, Koji Iriye, Kiyoshi Fujinami, Yoshiaki Amino, Stanley Honda.

Left to right: Row 1, Masako Konii, Chineko Mukai, Kiyoko Kobayashi, Masako Nagano, Emiko Kono, Shizuye Nakagawa, Fusako Okumura, Nobuko Nagashima, Edith Nishi, Irene Matsumoto, Ruth Koyama, Aiko Kurosimi.
Row 2, Mitose Kuramoto, Mary Matsuno, Aki Osawa, Ruby Oshio, Hideyo Nakaji, Kei Ono, Sumiko Osajima, Joy Kuse, Nancy Kuwata, Teruko Motooka, Noriko Minato, Betty Nojiri, Yoshiko Nagai, Yoshiko Okada.
Row 3, Ben Motoike, Bryce Nishimura, Jun Ogimachi, Shiro Matsumoto, Toshio Kuroyama, Tadao Marumoto, Shigeji Kuwahara Chiaki Nakata.
Row 4, Hidekichi Nagamine, Katsumi Kusaba, Mitsuomi Nishikawa, Davi Koga, Tony Masamitsu, Akira Minamiji, Takeshi Nakane, Takehiko Murata, Kiyoshi, Nakayu.

Left to right: Row 1, Lena Sawamura, Yoshiko Sugimoto, Miyoko Tachibana, Sachiko Sugimoto, Yoshiko Watanabe, Chizuko Sakaguchi, Tomeko Uyeda, Mary Seno Eileen Uchida, Amie Takahashi, Teiko Uyeda, Tomiko Takeda.
Row 2, Yoshiko Yamasaki, Bernice Sakurai, Taeko Yamashita, Kazumi Shono, Kayoko Wakita, Kimiko Takamoto, Dorothy Shindo, Seiko Uragami Masako Yuge, Mary Sakata, Masako Yano, Helen Uyeko, Lillian Wakatsuki.
Row 3, Takeshi Tanioka, Noboru Yamasaki, Miyoshi Sakamoto, Esamu Yokoyama, Hitoshi Toji, Taikyo Uyeshima, George Torii, Takeo Sato, Hiroshi Sato.
Row 4, Mamoru Shishido, Makio Tomita, Tadami Ushijima, Frank Takeyama, Tamotsu Yasuda, Masaru Shimoda.

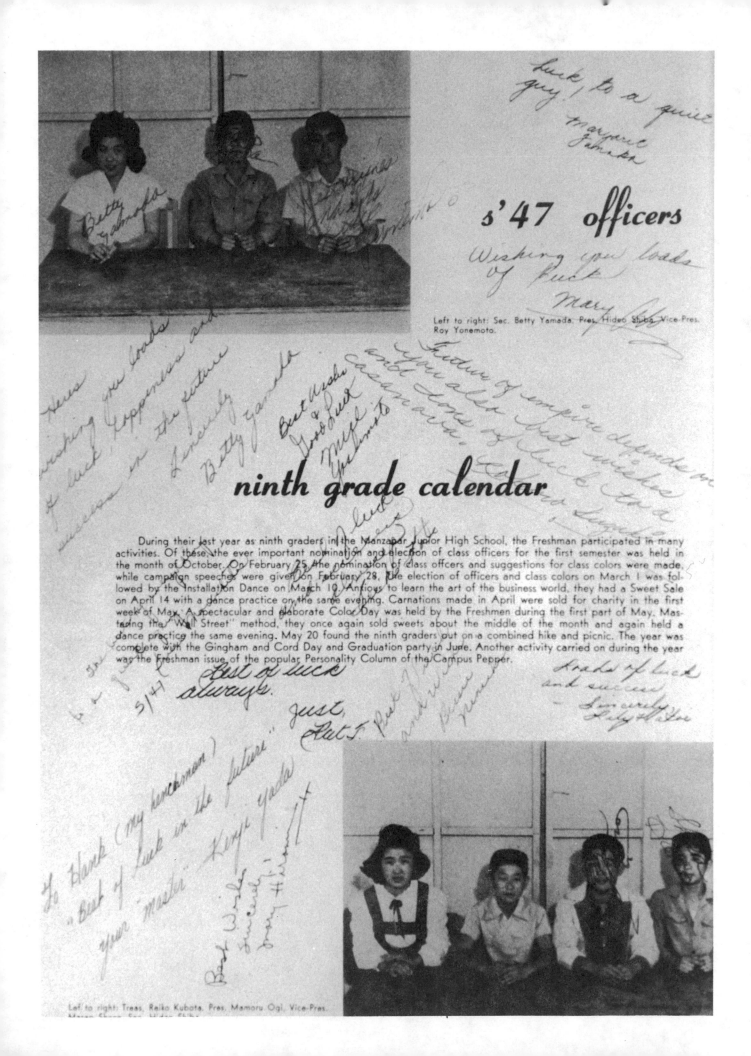

s'47 officers

Left to right: Sec. Betty Yamada, Pres. Hideo Shiba, Vice-Pres. Roy Yonemoto.

ninth grade calendar

During their last year as ninth graders in the Manzanar Junior High School, the Freshman participated in many activities. Of these, the ever important nomination and election of class officers for the first semester was held in the month of October. On February 25, the nomination of class officers and suggestions for class colors were made, while campaign speeches were given on February 28. The election of officers and class colors on March 1 was followed by the Installation Dance on March 10. Anxious to learn the art of the business world, they had a Sweet Sale on April 14 with a dance practice on the same evening. Carnations made in April were sold for charity in the first week of May. A spectacular and elaborate Color Day was held by the Freshmen during the first part of May. Mastering the "Wall Street" method, they once again sold sweets about the middle of the month and again held a dance practice the same evening. May 20 found the ninth graders out on a combined hike and picnic. The year was complete with the Gingham and Cord Day and Graduation party in June. Another activity carried on during the year was the Freshman issue of the popular Personality Column of the Campus Pepper.

Left to right: Treas. Reiko Kubota, Pres. Mamoru Ogi, Vice-Pres.

Left to right: Row 1, Emiko Hayashi, Nobuko Kakiuchi, (Jane Honda) Yuri Kageyama, Shigeko Sato, Kiku Komatsu, Yoko Inouye, Nakako Kodani, Reiko Kubota, Sachiko Kazunaga, Seiko Kato, Toshiko Akemoto.
Row 2, Yoshiko Kono, Mary Abe, Helen Katayama, Lilliam Kimura, Sumiko Azeka, Helen Matsumoto, Shitsuko Hiraide, Masako Kato Lily Kakoi, Miyeko Iwasaki, Masako Kusaba, Fumiyo Maeda, Mary Hirami, Mitsuka Kono.
Row 3, Kazuya Ando, Yukio Abii, Tetsuo Katayama, Lloyd Ide, Hajime Mato, Bobby Miyatake, Uwao Matsumura, Herbert Amamoto, Akira Ishii, Roy Kimura, Aro Ikeda.
Row 4, Shinji Arita John Kimura, Nori Marumoto, Hakashi Horii.

Left to right: Row 1, Shinako Okamoto, Helen Muraoka, Kiyoko Nakayu, Bessie Nenashi, Susie Morishita, Masako Motoyasu, Miyoko Nishi, Yuki Shigemori, Mitsuko, Sakuma, Aiko Shimobayashi, Katherine Nishimura, Flora Sakata.
Row 2: Faith Murakami, Chizuyo Ryono, Aika Murakami, Kimiko Suzuki, Miyeko Nakata.
Row 3: Noboru Sakaguchi, (Masahiro Nakajo) Seiji Saito, Raymond Oka, Lawrence Shinoda, Mamoru Ogi, Masami Nakashima, Harutoshi Nojima Fred Sakuda, Toshio Okui.
Row 4, Yukio Nakamura, Saburo Ogura, Shigeo Ogawa, Tadashi Ota, Hideo Shiba, Ray Motoike, Kiyomi Mizutani, Kenji Oye, (Mas Shono) Tom Sakaguchi, Wilbur Sato, Paul Okamura.

Left to right: Row 1, Pat Takeyama, June Yoshite, Misako Yamasaki, Sadako Taniota, Betty Yamada, Sumiko Uyemori, Margaret Tanaka, Haruko Watanabe, Sadako Yamashita, Kimiyo Toma, Kuniko Takeyama, Michiko Yoshimoto, Cherryko Yamada, Yoshiko Yamaguchi.
Row 2, Kenji Yada, Isamu Takedo, Billy Takemoto, Benny Tsukamoto, George Yamane, Michio Tanaka, Roy Yoshida, Mitsu Yamashita Richard Yamada Jim Tomita, Kokuro Suzuki, Tadashi Tatsui, Henry Umemoto.
Row 3, Ray Wakatsuki, Tetsuo Tateuchi, Takeshi Yamashita, Jun Tanaka, Tom Takahashi, Teddy Yamane, Toshio Yamashita, Noboru Yato, Henry Yoshino, Shiji Yamauchi, Ray Yamamoto, Norio Watanabe, George Uchida.

s'48 officers

Left to right: Vice-Pres. Rosie Kimura, Pres. Mutuso Kuram-
Sec. Mary Mato, Treas. Alan Ichida (Hospitalized)

eighth grade calendar

The eighth graders concluded early in the first semester that the class members arrived at decisions, responded more easily, and enjoyed their activities more when they worked in small social living groups. Consequently they passed the year in this manner. During the month of October, 1943, election of officers in various homerooms were held. On the 27th of that month, Miss Ely's Social Study Classes held a Halloween Party. Shortly before the season's vacation, Christmas Parties were held by small groups and other activities of the term were concluded. Being more enthusiastic about athletic events than parties and dances, the eighth graders held various interesting and exciting inter-homeroom activities in that field. The boys as well as the girls participated in sports when the weather permitted such activities during the second semester. The inter-homeroom athletic events were scheduled for the first semester, however weather conditions postponed all such events until the following semester. The Cornerstone Ceremony which was held on February 19, 1944, in dedication of the future "living room", was attended by the eighth graders as well as the other classes.

Left to right: Row 1, June Fukuda, Mary Honda, Grace Araishi, Tomiko Honda, Yachiyo Fukuda, Mary Anzai, Asako Hiraike, Rosie Kimura Masako Hata, Mitsuko, Ichida, Aileen Iwamizu, Sachiko Kusayanagi, Chiyoko Kusaba.
Row 2, Susumu Fukuchi, Ichiro Hamagiwa, Mickey Hiraga, Mutsu Kawamoto, Tadao Kamachi, Takeshi Fukushima, Hisao Anzai, Hideo Kishi.
Row 3, Jack Hayashi, Kiyoshi Hama, Sazoharu Enomoto, Hiroshi Kageyama, Mutsuo Kuramoto, William Hoshiko, Eddie Kato, Noboru Koshimizu.

Left to right: Row 1, Shizuka Sasahara, Stuneko Oye, Misako Okada, Mikiko Sakata, Michiko Oye, Mary Muraoka, Lillian Nagai, Alice Nakahama, Tatsuko Okumura, Lillian Neeno, Hideko Nakano Ayako Nishi.
Row 2, Bob Nakao, Stanley Mori, Kiyoshi Mikawa, Masako Nakajo, Yasuko Motooka, Dorothy Sakurai, Mary Muto, Setsuko Miki.
Row 3, Toshizo Saka, Michio Motoyasu, Takezo Sedohara, Toshio Nojiri, Yoshikazu Sakuma, James Nomura, Masaru Sagimoto, Shiso Matsuno, Kazutoshi Mayeda, Ryo Mukai, Masuo Okui, Harold Muraoka.

Left to right: Row 1, Lillian Watanabe, Merry Shinooka, Amy Sugihara, Atsuko Yamaguchi, Haruko Tachibana, Alice Takahashi, Dorothy Sugihara, Marjorie Tsukamoto, Angela Suzuki, Ruri Yamashina, Tsuyuko Shishido.
Row 2, Haruko Yoshimoto, Lily Yoshida, Jean Yamada, Atsuko Takechi, Yeko Yamamoto.
Row 3, Katsumi Tanimura, Hiroji Tomita, Yoshio Tsuda, Susumn Tanimura, Masami Toji, Michio Yoshii, Hisao Tani, Tsuneo Watanabe, Yashuka Shimizu, Shoji Anaka, Bobbie Yamashita, Henry Shinto, John Tomita.

s'49 officers

Left to right: Vice-Pres. Tomoji Saka, Pres. Toyoshi Asanuma, Sec. Haruko Isozaki.

seventh grade calendar

The seventh graders, alias the "scrubs", completed a year worthy of praise. Although the first semester was dull with only the Hallowe'en Party on October 29, 1943, the election of officers and the election of representatives to the Student Council to be accounted for, the second semester rolled along very smoothly. They started the second semester by attending the Cornerstone Ceremony on February 19, and went right on to the election of their officers on February 21 and 24. On March 6, 8, 13, and 15, an exciting Girls' Basketball tournament took place. On March 17, the class held a "Saint Patrick's Day Party," and on the 31st of the same month an Easter Party. To determine the champion speller of the "scrubs," a "Spelldown" contest was held from April 10 through April 14. During May an interesting "Science Quiz Kids Radio Program" was scheduled. The latter part of the month the boys participated in a baseball tournament while the girls participated in a softball tournament just as exciting. At this time many talented players were discovered. For their last activity for the year, the seventh graders went on a combined hike and picnic just before summer vacation.

Left to right: Treas. Yurika Fukushima, Vice-Pres. Eiichi Minami, Pres. Teruaki Takeda, Sec. Dorothy Takayama.

Left to right: Row 1, Naomi Inouye, Reiko Arai, Aiko Anzai, Keiko Fujino, Miyako Fujii, Frances Hatago, Doris Koga, Jane Harada, Toshiye Hori, Lily Abo, Yaeko Fukuda.
Row 2, James Hashimoto, Tommy Fujii Kanya Katano, Grace Hirata, Yuriko Fukushima, Midori Fujimori, Ayako Kawamoto, Haruko Isozaki, Yoko Kawaguchi, Tommy Hoshizaki, Minoru Hirano, Leo Kawamoto.
Row 3, Howard Kato, Ken Kimura, Nobuo Kawamura, Ryoyei Kitayama, Richard Kame, Frank Akiyama, Tomikazu Honda, Richard Honda, Toyoshi Asanuma, Tom Izuhara.

Left to right: Row 1, Shizuko, Emiko Motooka, Etsuko Namiyoshi, Tatsuko Matsuno, Hatsuki Nakauchi, Betty Matsushita, Mable Nakamura, Teruko Sakamoto, Grace Murakami, Frances Nishioka Tayeko Oda.
Row 2, Hisahi Sansui, Eiichi Minami, Iris Omura, Kazuko Sano, Janet Morimoto, Yoshiye Morita, Asako Masuda, Seiko Sato, Isao, Shigematsu, Tomoji Saka.
Row 3, Isao Murakami, Mitsuri Murakami, Kaname Okamoto, Tohoru Nakasuji, Sam Koyama, Katsumi Okuji, Tadayuki Marumoto, Shinichi Murakami, Toshio Middo, John Morita, Sam Nanashi, Roger Minami, Tetsuo Kunitomi, James Kuwata.

Left to right: Row 1, Michiko Takeda, May Wakatsuki, Mieko Yada, Noriko Sugimoto, Lucy Uyeda, Yukiko Shigetome, Florence Wada, Dorothy Takayama, Kimiko Tatsumi, Asako Shimizu, Anne Yamada, Rose Shiohama, Misako Shishido, Satsuko Shishido.
Row 2, Joe Watanabe, Hirosada Sugimoto, Takaya Uragami, Albert Taketa, Masami Tanaka, Isamu Yamashita, Hiroshi Takeshita, Katsumi Yoshimura, Hiro Shono, Susumu Shimizu, Hideo Yamashita, Ray Uyemori, Narumi Shimoda, Fumio Yamauchi, Chuichi Watanabe, Michio Yasuda, Kinya Tatsumi, Teruaki Takeda, Eddie Yyeda.

Associated

first semester

The Associated Student Body of Manzanar High School is comprised of the Junior High School, grades seven through nine, and the Senior High School, grades ten through twelve. Approximately 1,000 students were enrolled in the entire Student Body during the year.

Feeling that elections and campaigns are important to a democratic school system, campaign rallys and elections were stressed, and given much attention. The approach of elections meant the appearance on the school grounds of countless posters for various candidates. Rallys meant assemblies in Mess two and Library seven where speeches were made and a great deal of enthusiasm shown.

The Senior High School student body president for both semesters was George Nishimura, who won the second term after proving himself capable of the responsibilities of such a high office. In the Junior High School, for the first semester, Mamoru Ogi was president and the second semester president was Mary Hirami. Although student government was rather new to the Junior High students, much interest was shown and many activities were reported.

girls' and boys' courts

Student Body

second semester

As in any school there was heated rivalry among the classes. During assemblies and rallys much loyalty was demonstrated by the classes. Inter-class games in sports were played, and it was here that loyalties were seen to be the strongest. But when school activities needed support, the whole student body came out to make them successful.

The Student Council, made up of the cabinet members and faculty made plans providing for an Honor Society to which outstanding students of character, neatness, leadership, and scholarship were admitted. The students were also eager to have a Student Co-operative, and plans were made for the formation of one. This meant hard work and the shouldering of responsibilities, but the council showed themselves capable of such a task. The council also formed a student court, which had judges from the three Senior High School classes.

Through the Associated Student Body, the students are learning how to conduct school activities, and are participating in them as part of their educational program.

first semester

Girls'

Feeling there was a need for an organization to embrace all the girls in the high school a group of juniors and seniors met with Miss Janet Goldberg and as a result a Girls' League was established in October, 1943. After organization plans were completed an election of officers was held. Those chosen to serve the first semester were: "Pee Wee" Kusunoki, president; Lillian Igasaki, vic-president; Kiyo Yoshida, secretary; Teddy Hayashi, treasurer; Yuki Shiba, publicity manager; and Yuri Yamazaki, historian. Under the guidance of this group, the girls of Manzanar High held their first social in January, 1944. The "Spinsters' Skip", as it was called, proved to be one of the most successful dances of the year.

The Girls' Athletic Association, better known as the G.A.A., is an affiliate of the League. Their meetings are held on the first and third Fridays of each month. This organization directs the after school sports activities of high school girls. Intramural leagues for softball, speedball, volleyball, and basketball helped to create a very complete athletic program for the physical education classes. Cardinal and gold letters were later awarded to members of the championship softball team. Rosie Tamai, Toshiko Morishita and Ruby Oshio were chosen to act as yell leaders. The officers of the Girls' Athletic Association were: Chickie Hiraoka, president; Kazuko Yoshimura, vice-president; Yuri Yamazaki, secretary; Alice Kakoi, historian; and Yuki Shiba, Athletic Manager.

The "Boosters", a service club sponsored by the Girls' League, proved to be a valuable asset by ushering at the high school Open House and at the Senior Play. One of the most amusing incidents in school was their initiation of new members. Each so called victim was required to wear a very foolish headdress throughout the whole day. The cabinet of the Boosters consists of the following: Rosie Hanawa, president; Irene Kusayanagi, vice-president; Rosie Maruki, secretary; Kiyo Nishi, treasurer; Teddy Hayashi, historian.

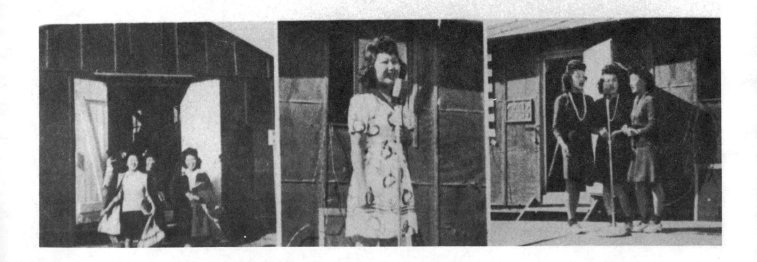

second semester

League

As it was decided by the Student Body Council that the student body Boys' and Girls Vice-Presidents should automatically take the leadership of their respective leagues, "Pee Wee" Kusunoki retained her office as president. An activity calendar was immediately drawn up and committees were appointed to plan the various activities of the semester. More than ever, these girls showed their willingness to help make Manzanar High School, one that would compare favorably with any of those on the outside. In order to bring about a better understanding between the high school girls and their mothers, the League sponsored a "Mothers Tea."

The Girls' Athletic Association also kept up their activities during the second semester. As soon as the term was under way, an election of new officers was held. Those chosen were President Kazuko Yoshimura, Vice-President Chickie Hiraoka, Secretary Yuri Yamazaki, Treasurer Yuki Shiba, and last but not least Publicity Manager Kiyo Nishi. Intramural leagues in basketball, softball, and volleyball followed in that order. Cardinal and gold emblems and sweaters were earned on the point system, whereas only members of the championship teams were given letters in the previous term. A field day in which the girls could partake in a number of recreational activities was planned by the cabinet.

The "Boosters" proved themselves again an asset to Manzanar High during the past semester. In their white blouses and dark skirts they participated in the talent assembly and helped in other school functions.

As the semester drew to an end Senior members of the Boosters were honored at a pot luck dinner. In June the girls ushered for the Baccalaureate and Graduation Exercises. They also helped serve at the Senior Reception following graduation. Six new Boosters will be elected to membership in the fall from the new Sophomore class.

Boys'

After a rather uncertain start, the Boys' League had come a long way by the end of the first semester. Under their reliable president, Seizo Tanibata, the boys held their first social event in December, 1943. The League owes a great deal of its success to Mr. Thomas Higa, who acted as advisor to the boys. His experience on the playing field has inspired the confidence of the boys in Manzanar High School.

Athletic activities of the Boys' League included intramural sports, such as six-man touch football, volleyball and ten-inch softball. The latter sport, by the way was first introduced in Manzanar by the League. In order to have a decent baseball diamond on which to play, many members spent three consecutive weekends hauling red surface dirt. Good sportsmanship and team spirit were displayed by every team entered in the intramural leagues. The nation wide physical fitness program was put into effect at Manzanar High this semester, when an obstacle course was constructed on the gym field. Although this course seemed quite strenuous to the boys at first, they soon got used to it and were able to go through the daily routine in regular fashion.

The Lettermen's Club, an exclusive organization under the Boys' League, was established during the early part of this semester. Membership included only those fortunate boys who received their cardinal and gold letters. These letters were awarded to the players on the championship teams.

second semester

.

League

Automatically the head of the Boys' League, since he was elected the Boys' Vice-President. George Takahashi took over the key to his office in the beginning of this semester. As he had no cabinet, George appointed different committees for the various school activities sponsored by the Boys' League.

Coming under the Boys' League are the intramural games, such as regulation softball, ten-inch softball and basketball. Enthusiastically the boys of Manzanar High School turned out for the hot competition that resulted in these contests.

During the semester the Boys' League sponsored dances, movies and field days. The movies, which were financed from the funds raised at the dances, were on different types of sports.

"The Girls' League has a Boosters Association, so why shouldn't we have a service club of our own," the boys argued. So this semester one was organized with successful results. This club is similar to the honor societies "back home"—the "Knights," "Squires," etc. Only a limited number of the outstanding boys in Manzanar High are elected for membership.

It was decided this year to have athletic letters awarded to the boys on the basis of points instead of giving them to the members of the winning team.

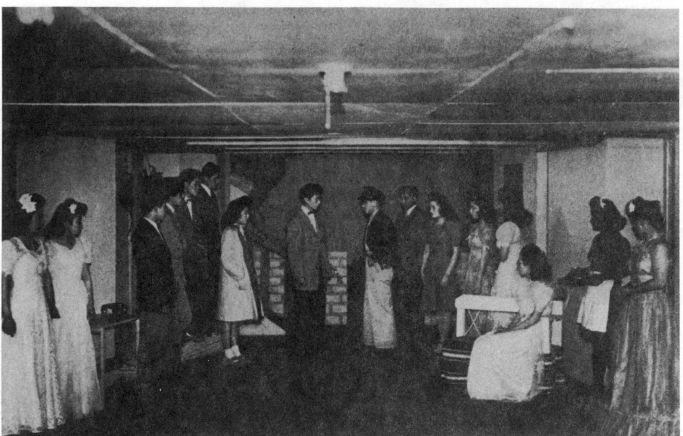

drama

Under the capable hands of Dramatic Instructor Louis Frizzell, the Drama Class presented the three acts of "Growing Pains", by Aurania Rouverol. This Senior Play tells the story of a typical American home, in this case that of the McIntyres. They see their boy and girl tossed into the normal awkward growing up stage but can offer little assistance or direction in their turbulent course. Any advice is always rejected by these adolescents.

The two youngsters, George and Terry, struggle and suffer through this trying phase of life together with their neighborhood friends. Many things happen to them, but the end is bright and promising.

The production staff was composed of Producer Masako Kimura, Director Rosie Maruki, Art Director Tanya Yoshida, Soundmen Tadao Shintani and Aiji Nagano, Prompter Ayako Kato, Make-up Artists Mary Toguchida and Shirley Tani, Secretary Lillian Igasaki, House Manager George Nishi, and staging was by Mr. Frizzell.

The cast included Shoji Katayama as George McIntyre, Takuko Ando as Terry McIntrye, Kazuko Nagai as Mrs. McIntyre, Arnold Maeda as Professor McIntyre, Yoshiko Kusunoki as Sophie, the maid, Suzanne Anzai as Mrs. Patterson, Junko Yoshimoto as Elsie Patterson, Tommy Uyeda as Traffic Officer, Mike Minato as Dutch, Benny Okami as Brian, Yoshindo Shibuya as Omar, Tadao Shintani as Hal, Lillian Uyemura as Prudence, Grace Odahara as Jane, Hideko Matsuno as Miriam, Diane Tani as Vivian and Terry Arita as Ann

have you got...

"Skindeep", by a senior, Tsugimaro Sakata relates the happenings in the camp Beauty Shoppe. This hilarious one act play was first presented at the Manzanar Fashion Show and had the audience fairly rolling in the aisles.

The all girl cast was composed of Grace Odahara, Rosie Maruki Nagai, Lillian Uyemura, Lillian Igasaki, Elsie Tatago, Aiko Yamashina, Yuki Inohara, and Ann Shimoda.

During the latter part of the semester the combined Drama, Choir, and Orchestra groups began rehearsal of an operetta. This undertaking was scheduled for the end of the semester for production in the new auditorium.

The progress of the inexperienced performers was indeed astounding and surprising. What they accomplished during the brief year was certainly a credit and honor to the school. With the completion of the theater, more plays will be produced.

growing pains?...

The Choral groups, consisting of the A Cappella and the newly added Girls' Choir are organizations which require no prerequisites other than the enjoyment of singing. Students of Senior High School are eligible to enter. They have presented programs before the Inyo County Teachers Meeting, Assemblies, and the Christmas Concert. The last part of the semester the Choral groups rehearsed for the spring musical.

The Orchestra is not based upon grade level. It is open to all students who have ability and the desire to participate in an activity which is most worthwhile, and which brings satisfaction to the individual and honor to the school. The Orchestra has performed at many of the assemblies throughout the year and is always ready to assist when musical accompaniment is needed.

The Music Theory Class, also under the tutelage of Mr. Frizzell, provides for instructions in harmony.

music to the right of you . . . .

Louis Frizzell and his two assistants, Lily Fukuhara and Yoshiteru Muraakmi, compose the staff of the music division of Manzanar High School, and much of the success of the department was due to their untiring and capable leadership.

The big program of the year sponsored by the Music Department was the Christmas Concert. The A Cappella Choir, Orchestra, and Girls' Choir, under the direction of Mr. Frizzell, unified their forces and presented a memorable and enjoyable two nights' performance of the Christmas Program. The Choral groups sang folksongs and carols while the Orchestra played various novelty pieces including selections from the "Wizard of Oz". Several compositions written by Mr. Frizzell were presented, including the cantata, "And Mary Wept", especially written for this occasion and sung by the guest soloist, Mary Kageyama. This program was the second outstanding musical event held in Manzanar, the first being the "Ballad for Americans" sung by the original A Cappella aggregation last spring.

music to the left of you...

Extra! Extra! This is the cry of the Campus Pepper Staff whenever they are able to scoop the Free Press, the community newspaper. Although there is a great rivalry between the two, the main job of the Campus Pepper is to advance the harmony and progress of the school, tell as complete a story as possible of school activities and bestow recognition on all achievements of merit. Under the supervision of Miss Janet Goldberg, adviser, the Pepper staff has worked tirelessly throughout the day and just as many hours during the night in editing the paper. Acting as a contributing factor to the success of many school dances and other activities, the Campus Pepper has had a cheerful reporter in attendance at all school functions to give them deserving publicity. For future newspaper men and women, the Pepper is an excellent training ground and the experiences that the reporters have had in meeting people and studying personalities will all prove valuable.

For Christmas, Thanksgiving and Hallowe'en, special issues were published. All stencils were cut and mimeographed by the students themselves. The two journalism classes of the first semester were combined for efficiency's sake during the second semester.

The first semester staff was: Editor Reggie Shikami, Associate Editor Masahiko Miyakoda, News Editor Aiji Nagano, Feature Editor Bennie Okami, Women's Page Editor Masako Kimura, Sports Editor Rabbit Katayama, Society Editor Hideko Matsuno, Assistant Sports Editor Ralph Lazo, Business Manager Harry Kikuta, Exchange Editor Suzanne Anzai, Make-Up Editor Nori Kuroyama, Assistant Make-Up Editors Teruko Kuwata, Arnold Maeda and Bruce Kaji.

great journalists...

The second semester staff included: Editor Nori Kuroyama, Associate Editor Bruce Kaji, News Editor Hideo Matsumoto, Feature Editor Rosie Hanawa, Women's Page Editor Hideko Matsuno, Society Editor Suzanne Anzai, Boys' Sports Editor Ralph Razo, Assistant Editor Yoshindo Shibuya, Girls' Sports Editor Teruko Kuwata, Business Manager Meito Hori, Exchange Editor Charles Sato, Make-Up Editors Arnold Maeda and Aiji Nagano.

Depicting pictorially a complete history of the life experiences in Manzanar throughout the year was the aim of the Our World staff. Since the year book takes into consideration not only school activities but general camp life too, the sale of the book was extended to persons not in school.

The staff was indebted to Mr. Toyo Miyatake for his excellent pictures of the classes, organizations, and the campus. Every student at one time faced the shutter of his camera, smiled and prayed that the picture would turn out good. During the March sales campaign, 1,000 annuals were sold. A "Photo Finish" dance was held to raise money and to give the annual publicity on October 30 in Library 7.

On the staff of the annual were Editor Reggie Shikami, Associate Editor Nori Kuroyama, Assistant Editor Masako Kimura, Business Manager Meito Hori, Senior Editors Taira Fukushima and Mary Yamashita, Class Editor Arnold Maeda, Administration Editor Aiji Nagano, Club Editor Bruce Kaji, Boys' Sports Editor Yoshindo Shibuya, Girls' Sports Editor "Pee Wee" Kusunoki.

...in the making

judicial committee

wood shop club

boosters club

baton
club

future
farmers

shorthand
club

latin club

spanish club

home economics club

g. a. a.

lettermen's

club

science

club

Boys' Sports

Under the watchful eye of Coach Thomas Higa, the Intramural Baseball League was started. Before the League began, the fundamentals of baseball were taught everyday after school, and later a varsity, B and C League were formed. Each league had four teams. The games were played after school as scheduled but the league was not completed due to the weather and segregation.

The highlight of the sports program in Manzanar High School was the football game between the Senior and Junior class in late October.

The Juniors threatened the Senior goal a number of times but were thrown back either by the powerful senior line or by penalties.

The first quarter showed hardly any action, with both sides following the other's defense and going through different plays.

In the second quarter, the Juniors threatened the Senior's goal seriously. From their own 30 yard line they booted the pigskin. Mike Minato, the safety man for the Seniors fumbled and the Juniors recovered the ball over the Senior's 10 yard line. Two line plunges failed. The third time they ran around the right and picked up about nine yards. Then a penalty was called for fifteen yards. This brought the ball back to the Seniors' 35 yard line. On fourth down and barely 15 to go, the Juniors took to the air. The pass was for about five yards gain as the half ended.

In the third quarter the seniors took to the air and went marching down the field only to lose the ball on downs. Then the juniors kicked and the seniors again started their march. With about five minutes to go, Co-captain Reggie Shikami displayed an array of passes. He let one fly for about 55 yards with Shoji Maruyama on the receiving end. There with first down and goal to go the seniors again took to the air.

Thomas Higa, Coach

Shig Shiba, Coach

Kay Osumi, Boys' Athletic Manager, 1st semester

Ralph Lazo, Boys' Athletic Manager, 2nd semester

On the second trial, Shikami passed to Taddy Nakashima in the end zone. It was completed but Nakashima was over the side line and the play was called back.

Third down and fifteen to go. This time Shikami threw the pigskin to Mas Imamoto, who went into the atmosphere to snag the ball. After a short conference with the head linesman, it was agreed that the ball would have been caught outside the end zone if the goal post had not been there.

Fourth down, and the pass didn't connect. After a few climaxing plays the game ended a tie, 0-0.

The Sophomores had a number of inter-homeroom games in which clean sportsmanship was displayed by the members participating in the sport.

Basketball proved to be the most crowd-gathering sport of the winter season. Leagues ranged from inter-block to camp-wide competition, however, due to bad weather conditions the season was extended to summer.

army overtures...

sports

Activity in the weightlifting division was influenced by a group of boys known as the Venice Barbell Club. They held regular work outs, and gave several public exhibitions. They also participated in a correspondence meet with weightlifting clubs of other centers.

During the month of May, 1942, many tennis enthusiasts got together and formed the Manzanar Tennis Club. As the club grew, the membership reached a high of about one hundred and thirty members. It was through the tennis club members that the four courts were made.

The Tennis Club has been very active and to date has had two tournaments. Trophies were awarded to the champions and finalists.

gridders, hoopsters display talent . . .

story

The club is lead by the able President Jimmy Ito and Vice-President Tom Morishita. The Treasurer's slot is filled by Roy Takenaka and Suzuki is the Secretary.

Recently the Tennis Club became a member of the Community Activities Co-operative Association. The membership dues are thirty-five cents for a period of three montnhs.

Many beginners are getting valuable tips and lessons from Roy Takenaka, the "A" champion. He is the coach and teaching beginners is his official job.

In the future the club intends to hold more meetings and if possible make a few more courts because of the increase in membership.

Coach Thomas Higa, coach of Manzanar High, has done much to improve and develop the Physical Education program.

His high school years were spent in McKinley High School, Hawaii, where he earned his athletic letters. At Los Angeles City College he studied Physical Education, Accounting and Music.

Deserving equal laurels is Coach Shig Shiba. He comes from Terminal Island, where he attended Banning High School. He takes interest in all kinds of sports, but his favorite is weightlifting.

horsehiders have active season . . .

Girls' Sports

Although the Girls Physical Education Department started with a very limited amount of equipment, it made great progress under the supervision of Miss Elizabeth Moxley and Mrs. Yaye Nakamura. The girls learned to play various games to the best of their ability with good sportsmanship as their goal. In the summer of 1943, Miss Elaine Clary, a graduate of U.C.L.A., was added to the teaching staff.

With the three Physical Education teachers and the Student Body Girl's Athletic Manager, Chickie Hiraoka, the Girls' Athletic Association was organized. The purposes were to encourage high physical efficiency, to promote cooperation and good fellowship among girls, to develop the highest ideals of sportsmanship, to develop leadership, to build a class and school loyalty by fastening an interest in physical education, particularly in the athletic activities among girls. Other officers were: Kazuko Yoshimura, vice-president; Yuri Yamazaki, secretary; Alice Kakoi, historian; Yuki Shiba, athletic manager; Rosie Tamai, head yell leader with Tosh Morishita and Ruby Oshio assisting her. Second semester found the G.A.A. under the leadership of Kazuko Yoshimura. Other officers were: Chickie Hiraoka, vice-president; Yuri Yamazaki, secretary; Yuki Shiba, treasurer; Seiko Kato, sports manager; Kiyo Nishi, publicity. The G.A.A. sweaters are cardinal in color with gold emblems. The sweaters and emblems are earned in the following point system: For Seniors, 350 points-emblem; 500 points-sweater. For all other students, 500 points-emblem; 700 points-sweater.

When the weather did not permit the girls to play, they were given lectures on health. As the weather became more favorable, the baseball season was inaugurated.

Elizabeth Moxley, Head of Physical Education Department

Elaine Clarey, Girls' Physical Education

Chickie Hiraoka, Girls' Athletic Manager

Kazuko Yoshimura and Sieko Kato, Girls' Athletic Managers

The girls became very enthusiastic about the game. With limited equipment and without a baseball diamond girls enjoyed playing with a make believe diamond. As the baseball intramural games started, all-star teams from each gym class were chosen. The games were played after school. Girls on each team played hard and showed remarkable sportsmanship in the games. Period three was victorious. This all-star team was captained by Chickie Hiraoka and supported by outstanding players such as Mary Myose, Masako Yano, Alice Kakoi and Tomoyo Kuramoto.

Volleyball was the next game played by the girls. At this time the girls were required to wear shorts for gym. Looking very uniform, they learned how to place the ball and make cross court plays. Outstanding players were known by this time; all-star teams were picked by the girls of each period. Such names as the Bombers, Huskies, Wheaties, Sockerettes, Pushovers, and Netsters were chosen to lead them to victory. The G.A.A. officiated at the intramural games. with their hopes high, a winning streak and luck with them, the Wheaties came out undefeated. This team was captained by Yoshiko Kusunoki with outstanding players as Yuki Shiba, Yuki Hara, Tasma Uyeno, Alice Kakoi, Clara Fukuda, and Mitsuye Kishishita.

girls shine in casaba season . . .

As the windy month of March came, the girls started to play basketball. Techniques, cross court, and straight plays were taught. Intramural games were played in firebreak 8. Many spectators gathered to watch the girls during the league and intramural games. All games were played after school with the G.A. A. members as officials. When the teams were evenly matched and great competition was expected, Miss Clary officiated. As this copy goes to press, the intramural games have started and winners have yet to be chosen.

Leading the tournament is period five by Masumi Ono, second place is tied between periods two, four, six and seven. Third place is held by third period.

Speedball was the only game that really had to be taught to the girls. The girls learned by bitter experience. Receiving many kicks in the shins that were intended for the ball, it was surprising that the girls came through with only a few minor bruises. Knowledge of this game, similar to basketball, added to the enjoyment of the sports program. With the completion of the new gym, the girls sports program will be enlarged in the coming seasons.

girls enjoy volleyball, baseball...

In years to come, when the war is over, and peace has returned to the world, people may say to you "What was Manzanar?" Then I hope you may say that Manzanar was a war time city that sprang up from the sands of the desert of Inyo and returned to desert with the end of the war. It was the largest city between Los Angeles and Reno. It was a city serving a war time purpose where people lived in peace and good will, where there was a school system that taught young citizens the ideals of American citizenship, where schools were of as high a rank as other California schools, and where students dedicated their future lives to the American way of living. I hope you may say that Manzanar was an experience worth living, where the important realities of life were made clear and where there was time and opportunity to prepare for participation in the work of winning the peace based on tolerance, understanding and good will. The graduates of Manzanar have a great contribution to make in determining the kind of world that is to come after the war.

Ralph P. Merritt,
Project Director

D
E
M
O
C
R
A
C
Y

Town Hall serves as an evacuee community government office, as it is the meeting place and office for the 34 Block Managers and Block Assistants. The policies of the WRA and the Department of the Interior, as well as the regular routine matters of maintenance of the blocks, are discussed. The executive body of the assembly is composed of a co-ordinator, secretary, stenographer, senior clerk and two messengers.

Once a day a messenger is sent to each block office with the latest administrative information and instructions. The block manager in turn submits a daily report of the happenings of the day within his block. Every Friday morning at nine the Block Managers meet with Project Director Ralph P. Merritt. At these meetings the managers receive first-hand information from the various departments, and the latest developments from Washington. Afterward they return to their respective blocks and inform residents of the proceedings.

The assembly, under the capable guidance of Mr. Merritt, has been instrumental in creating a feeling of peace and goodwill, not only among the evacuees, but also with the surrounding communities.

democracy at work . . .

INDUSTRY

In a community, the size of Manzanar, it is only natural that a great number of the necessities of the residents should be project made. Coming from our own production line are a number of useful articles for the evacuees.

The work and hospital clothing issued by the project and the ladies' apparel, children's clothing, and men's wear sold by the Co-op are produced by the clothing factory. The Industrial Division also manufactures all project office furniture and special orders for the Education Department and the hospital. Most of the signs around the center have been painted by the men in the project sign shop. The Industrial Division has its food department in which sections are devoted to shoyu, bean sprouts, tofu, pickling, and miso manufacturing. These are items which are familiar to Japanese, but not to most Caucasians. A new unit in foods is dehydration processing which was started this year. The storage plant handles the surplus vegetables that are kept for winter use. Other important departments are the mattress factory, community alterations shop (which alters and remodels G.I. clothing to fit the evacuees) and the domestic sewing machine repair shop.

The Industrial Division's manufacturing superintendent is H. R. Haberle and Aiji Hashii is his assistant in charge of general supervision and project improvement and development. Sumajiro Harada is the head of field supervision of operation and the technical supervisor for all food manufacturing and vegetable processing is Isomatsu Miyake.

on the production line...

AGRICULTURE

Enlarging their agricultural program to increase food production this year, the farming department is trying to make this center as self-sustaining as possible. Now that the livestock project is under way, another step in self-sustenance has been accomplished.

This department is divided into four main divisions with the main office located at warehouse 24. There are six crews in the field unit, each of which has a foreman who is in turn under the supervision of General Foreman Katsugoro Kawase.

The Nursery unit has all responsibilities in regard to propagation and seedlings on the farm project and Joe Kishi is head man.

The livestock units which include beef, cattle, swine and chickens are all located South of the center. Chickens have been consumed twice by camp residents and choice cuts of pork have also been served.

An important contribution to the whole country is being developed here in Manzanar at the guayle laboratory. Shimpei Nishimura, director of this section and the men under him are to be congratulated on the fine work they are doing.

residents consume manzanar products . . .

R
E
L
I
G
I
O
N

Religion has played such a large part in our limited lives and church attendance has grown in such proportions that the present accommodations are not sufficient. Organizing soon after the Manzanar Center was erected, the Protestant Church is attended by 2,009 people weekly at seven different locations. The members of the Ministerial Association are Reverends Junro Amos Kashitani, Ainosueke Ishida, Yukichi Naito, Takeshi Nishikawa, Masahiro Omi, Seiye Sakai, K. Suzuki and Junichi Fujimori.

The Catholic Church held its first mass on March 29, 1942. The Young Peoples' Study Club, Senior and Junior Sodality and the Holy Name Society are all under the supervision of the church. Father Hugh Lavery is the Superior, Father Leo Steinback, Pastor, with Sisters Mary Bernadette and Mary Suzanna assisting.

Holding its first service three months after the first volunteers arrived, the Buddhist Church has expanded to such a degree that it had to be divided into two sects. The Shinshu or the First Buddhist is directed by Reverend Shijo Nagatomi and the Nichiren or the Second Buddhist is headed by Reverend Hiromu Oda. Hana Matsuri celebrating the birth of Buddha, Mother's Day, Father's Day, and Gotanya were a few of the special services extended to the residents. Bon Odoris were also sponsored by this church. The Church Council, YBA Cabinet, Fujin Kai and other miscellaneous meetings rounded out the calendar.

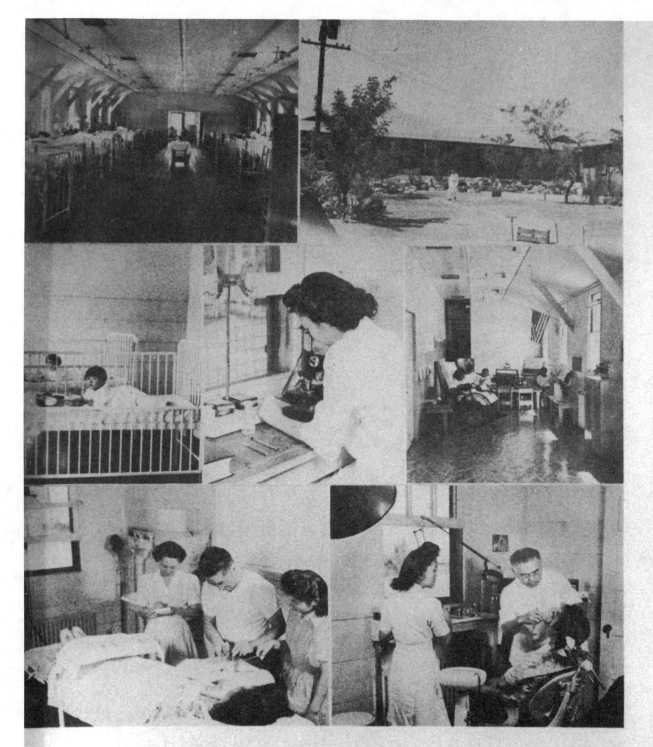

H
O
S
P
I
T
A
L

On March 21, 1942, Dr. James M. Goto, Miss Fumiko Gohata, R.N., and Mr. Frank Chuman, Medical Administrative Assistant, were asked by the United States Health Service to set up an emergency hospital unit until the 250-bed hospital was completed. This was to be headquarters for the health and welfare of the evacuees in the first assembly center under the Wartime Civilian Control Administration. In this bare room in Block 7 set up for the hospital was an operating table, instrument and medicine cabinets, a refrigerator, a place for one desk and two typewriters.

On July 22, 1942, the Ten-Bed hospital moved into the present beautiful 250-Bed hospital which includes the Administration Building, Doctors' and Nurses' Quarters, Seven Wards, Kitchen, Laundry Room, Boiler Room and Morgue. In the administration building are the offices of the Project Medical Officer Dr. Morse Little, Head Nurse Josephine Hawes, the Out-Patient Clinic, Eye, Ear, Nose and Throat Clinic, Pharmacy, X-Ray, Sterilizing Room, Minor Surgery, Surgery, Laboratory, Information and Ambulance Drivers' Room.

Throughout its development it may be clearly seen that the hospital has served as the fountain head for the health and welfare of the entire center and in doing so the growth of the hospital has reflected the growth of the community.

residents given medical care . . .

COMMUNITY

Recreation being one of the best morale builders, the Community Activities directed by Mr. Aksel Nielsen has developed a program to interest all age levels in camp. For the young people there are talent shows, dances, softball, basketball, football and tennis games, weight lifting contests, song fests, folk dances, parties, ping pong and movies. Mothers have the opportunity to learn and do embroidery, flower making, knitting, leathercraft, sewing, dramas and musicals, while fathers' pastimes are goh, shogi, drama, musicals, woodcarving and gardening.

The work of Community Activities is divided into five main departments. The heads of the five departments are: Arts and Crafts, Mr. M. Ichien; Sports, Mr. Shig Nakaji; Music, Mr. M. Shiozaki; Social, Entertainment, and Youth Activities, Mr. Shig Ishii; and Gardening, Mr. B. Kitazawa.

Although faced with inadequate funds and equipment the Community Activities division has organized various recreational cooperatives through which necessary funds are being raised to carry on the work. For public benefit, ground facilities located along Baird's creek are being used for picnics, golf and a general recreational area.

The community band is under the leadership of Mrs. Melba Nielson. Class instructions are in: harmony, voice, piano, string, woodwind, brass and percussion instruments.

In planning such an extensive recreational program Community Activities becomes an instrument for the development of a more wholesome center life for the young people and their parents.

C O N S U M E R S   E N T E R P R I S E S

Recognizing the need for distribution to the community of material goods at the lowest price possible for the customer, the Manzanar Consumer Enterprises was organized to accomplish this purpose.

The people of Manzanar, as members of this co-operative and as ultimate consumers, own, operate and conduct it for their collective benefit.

Co-op history began in Block 1, but today, two years later, it has developed into a very stable enterprise with aggregate annual sales in excess of three quarters of a million dollars. Its shops and services include: the Canteen, Dry Goods Store, Shoe Repair Shop, Laundry Depot, Watch Repair, Beauty Parlor, Barber Shop, Photo Studio, Sporting Goods, Flower Shop, Movie Department, Manzanar Free Press, Check Cashing Department and Sewing Department.

The Manzanar Cooperative is made up of 6377 members who elect representatives to a Congress of Delegates one for each 50 members in a block, who in turn elect a Board of Directors of fifteen to serve a term of six months for the general administration of the enterprises. The Board of Directors in turn appoint a Managerial Staff of four to conduct and manage its various shops and services. Chokichi Nakano is the President of the Board of Directors.

co-operative enterprise...

Today as the sun disappears behind the peak of Mount Williamson the typical block in Manzanar takes it easy. Now in the early summer, twilight heralds the approach of the evening's activity. The young people gather on the cool green lawns for a record session or saunter off to the firebreak to watch the baseball games. Their younger brothers and sisters run noisily between the barracks busy with cowboys and Indians. The older women gather to talk and knit . . . the men to smoke and talk. The day is over; the block relaxes. And yet several hours earlier this same setting was a scene of great activity.

To house and feed approximately 200 people there are in each of the 36 blocks, 15 tar papered barracks for living quarters, a laundry barrack, an ironing barrack, two latrines and most important of all, a mess hall. The block government consists of a block manager, assistant block manager and barrack representatives, all of whom are elected by the residents. All block activities, dances or other social functions sponsored by the younger generation, or goh, shogi, talent shows, song fests and English grammar classes which their elders attend are all indirectly run by the governing body which has as its meeting place, apartment 1-1.

Since the WRA has furnished grass seed, ambitious residents have planted gardens and lawns around their apartments. A number of residents have donated basketball courts for the young people in their blocks. As a precaution against fire, each

active season . . .

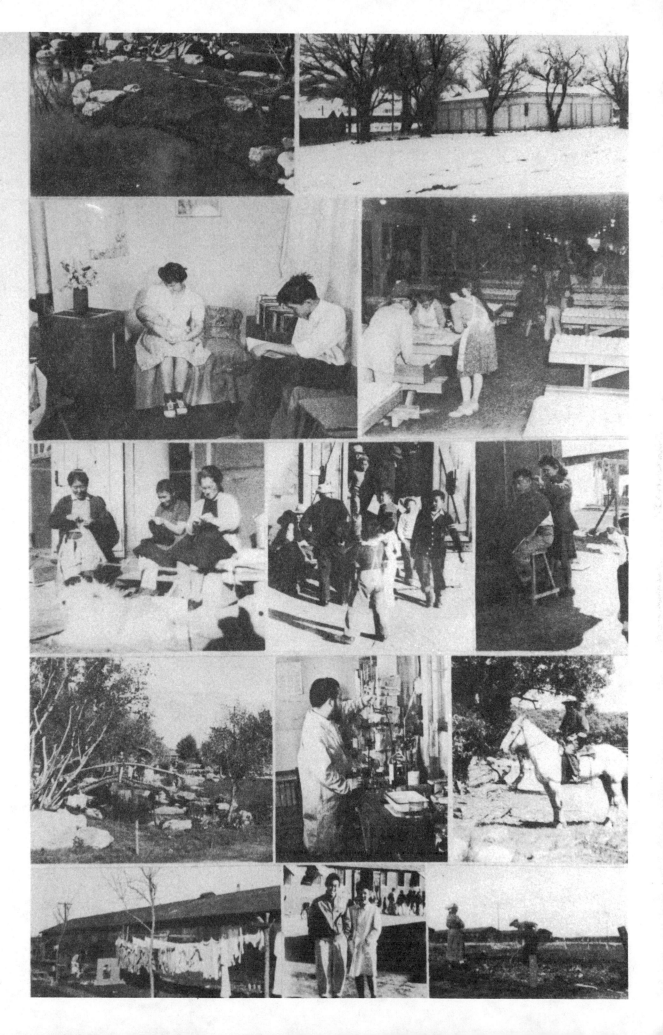

TAKING IT EASY

BLOCK BY BLOCK

R
E
A
D
I
N
G
,

R
I
T
I
N
G

AND, RITHMETIC

THESE FOND

MEMEORIES

DEAR READER:

AS YOU TURN TO THE LAST PAGE IN THIS BOOK, WE HOPE THAT YOU WILL DO SO WITH A SATISFIED
FEELING. FOR IT IS VERY IMPORTANT TO US THAT YOU WILL FIND IN THIS STORY AN ACCURATE
PICTURE OF THE SCHOOL AND COMMUNITY LIFE THAT YOU ARE ACTUALLY LIVING. WE HAVEN'T
INCLUDED ANYTHING JUST BECAUSE IT WAS BEAUTIFUL OR UNUSUAL. WE WERE NOT INTERESTED IN
PICTURING FOR YOU ISOLATED CASES THAT ARE FEW AND FAR BETWEEN. AS YOU LOOK AT THE
PICTURES IN THIS BOOK WE WANT YOU TO BE FAMILIAR WITH EVERY ONE OF THEM. FOR THIS IS
THE STORY OF THE TYPICAL 'TEEN AGED YOUNGSTER IN MANZANAR.

WE ARE INDEBTED TO A NUMBER OF PEOPLE WHO HAVE HELPED US TO MAKE THIS BOOK SUCCESSFUL.
WE ARE ESPECIALLY APPRECIATIVE OF THE ASSISTANCE GIVEN TO US BY OUR ADVISOR JANET
GOLDBERG. TO OUR PHOTOGRAPHER TOYO MIYATAKE AND HIS STAFF, HISAO KIMURA, TIMOTHY
SAITO, GEORGE SHIRA AND KATSUMI IGARASHI, WE CAN ONLY SAY THAT WITHOUT THEIR UNTIRING
EFFORTS THIS BOOK WOULD NOT HAVE BEEN POSSIBLE. WE APPRECIATE THE SUPPORT GIVEN TO
US BY OUR PRINCIPAL ROLLIN C. FOX AND ASSISTANT PROJECT DIRECTOR LUCY ADAMS. WITHOUT
THE GENEROUS FINANCIAL ASSISTANCE OF THE COMMUNITY FUND THIS BOOK WOULD NOT HAVE BEEN
ABLE TO TELL AS COMPLETE A STORY. THE SENIOR PLAY PICTURES OF ANSEL ADAMS, THE CAMP
SHOTS OF FREDERICK R. THORNE, AND THOSE OF THE REPORTS OFFICE CONTRIBUTE MUCH TO OUR
UNDERTAKING.

TO THE RESIDENTS OF THE CENTER: TO EACH AND EVERY ONE OF YOU WE ARE TRULY GRATEFUL AND
WE HOPE THAT YOU WILL ENJOY READING THIS ANNUAL AS MUCH AS WE HAVE ENJOYED EDITING IT.

Masako Kimura   *Nori Kuroyama*   *Reggie Shikami*

Meito Hori   *Taira Fukushima*   *Mary Yamashita*

Arnold Maeda   *Aiji Nagano*   *Yoshiko Kusunoki*

Hideko Matsuno   *Yoshindo Shibuya*   *Bruce Kaji*

An unforgettable
sight this Tower
an unforgettable place
— this Manzanar.
Here's to a happy future.
M.H. Wolff

Appendix B

PUBLIC LAW 100-383—AUG. 10, 1988   102 STAT. 903

Public Law 100-383
100th Congress

An Act

Aug. 10, 1988
_____
[H.R. 442]

Human rights.

To implement recommendations of the Commission on Wartime Relocation and Internment of Civilians.

Be it enacted by the Senate and House of Representatives of the United States of America in Congress assembled,

50 USC app.
1989.

SECTION 1. PURPOSES.

The purposes of this Act are to—

(1) acknowledge the fundamental injustice of the evacuation, relocation, and internment of United States citizens and permanent resident aliens of Japanese ancestry during World War II;

(2) apologize on behalf of the people of the United States for the evacuation, relocation, and internment of such citizens and permanent resident aliens;

Public
information.

(3) provide for a public education fund to finance efforts to inform the public about the internment of such individuals so as to prevent the recurrence of any similar event;

(4) make restitution to those individuals of Japanese ancestry who were interned;

(5) make restitution to Aleut residents of the Pribilof Islands and the Aleutian Islands west of Unimak Island, in settlement of United States obligations in equity and at law, for—

(A) injustices suffered and unreasonable hardships endured while those Aleut residents were under United States control during World War II;

Real property.

(B) personal property taken or destroyed by United States forces during World War II;

(C) community property, including community church property, taken or destroyed by United States forces during World War II; and

(D) traditional village lands on Attu Island not rehabilitated after World War II for Aleut occupation or other productive use;

(6) discourage the occurrence of similar injustices and violations of civil liberties in the future; and

(7) make more credible and sincere any declaration of concern by the United States over violations of human rights committed by other nations.

50 USC app.
1989a.

SEC. 2. STATEMENT OF THE CONGRESS.

(a) WITH REGARD TO INDIVIDUALS OF JAPANESE ANCESTRY.—The Congress recognizes that, as described by the Commission on Wartime Relocation and Internment of Civilians, a grave injustice was done to both citizens and permanent resident aliens of Japanese ancestry by the evacuation, relocation, and internment of civilians during World War II. As the Commission documents, these actions were carried out without adequate security reasons and without any acts of espionage and sabotage documented by the Commission, and were motivated largely by racial prejudice, wartime hysteria, and a failure of political leadership. The excluded individuals of Japanese ancestry suffered enormous damages, both material and intangible, and there were incalculable losses in education and job training, all of which resulted in significant human suffering for which appropriate compensation has not been made. For these fundamental violations of the basic civil liberties and constitutional rights of these individuals of Japanese ancestry, the Congress apologizes on behalf of the Nation.

(b) WITH RESPECT TO THE ALEUTS.—The Congress recognizes that, as described by the Commission on Wartime Relocation and Internment of Civilians, the Aleut civilian residents of the Pribilof Islands and the Aleutian Islands west of Unimak Island were relocated during World War II to temporary camps in isolated regions of southeast

Alaska where they remained, under United States control and in the care of the United States, until long after any potential danger to their home villages had passed. The United States failed to provide reasonable care for the Aleuts, and this resulted in widespread illness, disease, and death among the residents of the camps; and the United States further failed to protect Aleut personal and community property while such property was in its possession or under its control. The United States has not compensated the Aleuts adequately for the conversion or destruction of personal property, and the conversion or destruction of community property caused by the United States military occupation of Aleut villages during World War II. There is no remedy for injustices suffered by the Aleuts during World War II except an Act of Congress providing appropriate compensation for those losses which are attributable to the conduct of United States forces and other officials and employees of the United States.

TITLE I—UNITED STATES CITIZENS OF JAPANESE ANCESTRY AND RESIDENT JAPANESE ALIENS

Civil Liberties Act of 1988.

50 USC app. 1989b.

SEC. 101. SHORT TITLE.

This title may be cited as the "Civil Liberties Act of 1988".

50 USC app. 1989b-1.

SEC. 102. REMEDIES WITH RESPECT TO CRIMINAL CONVICTIONS.

(a) REVIEW OF CONVICTIONS.—The Attorney General is requested to review any case in which an individual living on the date of the enactment of this Act was, while a United States citizen or permanent resident alien of Japanese ancestry, convicted of a violation of—

(1) Executive Order Numbered 9066, dated February 19, 1942;

(2) the Act entitled 'An Act to provide a penalty for violation of restrictions or orders with respect to persons entering, remaining in, leaving, or committing any act in military areas or zones", approved March 21, 1942 (56 Stat. 173); or

(3) any other Executive order, Presidential proclamation, law of the United States, directive of the Armed Forces of the United States, or other action taken by or on behalf of the United States or its agents, representatives, officers, or employees, respecting the evacuation, relocation, or internment of individuals solely on the basis of Japanese ancestry; on account of the refusal by such individual, during the evacuation, relocation, and internment period, to accept treatment which discriminated against the individual on the basis of the individual's Japanese ancestry.

(b) RECOMMENDATIONS FOR PARDONS.—Based upon any review under subsection (a), the Attorney General is requested to recommend to the President for pardon consideration those convictions which the Attorney General considers appropriate.

(c) ACTION BY THE PRESIDENT.—In consideration of the statement of the Congress set forth in section 2(a), the President is requested to offer pardons to any individuals recommended by the Attorney General under subsection (b).

50 USC app. 1989b-2.

SEC. 103. CONSIDERATION OF COMMISSION FINDINGS BY DEPARTMENTS AND AGENCIES.

(a) REVIEW OF APPLICATIONS BY ELIGIBLE INDIVIDUALS.—Each department and agency of the United States Government shall review with liberality, giving full consideration to the findings of the Commission and the statement of Congress set forth in section 2(a), any application by an eligible individual for the restitution of any position, status, or entitlement lost in whole or in part because of any discriminatory act of the United States Government against such individual which was based upon the individual's Japanese ancestry and which occurred during the evacuation, relocation, and internment period.

(b) NO NEW AUTHORITY CREATED.—Subsection (a) does not create any authority to grant restitution described in that subsection, or establish any eligibility to apply for such restitution.

50 USC app. 1989b-3.

SEC. 104. TRUST FUND.

(a) ESTABLISHMENT.—There is established in the Treasury of the United States the Civil Liberties Public Education Fund, which shall be administered by the Secretary of the Treasury.

(b) INVESTMENT OF AMOUNTS IN THE FUND.—Amounts in the Fund shall be invested on accordance with section 9702 of title 31, United States Code.

(c) USES OF THE FUND.—Amounts in the Fund shall be available only for disbursement by the Attorney General under section 105 and by the Board under section 106.

(d) TERMINATION.—The Fund shall terminate not later than the earlier of the date on which an amount has been expended from the Fund which is equal to the amount authorized to be appropriated to the Fund by subsection

(e), and any income earned on such amount, or 10 years after the date of the enactment of this Act. If all of the amounts in the Fund have not been expended by the end of that 10-year period, investments of amounts in the Fund shall be liquidated and receipts thereof deposited in the Fund and all funds remaining in the Fund shall be deposited in the miscellaneous receipts account in the Treasury.

(f)AUTHORIZATION OF APPROPRIATIONS.—There are authorized to be appropriated to the Fund $1,250,000,000, of which not more than $500,000,000 may be appropriated for any fiscal year. Any amounts appropriated pursuant to this section are authorized to remain available until expended.

50 USC app.
1989b-4.

SEC. 105. RESTITUTION.

(a) LOCATION AND PAYMENTS OF ELIGIBLE INDIVIDUALS.—

(1) IN GENERAL.—Subject to paragraph (6), the Attorney General shall, subject to the availability of funds appropriated to the Fund for such purpose, pay out of the Fund to each eligible individual the sum of $20,000, unless such individual refuses, in the manner described in paragraph (4), to accept the payment.

(2) LOCATION OF ELIGIBLE INDIVIDUALS.—The Attorney General shall identify and locate, without requiring any application for payment and using records already in the possession of the United States Government, each eligible individual. The Attorney General should use funds and resources available to the Attorney General, including those described in subsection (c), to attempt to complete such identification and location within 12 months after the date of the enactment of this Act. Any eligible individual may notify the Attorney General that such individual is an eligible individual, and may provide documentation therefor. The Attorney General shall designate an officer or employee to whom such notification and documentation may be sent, shall maintain a list of all individuals who submit such notification and documentation, and shall, subject to the availability of funds appropriated for such purpose, encourage, through a public awareness campaign, each eligible individual to submit his or her current address to such officer or employee. To the extent that resources referred to in the second sentence of this paragraph are not sufficient to complete the identification and location of all eligible individuals, there are authorized to be appropriated such sums as may be necessary for such purpose. In any case, the identification and location of all eligible individuals shall be completed within 12 months after the appropriation of funds under the preceding sentence. Failure to be identified and located by the end of the 12-month period specified in the preceding sentence shall not preclude an eligible individual from receiving payment under this section.

(3) NOTICE FROM THE ATTORNEY GENERAL.—The Attorney General shall, when funds are appropriated to the Fund for payments to an eligible individual under this section, notify that eligible individual in writing of his or her eligibility for payment under this section. Such notice shall inform the eligible individual that—

(A) acceptance of payment under this section shall be in full satisfaction of all claims against the United States arising out of acts described in section 108(2)(B), and

(B) each eligible individual who does not refuse, in the manner described in paragraph (4), to accept payment under this section within 18 months after receiving such written notice shall be deemed to have accepted payment for purposes of paragraph (5).

(4) EFFECT OF REFUSAL TO ACCEPT PAYMENT.—If an eligible individual refuses, in a written document filed with the Attorney General, to accept any payment under this section, the amount of such payment shall remain in the Fund and no payment may be made under this section to such individual at any time after such refusal.

(5) PAYMENT IN FULL SETTLEMENT OF CLAIMS AGAINST THE UNITED STATES.—The acceptance of payment by an eligible individual under this section shall be in full satisfaction of all claims against the United States arising out of acts described in section 108(2)(B). This paragraph shall apply to any eligible individual who does not refuse, in the manner described in paragraph (4), to accept payment under this section within 18 months after receiving the notification from the Attorney General referred to in paragraph (3).

(6) EXCLUSION OF CERTAIN INDIVIDUALS.—No payment may be made under this section to any individual who, after September 1, 1987, accepts payment pursuant to an award of a final judgment or a settlement on a claim against the United States for acts described in section 108(2)(B), or to any surviving spouse, child, or parent of such individual to whom paragraph (6) applies.

(7) PAYMENTS IN THE CASE OF DECEASED PERSONS.—(A) In the case of an eligible individual who is deceased at the time of payment under this section, such payment shall be made only as follows:

(i) If the eligible individual is survived by a spouse who is living at the time of payment, such payment shall be made to such surviving spouse.

(ii) If there is no surviving spouse described in clause (i), such payment shall be made in equal shares to all children of the eligible individual who are living at the time of payment.

(iii) If there is no surviving spouse described in clause (i) and if there are no children described in clause (ii), such payment shall be made in equal shares to the parents of the eligible individual who are living at the time of payment. If there is no surviving spouse, children, or parents described in clauses (i), (ii), and (iii), the amount of such payment shall remain in the Fund, and may be used only for the purposes set forth in section 106(b).

(B) After the death of an eligible individual, this subsection and subsections (c) and (f) shall apply to the individual or individuals specified in subparagraph (A) to whom payment under this section will be made, to the same extent as such subsections apply to the eligible individual.

(C) For purposes of this paragraph—

(i) the "spouse" of an eligible individual means a wife or husband of an eligible individual who was married to that eligible individual for at least 1 year immediately before the death of the eligible individual;

(ii) a "child" of an eligible individual includes a recognized natural child, a stepchild who lived with the eligible individual in a regular parent-child relationship, and an adopted child; and

(iii) a "parent" of an eligible individual includes fathers and mothers through adoption.

(b) ORDER OF PAYMENTS.—The Attorney General shall endeavor to make payments under this section to eligible individuals in the order of date of birth (with the oldest individual on the date of the enactment of this Act (or, if applicable, that individual's survivors under paragraph (6)) receiving full payment first), until all eligible individuals have received payment in full.

(c) RESOURCES FOR LOCATING ELIGIBLE INDIVIDUALS.—In attempting to locate any eligible individual, the Attorney General may use any facility or resource of any public or nonprofit organization or any other record, document, or information that may be made available to the Attorney General.

Records.
Public
information.

Appropriation
authorization.

Claims.

Claims.

Records.

185

(d) ADMINISTRATIVE COSTS NOT PAID FROM THE FUND.—No costs incurred by the Attorney General in carrying out this section shall be paid from the Fund or set off against, or otherwise deducted from, any payment under this section to any eligible individual.

(e) TERMINATION OF DUTIES OF ATTORNEY GENERAL.—The duties of the Attorney General under this section shall cease when the Fund terminates.

(f) CLARIFICATION OF TREATMENT OF PAYMENTS UNDER OTHER LAWS.—Amounts paid to an eligible individual under this section—

(1) shall be treated for purposes of the internal revenue laws of the United States as damages for human suffering; and

(2) shall not be included as income or resources for purposes of determining eligibility to receive benefits described in section 3803(c)(2)(C) of title 31, United States Code, or the amount of such benefits.

50 USC app. 1989b-5.

Research and development. Education. Public information.

SEC. 106. BOARD OF DIRECTORS OF THE FUND.

(a) ESTABLISHMENT.—There is established the Civil Liberties Public Education Fund Board of Directors, which shall be responsible for making disbursements from the Fund in the manner provided in this section.

(b) USES OF FUND.—The Board may make disbursements from the Fund only—

(1) to sponsor research and public educational activities, and to publish and distribute the hearings, findings, and recommendations of the Commission, so that the events surrounding the evacuation, relocation, and internment of United States citizens and permanent resident aliens of Japanese ancestry will be remembered, and so that the causes and circumstances of this and similar events may be illuminated and understood; and

(2) for reasonable administrative expenses of the Board, including expenses incurred under subsections (c)(3), (d), and (e).

(c) MEMBERSHIP.—

(1) APPOINTMENT.—The Board shall be composed of 9 members appointed by the President, by and with the advice and consent of the Senate, from individuals who are not officers or employees of the United States Government.

(2) TERMS.—(A) Except as provided in subparagraphs (B) and (C), members shall be appointed for terms of 3 years.

(B) Of the members first appointed—

(i) 5 shall be appointed for terms of 3 years, and

(ii) 4 shall be appointed for terms of 2 years,

as designated by the President at the time of appointment.

(C) Any member appointed to fill a vacancy occurring before the expiration of the term for which such member's predecessor was appointed shall be appointed only for the remainder of such term. A member may serve after the expiration of such member's term until such member's successor has taken office. No individual may be appointed as a member for more than 2 consecutive terms.

(3) COMPENSATION.—Members of the Board shall serve without pay, except that members of the Board shall be entitled to reimbursement for travel, subsistence, and other necessary expenses incurred by them in carrying out the functions of the Board, in the same manner as persons employed intermittently in the United States Government are allowed expenses under section 5703 of title 5, United States Code.

(4) QUORUM.—5 members of the Board shall constitute a quorum but a lesser number may hold hearings.

(5) CHAIR.—The Chair of the Board shall be elected by the members of the Board.

(d) DIRECTOR AND STAFF.—

(1) DIRECTOR.—The Board shall have a Director who shall be appointed by the Board.

(2) ADDITIONAL STAFF.—The Board may appoint and fix the pay of such additional staff as it may require.

(3) APPLICABILITY OF CIVIL SERVICE LAWS.—The Director and the additional staff of the Board may be appointed without regard to section 531(b) of title 5, United States Code, and without regard to the provisions of such title governing appointments in the competitive service, and may be paid without regard to the provisions of chapter 51 and subchapter III of chapter 53 of such title relating to classification and General Schedule pay rates, except that the compensation of any employee of the Board may not exceed a rate equivalent to the minimum rate of basic pay payable for GS-18 of the General Schedule under section 5332(a) of such title.

(e) ADMINISTRATIVE SUPPORT SERVICES.—The Administrator of General Services shall provide to the Board on a reimbursable basis such administrative support services as the Board may request.

(f) GIFTS AND DONATIONS.—The Board may accept, use, and dispose of gifts or donations of services or property for purposes authorized under subsection (b).

(g) ANNUAL REPORTS.—Not later than 12 months after the first meeting of the Board and every 12 months thereafter, the Board shall transmit to the President and to each House of Congress a report describing the activities of the Board.

(h) TERMINATION.—90 days after the termination of the Fund, the Board shall terminate and all obligations of the Board under this section shall cease.

50 USC app. 1989b-6.

Public information.

SEC. 107. DOCUMENTS RELATING TO THE INTERNMENT.

(a) PRESERVATION OF DOCUMENTS IN NATIONAL ARCHIVES.—All documents, personal testimony, and other records created or received by the Commission during its inquiry shall be kept and maintained by the Archivist of the United States who shall preserve such documents, testimony, and records in the National Archives of the United States. The Archivist shall make such documents, testimony, and records available to the public for research purposes.

(b) PUBLIC AVAILABILITY OF CERTAIN RECORDS OF THE HOUSE OF REPRESENTATIVES.—(1) The Clerk of the House of Representatives is authorized to permit the Archivist of the United States to make available for use record the House not classified for national security purposes, which have been in existence for not less than thirty years,, relating to the evacuation, relocation, and internment of individuals during the evacuation, relocation, and internment period.

(2) This subsection is enacted as an exercise of the rulemaking power of the House of Representatives, but is applicable only with respect to the availability of records to which it applies, and supersedes other rules only to the extent that the time limitation established by this section with respect to such records is specifically inconsistent with such rules, and is enacted with full recognition of the constitutional right of the House to change its rules at any time, in the same manner and to the same extent as in the case of any other rule of the House.

SEC. 108. DEFINITIONS.

For the purposes of this title—

(1) the term "evacuation, relocation, and internment period" means that period beginning on December 7, 1941, and ending on June 30, 1946;

(2) the term "eligible individual" means any individual of Japanese ancestry who is living on the date of the enactment of this Act and who, during the evacuation, relocation, and internment period—

(A) was a United States citizen or a permanent resident alien; and

(B)(i) was confined, held in custody, relocated, or otherwise deprived of liberty or property as a result of—

(I) Executive Order Numbered 9066, dated February 19, 1942;

(II) the Act entitled "An Act to provide a penalty for violation of restrictions or orders with respect to persons entering, remaining in, leaving, or committing any act in military areas or "zones", approved March 21, 1942 (56 Stat. 173); or

(III) any other Executive order, Presidential proclamation, law of the United States, directive of the Armed Forces of the United States, or other action taken by or on behalf of the United States or its agents, representatives, officers, or employees, respecting the evacuation, relocation, or internment of individuals solely on the basis of Japanese ancestry; or

(ii) was enrolled on the records of the United States Government during the period beginning on December 7, 1941, and ending on June 30, 1946, as being in a prohibited military zone;

except that the term "eligible individual" does not include any individual who, during the period beginning on December 7, 1941, and ending on September 2, 1945, relocated to a country while the United States was at war with that country;

(3) the term "permanent resident alien" means an alien lawfully admitted into the United States for permanent residence;

(4) the term "Fund" means the Civil Liberties Public Education Fund established in section 104;

(5) the term "Board" means the Civil Liberties Public Education Fund Board of Directors established in section 106; and

(6) the term "Commission" means the Commission on Wartime Relocation and Internment of Civilians, established by the Commission on Wartime Relocation and Internment of Civilians Act (Public Law 96-317; 50 U.S.C. App. 1981 note).

SEC. 109. COMPLIANCE WITH BUDGET ACT.

No authority under this title to enter into contracts or to make payments shall be effective in any fiscal year except to such extent and in such amounts as are provided in advance in appropriations Acts. In any fiscal year, total benefits conferred by this title shall be limited to an amount not in excess of the appropriations for such fiscal year. Any provision of this title which, directly or indirectly, authorizes the enactment of new budget authority shall be effective only for fiscal year 1989 and thereafter.

TITLE II—ALEUTIAN AND PRIBILOF ISLANDS RESTITUTION

SEC. 201. SHORT TITLE.

This title may be cited as the "Aleutian and Pribilof Islands Restitution Act".

SEC. 202. DEFINITIONS.

As used in this title—

(1) the term "Administrator" means the person appointed by the Secretary under section 204,

(2) the term "affected Aleut villages" means the surviving Aleut villages of Akutan, Atka, Nikolski, Saint George, Saint Paul, and Unalaska, and the Aleut village of Attu, Alaska;

(3) the term "Association" means the Aleutian/Pribilof Islands Association, Inc., a nonprofit regional corporation established for the benefit of the Aleut people and organized under the laws of the State of Alaska;

(4) the term "Corporation" means the Aleut Corporation, a for-profit regional corporation for the Aleut region organized under the laws of the State of Alaska and established under section 7 of the Alaska Native Claims Settlement Act (Public Law 92-203; 43 U.S.C. 1606);

(5) the term "eligible Aleut" means any Aleut living on the date of the enactment of this Act—

(A) who, as a civilian, was relocated by authority of the United States from his or her home village on the Pribilof Islands or the Aleutian Islands west of Unimak Island to an internment camp, or other temporary facility or location, during World War II; or

(B) who was born while his or her natural mother was subject to such relocation;

(6) the term "Secretary" means the Secretary of the Interior;

(7) the term "Fund" means the Aleutian and Pribilof Islands Restitution Fund established in section 203; and

(8) the term "World War II" means the period beginning on December 7, 1941, and ending on September 2, 1945.

50 USC app.
1989c-2.

SEC. 203. ALEUTIAN AND PRIBILOF ISLANDS RESTITUTION FUND.

(a) ESTABLISHMENT.—There is established in the Treasury of the United States the Aleutian and Pribilof Islands Restitution Fund, which shall be administered by the Secretary. The Fund shall consist of amounts appropriated to it pursuant to this title.

(b) REPORT.—The Secretary shall report to the Congress not later than 60 days after the end of each fiscal year, on the financial condition of the Fund, and the results of operations of the Fund, during the preceding fiscal year and on the expected financial condition and operations of the Fund during the current fiscal year.

(c) INVESTMENT.—Amounts in the Fund shall be invested in accordance with section 9702 of title 31, United States Code.

Securities.

(d) TERMINATION.—The Secretary shall terminate the Fund 3 years after the date of the enactment of this Act, or 1 year following disbursement of all payments from the Fund, as authorized by this title, whichever occurs later. On the date the Fund is terminated, all investments of amounts in the Fund shall be liquidated by the Secretary and receipts thereof deposited in the Fund and all funds remaining in the Fund shall be deposited in the miscellaneous receipts account in the Treasury.

50 USC app.
1989c-3.
Contracts.

SEC. 204. APPOINTMENT OF ADMINISTRATOR.

As soon as practicable after the date of the enactment of this Act, the Secretary shall offer to undertake negotiations with the Association, leading to the execution of an agreement with the Association to serve as Administrator under this title. The Secretary may appoint the Association as Administrator if such agreement is reached within 90 days after the date of the enactment of this title. If no such agreement is reached within such period, the Secretary shall appoint another person as Administrator under this title, after consultation with leaders of affected Aleut villages and the Corporation.

50 USC app.
1989c-4.

SEC. 205. COMPENSATION FOR COMMUNITY LOSSES.

(a) IN GENERAL.—Subject to the availability of funds appropriated to the Fund, the Secretary shall make payments from the Fund, in accordance with this section, as restitution for certain Aleut losses sustained in World War II.

(b) TRUST.—

(1) ESTABLISHMENT.—The Secretary shall, subject to the availability of funds appropriated for this purpose, establish a trust for the purposes set forth in this section. Such trust shall be established pursuant to the laws of the State of Alaska, and shall be maintained and operated by not more than seven trustees, as designated by the Secretary. Each affected Aleut village may submit to the Administrator a list of three prospective trustees. The Secretary, after consultation with the Administrator, affected Aleut villages, and the Corporation, shall designate not more than seven trustees from such lists as submitted.

(2) ADMINISTRATION OF TRUST.—The trust established under this subsection shall be administered in a manner that is consistent with the laws of the State of Alaska, and as prescribed by the Secretary, after consultation with representatives of eligible Aleuts, the residents of affected Aleut villages, and the Administrator.

(c) ACCOUNTS FOR THE BENEFIT OF ALEUTS.—

(1) IN GENERAL.—The Secretary shall deposit in the trust such sums as may be appropriated for the purposes set forth in this subsection. The trustees shall maintain and operate 8 independent and separate accounts in the trust for purposes of this subsection, as follows:

(A) One account for the independent benefit of the wartime Aleut residents of Attu and their descendants.

(B) Six accounts for the benefit of the 6 surviving affected Aleut villages, one each for the independent benefit of Akutan, Atka, Nikolski, Saint George, Saint Paul, and Unalaska, respectively.

(C) One account for the independent benefit of those Aleuts who, as determined by the Secretary, upon the advice of trustees, are deserving but will not benefit directly from the accounts established under subparagraphs (A) and (B).

The trustees shall credit to the account described in subparagraph (C) an amount equal to 5 percent of the principal amount deposited by the Secretary in the trust under this subsection. Of the remaining principal amount, an amount shall be credited to each account described in subparagraphs (A) and (B) which bears the same proportion to such remaining principal amount as the Aleut civilian population, as of June 1, 1942, of the village with respect to which such account is established bears to the total civilian Aleut population on such date of all affected Aleut villages.

(2) USES OF ACCOUNTS.—The trustees may use the principal, accrued interest, and other earnings of the accounts maintained under paragraph (1) for—

Aged persons.
Handicapped persons.
Education.
Historic preservation.
Community development.

(A) the benefit of elderly, disabled, or seriously ill persons on the basis of special need;

(B) the benefit of students in need of scholarship assistance;

(C) the preservation of Aleut cultural heritage and historical records;

(D) the improvements of community centers in affected Aleut villages; and

(E) other purposes to improve the condition of Aleut life, as determined by the trustees.

(3) AUTHORIZATION OF APPROPRIATIONS.—There are authorized to be appropriated $5,000,000 to the Fund to carry out this subsection.

(d) COMPENSATION FOR DAMAGED OR DESTROYED CHURCH PROPERTY.—

Records.

(1) INVENTORY AND ASSESSMENT OF PROPERTY.—The Administrator shall make an inventory and assessment of real and personal church property of affected Aleut villages which was damaged or destroyed during World War II. In making such inventory and assessment, the Administrator shall consult with the trustees of the trust established under subsection (b), residents of affected Aleut villages, affected church members and leaders, and the clergy of the churches involved. Within 1 year after the date of the enactment of this Act, the Administrator shall submit such inventory and assessment, together with an estimate of the present replacement value of lost or destroyed furnishings and artifacts, to the Secretary.

(2) REVIEW BY THE SECRETARY; DEPOSIT IN THE TRUST.—The Secretary shall review the inventory and assessment provided under paragraph (1), and shall deposit in the trust established under subsection (b) an amount reasonably calculated by the Secretary to compensate affected Aleut villages for church property lost, damaged, or destroyed during World War II.

(3) DISTRIBUTION OF COMPENSATION.—The trustees shall distribute the amount deposited in the trust under paragraph (2) for the benefit of the churches referred to in this subsection.

(4) AUTHORIZATION OF APPROPRIATIONS.—There are authorized to be appropriated to the Fund $1,400,000 to carry out this subsection.

(c) ADMINISTRATIVE AND LEGAL EXPENSES.—

(1) REIMBURSEMENT FOR EXPENSES.—The Secretary shall reimburse the Administrator, not less often than annually, for reasonable and necessary administrative and legal expenses in carrying out the Administrator's responsibilities under this title.

(2) AUTHORIZATION OF APPROPRIATIONS.—There are authorized to be appropriated to the Fund such sums as are necessary to carry out this subsection.

50 USC app.
1989c-5.

SEC. 206. INDIVIDUAL COMPENSATION OF ELIGIBLE ALEUTS.

(a) PAYMENTS TO ELIGIBLE ALEUTS.—In addition to payments made under section 205, the Secretary shall, in accordance with this section, make per capita payments out of the Fund to eligible Aleuts. The Secretary shall, in accordance with this section, make per capita payments out of the Fund to eligible Aleuts. The Secretary shall pay, subject to the availability of funds appropriated to the Fund for such payments, to each eligible Aleut the sum of $12,000.

(b) ASSISTANCE OF ATTORNEY GENERAL.—The Secretary may request the Attorney General to provide reasonable assistance in locating eligible Aleuts residing outside the affected Aleut villages, and upon such request, the Attorney General shall provide such assistance. In so doing, the Attorney General may use available facilities and resources of the International Committee of the Red Cross and other organizations.

(c) ASSISTANCE OF ADMINISTRATOR.—The Secretary may request the assistance of the Administrator in identifying and locating eligible Aleuts for purposes of this section.

(d) CLARIFICATION OF TREATMENT OF PAYMENTS UNDER OTHER LAWS.—Amounts paid to an eligible Aleut under this section—

(1) shall be treated for purposes of the internal revenue laws of the United States as damages for human suffering, and

(2) shall not be included as income or resources for purposes of determining eligibility to receive benefits described in section 3803(c)(2)(C) of title 31, United States Code, or the amount of such benefits.

(e) PAYMENT IN FULL SETTLEMENT OF CLAIMS AGAINST THE UNITED STATES.—The payment to an eligible Aleut under this section shall be in full satisfaction of all claims against the United States arising out of the relocation described in section 202(5).

(f) AUTHORIZATION OF APPROPRIATIONS.—There are authorized to be appropriated to the Fund such sums as are necessary to carry out this section.

Public lands.
National Wildlife Refuge System.
Conservation.
50 USC app.
1989c-6.

SEC. 207. ATTU ISLAND RESTITUTION PROGRAM.

(a) PURPOSE OF SECTION.—In accordance with section (3)(c) of the Wilderness Act (78 Stat. 892; 16 U.S.C. 1132(c)), the public lands on Attu Island, Alaska, within the National Wildlife Refuge System have been designated as wids Conservation Act (94 Stat. 2417; 16 U.S.C. 1132 note). In order to make restitution for the loss of traditional Aleut lands and village properties on Attu Island, while preserving the present designation of Attu Island lands as part of the National Wilderness Preservation System, compensation to the Aleut people, in lieu of the conveyance of Attu Island, shall be provided in accordance with this section.

(b) ACREAGE DETERMINATION.—No later than 90 days after the date of the enactment of this Act, the Secretary shall, in accordance with this subsection, determine the total acreage of land on Attu Island, Alaska, that, at the beginning of World War II, was subject to traditional use by the Aleut villagers of that island for subsistence and other purposes. In making such acreage determination, the Secretary shall establish a base acreage of not less than 35,000 acres within that part of eastern Attu Island traditionally used by the Aleut people, and shall, from the best available information, including information that may be submitted by representatives of the Aleut people, identify any such additional acreage on Attu Island that was subject to such use. The combination of such base acreage and such additional acreage shall constitute the acreage determination upon which payment to the Corporation under this section is based. The secretary shall promptly notify the Corporation of the results of the acreage determination made under this subsection.

(c) VALUATION.—

(1) DETERMINATION OF VALUE.—Not later than 120 days after the date of the enactment of this Act, the Secretary shall determine the value of the Attu Island acreage determined under subsection (b), except that—

(A) such acreage may not be valued at less than $350 per acre nor more than $500 per acre; and

(B) the total valuation of all such acreage may not exceed $15,000,000.

(2) FACTORS IN MAKING DETERMINATION.—In determining the value of the acreage under paragraph (1), the Secretary shall take into consideration such factors as the Secretary considers appropriate, including—

(A) fair market value;

(B) environmental and public interest value; and

(C) established precedents for valuation of comparable wilderness lands in the State of Alaska.

(3) NOTIFICATION OF DETERMINATION; APPEAL.—The Secretary shall promptly notify the Corporation of the determination of value made under this subsection, and such determination shall constitute the final determination of value unless the Corporation, within 30 days after the determination is made, appeals the determination to the Secretary. If such appeal is made, the Secretary shall, within 30 days after the appeal is made, review the determination in light of the appeal, and issue a final determination of the value of that acreage determined to be subject to traditional use under subsection (b).

(d) IN LIEU COMPENSATION PAYMENT.—

(1) PAYMENT.—The Secretary shall pay, subject to the availability of funds appropriated for such purpose, to the Corporation, as compensation for the Aleuts' loss of lands on Attu Island, the full amount of the value of the acreage determined under subsection (c), less the value (as determined under subsection (c)) of any land conveyed under subsection (e).

(2) PAYMENT IN FULL SETTLEMENT OF CLAIMS AGAINST THE UNITED STATES.—The payment made under paragraph (1) shall be in full satisfaction of any claim against the United States for the loss of traditional Aleut lands and village properties on Attu Island.

(3) VILLAGE SITE CONVEYANCE.—The Secretary may convey to the Corporation all right, title, and interest of the United States to the surface estate of the traditional Aleut village site on Attu Island, Alaska (consisting of approximately 10 acres) and to the surface estate of a parcel of land consisting of all land outside such village that is within 660 feet of any point on the boundary of such village. The conveyance may be made under the authority contained in section 14(h)(1) of the Alaska Native Claims Settlement Act (Public Law 92-203; 43 U.S.C. 1613(h)(1)), except that after the enactment of this Act, no site on Attu Island, Alaska, other than such traditional Aleut village site and such parcel of land, may be conveyed to the Corporation under section 14(h)(1).

(f) AUTHORIZATION OF APPROPRIATIONS.—There are authorized to be appropriated $15,000,000 to the Secretary to carry out this section.

Contracts.
50 USC app.
1989c-7.

SEC. 208. COMPLIANCE WITH BUDGET ACT.

No authority under this title to enter into contracts or to make payments shall be effective in any fiscal year except to such extent and in such amounts as are provided in advance in appropriations Acts. In any fiscal year, the Secretary with respect to—

(1) the Fund established under section 203,

(2) the trust established under section 205(b), and

(3) the provisions of sections 206 and 207,

shall limit the total benefits conferred to an amount not in excess of the appropriations for such fiscal year. Any provision of this title which, directly or indirectly, authorizes the enactment of new budget authority shall be effective only for fiscal year 1989 and thereafter.

Effective date.

SEC. 209. SEVERABILITY.

50 USC app.
1989c-8.

If any provision of this title, or the application of such provision to any person or circumstance, is held invalid, the remainder of this title and the application of such provision to other persons not similarly situated or to other circumstances shall not be affected by such invalidation.

TITLE III—TERRITORY OR PROPERTY CLAIMS AGAINST UNITED STATES

SEC. 301. EXCLUSION OF CLAIMS.

Mexico.
Indians.
50 USC app.
1989d.

Notwithstanding any other provision of law or of this Act, nothing in this Act shall be construed as recognition of any claim of Mexico or any other country or any Indian tribe (except as expressly provided in this Act with respect to the Aleut tribe of Alaska) to any territory or other property of the United States, nor shall this Act be construed as providing any basis for compensation in connection with any such claim.

Approved August 10, 1988.

LEGISLATIVE HISTORY—H.R. 442:

HOUSE REPORTS: No. 100-278 (Comm. on the Judiciary) and No. 100-785 (Comm. of Conference).
CONGRESSIONAL RECORD:
Vol. 133 (1987): Sept. 17, considered and passed House.
Vol. 134 (1988): Apr. 20, considered and passed Senate, amended.
July 27, Senate agreed to conference report.
Aug. 4, House agreed to conference report.
WEEKLY COMPILATION OF PRESIDENTIAL DOCUMENTS, Vol. 24 (1988): Aug. 10, Presidential remarks.

Nowhere in P.L.100-383, or in the "automatic entitlement" appropriated in the 1991 budget, do the words "Redress & Reparations" appear. The monetary "damages for human suffering" is called: "settlement," "appropriations," "payments," "funds," "restitution," "disbursements." (See "Redress" and "Reparations" in GLOSSARY)

Appendix C

Public Law 100-383
100th Congress

An Act

To implement recommendations of the Commission on Wartime Relocation and Internment of Civilians

Be it enacted by the Senate and House of Representatives of the United States of America in Congress assembled,

SEC. 2. STATEMENT OF THE CONGRESS.

(a) WITH REGARD TO INDIVIDUALS OF JAPANESE ANCESTRY.—The Congress recognizes that, as described by the Commission on Wartime Relocation and Internment of Civilians, a grave injustice was done to both citizens and permanent resident aliens of Japanese ancestry by the evacuation, relocation, and internment of civilians during World War II. As the Commission documents, these actions were carried out without adequate security reasons and without any acts of espionage or sabotage documented by the Commission, and were motivated large by racial prejudice, wartime hysteria, and a failure of political leadership. The excluded individuals of Japanese ancestry suffered enormous damages, both material and intangible, and there were incalculable losses in education and job training, all of which resulted in significant human suffering for which appropriate compensation has not been made. For these fundamental violations of the basic civil liberties and constitutional rights of these individuals of Japanese ancestry, the Congress apologizes on behalf of the Nation.

TITLE I—UNITED STATES CITIZENS OF JAPANESE ANCESTRY AND RESIDENT JAPANESE ALIENS

SEC. 101. SHORT TITLE.

This title may be cited as the "Civil Liberties Act of 1988".

SEC. 102. REMEDIES WITH RESPECT TO CRIMINAL CONVICTIONS.

(a) REVIEW OF CONVICTIONS.—The Attorney General is requested to review any case in which an individual living on the date of the enactment of this Act was, while a United States citizen or permanent resident alien of Japanese ancestry, convicted of a violation of—

(1) Executive Order Numbered 9066, dated February 19, 1942;

(2) the Act entitled "An Act to provide a penalty for violation of restrictions or orders with respect to persons entering, remaining in, leaving, or committing any act in military areas or zones", approved March 21, 1942 (56 Stat. 173); or

(3) any other Executive order, Presidential proclamation, law of the United States, directive of the Armed Forces of the United States, or other action taken by or on behalf of the United States or its agents, representatives, officers, or employees, respecting the evacuation, relocation, or internment of individuals solely on the

basis of Japanese ancestry; — — — —

— — — —

on account of the refusal by such individual, during the evacuation, relocation, and internment period, to accept treatment which discriminated against the individual on the basis of the individual's Japanese ancestry.

(b) RECOMMENDATIONS FOR PARDONS.—Based upon any review under subsection (a), the Attorney General is requested to recommend to the President for pardon consideration those convictions which the Attorney General considers appropriate.

(c) ACTION BY THE PRESIDENT.—In consideration of the statement of the Congress set forth in section 2(a), the President is requested to offer pardons to any individuals recommended by the Attorney General under subsection (b).

SEC. 108. DEFINITIONS.

For the purposes of this title—

(1) the term "evacuation, relocation, and internment period" means that period **beginning on December 7, 1941,** and ending on June 30, 1946;

(2) the term "eligible individual" means any individual of Japanese ancestry who is living on the date of the enactment of this Act and who, during the evacuation, relocation, and internment period—

(A) was a United States citizen or a permanent resident alien; and

(B)(i) was confined, held in custody, relocated, or otherwise deprived of liberty or property as a result of—

(I) Executive Order Numbered 9066, dated February 19, 1942;

(II) the Act entitled "An Act to provide a penalty for violation of restrictions or orders with respect to persons entering, remaining in, leaving, or committing any act in military areas or zones", approved March 21, 1942 (56 Stat. 173); or

(III) any other Executive order, Presidential proclamation, law of the United States, directive of the Armed Forces of the United States, or other action taken by or on behalf of the United States or its agents, representatives, officers, or employees, respecting the evacuation, relocation, or internment of individuals solely on the basis of Japanese ancestry; or

(ii) was enrolled on the records of the United States Government during the period **beginning on December 7, 1941,** and ending on June 30, 1946, as being in a prohibited military zone; except that the term "eligible individual" does not include any individual who, during the period **beginning on December 7, 1941,** and ending on September 2, 1945, relocated to a country while the United States was at war with that country;

(3) the term "permanent resident alien" means an alien lawfully admitted into the United States for permanent residence;

Author's Comments:
Political Machinations Made This Law;
The Proof Is in The Congressional Record

Congressional Record July 27, 1988: Senator Spark Matsunaga (D-HI), commented, "...the House never *formally* accepted the Report of the commission"—the Report which was the basis for legislative action in both Houses of Congress.

Senator Matsunaga introduced the "Conference" Report" to accompany H.R. 442, 100th Congress, 2nd Session.

House of Representatives, Report 100-785, submitted by Mr. Barney Frank, which had been *ordered to be printed July 26, 1988*—and was not yet available for legislators to read, let alone contest.

Details of the Conference Report were not discussed on the Senate floor when on July 27, 1988, at 10:00 o'clock at night and with fewer than a dozen Senators present, it was passed by voice vote.

The Conference Report, which became P.L. 100-383, was never *read* nor was it available for study *prior to its passage!*

The House of Representatives, in considering its vote, was told that the Senate had passed the Conference Report by "unanimous voice vote." This report does *not* appear in the *Congressional Record* nor was it distributed to anyone for study of its contents.

It appears that Senator Matsunaga succeeded in creating another day which will live in infamy—a day when political machination at its worst ruled the United States Congress and the Executive Branch of the government. ☐

Marriages were frequent in the relocation centers and at the family internment center in Texas. This couple, if living on August 10, 1988, would be in their sixties and each is entitled to $20,000 from American taxpayers for the "human suffering" they endured for being evacuated. National Archives Photo 210-GD-273.

Appendix D

"In the Interest of National Defense..."

A True Copy

COORDINATOR OF INFORMATION
Washington, D.C.

October 31, 1941

Mr. J. Edgar Hoover, Director
Federal Bureau of Investigation
U.S. Department of Justice
Washington, D.C.

My dear Mr. Hoover:

On Colonel Donovan's request, I am enclosing herewith, as of possible interest to you, a copy of a communication sent by Mr. Kilsoo K. Haan to the Honorable Frank Knox on September 30, 1941, the copy having been sent to this office.

Sincerely,

(Signed)
Turner McBaine, Special Assistant
to the Coordinator

A True Copy of Above Letter Enclosure

Sept. 30, 1941

Honorable Frank Knox
U.S. Secretary of Navy
Navy Department
Washington, D.C.

My dear Secretary Knox:

We hereby submit the following information in the hope that your Department will help us expose the anti-American Japanese activities in Hawaii and mainland America.

We sincerely believe unless a public exposure is made of all anti-American activities the average American cannot evaluate the facts and factors and hence it would be impossible to aid the U.S. National Defense effectively.

Reason and Free Inquiry a necessity

"Reason and free inquiry is the only effective agent
against error," advised Thomas Jefferson.

194

The Japanese Consulate agents have been given too much free rein to carry on their activities against America, both in Hawaii and on mainland U.S.A. I honestly believe if America treated them as the German and Italian Consular agents, under similar situations have been treated, it would help eliminate and prevent most of the Japanese anti-U.S. activities.

Preventive Measures Our Desire

Why let the Japanese go on as they do now—with the wishful thinking that America may "bag" them in the act of sabotage, etc.?

In the first place, the Japanese will not take any step unless they are ready and when they do, much damage will have been done.

The only and best policy I believe is to help the few loyal Japanese Americans in their fight against Japanism and follow up with public exposure.

Hawaiian Jap Consulate Activities

As you know we have reported in my testimony before the Joint Hawaii Statehood Investigation Committee, Oct. 1937, some of the Japanese un-American activities there.

Iizuka Tadaaiki - Secretary Iizuka Tadaaiki was sent from Japan to Hawaii and organized the following groups:
First, Consolidation of all Orientals under the Japanese
leadership and push statehood for Hawaii.

Second, Organize patriotic groups of Japanese and American
citizens of Japanese ancestry to assist Japan in the event
of war with the U.S.

Significant:

100 American citizens of Japanese ancestry were chosen as "Suicide Troops," better termed as "Human Bombs," to spread "contagious disease germs" in Pearl Harbor and the U.S. Army Reservation in order to "Quarantine U.S. Navy and Army" in Hawaii.

Nippon to America February 1941 issue
"Loyalty of Nisei or Second Generation"

"Loyalty of nisei. The number of nisei who have become Japanese nationals and who are serving in the army or navy is gradually increasing.

"Previously, Lieutenant Kurokawa, born in Hawaii, who succeeded to a baron's title, died a hero in action on the Shanghai front, thus showing nisei's loyalty.

"Recently American-born Risshin Nakamura, second son of Mr. Nakaemon Nakamura of San Francisco, was made sub-lieutenant in the army medical corps after graduating from the Showa Medical College in Tokyo.

"Passing a physical examination, Donald Seiichi Murata went to camp last January. A graduate of Waseda University and a radio announcer in the International Department of the Japanese Broadcasting Society, he is the third son of Mr. Ryuichi Murata, principal of Manoa Japanese School in Honolulu, T.H."

Nippon to America January 1941 issue
"Japanese-American Citizen Sent Back Before U.S. Draft"

"In view of the latest Japanese-American relations and in anticipation of the enactment of the peace time conscription of the law in America, many Japanese parents, fearing their sons pointing guns against their parent Country, have sent them back to Japan, where all available man power is sorely needed."

U.S.-Dual Citizens of Japanese Ancestry

According to our agent's report from the Orient, that there are 159,565 Japanese Americans in Hawaii and mainland U.S.A.,—this is information based on the statistics compiled by the Japanese Home Ministry after the Japanese Government Cencus conducted Dec. 1940 to Jan. 1941. Last January 1941 we made strong protest to the State Department against permitting the taking census of all Japanese Americans in Hawaii and America. The 159,565 are "dual citizens."

West Coast States—Japanese Activities

After almost three years of ceaseless investigation of Mr. Tadaaiki Iizuka's activities in the Western States, I am convinced that this is the time to expose the following information to the public in America:

Iizuka Organizes Subversive Groups in the Western States
Mr. Iizuka after completion of his work in Hawaii left April 1937 for Los Angeles to the Japanese Consulate. He organized:

First, the Japanese Military Servicemen's League, or *Zaibei Heimusha Kai*

Second, strengthened and reorganized the already existing "The Imperial Comradeship Society," a Japanese ex-servicemen's organization, by enlisting American citizens of Japanese ancestry to cooperate with the two groups.

The *Japanese Military Servicemen's League*. This organization with headquarters in San Francisco was formed in August 1937, one month after Japan's undeclared war with China. There are 7,200 members, consisting of Japanese subjects and dual-citizens of Japanese ancestry, who annually apply for deferment of military service in Japan to the Japanese Consulates.

As of May 1941 it is stated that 650,000 yen of Japanese War Funds were sent to Japan by this organization. They have branches in the States of Washington, Oregon, Utah and northern California. Each member is said to have pledged to die for Japan. They too are called "Suicide Troops." This organization has close connection with the Imperial Comradeship Society of Los Angeles.

The *Imperial Comradeship Society,* headquarters in Los Angeles. This society was in existence for many years. Since Mr. Iizuka's arrival in Los Angeles at the Japanese Consulate it has been strengthened, reorganized and includes patriotic Japanese of the second generation.

The *leader, Mr. Sakutaro Kubota*, is a retired Japanese officer. His son, *Takashi Kubota*, an *American citizen*, is one of the active leaders in the Japanese American Citizens League of Los Angeles, and an *able assistant*.

Last year the elder Kubota was sent to Japan to attend the "Oversea Japanese Congress" as delegate, and is said to have completed the final preparations for any emergency.

The total members are 4,800, spread throughout southern California, Arizona, and Texas.

Two Organizations operate in 65 localities—have 74 branches

The Japanese American Citizens League—with branches all over the Western States, headquarters in San Francisco. For the past several years Mr. Takashi has taken an unusually active part in the JACL in Los Angeles. He was for some time the editor of a monthly called *The Citizens' Friend*. He succeeded in bringing about the cooperation and collaberation of JACL with the Japanese Imperial Comradeship Society and the Japanese Military Servicemen's League in the campaign to sell Japanese War Bonds to the Japanese in the Western States.

1. The Japanese War Ministry sent 100 war propaganda films to this group to be shown throughout America.

2. The Japanese Finance Minister, Seinen Ikeda, requested of the JACL to raise one million yen and designated the Yokohama Specie Bank of Japan, with branch in San Francisco, as agent to receive the money.

I am told a large portion of the one million yen was collected—however, the Federal agents stepped in last year and stopped the sale of war bonds on the ground it was not registered with the State Department or with the Treasury. You can check this for confirmation.

A Japanese American Demands Immediate Dissolution of these Subversive Organizations in America.

Recently a courageous Japanese-American citizen, Mr. Shujii Fuji, editor of a small tri-monthly publication, demanded the dissolution of the Japanese Military Servicemen's League, and decried the denials of Fred Yoyamia, the president of the Japanese America Citizens League, as to the existence of such organization, as "deplorable ignorance" or "an asinine attempt at concealment of fact." He further charged that "Due to the character of its membership it has often been regarded as a potential fifth columnist organization" against the U.S.A.

Another Japanese in 1934 Charged Japanese-Americans Camouflaging.

You may recall my testimony in Hawaii and the presentation of a photostat copy of statement made by Rev. Shimnyu Umihara, who said (Hearing—Joint Congressional Statehood Investigation, Oct. 1937, Honolulu):

> It appears that the Japanese are afraid of other
> people's reproach and in order not to become the target
> of their criticism they are camouflaging their activities.

These two un-American Japanese subversive groups should be dissolved immediately and this can only be done through exposure and publicity.

Accordingly, I have requested Senator Guy M. Gillette, of the Senate Naval and Foreign Relations Committee, if he would do so.

In the interest of National Defense,

Gratefully yours,

Kilsoo K. Haan

Author's Notes:

Pursuant to a 7 October 1987 Freedom of Information Act (FOIA) the Central Intelligence Agency, Washington, D.C., released through its forerunner organization, the Coordinator of Information (COI), the letter from Kilsoo K. Haan to Secretary of the Navy Frank Knox. The document was released from the Federal Bureau of Investigation (FBI), from its records pertaining to Japanese Military Servicemen's League and the Imperial Comradeship Society. The 31 October 1941 letter, with attachment, was released in its entirety, and *APPROVED FOR RELEASE IN JUNE 1988, approximately two months before President Ronald Reagan signed into law, P.L. 100-383, August 10, 1988.* The declassified documents were forwarded to the President, the Senate and House Judiciary Committees, and to every member of the United States Congress who were responsible for investigating the background and factual evidence related to H.R. 442 and S. 1009—bills which would implement the payment of $20,000 to *every person of Japanese descent,* plus providing a written apology on behalf of the Nation for "wrong doing." [Who was responsible for covering-up documentation which would have proven tha the CWRIC's report, *Personal Justice Denied,* was ill-conceived and based on predetermined conclusions rather than on factual, documented evidence?]

Appendix to the Congressional Record, 77th Congress 2nd Session, 1942
(A1893-4) and 78th Congress 1st Session, 1943 (A5006-7)

Kilsoo K. Haan's radio address, Monday, May 25, 1942, was entered into the above-referenced Congressional Record, followed by further reference in 1943, about aid to the Korean people.

Mr. Haan's radio address, Monday, May 25, 1942, ended with these words:

> Koreans everywhere pray and urge the United States to attack Japan at her heart. I say this knowing full well than when the American bombers range over the industrial cities of Jap-dominated Korea my people will be killed. But I say, and my people say, "Let it come": we would rather die by American bombs than live as servants to the Japanese. □

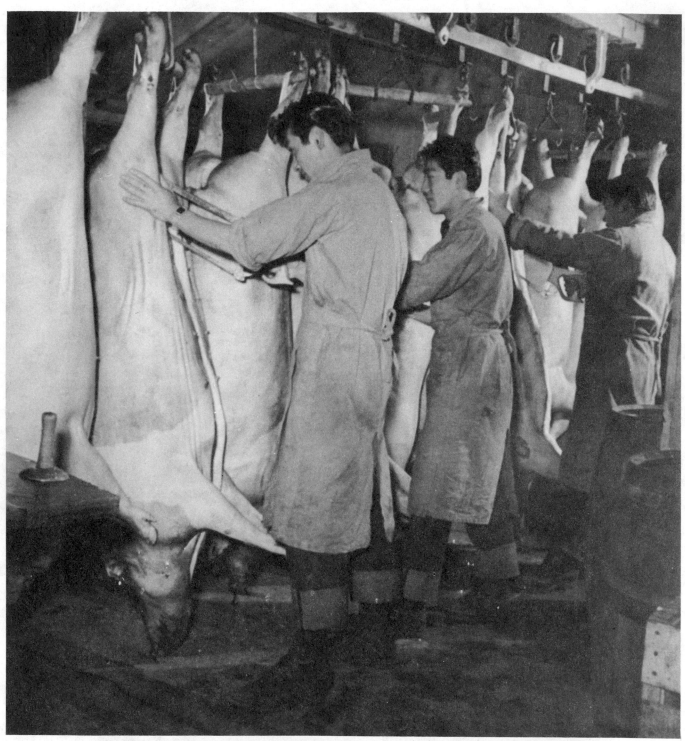

All the relocation centers operated huge farms with intention that the centers be as self-sufficient as possible. Evacuee butchers dress pork from the hog farm at Tule Lake. Over 100,000 evacuees received three meals a day without concern for rationing or shortages as faced by the nation's people who maintained their own households. The evacuees are to receive $20,000 each for "human suffering," under Public Law 100-383, August 10, 1988. (Photo from the National Archives 210-GB-158.

Appendix E

So Nothing Happened in Hawaii? False!

Today's revisionist historians claim that "there was nothing done in Hawaii" where almost half the population consisted of first and second generation Japanese (Issei and Nisei). This claim is completely false.

In the first place, Martial Law was declared immediately upon declaration of war, December 8, 1941, suspending the writ of *habeas corpus*. Thus civil rights were subservient to the military rule which existed in Hawaii.

The territorial governor invoked the Hawaii Defense Act and furthermore, he formally handed over to the military authorities all of his and other judicial employees of the Territory legal and political powers normally exercised in peacetime. Thus, without hinderance and with logical decision-making in time of war, the Army and Navy Intelligence was able by December 10, 1941, to round up almost 500 Japanese, German and Italian nationals who were enemy aliens with security charges against them. These people were interned on Sand Island. In stark contradiction to the Report *Personal Justice Denied* by the Commission (which claimed there were no disloyalties), 43 American citizens were also picked up by Army Intelligence for security reasons. According to the Pearl Harbor investigation report, in which there appeared a Feb. 9, 1942, *Memo from the District Intelligence Officer*, Fourteenth Naval District, the Joint Committee appointed by the 79th Congress to investigate "that day of infamy" at Pearl Harbor, the officer reported, "There were, prior to December 7, 1941, Japanese spies on the island of Oahu. Some were Japanese consular agents and others were persons having no open relations with the Japanese foreign service." On January 20, 1942,

Secretary Stimson entered into his diary that others in high office were fearful that ethnic Japanese in Hawaii posed a major risk of espionage, sabotage and fifth-column activity. Because of intelligence reports and personal reports of investigations into these threats, Secretary of the Navy Knox recommended that the war office remove all Japanese aliens in the Hawaiian Islands and intern them for security reasons in an already established internment center on Sand Island.

Nisei already in the military were segregated, given restricted orders on the basis that were Japan to invade the islands Nisei would not be distinguishable. By June 1942, the Hawaiian Nisei battalion and the Japanese American National Guardsmen were transferred from Hawaii to Camp McCoy, Wisconsin, and redesignated as the 100th Infantry Battalion.

All ethnic Japanese were removed from guarding public utilities and vital waterfronts.

Although only alien German, Italian, and Japanese on the mainland were ordered to turn in firearms, explosives, cameras, shortwave receivers, and other restricted items, in Hawaii during the months following Pearl Harbor bombing, all American citizens of Japanese, German, and Italian ancestry were ordered to comply with the same military proclamation.

On December 7, 1941, martial law resulted in a curfew to all residents, citizen and non-citizen. Censorship, including mail, and listening-posts to all telephone calls leaving the islands plus English-only conversations were allowed. The media (print and broadcast) was under strict censorship until formally ended on August 15, 1945.

The Federal Government was so concerned that the Japanese military might invade Hawaii, that all U.S. currency was exchanged for special paper money on which the name H A W A I I had been overprinted. In the event of invasion, all this special money could be immediately declared invalid.

On December 27, 1941, all civilians over the age of six were required to register and be fingerprinted; all residents (citizen and alien alike) were required to carry identification cards at all times. Civil law was only partially returned to Hawaii on March 10, 1943. Presidential Proclamation No. 2627 ended martial law in Hawaii on October 24, 1944, but the control of enemy aliens continued, including curfew.

On July 17, 1942, President Roosevelt in a secret memo, authorized the resettlement on the mainland of up to 15,000 persons, *in family groups*, who were "considered as potentially dangerous to national security." Those evacuated from Hawaii proved by their subsequent actions that they were, indeed, pro-Japan and a danger to national security.

Dillon S. Myer, Director of the WRA, and responsible for those evacuated from Hawaii to the Jerome Relocation Center (Arkansas), requested that "no more of these troublemakers be brought to the relocation centers." He stated for the record that "Half of them had answered 'no' to the loyalty question number 28 in the selective service registration form...and they "definitely are not the kind of people who should be scattered among the West Coast evacuees" already in the relocation centers. (Feb. 27, 1943, letter to McCloy, NARS. RG 107).

Hundreds of detained aliens were at Haiku, Maui and upon conviction were transferred to Sand Island Detention Center or Camp Honoluliuli (Oahu).

On August 30, 1942, Joseph C. Grew, U.S. Ambassador to Japan (1932-1942), by now returned to the United States on an exchange ship, delivered a radio address over CBS network to the American people. In describing imprisonment in Japan, he stated: "Among us were many Americans—missionaries, teachers, newspaper correspondents, businessmen—who had spent the preceding six months in solitary confinement in small, bitterly cold prison cells, inadequately clothed and inadequately fed and at times subjected to the most cruel and barbaric tortures.... Nearly all of the American missionaries, teachers, newspaper correspondents, and businessmen were regarded as potential spies. The stupidity of those Japanese police was only surpassed by their utter cruelty.... Do you wonder that during those seven days of waiting in the harbor of Yokohama several of those people (who had been tortured) told me that if the negotiations for our exchange failed they would commit suicide rather than return to their imprisonment in Japan? I know that they would have done so." [Quoted from *Ten Years in Japan: A Contemporary Record Drawn from the Diaries and Private and Official Papers of Joseph C. Grew.*

Simon and Schuster, 1944.]

Japan is not criticized for interning all Caucasian missionaries, teachers, newspaper correspondents, businessmen, and leaders in the "European Community"; yet Senator Spark Matsunaga has continually expressed his personal sentiment that the United States was "racist" in removing all "leaders in Hawaii of the Japanese community [including Senator Matsunaga's father] including church leaders, newspapermen, teachers of Japanese language schools," etc. What should be remembered is the humane treatment of those picked up in Hawaii by the United States military forces. Readers are urged to study Ambassador Grew's writings and then judge more honestly the actions of a wartime government confronted with a sneak attack on its forces at Pearl Harbor.

The bottom line is this: are those brought over from Hawaii to the mainland because of presumptive action or for security reasons, entitled to $20,000 and an apology as "damages for human suffering"? Yet because of the Dec. 7, 1941, "eligibility" date, and the inclusion of the words "evacuated" and "interned," all alien enemies and American Japanese proven to be *disloyal* to the United States, will be given an "automatic entitlement" of $20,000 under Senator Dan Inouye's "automatic entitlement program" passed by the United States Senate, October 4, 1989.

Under the present law, P.L. 100-383, August 10, 1988, 1,875 Hawaiian residents of Japanese ancestry are eligible for $20,000 plus hundreds of children born to the 1,118 who spent the war-years at WRA camps. Over 600 of those evacuated to the mainland were interned in Dept. of Justice Internment Camps, with approximately 150 of them choosing voluntary internment at Crystal City, Texas, family camp to join families together.

Public Broadcasting station KOCE sponsored the program *Super Chief: Life & Legacy of Earl Warren*, in which the narrator stated that "parents were separated from children." The fact is that the United States was the *only nation during World War II* which specifically worked to keep *families together*, including those who were *alien enemies*. □

NOTE: On November 21, 1989, President George Bush signed an appropriations bill for $17.2 billion for State, Justice and Commerce Departments which includes up to $500 million as an automatic "entitlement" (as is Social Security and Medicare), for **"damages for human suffering"** to Japanese who were relocated in WWII—$20,000 each, is payable in 3 years beginning 1991. It is noted that Public Law 100-383, August 10, 1988, specifies payments of $20,000 to Japanese and only $12,000 to Aleut Indians (Alaska), some of whom had been whisked out from under the very teeth of a Japanese invasion by the U.S. Navy. But the new "entitlement" pays only the Japanese. The Aleut Indians were left out! Why?

Special U.S. currency (page 199) used in Hawaii soon after Pearl Harbor attack. Japanese "dollar" currency (pages 200, 201) printed for use in Malaya could have been used in Hawaii and on American mainland if Japanese had invaded there. Data about "payable in dollars" Japanese occupation money is elusive. Examples shown owned by Earl Bayless who was in U.S. Occupation Force in Japan and recalls witnessing money being burned by the Japanese.

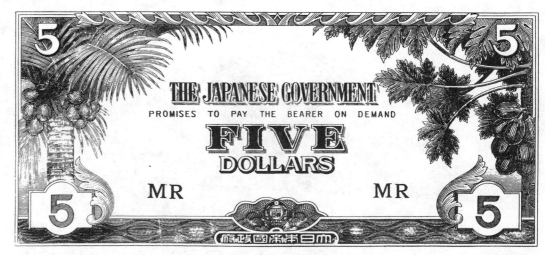

Drum Majorette and members of Twirlers Club participate in Labor Day Parade at Tule Lake Relocation Center, 1942 as seen in this National Archives picture 210-GD-223. Under Public Law 100-383, these girls are each paid $20,000 for "human suffering."

Appendix F

How To Leave A Relocation Center

A True Copy

Source: War Relocation Authority   Washington, D.C.
         February 1943 [6-5154-P4 Final BU-COS-WP]

The growing scarcity of manpower resulted in demands early in 1942 that evacuees be available for some of the agricultural work in western states which ordinarily is performed by itinerant workers. During the spring and summer months of 1942, over 1,600 evacuees from assembly centers and relocation centers were recruited to cultivate sugar beets in states outside the evacuated area. In the fall, the demand for labor to harvest sugar beets and other crops was much greater and about 10,000 were granted short term permits for work in the harvest fields. It is estimated that the sugar beets harvested by the evacuee workers in 1942 would make about 297,000,000 pounds of refined sugar. **Many of the harvest workers were hired on a permanent basis by their employers and have not returned to relocation centers. [Author's Note: Hardly "prisoners" and "unable to leave."]**

In July 1942, the War Relocation Authority announced a policy of permitting qualified American citizens among the evacuees to leave relocation centers to accept permanent jobs. On October 1, this policy with the approval of the War and Justice Departments, was broadened to include aliens as well as citizens. Under present policies of the War Relocation Authority, any evacuee may apply for a permit of indefinite leave. The permit will be granted under the following conditions:

a. He has a place to go and means of supporting himself;

b. A check of records of the FBI and other intelligence agencies, plus the applicant's record of behavior in the relocation center indicates that he would not endanger national security;

c. There is evidence that his presence in the community in which he proposes to go is not likely to cause a public disturbance;

d. He agrees to keep the War Relocation Authority informed of his address at all times. **[Author's Note: The I.D. card and Alien Enemy Registration Card was required of all *German, Italian and Japanese* nationals. American citizens were not required to carry I.D. cards.]**

In addition to the several hundred evacuees who left relocation centers for harvest work and obtained permanent jobs, about 2,000 had been granted permits of indefinite leave up to February 10, 1943. These people were widely scattered throughout the interior of the country, but most of them were in the intermountain or middle western states.

The largest number of indefinite leave permits for a specific purpose was granted to students who wished to continue their education. **[Author's NOTE: Senator Spark Matsunaga of Hawaii, most active proponent for monetary "reparations" and a government "apology" to alien Japanese and American Japanese, stated for the record that evacuees "suffered the loss of educational benefits." In reality, approximately 4,300 students— citizen and alien—spent the war-years at colleges and universities away from the west coast.]**

The next largest group receiving indefinite leave permits was household workers; agricultural workers were next in numerical order, and the next largest category was composed of girls leaving the center to join husbands or *fiances* in the United States Army. Others who have been granted permits of indefinite leave are now employed as cooks, clerks, photographers, mechanics, chick sexers, secretaries, engineers, and in a wide variety of other occupations. □

Author's Comment: *Proponents for legislation which was enacted into Public Law 100-383, August 10, 1988, insist that any other term but "concentration camp" when describing the War Relocation Centers is a "euphemism."*

Source: Declassified
E.O. 116252, Sec. 3(E) and 5(d) or (e)
NND 770091 NARS
June 7, 1977

A True Copy

CONFIDENTIAL
El Centro, California
December 6, 1942

MEMORANDUM FOR THE OFFICER IN CHARGE
SUBJECT: Conditions at Poston Relocation Center,
Poston, Arizona

Appendix G

Conditions at Poston Relocation Center

A reliable informant has supplied agents with the following information:

Many of the more dangerous Japanese, after they were apprehended, were interned instead of being sent to a relocation center. After a period of internment, they were removed to the relocation center. Prior to their removal to the center, there were printed in the center the rules and regulations promulgated for the conduct of the Japanese occupants of the camp. These rules and regulations were printed in the JAPANESE LANGUAGE and constituted the only matter of any kind which was permitted to be printed in any language other than English. Immediately upon their arrival at Poston, the former internees went to the office of the camp and requested that they be given printed copies of all regulations which had theretofore been printed, giving us the pretext that they were unacquainted with the regulations and wanted to "study them." Copies were given to them as requested. But, instead of their being kept in the camp for study purposes, these former internees immediately mailed them intact to the SPANISH CONSUL IN SAN FRANCISCO, CALIF., who in turn is reported to have, using his diplomatic immunity, mailed them direct to JAPAN, to be used for propaganda and other purposes. This information was given to informant by TOY NAKASHIMA, a loyal Japanese, who has twice been brutally beaten. It is assumed by agents that WDC Headquarters knows the names of many of the above-referred to offenders, since NAKASHIMA furnished to the informant a list of thirty-five names of men he knew were members of the pro-Axis group, which list in turn was given to NORRIS JAMES, Press and Intelligence Officer at Poston. Informant, who has had a long acquaintance with the Japanese in the Imperial Valley, and who, agents know, was of great aid to the Federal Bureau of Investigation, prior to, and after, Pearl Harbor, is of the opinion that all of the trouble in the relocation camps is part of a well-organized scheme directed from Tokyo, and that the SPANISH CONSULATES are acting as mediums for the exchange of information.

A. H. Moore, Special Agent, CIC
Albert M. Franco, Agent, CIC
Received Dec 23 P.M.(1942) WDC & FOURTH ARMY WCCA □

Source: UOP Archives
WRA/Barrows 36.310
Stuart Library,
University of the Pacific
California

Minidoka War Relocation Project
Hunt, Idaho

Welfare Section   April 8, 1944

Mr. Leland Barrows, Assistant Director
War Relocation Authority
Barr Building
Washington (25), D.C.

Appendix H

Draft Evasion at Minidoka

Dear Mr. Barrows:

In reply to your teletype of March 29, 1944, relative to the factors motivating repatriation and expatriation since the time of the last segregation from this Center in September 1943, we have gleaned the following information.

On March 20, 1944, we prepared the list of all persons subject to segregation dating from the time of the last segregation to March 20th, inclusive. Our analysis has been taken from this group which on March 20th numbered 190 persons subject to segregation for reasons of repatriation or expatriation. Out of this number 12 had been deferred from the last segregation movement because of illness. In another group and also included in the above figure are 5 people who have requested expatriation or repatriation and who have also requested permission to go to the family internment camp. The 190 figure is exclusive of accompanying family members.

We have broken this analysis down into two categorical parts, namely, those requesting expatriation or repatriation prior to January 20, 1944, or the date upon which Japanese were declared eligible for selective service, and those making requests after that date. Of the 190 segregants, 35 families consisting of 81 people applied prior to January 20, 1944, 42 families involving 99 persons applied after that date. We have attempted as nearly as possible to categorize the reasons which these individuals gave for their request and from the total group, we picked at random 89 cases, 50 of which requested expatriation or repatriation after January 20, 1944, and 39 requested prior to that time. The difference in these numbers is explained by the fact that there were more individual requests after January 20, 1944. Those prior to that date included many family members.

Our analysis will be found on the enclosed forms.

In this information we enumerated the respective ages. In that group signing prior to January 20, 1944, the average age was 35 years, which figure was lowered due to the fact there are many family members in the early adolescent years. In that group requesting expatriation or repatriation after January 20, 1944, the average age was found to be 27 years.

We would like to draw your attention to the trend which we believe to be significant and which was **not brought by evacuation or segregation. It appears that the coming of selective service to Japanese has definitely increased requests for expatriation and repatriation, many of which we presume would not have been made had they not been subject to military duty.** There seems to be quite a bit of feeling on the part of the people dealing with these persons such as members of the local hearing board, that the real reason for expatriation on the part of the draft age men is hidden by more acceptable reasons than that of the **frank admission of draft evasion,** which it would appear, is present in many cases.

Before having advanced this report to you, it was submitted to people on the hearing board, relocation program officers, statistician, and leaves officers who have concurred that this represents a fair cross-section on the matter of repatriation and expatriation. We trust that this meets with your request.

(signed) W. L. Stafford, Project Director ☐

Residents of Tule Lake Segregation Center have put out "welcome" signs for expatriates and repatriates and their families expected to arrive by trains from the other nine relocation centers. The incoming segregees would legally give up their American citizenship in favor of Japan then be interned to await deportation to Japan. Photographed September 26, 1943. (From National Archives No. 210-GH-328)

Source: National Archives

Appendix I

Alien Enemy Control Section and Japanese Peruvians

Department off State

FOR THE PRESS   November 2, 1945
                                     No. 826

By Departmental Order dated October 24, the Secretary of State has established under Assistant Secretary Braden, an Alien Enemy Control Section to handle the cases of enemy aliens who were brought to this country from other American republics during the course of the war and remain in the custody of this Government. The directive provides for the establishment of an orderly procedure for disposing of these cases on an individual basis in accordance with standards to be approved by the Secretary.

Immediately after the attack on Pearl Harbor and on a number of occasions thereafter, groups of enemy aliens considered to be dangerous to hemispheric security were deported to the United States from various of the other American republics for internment here with a view of later repatriation. A large number of these persons have already been repatriated to Germany, Italy and Japan at their own request or with their consent, most of them during the war in exchange for Americans interned in enemy countries. A considerable number of others, including many who were leaders in anti-American activities, now decline to return to their native countries, wishing to move back to Latin America or to remain here. It is the disposition of the latter cases with which the new Alien Enemy Control Section is concerned.

The desirability of ridding this Hemisphere of dangerous Axis nationals was recognized by all the American republics at the Mexico City Conference last Winter; the Final Act of that Conference included a recommendation that measures be taken "to prevent any person whose deportation was deemed necessary for reasons of security of the Continent from further residing in this Hemisphere, if such residence would be prejudicial to the future security or welfare of the Americas." Pursuant to that recommendation, on September 8, the President of the United States by Proclamation authorized the Secretary of State to order the repatriation of dangerous alien enemies deported to this country during the war.

In proceeding with this program the Department intends to follow an orderly procedure wholly consistent with American concepts of fairness and equity. A preliminary review of the cases is now going on, with a view of releasing as quickly as possible those persons who may safely be allowed to remain in this Hemisphere. Any person who appears to be so clearly dangerous as to make his repatriation desirable will be given ample opportunity for a hearing, and before a repatriation order is issued his case will be reviewed by a high officer of the Department. Finally, the Department does not propose to order repatriation in any case until after consultation with the other American republics concerned.

The overall objective of this program is to accomplish the purposes of Resolution VII of the Mexico City Conference, especially "to prevent Axis-inspired elements from securing or regaining vantage points from which to disturb or threaten the security or welfare of any American republic." It is the policy of the Department to pursue that objective in close cooperation with the other American republics.

● ● ●

Author's Note: Although those persons of Japanese descent who were considered "dangerous alien enemies" were interned for the duration of the war, today they are "eligible" for $20,000 each along with a public apology for "human suffering" by virtue of their *residence*. The so-called logic of "eligibility" is explained by the Department of Justice, printed in *The Federal Register* Vol. 54, No.

159, Friday, August 18, 1989, Rules and Regulations P. 34160:

"II. Responses to Comments and Summary of the Regulations and Revisions

The last major eligibility issue pertains to persons of Japanese ancestry who were sent to the United States from other American countries for restraint and repatriation pursuant to international commitments of the United States Government for the security of the United States and its associated powers. We received 77 comments advocating that all such individuals should be eligible for redress. The plight of these persons is described in the Appendix to Part I of *Personal Justice Denied*.[1] Although these individuals were evacuated, relocated or interned similarly to those of Japanese ancestry evacuated from the West Coast, the statute's threshold requirement that an eligible person must be a citizen of the United States or a permanent resident alien[2] excludes most of these persons from redress payment. Records indicate that the people who entered the United States under these international agreements were determined by the Department of Justice to be illegal aliens. As such, they were not lawfully admitted to the United States for permanent residence. Consequently, the restrictive language of the Act pertaining to citizenship status renders such person ineligible. On the other hand, after World War II some of the Latin American Japanese who were brought to the United States from other American republics for internment were permitted, under applicable statutes[3] to apply to the Attorney General of the United States for an adjustment of their immigration status; these individuals obtained the status of *permanent resident alien extending retroactively to the internment period*. Such persons would meet the threshold statutory requirement under the regulations of being permanent resident aliens during the evacuation, relocation and internment period and, as such, be eligible for compensation. In addition, children born in the United States to the Latin American Japanese during their internment would, by virtue of their place of birth, be United States citizens and therefore meet the threshold requirement for eligibility." [Italic added].

---

[1] The Commission's report, *Personal Justice Denied* states: "Historical documents concerning the ethnic Japanese in Latin America are, of course, housed in distant archives, and the Commission has not researched that body of material," and therefore the CWRIC has not based its "findings and recommendations" regarding these specific internees on documentation. However, the Commission does not deny that these alien enemies interned in the INS camps were anything but "dangerous to the national security" when they were deported from Peru and other American republics.

[2] The term "permanent resident alien" was given only to the Peruvian Japanese internees when Peru refused to accept any non-citizens (Japanese deportees). In Spring 1949, approximately 300 Japanese who refused repatriation back to Japan, and would not be accepted by the Peruvian government, remained as "people without a country." The United States State Department solved the problem by giving this small group a special status of "permanent legally admitted immigrants." Those immigrants who resided in the United States for 7 years (including the internment period), were given "permanent resident alien" status officially in July 1952, under a special Act of Congress which suspended deportation orders (1953).

[3] The term "permanent resident aliens" was extended to include all Japanese Nationals residing in the United States at the time of Japan's attack on Pearl Harbor—a term illogically applicable to known alien enemies. Under P.L. 100-383, Aug. 10, 1988, these known alien enemy Japanese or their heirs will be paid $20,000 each, as well as those born in the internment camps. Similarly situated Germans and Italians need not apply. *The Act thus discriminates on the basis of National Origin.* □

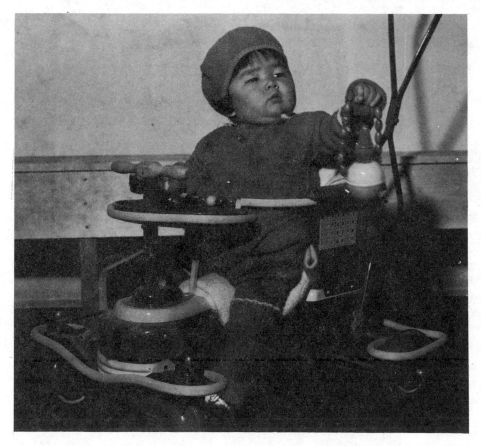

Could this child plausibly be today's Congressman Matsui who, at 10 months, went with his father and mother and sister to live at Tule Lake Relocation Center? Matsui testified before the Committee on Wartime Relocation and Internment of Civilians (CWRIC) in 1981 that after nine months at Tule Lake they left to farm in Idaho. In 1989, Congressman Matsui declared his family was "interned for 3½ years at Tule Lake." Which story is true? Photo by F. Stewart on September 10, 1942 at Tule Lake. (N.A.210-GD-254)

Remnants of buildings at Tule Lake Relocation/Segregation Center as viewed in 1973. (Photo by Bert Webber)

Source: *Stuart Library,*
University of the Pacific,
Stockton, California
[File: Jacoby MS 27 1.23]

A True Copy

OFFICE OF WAR INFORMATION   [OWI 2712]
WAR RELOCATION AUTHORITY   x022797

ADVANCE RELEASE: To Be Held in STRICTEST CONFIDENCE and NOT to Be Used by PRESS or RADIO BEFORE 8:p.m., EWT, SATURDAY November 13, 1943

Appendix J

Segregation and Riot at Tule Lake

Dillon S. Myer, director of the War Relocation Authority, today issued the following statement regarding the events that occurred between November 1, and November 4, at the Tule Lake Center in northern California:

1. Tule Lake is the only center maintained by the War Relocation Authority for segregation purposes. It was established originally in 1942 as one of 10 relocation centers for persons of Japanese ancestry who were evacuated from the West Coast military area. In September of this year, however, it was made the focal point in a segregation program carried out by the War Relocation Authority and since that time has occupied a peculiar status among WRA centers.

During February and March of this year a registration program was conducted at all relocation centers for the purpose of accumulating information on the background and attitudes of all adult residents. As part of this program, citizen evacuees at the centers were questioned concerning about their willingness to abide by the Nation's laws. After the results of registration were compiled and analyzed, W.R.A. began a program to separate from the bulk of the population at relocation centers, those evacuees who have indicated by word or action that their loyalties lie with Japan.

Four major groups were designated for segregation:

(1) Those who requested repatriation or expatriation to Japan;

(2) Citizens who refused during registration to state unqualified allegiance to the United States; and aliens who refused to agree to abide by the laws of the United States;

(3) Those with intelligence records or other records indicating that they might endanger the national security or interfere with the war effort;

(4) Close relatives of persons in the above three groups who expressed a preference to remain with the segregants rather than disrupt family ties. [Proponents for "redress" declare that the U.S. government "separated families."]

The major movement of segregants into Tule Lake from other WRA centers and of non-segregants from Tule Lake to other WRA centers was started in early September and completed about the middle of October. The process, which was carried out jointly by WRA and the Army involved the movement of approximately 9,000 evacuees from other centers into Tule lake and the removal from Tule Lake to other centers of approximately the same number. Slightly more than 6,000 residents of Tule Lake who had been designated for segregation or who wish to remain with segregated relatives were retained there. At the present time, there are at the Manzanar Relocation Center in California approximately 1,900 evacuees who are awaiting transfer to Tule Lake. They will be transferred as soon as necessary housing can be completed, probably in the early part of 1944.

2. The Army has the responsibility of providing full protection of the area surrounding the Tule Lake Center. A man-proof fence surrounds the external boundaries of the center; troops patrol that fence; other necessary facilities are at all times in readiness. In September, when Tule Lake was transformed into a segregation center, the Army substantially increased the number of troops assigned to guard duty at the center and built the present man-proof fence around the external boundary outside the ordinary wire fence which was erected at the time of the center's establishment. At this time also additional military equipment was provided.

During the recent disturbance at the Tule Lake Center, the War Relocation Authority and the Army have been in constant contact regarding the necessary safety measures. Special arrangements were made for prompt communication between the WRA staff and the officer commanding the troops at Tule Lake.

Like all WRA centers, Tule Lake has been operated, ever since the time of establishment in 1942, under the terms of an agreement between WRA and the War Department. WRA is responsible for all phases of internal administration of the center. The Army, from the beginning, has been responsible for guarding the external boundaries of the center, and for controlling the entry and departure of all persons of Japanese descent.

WRA maintains order within the center through civilian guards assisted by a staff of evacuees. The understanding with the Army provides that when a show of greater force is necessary to maintain order within the center, WRA will call upon the Army to move inside the center and take full control.

3. Immediately following the segregation movement, some of the evacuees at the Tule Lake Center began to create difficulties. All available evidence indicates that a small, well-organized group—composed chiefly of persons transferred to Tule Lake from the other centers—was attempting to gain control of the community and disrupt the orderly process of administration. Against this background, a serious accident occurred at the center on October 15. A truck, carrying 29 evacuee workers and driven by an evacuee, was over-turned while attempting to pass another truck on the road from the center to the WRA farm. All occupants of the truck were injured and one of them subsequently died. On the day following the accident, no evacuee workers reported for duty at the farm.

For a period of approximately 10 days thereafter, work on the harvesting of crops stopped, but no formal representations were made to WRA by evacuee workers. Then on October 25, a group of evacuees who claimed to represent the community, met with Project Director Ray Best and submitted a series of questions and demands. Among other things, this committee asked whether the residents of Tule Lake were regarded by the United States government as prisoners of war and stated that the residents would not engage in the harvesting of crops for use at other WRA centers. Project Director Best told the committee: (1) that the residents of Tule Lake were regarded as segregants and not as prisoners of war, (2) that WRA does not operate on the basis of demands, and (3) that if the residents of Tule Lake were unwilling to harvest the crops, some other method of harvesting them would be found.

Faced with the onset of winter and the possibility of losing approximately $500,000 worth of vegetables, WRA immediately began recruiting loyal evacuees from other centers to carry out the harvesting work at Tule Lake. A crew of 234 was recruited and is still engaged in harvesting work on the Tule Lake Farm. These evacuees are quartered outside the boundaries of the center, wholly apart from the population of the center. [It was necessary to segregate loyal evacuees from the disloyal as the latter used terrorist tactics against any evacuee who was pro-America.]

4. On the morning of Monday, November 1, D. S. Myer, national director of the War Relocation Authority, and Robert B. Cozzens, assistant director of the Authority in San Francisco, arrived at Tule Lake center for an inspection and consultation with key WRA staff members and with evacuee representatives. The original arrangement called for Mr. Myer and Mr. Cozzens to meet with evacuee representatives on the day following their arrival. However, during the lunch hour, a report was received by Project Director Best that certain evacuees were making unauthorized announcements in the mess halls. Residents were being told, according to this report, that Mr. Myer was to make a speech from the main administration building shortly after lunch. On receiving this report, Mr. Myer and Mr. Best immediately made a quick automobile inspection trip through the evacuee section of the center. They observed that large numbers of men, women and children were proceeding in an orderly manner from the evacuee barracks in the direction of the administration building.

By 1:30 p.m. Mr. Myer and Mr. Best had returned to the administration building and a crowd estimated between 3,500 & 4,000 had congregated immediately outside. One young man from the evacuee group then entered the administration building and asked whether a committee of 17 evacuees might have a conference with Mr. Myer. This request was granted, and Mr. Myer, Mr. Cozzens, Mr. Best and other staff members met with the committee. The committee presented a series of demands including the resignation of Project Director Best and several other WRA staff members at the center.

While the discussion was going on, word was received that a group **of about a dozen evacuees had entered the center hospital and beaten the chief medical officer, Dr. Reece M. Pedicord. The conference was interrupted while one WRA staff member left the administration building, passed through the crowd, and went to the hospital for a check up on the situation there. After this man had returned—wholly unmolested—with the report that Dr. Pedicord had been badly battered but was receiving adequate medical attention** and that order prevailed in the hospital, the conference was resumed. Meanwhile, a small group of evacuees had gone into the administration building and installed a public address system with WRA permission.

At the conclusion of the conference, Director Myer was asked to address the crowd briefly over the address system and agreed to do so. Mr. Myer told the crowd substantially what he had told the committee, (1) that WRA would consider requests made by the evacuee population provided they were in the framework of national policy; (2) that WRA would not accede to demands; (3) that WRA was under the impression that the majority of residents at Tule Lake wanted to live in a peaceful and orderly atmosphere; (4) that if the residents of the center could not deal peacefully with WRA they would have to deal with someone else; and (5) that once the segregation process was wholly completed with the movement from Manzanar, the community at Tule Lake should attempt to select a committee—more directly representative of its wishes than the current one—to deal with the War Relocation Authority. After Mr. Myer had concluded his remarks, two members of the evacuee committee addressed the crowd briefly in Japanese. Immediately following the completion of these speeches, at about 4:30 p.m., the crowd broke up quickly and peacefully and returned to family living quarters. During the entire conference and the time when committee members were addressing the crowd, a member of the War Relocation Authority staff who is fully competent in the Japanese language was present and was able to indicate to Mr. Myer and Mr. Best the nature of all remarks made in Japanese.

5. While the meeting was in progress in the administration building a number of automobiles at the center were slightly damaged. Some of these automobiles belonged to visitors and some to WRA personnel. One visitor reported that a window of his car was broken

and a sun visor removed. (This statement has not been verified by other evidence.) A door handle was broken off one car. Radio aerials were removed from two cars and windshield wipers from about twelve cars. Air was released from tires of several cars. The paint on two cars was scratched.

In the struggle during which Dr. Pedicord was beaten, a wooden railing in the hospital office was knocked down. A careful investigation has revealed no reliable evidence of any property damage during this incident other than that listed here.

Several WRA employees and visitors to the centers who were in the area outside the administration building at the time the crowd was forming were approached by some of the evacuees directing the movements of the crowd and told to go inside the building. Aside from Dr. Pedicord, however, no WRA employees or visitors were beaten or injured during this incident. The evacuee employees in the administration office left their work. A few individuals reported they saw knives and clubs in the hands of some of the evacuees. The great majority of WRA personnel reported following the meeting that they had seen no weapons of any kind.

6.   After dispersal of the crowd on Monday afternoon, a calm marked by some evidence of sub-surface tension prevailed in the evacuee community for approximately three days. Orders were sent out following the Monday meeting forbidding any meetings or assembly of evacuees in the administration area. The internal security force was strengthened and authority was given for any member of the internal security staff, under certain specified conditions, to summon the Army directly without consultation with the project director or any other superior officer.

On Thursday afternoon, November 4, work was started on a fence separating the evacuee community from the section of the center where the administrative buildings are located and WRA staff members are housed. That evening a crowd of about 400 evacuees, mainly young men—many of them armed with clubs—entered the administration area. Most of the crowd entered the warehouse area. A few entered the motor pool area and some surrounded the project director's residence. The advance of this crowd was resisted by several WRA internal security officers, one of whom was tripped, struck his head on a stone, and was then struck by evacuees with clubs. No other persons were injured. As the crowd closed in around Mr. Best's home, he telephoned Lt. Col. Verne Austin, commanding officer of the military outside the center, and asked the Army to assume full control of the project area. Troops entered the center at once. [The Army was never stationed *inside* the WRA centers and never on duty *inside* the centers unless it was called in to settle a disturbance.]

7.   During and immediately following the evacuee meeting on Monday, a number of the WRA staff became apprehensive concerning their personal safety. Most of them remained calm but a few became almost hysterical. All were offered the opportunity to leave the center until they felt secure in returning there, and a number of them did so. Since the incident on Monday, twelve people have resigned voluntarily, and two have resigned or were separated at the request of the Authority. [Dillon Myer requested resignation of some WRA staff who sought "retribution."]

8.   A large number of the evacuees at Tule Lake are citizens of the United States, with constitutional rights of citizens. Many of them are children under 17, and they, together with a very large number of the adults, have no responsible part in the recent events.

In presenting this factual statement, the War Relocation Authority wants to emphasize that reports of the events at Tule Lake are being watched in Tokyo. Already some of the recent newspaper accounts have been used by the Japanese Government for propaganda purposes. There is every possibility that they may be used as a pretext for retaliatory action against American civilians and prisoners of war under Japanese control. [Japan's atrocities against civilians and POWs in Japan and in Japanese conquered territories occurred *before* this incident. Myer's statement was intended to protect American Japanese who had already been relocated.] Under these circumstances, it is imperative that the situation at Tule Lake he handled with a *scrupulous regard for accuracy*. [Emphasis Added]

9.   In view of the serious international implications in the situation at Tule Lake, the War Relocation Authority has been particularly careful in preparing the information contained in this statement. There have been so many exaggerated, even hysterical reports that the staff at Tule Lake, confronted with an otherwise complicated and difficult situation, has been able to verify conclusively only the information presented in this statement. As this is written, further investigation is being made to check the accuracy of many of the allegations that have appeared in the press and to complete this story in all its pertinent details. The major events, however, have now been fully documented and can for the first time be presented to the public in an official statement. □

Source: The San Francisco *Chronicle*
February 29, 1944
Headline: "The Nisei Problem"

A True Copy

**EVACUATED JAPANESE FIND
A 'NEW AMERICA' IN THE EAST**

**WRA RECORDS SHOW GROWING RUSH TO DISPOSE
OF WEST COAST PROPERTY
By William Flynn**

Chronicle Staff Writer

Appendix K

Fallacy:
"We Lost Everything ...We Were Prisoners"

DENVER, Col., Feb. 27—More than 20,000 of the 112,353 individuals of Japanese ancestry who were removed by the military from the Pacific Coast almost two years ago already have established permanent new homes in the "New America" they discovered east of the Sierra Nevada mountains.

The number is increasing each day. News of the success of those who have ventured out of the relocation centers is encouraging others to undertake the pioneering task of resettlement. The War Relocation Authority is increasing its efforts to place those anxious to begin anew in communities where they will be accepted.

Currently, more than 50,000 of the participants in the greatest controlled mass migration in the history of the United States are determined never to return to their former homes. Forty per cent are undecided at the moment what to do with their future when they are free to determine their action. Only 10 percent, according to qualified estimates, are determined to return to the Pacific Coast.

COAST PROPERTY

Ownership of Pacific Coast property is the factor which ties the evacuated Japanese-Americans to their former homes. But they are becoming more and more convinced that their future does not lie in California, Washington, and Oregon, and they are disposing of that property.

The rate of disposal of property has been slow, but it is increasing as the period of evacuation extends toward its third year and the greater opportunity of voluntary pioneering eastward becomes more and more apparent.

During the first months of evacuation the Japanese Americans were of the opinion that their exclusion would be only a matter of months. They held their property. They "hoarded" their assets with the hope they would be able to take up life where they had dropped it.

The opportunity did not materialize. Now they believe that even if it did they would be unwise to return. As a result the rate of disposal is being accelerated. The transfer of property held by Japanese Americans throughout California already is almost 20 percent of the total number of titles held.

In Alameda county, for example, the Japanese Americans owned 15 farm properties. Four of them have been transferred to non-evacuees. Farms owned by Japanese Americans in Fresno county totaled 282. Seventy of those titles have been transferred. Santa Clara county Japanese American farm properties totaled 117, according to the WRA property division records, and 30 have been transferred.

The rate of transfer of non-agriculture properties is proceeding at about the same rate. In San Francisco, the WRA records reveal, the Japanese Americans possessed title to 139 business institutions and firms. Seven have been transferred according to available records.

The Contra Costa business holdings of Japanese Americans totaled 92, and 17 have been transferred. In Merced county the Japanese Americans owned three business firms. One of them has been transferred to non-evacuees. The San Mateo urban property holdings of Japanese Americans totaled 85, and six have been sold or transferred.

The available WRA figures do not cover the property that was owned, in fact, by the Japanese aliens who registered the titles in the names of citizen relatives to circumvent the prohibitions of the California alien land law. But they, too, are becoming more and more determined to turn their backs forever on the Pacific Coast.

The change in mood is caused by the maturity of the American-born members of the family. As they grow older they are realizing with astonishing clarity that they do not wish to return to the Pacific Coast because they see greater opportunity for them in other sections of the United States. As a result, their determination and decisions are the vital factors in determining the future of the family, and Pacific Coast holdings are being disposed of to a large degree.

The 20,000 evacuees who have already established their new homes in the "new America" are those who have been released on indefinite leave from the war relocation centers. None from the Tule Lake Segregation Camp, established for control of Japanese Americans who have professed loyalty to the Japanese Empire, are included in the number.

To qualify for indefinite leave, the Japanese American must meet two standards. They are:

    1—He must be loyal to the United States.

    2—He must have sufficient economic resources or money earning ability to guarantee he will not become a public charge.

The question of loyalty is the most difficult to determine. The test is made through study of reports on character and activity prepared by the WRA, the Federal Bureau of Investigation, and military intelligence units.

If no instances of subversive activity are discovered and listed in the individual's dossier, it is presumed that he is a loyal citizen of the United States, and worthy of the opportunity of resettlement.

[End of Article]

Fallacy: "There were no disloyal American or Japanese evacuees..."

Fallacy: "We were prisoners and couldn't leave..."

Fallacy: "There were armed guards with machine guns facing inward at us through the barbed wire fences..."

Fallacy: "We lost everything..."

FACTS

Source: HEADQUARTERS WESTERN DEFENSE COMMAND AND FOURTH ARMY, OFFICE OF THE COMMAND GENERAL, PRESIDIO OF SAN FRANCISCO, CALIFORNIA

1 September 1943
STANDARD OPERATING PROCEDURE FOR MILITARY POLICE AT TULE LAKE CENTER

1 September 1943
USE OF TROOPS WITHIN RESIDENTIAL AREA
(LIVING QUARTERS OF ALL EVACUEES)

1. The Commanding Officer, upon such occasions as he causes troops of his command to enter the Residential Area, will cause them to do so in force, and he will assume absolute command and full control.

2. The Commanding Officer will cause troops of his command to enter the Residential Area *only in the following cases*:

    a. When the Project Director states that he is no longer able to maintain order and requests the Commanding Officer to enter and assume command. [See APPENDIX J]

    b. When, in the opinion of the Commanding Officer, the situation within the Residential Area has reached such a degree of disorder that it endangers the external security. ☐

Appendix L

Documented Disloyalties by Japanese Nationals and American Japanese—No. 1

A True Copy

Source: National Archives

WAR DEPARTMENT
M. I. D.

MID 336.8 Japan 10-14-41

MILITARY INTELLIGENCE DIVISION
CONTACT OFFICE
205 Dillingham Building
CONFIDENTIAL   Honolulu, T. H.
14 October 1941

Subject: JAPANESE EX-SERVICEMEN'S ORGANIZATION

Summary of Information:

1.   ZAIBEI HEIMUSAI (Japanese Military Service Men League). This organization was organized in August, 1937, by Tadasiki Izuka, Assistant Chief of Japanese Foreign Information Bureau Headquarters in San Francisco.

There are 7,200 members in northern California, Washington, Oregon and Utah. Each member gives $1.00 to a Japanese War Fund, and others engage in intelligence activities. **This includes military age nisei as well as Japanese aliens.** Y650,000.00 were sent to Japan as of May 1941.

2.   IMPERIAL COMRADESHIP SOCIETY (Japanese Ex-Service men League). This organization is headed by Sakutaro Kuboda, owner of Market Hotel, a retired officer. Kuboda visited Japan last year and attended *Japanese Overseas Congress*. He is especially recognized by Japanese army to carry on the work. His son Takashi is an active member of *Japanese American Citizen League*; he is also the editor of *Shinsin no Tomo* (Citizen Friend). This Society raised fund of Y1,000,000.00 at the request of Finance Minister, Mr. Ikeda, through Yokohama Specie Bank in San Francisco and Los Angeles, Headquarters at Los Angeles.

These two organizations are the same in nature. It is further stated that these two organizations have pledged to do sabotage (railroads and harbors) in the states mentioned above, in time of emergency. Similar organizations are in Hawaii. Sixty-nine local units of these two organizations are said to be carrying on activities.

Distribution
MID, Washington, D.C.
FBI, Honolulu
ONI, Honolulu
File

**UPGRADED/UNCLASSIFIED
1 MAY 1988**

214

Author's Note: This is a portion of the PRINGLE REPORT that was deleted from CWRIC Report and Findings.

A True Copy

BIO/KD/KF37/A8-5
Serial LA/1055/re   26 JAN 1942

DECLASSIFIED (Previously classified CONFIDENTIAL)

From: LIEUTENANT COMMANDER K. D. RINGLE, USN
To   : The Chief of Naval Operations
Via : The Commandant, Eleventh Naval District

Subject: Japanese Question, Report on.

Appendix M

Documented Disloyalties by Japanese Nationals and American Japanese—No. 2

(b) That of the Japanese-born alien residents, the large majority are at least passively loyal to the United States. That is, they would knowingly do nothing whatever to the injury of the United States, but at the same time would not do anything to the injury of Japan. Also, most of the remainder would not engage in active sabotage or insurrection, but might well do surreptitious observation work for Japanese interests if given a convenient opportunity.

(c) That, however, there are among the Japanese both alien and United States citizens, certain individuals, either deliberately placed by the Japanese government or actuated by a fanatical loyalty to that country, who would act as saboteurs or agents. This number is estimated to be less than three percent of the total, or about 3,500 in the entire United States.

(d) That of the persons mentioned in (c) above, the most dangerous are either already in custodial detention or are members of such organizations as the Black Dragon Society, the Kaigun Kyokai (Navy League), or the Hoirusha Kai (Military Service Man's League), or affiliated groups. The membership of these groups is already fairly well known to the Naval Intelligence Service or the Federal Bureau of Investigation and should immediately be placed in custodial detention, irrespective of whether they are alien or citizen. (See reference (c) and (f)).

(f) That in spite of paragraph (c) above, the most potentially dangerous element of all are those American citizens of Japanese ancestry who have spent the formative years of their lives, from 10 to 20, in Japan and have returned to the United States to claim their legal American citizenship within the last few years. Those people are essentially and inherently Japanese and may have been deliberately sent back to the United States by the Japanese government to act as agents. In spite of their legal citizenship and the protection afforded them by the Bill of Rights, they should be looked upon as enemy aliens and many of them placed in custodial detention. This group numbers between 600 and 700 in the Los Angeles metropolitan area and at least that many in other parts of Southern California. □

In this appendix, the author's emphasis appear in bold print. Author's comments appear in (brackets) to set apart her remarks from that of the Supreme Court decision.

SUPREME COURT OF THE UNITED STATES

October Term 1944

FRED TOYOSABURO KOREMATSU
Petitioner,

v

UNITED STATES OF AMERICA
(323 US 214-248)

[The 6-3 *affirmative ruling upholds constitutionality* of the mandatory evacuation under Executive Order 9066, February 19, 1942 as nothing more than an *exclusion* order.]

Mr. Justice Black delivered the opinion of the Court:

The petitioner, an American citizen of Japanese descent, was convicted in a Federal district court for remaining in San Leandro, California, a "Military Area," contrary to Civilian Exclusion Order No. 34 of the Commanding General of the Western Command, U. S. Army, which directed that after May 9, 1942, all persons of Japanese ancestry should be excluded from that area. No question was raised as to petitioner's loyalty to the United States. The Circuit Court of Appeals affirmed, and the importance of the constitutional question involved caused us to grant certiorari.

It should be noted, to begin with that all legal restrictions which curtail the civil rights of a single racial group are immediately suspect. **That is not to say that all such restrictions are unconstitutional.** It is to say that courts must subject them to the most rigid scrutiny. Pressing public necessity may sometimes justify the existence of such restrictions; racial antagonism never can.

In the instant case prosecution of the petitioner was begun by information charging violation of an Act of Congress, of March 21, 1942, which provides that "...whoever shall enter, remain in, leave, or commit any act in any military area or military zone prescribed, under the authority of an Executive order of the President, by the Secretary of War, or by any military commander designated by the Secretary of War, contrary to the restrictions applicable to any such area or zone or contrary to the order of the Secretary of War or anyy such military commander, shall, if it appears that he knew or should have known of the existence and extent of the restrictions or order and that his act was in violation thereof, be guilty of a misdemeanor and upon conviction shall be liable to a fine of not to exceed $5,000 or to imprisonment for not more than one year, or both, for each offense."

Exclusion Order No. 34, which petitioner knowingly and admittedly violated, was one of a number of military orders and proclamations, all of which were substantially based upon Executive Order No. 9066, 7 Fed Reg 1407. That order, issued after we were at war with Japan, declared that "the successful prosecution of the war requires every possible protection against espionage and against sabotage to national-defense material, national-defense premises, and national-defense utilities...."

One of the series of orders and proclamations, a curfew order, which like the exclusion order here was promulgated pursuant to Executive Order 9066, subjected all persons of Japanese ancestry in prescribed West Coast military areas to remain in their residence from 8 p.m. to 6 a.m. As is the case with the exclusion order here, that prior curfew order was designed as a "protection against espionage and against sabotage." In Hirabayashi v. United States, we sustained a conviction obtained for violation of the curfew order. The Hirabayashi conviction and this one thus rest on the same 1942 Congressional Act and the same basic executive and military orders, all of which orders were aimed at the twin dangers of espionage and sabotage.

The 1942 Act was attacked in the Hirabayashi Case as an

unconstitutional delegation of power; it was contended that the curfew order and other orders on which it rested were beyond the war powers of Congress, the military authorities and of the President, as Commander in Chief of the Army; and finally that to apply the curfew order against none but citizens of Japanese ancestry amounted to a constitutionally prohibited discrimination solely on account of race. To these questions, we gave the serious consideration which their importance justified. **We upheld the curfew order as an exercise of the power of the government to take steps necessary to prevent espionage and sabotage in an area threatened by Japanese attack.**

In the light of the principles we announced in the Hirabayashi Case [hearings before the Subcommittee on the National War Agencies Appropriations Bill for 1945, Part II, 608-726; Final Report, Japanese Evacuation from the West Coast, 1942, 309-327; Hearings before the Committee on Immigration and Naturalization, House of Representatives, 78th Cong., 2d Sess. on H.R. 2701 and other bills to expatriate certain nationals of the United States, pp. 37-42, 49-58] we are unable to conclude that it was beyond the war power of Congress and the Executive to exclude those of Japanese ancestry from the West Coast war area at the time they did. True, exclusion from the area in which one's home is located is a far greater deprivation than constant confinement to the home from 8 p.m. to 6 a.m. Nothing short of apprehension by the proper military authorities of the gravest imminent danger to the public safety can constitutionally justify either. But exclusion from a threatened area, no less than curfew, has a definite and close relationship to the prevention of espionage and sabotage. The military authorities, charged with the primary responsibility of defending our shores, concluded that curfew provided inadequate protection and ordered exclusion. They did so, as pointed out in our Hirabayashi opinion, in accordance with congressional authority to the military to say who should, and who should not, remain in the threatened areas.

In this case the petitioner challenges the assumptions upon which we rested our conclusions in the Hirabayashi Case. He also urges that by May 1942, when Order No. 34 was promulgated, all danger of Japanese invasion of the West Coast had disappeared. After careful consideration of these contentions we are compelled to reject them.

Here, as in the Hirabayashi Case, "we cannot reject as unfounded the judgment of the military authorities and of Congress that there were disloyal members of that population, whose number and strength could not be precisely and quickly ascertained. We cannot say that the war-making branches of the Government did not have ground for believing that in a critical hour such persons could not readily be isolated and separately dealt with, and constituted a menace to the national defense and safety, which demanded that prompt and adequate measures be taken to guard against it."

Like curfew, exclusion of those of Japanese origin was deemed necessary because of the presence of an **unascertained number of disloyal members of the group**, most of whom we have no doubt were loyal to this country. It was because we could not reject the finding of the military authorities that it was impossible to bring about an immediate segregation of the disloyal from the loyal that we sustained the validity of the curfew order as applying to the whole group. In the instant case, temporary exclusion of the entire group was rested by the military on the same ground. The judgment that exclusion of the whole group was for the same reason a military imperative answers the contention that the exclusion was in the nature of a group punishment based on antagonism to those of Japanese origin. **That there were members of the group who retained loyalties to Japan has been confirmed by investigations made subsequent to the exclusion. Approximately five thousand American citizens of Japanese ancestry refused to swear unqualified allegiance to the United States and to renounce allegiance to the Japanese Emperor, and several thousand evacuees requested repatriation to Japan.**

We uphold the exclusion order as of the time it was made and when the petitioner violated it. In doing so, we are not unmindful of the hardships imposed by it upon a large group of American citizens.

But hardships are part of war, and war is an aggregation of hardships. All citizens alike, both in and out of uniform, feel the impact of war in greater or lesser measure. Citizenship has its responsibilities as well as its privileges, and in time of war the burden is always heavier. Compulsory exclusion of large groups of citizens from their homes, except under circumstances of direst emergency and peril, is inconsistent with our basic governmental institutions. But **when under conditions of modern warfare our shores are threatened by hostile forces, the power to protect must be commensurate with the threatened danger.**

It is argued that on May 30, 1942, the date the petitioner was charged with remaining in the prohibited area, there were conflicting orders outstanding, forbidding him both to leave the area and to remain there. Of course, a person cannot be convicted for doing the very thing which it is a crime to fail to do. But the outstanding orders here contained no such contradictory commands.

There was an order issued March 27, 1942, which prohibited petitioner and others of Japanese ancestry from leaving the area, but its effect was specifically limited in time "until and to the extent that a future proclamation or order should so permit or direct." That "future order," the one for violation of which petitioner was convicted, was issued May 3, 1942, and it did "direct" exclusion from the area of all persons of Japanese ancestry, before 12 o'clock noon, May 9; furthermore it contained a warning that all such persons found in the prohibited area would be liable to punishment under the March 21, 1942 Act of Congress. Consequently, the only order in effect touching the petitioner's being in the area on May 30, 1942, the date specified in the information against him, was the May 3 order which prohib-ited his remaining there, and it was that same order, which he stipulated in his trial that he had violated, knowing of its existence. There is therefore no basis for the argument that on May 30, 1942, he was subject to punishment, under the March 27 and May 3 orders, whether he remained in or left the area.

It does appear, however, that on May 9, the effective date of the exclusion order, the military authorities had already determined that the evacuation should be effected by assembling together and placing under guard all those of Japanese ancestry, at central points, designated as "assembly centers," in order "to insure the orderly evacuation and resettlement of Japanese voluntarily migrating from military area No. 1 to restrict and regulate such migration." And on May 19, 1942, eleven days before the time petitioner was charged with unlawfully remaining in the area, Civilian Restrictive Order No. 1, 8 Fed Reg 982, provided for detention of those of Japanese ancestry in assembly or relocation centers. It is now argued that the validity of the exclusion order cannot be considered apart from the orders requiring him, after departure from the area, to report and to remain in an assembly or relocation center. The contention is that we must treat these separate orders as one and inseparable; that, for this reason, if detention in the assembly or relocation center would have illegally deprived the petitioner of his liberty, the exclusion order and his conviction under it cannot stand.

We are thus being asked to pass at this time upon the whole subsequent detention program in both assembly and relocation centers, although the only issues framed at the trial related to petitioner's remaining in the prohibited area in violation of the exclusion order. Had petitioner here left the prohibited area and gone to an assembly center we cannot say **either as a matter of fact or law, that his presence in that center would have resulted in his detention in a relocation center. Some who did report to the assembly center were not sent to relocation centers, but were released upon condition that they remain outside the prohibited zone until the military orders were modified or lifted.** This illustrates that they pose different problems and may be governed by different principles. The lawfulness of one does not necessarily determine the lawfulness of the others. This is made clear when we analyze the requirements of the separate provisions of the separate orders. These separate requirements were that those of Japanese ancestry (1) depart from the area; (2) report to and temporarily remain in an assembly center; (3) go under military control to a relocation center there to remain for an indeterminate period until released conditionally or unconditionally by the military authorities. Each of these requirements, it will be noted, imposed distinct duties in connection with the separate steps in a complete evacuation program. Had Congress directly incorporated into one Act the language of these separate orders, and provided sanctions for the violations, disobedience of any one would have constituted a separate offense. There is no reason why violations of these orders, insofar as they were promulgated pursuant to congressional enactment, should not be treated as separate offenses.

The **Endo Case,** decided today (323 US 283, post, 243, 65 S Ct 208) graphically illustrates the difference between the validity of a detention order after exclusion has been effected.

Since the petitioner has not been convicted of failing to report or to remain in an assembly or relocation center, we cannot in this case determine the validity of those separate provisions of the order. It is sufficient here for us to pass upon the order which petitioner violated. To do more would be to go beyond the issues raised, and to decide momentous questions not contained within the framework of the pleadings or the evidence in this case. It will be time enough to decide the serious constitutional issues which petitioner seeks to raise when an assembly or relocation order is applied or is certain to be applied to him, and we have its terms before us.

Some of the members of the Court are of the view that evacuation and detention in an Assembly Center were inseparable. After May 3, 1942, the date of Exclusion Order No. 34, Korematsu was under compulsion to leave the area not as he would choose but via an Assembly Center. The Assembly Center was conceived as a part of the machinery for group evacuation. The power to exclude includes the power to do it by force if necessary. And any forcible measure must necessarily entail some degree of detention or restraint whatever method of removal is selected. But whichever view is taken, it results in holding that the order under which the petitioner was convicted was valid.

It is said that we are dealing here with the case of imprisonment of a citizen in a concentration camp solely because of his ancestry, without evidence or inquiry concerning his loyalty and good disposition towards the United States. Our task would be simple, our duty clear, were this a case involving the imprisonment of a loyal citizen in a concentration camp because of racial prejudice. Regardless of the true nature of the assembly and relocation centers—and we deem it unjustifiable to call them concentration camps with all the ugly connotations that term implies—we are dealing specifically with nothing but an exclusion order. To cast this case into outlines of racial prejudice, without reference to the real military dangers which were presented, merely confuses the issue. Korematsu was not excluded from the Military Area because of hostility to him or his race. He was excluded because we are at war with the Japanese Empire, because the properly constituted military authorities feared an invasion of our West Coast and felt constrained to take proper security measures, because they decided that the military urgency of the situation demanded that all citizens of Japanese ancestry be segregated from the West Coast temporarily, and finally, because Congress, reposing its confidence in this time of war in our military leaders—as inevitably it must—determined that they should have the power to do just this. **There was evidence of disloyalty on the part of some,** the military authorities considered that the need for action was great, and time was short. We cannot—by availing ourselves of the calm perspective of hindsight— now say that at that time these actions were unjustified.

Affirmed.

Mr. Justice Frankfurter, concurring:

According to my reading of Civilian Exclusion Order No. 34, it was an offense for Korematsu to be found in Military Area No. 1, the territory wherein he was previously living, except within the bounds of the established Assembly Center of that area. Even though the various orders issued by General DeWitt be deemed a comprehensive code of instructions, their tenor was clear and not contradictory. They put upon Korematsu the obligation to leave Military Area No. 1, but only by the method prescribed in the instructions, i. e., by reporting to the Assembly Center. I am unable to see how the legal considerations that led to the decision in **Hirabayashi v. United States,** 320 US 81, 87 L ed 1774, 63 S Ct 1375, fail to sustain the military order which made the conduct now in controversy a crime. And so I join in the opinion of the Court, but should like to add a few words of my own.

The provisions of the Constitution which confer on the Congress and the President powers to enable this country to wage war are as much part of the Constitution as provisions looking to a nation at peace. And we have had recent occasion to quote approvingly the statement of former Chief Justice Hughes that the war power of the Government is "the power to wage war successfully." Therefore, the **validity of action under the war power must be judged wholly in the context of war. That action is not to be stigmatized as lawless because like action in times of peace would be lawless.** To talk about a military order that expresses an allowable judgment of war need by those entrusted with the duty of conducting war as "an unconstitutional order" is to suffuse a part of the Constitution with an atmosphere of unconstitutionality. The respective spheres of action of military authorities and of judges are of course very different. But within their sphere, military authorities are no more outside the bounds of obedience to the Constitution than are judges within theirs. "The war power of the Unites States, like its other powers...is subject to applicable constitutional limitations." To recognize that military orders are "reasonably expedient military precautions" in time of war and yet to deny them constitutional legitimacy makes of the Constitution an instrument for dialetic (*sic*) subtleties not reasonably to be attributed to the hard-headed Framers, of whom a majority had had actual participation in war. If a military order such as that under review does not transcend the means appropriate for conducting war, such action by the military is as constitutional as would be any authorized action by the Interstate Commerce Commission within the limits of the constitutional power to regulate commerce. And being an exercise of the war power explicitly granted by the Constitution for safe-guarding the national life by prosecuting war effectively, I find nothing in the Constitution which denies to Congress the power to enforce such a valid military order by making its violation an offense triable in the civil courts. Compare **Interstate Commerce Commission v. Brimson.** To find that the Constitution does not forbid the military measures now complained of does not carry with it approval of that which Congress and the Executive did. That is their business, not ours. □

Glossary

ASSEMBLY CENTER
Temporary places for evacuees while awaiting decision by the Wartime Civil Control Commission whether they could be released to locations away from the "red zone" (designated military areas), as students for colleges, work locations, or resettlement into the temporary wartime housing of the War Relocation Centers.

COI
Coordinator of Information; FBI, Washington, D.C.

COMINT
Jargon for "communications intelligence" which is the analysis and exploitation of one's opponent's radio communications. This involves intercepting an opponent's messages from the airwaves or any other way to get them, then breaking the codes and ciphers through cryptanalysis in order to read the underlying plain text.

COMMISSION ON WARTIME RELOCATION AND INTERNMENT OF CIVILIANS   See CWRIC

CRYSTAL CITY   See also: Internment Camp
Crystal City Internment Camp (Texas) was the family camp for German, Italian and Japanese enemy aliens who had valid security charges against them. To be "interned" meant deportation at the convenience of the U.S. government. In the U.S., those interned at Crystal City were permitted to have their families with them, which in some cases included an American citizen wife and/or American citizen children. Entire families were often there when the breadwinner, who had been interned by the Department of Justice, had no way of supporting his family.

CWRIC
The Commission on Wartime Relocation and Internment of Civilians, initiated in 1980 to investigate the effect of E.O. 9066, Feb. 19, 1942 (under which the exclusion of persons of Japanese descent took place in the West Coast designated military zones), upon American citizens of Japanese origin and resident Japanese aliens.

Commissioners Appointed by President Carter were:

Joan Z. Bernstein, *Chair*

Daniel E. Lungren, *Vice-Chair*	Arthur J. Goldberg
Edward W. Brooke	Ishmael V. Gromoff
Robert F. Drinan	William M. Marutani
Arthur S. Flemming*	Hugh B. Mitchell

Angus Macbeth, *Special Counsel*

*Please advise when hearings will be held relating to H.R.442. I wish to present oral testimony and trust there will be a more democratic forum than had greeted me by the CWRIC, *26 Aug, 1981*. I tried to give testimony before the Commission in Seattle. *However, I was drummed out by a lecture on "racism" delivered by Dr. Arthur S. Flemming, the member of the CWRIC who was subsequently dismissed "without comment" by President Reagan.* This was but one instance of the scandalous, shameful and ignominious behavior of this Commission. I find it shocking that our

Congress should be considering legislation based on the findings and recommendations of a Commission so utterly flawed from its inception.

Br. General A. W. Beeman, USA(Ret)
Letter to Janet Potts, Counsel, Subcommittee on Administrative Law and Governmental Relations, House of Representatives. March 26, 1986.

In 1983, the CWRIC published its findings in a report titled, *Personal Justice Denied*. This report became the basis for legislation, and eventually was signed into law by President Reagan on August 10, 1988 (P.L. 100-383, "Civil Liberties Act of 1988). This act is being challenged in the Federal Court for the District of Columbia, under filing for injunctive relief (March 9, 1989), by Coale, Kananack & Murgatroyd on behalf of Arthur D. Jacobs. Jacobs is an American citizen of German descent. His father was interned by the Department of Justice at Crystal City Internment Camp and Jacobs, and others in his family, went with him.

DEPORTATION
A legal act, usually following internment, resulting in the removal of an *alien* considered to be dangerous to the national security or to the public welfare. Deportation is the Act of deporting an *alien* or one who has asked for expatriation or repatriation, or is a renunciant. (See GLOSSARY for terms: *expatriation, repatriation,* and *renunciant)*

DETENTION CENTER
A place where an American citizen could be detained and separated from others at relocation centers because that person was a known security risk, a "troublemaker," or had other charges against him. If that evacuee renounced citizenship, he could then be interned as an alien enemy in a Dept. of Justice internment camp.

DOHO
Japanese government's name referring to all persons of Japanese descent living abroad who were considered by the Empire of Japan to be, literally, "compatriots" and extensions of the Japanese nation.

ELINT
Electronic intelligence is a related field to COMINT, but is more concerned with electronic emissions such as those from radar.

E.O. 9066
The executive order, February 19, 1942, under which the military commander on the West Coast was given the authority by the President and Secretary of War, to exclude "any and all persons" deemed to be a danger to national security. Under this power, the military in the declared "war zones on the Pacific Frontier," initiated curfew for all persons of Japanese descent and eventually the exclusion of these persons from the military designated areas. E.O. 9066, Feb. 19, 1942, was the landmark test case in 1943 and 1944, (Hirabayashi, Yasui and Korematsu cases). Curfew was upheld unanimously by the U.S. Supreme Court for public safety and national security, and for the same reasons the highest Court ruled 6-3 that E.O. 9066, Feb. 19, 1942, was constitutional on the grounds that it was "nothing more than an exclusion order" not based on "racism" but because we were at war with the Empire of Japan; because "there were disloyalties"; and because in wartime the government must place its confidence in its military leaders "as inevitably it must." Despite the lower courts vacating some of the charges in these cases, the decisions of the U.S. Supreme Court cannot be reversed by any lower court thus still stand in 1989.

E.O. 9102   (See WRA)

EVACUEE
Persons of German, Italian and Japanese descent who were required to remove from the "red zone" of the west coast and lower area of Arizona.

EXPATRIATE
To renounce the rights and liabilities of citizenship where one is born, and to become a citizen of another country. (Also see *renunciant)*

FBI
Federal Bureau of Investigation

INTERNMENT CAMP
Under the Department of Justice, camps were operated by the Immigration and Naturalization Dept. Persons interned by the Dept. of Justice—after formal hearings on specific charges—were either interned for the duration of the war and subject to deportation, or they could be paroled. Internment camps should never be confused with the relocation centers operated by the WRA (See WRA). See map for locations.

ISOLATION CENTER
A public jail or place for temporary isolation of an evacuee until hearings could be held and a decision made as to whether the evacuee should be placed in detention or in an interment camp.

ISSEI
Nationals of Japanese; also known as "first generation" Japanese in America.

JOHO KYOKU
The Third Bureau of the Imperial Naval General Staff or Naval Intelligence of Japan with responsibility for intelligence in the Western Hemisphere. Third Bureau agents, normally, were naval officers who wore civilian clothing and posed as language and cultural students throughout the United States, Canada and in Latin and South American countries. The JOHO KYOKU operated separately from Japan's registered agents who held diplomatic posts in Japan's Foreign Ministry stations in the major cities of the Western Hemisphere.

KIBEI
American citizens of Japanese descent (second generation), who spent most of their informative years in Japan and in the words of University of Hawaii sociologist Andrew Lind, were "more fanatically Japanese in their disposition than their own (Issei) parents." (It is estimated that in 1938 there were 20,000 American citizens studying in Japan.)

MAGIC
Cover-name for messages coming from Tokyo to the

Japanese Consulates in the United States and elsewhere. MAGIC came to be known as the intelligence acquired from reading the "purple" diplomatic cipher of the Japanese. The cracking of the Japanese Purple Code is classed as the greatest intelligence feat of World War II and some researchers state the ability to keep silent about the feat was the best kept secret on the war.

MID
Army G-2 or Military Intelligence Division

NISEI
American citizens of Japanese descent; also known as "second generation" Japanese-Americans.

ONI
Office of Naval Intelligence

PRISONER OF WAR CAMPS (P.O.W.)
These camps were specifically for actual prisoners of war (military or naval), and were under jurisdiction of the Armed Forces. P.O.W. Camps were not related to the War Relocation Authority or to the Justice Department's Internment Camps in any way.

PURPLE
The name the Unites States intelligence community gave to the crypt system and its accompanying machine which was used by Japan's Foreign Ministry almost exclusively at embassy level. In Japan it was called *97-shiki O-bun In-ji-ki* which meant alphabetical typewriter with 14 separate crypt systems. But in Japanese communications it was referred to simply as "the Machine." The "97" was an abbreviation for the year 2597 of the Japanese calendar, corresponding to 1937 in the Western calendar. Shortly after PURPLE made its appearance in 1939, a special team of cryptanalysts from the U.S. Army's Signal Intelligence Service (SIS) was organized to tackle the incredibly difficult task of solving the PURPLE system. After eighteen months of exhausting mental labor, the team, led by William F. Freidman, who was generally acknowledged to be the world's greatest cryptanalyst, broke the PURPLE system and created an analogue machine which deciphered the Japanese messages. (Ref.: David D. Lowman's *amicus curiae,* August, 1989, *C.A. No. 89-607-JGP,* in the United States District Court for the District of Columbia.)

Japan considered the PURPLE system unbreakable. After the war those Japanese involved with "the machine," refused to believe that it had been broken by analytic means. They went to their graves believing someone had betrayed their system to the Americans. (See also: MAGIC)

REDRESS
A constitutional privilege which allows, through a Congressional Act or judicial law, to set right a wrong; to make amends; to remedy. During WWII, the right of redress through the judicial system, was intact and through such process came the test cases for curfew (Yasui & Hirabayashi, U.S. Supreme Court 1943 Term), and the test for constitutionality of E.O.9066, Feb. 19, 1942, for exclusion of persons of Japanese descent, (Korematsu, U.S. Supreme Court, 1944). Curfew was upheld unanimously; E.O.9066, Feb. 19, 1942, was ruled 6-3 as constitutionally correct.

RELOCATION CENTER   (See War Relocation Authority)

RENUNCIANT
One who renounces, repudiates, rejects, and disowns allegiance thereby abandoning citizenship. The Act of renunciation is ordinarily not lawful while on native soil in time of war. However, during World War II, when thousands of American citizens of Japanese descent refused to sign a loyalty oath and give unqualified allegiance to the United States while at the same time asked for expatriation, the United States passed Public Law No. 405, July 1, 1944, 78th Congress. This law was an amendment to the National Act of 1940 which allowed *in time of war,* and *while on U.S. soil,* scores of disloyal American Japanese to renounce citizenship and allegiance to the United States. These renunciants, having formally taken this step, became *alien enemies* subject to *internment* and *deportation.* Since no *American citizen* can be *interned,* it served the United States interests to pass such a law so that the troublemakers and terrorists residing in the relocation centers and segregation center, could be removed. Once removed, there were no further uprisings or riots in the centers run by the War Relocation Authority in WWII.

AMENDMENT TO THE NATIONAL ACT OF 1940, PUBLIC LAW No. 405, 78th Congress
July 1, 1944

(i)Making in the United States a formal written renunciation of nationality in such form as may be prescribed by and before such officer as may be designated by, the Attorney General, whenever the United States shall be in a state of war and the Attorney General shall approve such renunciation as not contrary to the interest of national defense.

Signed by the President on July 1, 1944
as Public Law 405 (78th Congress)

REPARATIONS
Compensation for a wrong or injury suffered. Under the *Evacuation Claims Statute,* Public Law #886, July 2, 1948, the law reads: "The Attorney General shall receive claims for a period of eighteen months from the date of enactment of this act [and] all claims not presented within that time shall be forever barred on this subject." Ultimately, 26,568 settlements of $147 million were made to family groups for "personal injury, personal inconvenience, physical hardship...for all purposes...on this subject." The payments were compensation for "any claim" for damages to or loss of real or personal property as "a reasonable natural consequence of the evacuation or exclusion" of persons of Japanese ancestry as a reesult of governmental action during World War II [50 U.S.C. App. 1981-1987]. Nowhere in the "Civil Liberties Act of 1988," signed into law by President Ronald Reagan, Aug. 10, 1988, are the words "redress" and/or "reparations" used for the simple reason that both had been accomplished and satisfied by previous Courts and post-war Congress. P.L.100-383 specifically *avoids* the terms "redress and reparations" by referring to the $20,000 amount payable to eligible individuals as amounts paid and "treated for the purposes of internal revenue laws of the United States as *damages for human suffering,"* and *not* taxable "income." (Italic added) See Appendixes B and C.

REPATRIATION

To restore citizenship or to return to one's country, giving it allegiance and thereby restoration of citizenship, i.e., to *repatriate* prisoners of war or alien enemy internees upon the end of hostilities and the coming of peace between nations at war.

SEGREGATION CENTER

Evacuees from relocation centers who had asked for expatriation or repatriation to Japan were segregated from evacuees in the nine other relocation centers. The Segregation Center was established in 1943 at Tule Lake, which had formerly been a relocation center. Tule Lake was chosen because it was the most self-supporting of the centers and had the largest population of expatriates and repatriates already residing there prior to segregation.

SEGINT

COMINT and ELINT combined or grouped under the general term, "Signals intelligence," or SEGINT.

SIS

(See PURPLE) Members of the Army Signal Intelligence Service, led by Freidman, without having seen the original Japanese apparatus, built a machine that did exactly the same thing as Japan's *97-shiki-O-bun In-ji-ki*. The American contraption was assembled with ordinary hardware, miles of wire and selector switches as used in that period for handling telephone calls through automatic dialing apparatus. The first complete PURPLE solution was accomplished in August 1940. The sustained pressure on the team over the months of day-and-night analysis and experimenting, caused Freidman to collapse from exhaustion and emotional strain that lead to his hospitalization for almost four months.

TULE LAKE   (See SEGREGATION CENTER)

ULTRA

Code name used in the European theatre by the allies, and by the United States in the Pacific theatre for Army Signal Corps and *military messages*, as opposed to MAGIC which was used on an international level for diplomatic/consulate messages.

WAR RELOCATION AUTHORITY

Established under E.O. 9102, March 18, 1942, to provide "wayside shelters" for evacuees. The relocation center's primary duty was to assist evacuees in relocating and resettling in areas not restricted by military zoning. Evacuees were free to leave providing those with dual-citizenship took unqualified allegiance to the United States; had employment waiting so that evacuee would not become a burden to any community; was accepted in a university or college for continuing education. (See also: WRA)

WCCA

Wartime Civil Control Administration, headed by Col. Karl R. Bendetsen, former Assistant Chief of Staff, Western Defense Command and Fourth Army. Bendetsen was in charge of the Civil Affairs Division relative to the evacuation and assembly centers.

WDC

Western Defense Command under Lieut. General John L. DeWitt, which encompassed all the Pacific Coast States as well as five other Western States and the Territory of Alaska.

WRA

War Relocation Authority, established under President Roosevelt's Executive Order 9102, March 18, 1942. Dr. Milton S. Eisenhower was its first Director; he relinquished the post within 3 months to Dillon S. Myer who served until the closing of the relocation centers in 1945. On May 8, 1946, WRA Director Myer received the "Medal for Merit" for his work with the WRA during the war. The WRA program, which included administration of the Oswego, New York, refugee camp (for European refugees), was officially ended June 30, 1946.

WRA CENTERS

Communities (cities) operated by the WRA. See map for locations.

About the Author

Lillian Baker established her professional status in fiction and non-fiction with her WWII experience as a continuity writer for WINS radio in New York, the State in which she was born. Resettled in California in late 1940, she continued with works of award-winning poetry, articles, and weekly columns for 12 years in *The Gardena Valley News,* Gardena, California. Her columns, editorials, and special features covered politics, history, current events, theatre reviews, religion, philosophy, antiques and collectibles.

She is recipient of many awards including: Freedoms Foundation at Valley Forge for "promoting a better understanding of America and Americans"; National Association of Pro-America "for contribution to her fellow citizens and to the preservation of the Constitutional Form of Government"; American Biographic Institute "Community Leader of America" medal (1986).

Her 1983 book, *The Concentration Camp Conspiracy: A Second Pearl Harbor,* was chosen top award (scholastic category) by The Conference of California Historical Societies for "distinguished contributions to California history." In 1984, she wrote *Redress & Reparations Demands by Japanese-Americans,* (expanded 1989). In 1985, The Hoover Institution on War, Revolution and Peace at Stanford University, invited her to place her compilation of letters, manuscripts and documents about the WWII exclusion of persons of Japanese descent from the west coast, in their

223

permanent archives for future historical research, and have since established *The Lillian Baker Collection* under a Deed of Ownership.

She is Director of Americans for Historical Accuracy, (P.O. Box 372, Lawndale, CA 90260), and its chief spokesperson on the subject of the WWII relocation. She has made numerous public appearances on platform and in the media, and was an expert witness before the Commission on Wartime Relocation and Internment of Civilians (CWRIC, 1981); the U.S. Senate Judiciary Committee (1983-1984); U.S. House of Representatives Judiciary (1986) and its Subcommittee on Appropriations (1989).

In 1988, she edited *Dishonoring America: The Collective Guilt of American Japanese*. A diversive author, her definitive work on the decorative, functional, political, and historical collectible, the *hatpin,* is recognized worldwide. Published in 1976, *The Collector's Encyclopedia of Hatpins*

and Hatpin Holders had a second limited edition printed in 1989. The supplemental work, *Hatpins and Hatpin Holders* (1983, reprinted 1989), adds to the titles of her other books: *100 Years of Collectible Jewelry: 1850-1950* (8th edition 1989); *Art Nouveau & Art Deco Jewelry* (5th edition 1988); *Creative & Collectible Miniatures* (1983); *Fifty Years of Collectible Fashion Jewelry: 1925-1975* (3rd edition 1989) (Collector Books, Publisher)

Mrs. Baker is a member of the National League of American Pen Women, The National Writers Club, the Art Students League of New York (Life Member), Life Fellow IBA, Cambridge, England and appears in major anthologies such as *Who's Who in American Women, Who's Who in the World, International Authors and Writer's Who's Who, Who's Who in California,* etc. Mother of a son and a daughter, Lillian Baker and her husband make their home in Gardena, California. □

General References

"...the fifties had seen a spate of books by so-called revisionist historians [then] a massive amount of hitherto classified naval records became available in the National Archives [in 1980] when President Jimmy Carter effected the release of WWII intelligence records. This meant that all previous histories were to a degree rendered obsolete."

—Rear Admiral Edwin T. Layton
author, *And I Was There: Pearl Harbor and Midway— Breaking the Secrets.* (1985)

BOOKS

Abernathy, M. Glenn. *Civil Liberties Under the Constitution.* 2nd Ed. Dodd, Mead. 1972.

Anthony, J. Garner. *Hawaii Under Army Rule.* Univ. of Hawaii Press. 1955.

Arthur, Anthony. *Deliverance at Los Baños.* St. Martin. 1985.

Bailey, Paul. *City in the Sun.* Westernlore. 1971.

Baker, Lillian. *The Concentration Camp Conspiracy: A Second Pearl Harbor.* AfHA Publications. 1981.

_____. *Dishonoring America: The Collective Guilt of American Japanese.* Webb Research Gp. 1988.

_____. *Redress and Reparations Demands by Japanese-Americans.* Webb Research Gp. 1984, expanded ed. 1989.

Bergamini, David. *Japan's Imperial Conspiracy.* Vols. I & II. Morrow. 1971.

Bergee, Lee K. *Guest of the Emperor.* Four Freedoms Press, High Ridge, MO. 1987.

Biddle, Francis. *In Brief Authority.* Doubleday. 1962.

Boddy, E. Manchester. *Japanese in America.* (Private print) 1921.

Bosworth, Allan R. *American Concentration Camps.* Norton. 1967.

Brown, Courtney. *Tojo: The Last Banzai.* Kinney. 1972.

Burns, James MacGregor. *Roosevelt: The Soldier of Freedom 1940-1945.* Harcourt. 1970.

Capra, Frank. *The Name Above the Title.* Macmillan. 1971.

Cates, Teressa R., R.N. *Infamous Santo Tomas.* 2nd Ed. Pacific Press. 1981.

Christgau, John. *Enemies.* Iowa State Univ. Press. 1985.

Close, Upton. *Challenge: Behind the Face of Japan.* Grosset. 1934.

Conn, Stetson. *The Decision to Evacuate the Japanese from the Pacific Coast.* Command Decisions Office of the Chief of Military History, Department of the Army, Washington, D.C. 1960.

Conn, Stetson, Rose E. Engleman and Byron Fairchild. *Japanese Evacuation from the United States, Guarding the United States and Its Outposts.* Office of the Chief of Military History, Department of the Army, Washington, D.C. 1964.

Costello, John. *The Pacific War: 1941-1945*. Quill. 1981.

Daniels, Roger. *Concentration Camps U.S.A.: Japanese Americans and World War II*. Holt. 1972.

_____. *The Decision to Relocate the Japanese Americans*. Lippincott. 1975.

Douglas, William O. *The Anatomy of Liberty—The Rights of Man Without Force*. Trident-Pocket. 1963.

Dunne, Gerald T. *Hugo Black and the Judicial Revolution*. Simon and Schuster. 1977.

Duus, Masayo Unezawa. *Unlikely Liberators: The Men of the 100th and 442nd*. [English translation] Univ. of Hawaii Press. 1987.

Eaton, Allen H. *Beauty Behind Barbed Wire: The Arts of the Japanese in Our War Relocation Camps*. Harper's. 1952.

Edell, Edward. *An American With Guts*. Cole-Holmquist Press, Los Angeles. 1961.

Edmiston, James. *Home Again*. Doubleday. 1955.

Embree, John F. *Suye Mura—A Japanese Village*.

Endo, Shusaku. *The Sea and Poison*. Taplinger. 1972.

Farago, Ladislas. *The Broken Seal*. Random Hse. 1967.

Flowers, Montaville. *The Japanese Conquest of American Opinion*. Doran. 1917.

Goldman, Eric. F. *Rendezvous With Destiny*. Vintage-Random Hse. 1956.

Goralski, Robert. *World War II Almanac—1931-1945*. Hamish-Hamilton (London) 1981.

Grew, Joseph. *Ten Years in Japan*. Simon & Schuster. 1944.

Grodzins, Morton. *Americans Betrayed: Politics and the Japanese Evacuation*. Univ. of Chicago Press. 1949.

_____. *The Loyal and the Disloyal*. Univ. of Chicago Press. 1956.

Gulick, Sidney L. *The American Japanese Problem*. Scribners. 1914.

_____. *The East and the West*. Tuttle. 1963.

_____. *Japan and the Gentleman's Agreement*. Fed. Council of Churches in America. 1920.

Hansen, Arthur A. and Betty E. Mitson. *Voices Long Silent*. Calif. State Univ. 1974.

Hembree, Charles R. *From Pearl Harbor to the Pulpit*. Rex Humbard Ministry. 1975.

Herman, Masako. *The Japanese in America 1943-1973*. Oceana. 1974.

Hersey, John. *Hiroshima*. Knopf. 1965.

Holmes, W. J. *Double-Edged Secrets*. U.S. Naval Inst. 1979.

Houston, J. W. *Farewell to Manzanar*. Houghton Mifflin. 1973.

Hoyt, Edwin P. *Japan's War: The Great Pacific Conflict*. McGraw. 1986.

Hull, Eleanor. *Suddenly the Sun*. Friendship (NY). 1957.

Hynd, Alan. *Betrayal from the East. The Inside Story of Japanese Spies in America*. McBride. 1957.

Ichihashi, Yamato. *Japanese in the United States, A Critical Study of the Problems of the Japanese Immigrants and their Children*. Stanford Univ. Press. 1932.

_____. *Japanese Immigration—Its Status in California*. Marxhall. 1915.

Ienaga, Saburo. *The Pacific War: 1931-1945*. Pantheon. 1978.

Ike, Nobutaka. *The Beginnings of Political Democracy in Japan*. Johns Hopkins Univ. Press. 1950.

Irons, Peter. *Justice at War*. Oxford. 1983.

Jung, Robert T. *Brighter Than A Thousand Suns*. Harcourt. 1958.

Kahn, David. *The Code-Breakers*. Macmillan. 1968.

Kase, Toshikazu. *Journey to the Missouri*. Yale Univ. Press. 1950.

Kawakami, K. K. *The Real Japanese Question*. Macmillan. 1921.

Keith, Agnes N. *Three Came Home*. Little, Brown. 1947.

Kelsey, Carl. Editor. *Present-Day Immigration*. American Academy of Political and Social Science. 1921.

Kitagawa, Daisike. *Issei and Nisei: The Internment Years*. Seabury. 1967.

Knox, Donald. *Death March: The Survivors of Bataan*. Harcourt. 1981.

Kurzman, Dan. *Day of the Bomb: Countdown to Hiroshima*. McGraw-Hill. 1984.

Lawton, Manny. *Some Survived*. Algonquin. 1984.

Layton, R.Adm. Edwin T. with Captain Roger Pineau, U.S.N.R. and John Costello. *And I Was There*. Morrow. 1985.

Leighton, Alexander H. *The Governing of Men*. Princeton Univ. Press. 1945.

Lewin, Ronald. *The American Magic*. Farrar. 1982.

Leyman, Anthony L. L. *Birthright of Barbed Wire: The Santa Anita Assembly Center for the Japanese*. Westernlore. 1970.

Lind, Andrew W. *Hawaii's Japanese—An Experiment in Democracy*. Princeton Univ. Press. 1946.

Machi, Mario. *The Emperor's Hostages*. Vantage. 1982.

Manning, Paul. *Hirohito, The War Years*. Dodd, Mead. 1986.

Matsumoto, Toru. *Beyond Prejudice: A Story of the Church and Japanese Americans*. Friendship Press, NY. 1946.

Matsuo, Kinoaki. *How Japan Plans to Win*. Little, Brown. 1942.

Matsuoka, Jack. *Camp II, Block 211*. Japan Publications. 1974.

Morison, Samuel Eliot. *History of United States Naval Operations in World War II*, (Volume 3), *The Rising Sun in the Pacific: 1931-April 1942*. Little, Brown. 1948.

Mosley, Leonard. *Hirohito, Emperor of Japan*. Prentice-Hall. 1966.

_____. *Marshall, Hero for Our Times*. Hearst. 1982.

Myer, Dillon S. *Uprooted Americans*. Univ. of Arizona Press. 1971.

Noda, Kesa. *Yamato Colony: 1906-1960*. Livingston-Merced JACL Chapter. 1981.

O'Brien, Robert W. *The College Nisei*. Pacific Books. 1949.

O'Connor, Richard. *Pacific Destiny*. Little, Brown. 1969.

Oda, James. *Heroic Struggles of Japanese Americans*. Printed in U.S. by KNI. 1980.

Okada, John. *No-No Boy*. Tuttle. 1957.

Okubo, Mine. *Citizen 13660*. Univ. of Washington Press. 1946, 1973, 1983.

Olson, John E. *O'Donnell, Andersonville of the Pacific*. (Private print) 1985.

Pogue, Forrest C. *George C. Marshall, Organizer of Victory 1943-1945*. Viking. 1973.

Prange, Gordon W. *At Dawn We Slept, the Untold Story of Pearl Harbor*. McGraw-Hill. 1981.

_____ with Donald M. Goldstein and Katherine V. Dillon. *Miracle at Midway*. McGraw-Hill. 1982.

_____ with Donald M. Goldstein and Katherine V. Dillon. *Pearl Harbor the Verdict of History*. McGraw-Hill. 1986.

Reischauer, Edwin O. *Japan: Past and Present*. Knopf. 1964.
_____. *My Life Between Japan and America*. Harper and Row. 1986.
Rhee, Syngman. *Japan Inside Out: The Challenge of Today*. 2nd Edition. Revell. 1941.
Scalapino, Robert A. *Democracy and the Party Movement in Prewar Japan—The Failure of the First Attempt*. Univ. of California Press. 1953.
Scherer, James A. B. *Japan Defies the World*. Bobbs-Merrill. 1938.
Seth, Donald. *Secret Servants: A History of Japanese Espionage*. Farrar, Straus and Cudahy. 1957.
Shub, Anatole. *An Empire Loses Hope*. Norton. 1970.
Spicer, Edward H., Asael T. Hansen, Katherine Luomala, and Marvin K. Opler. *Impounded People: Japanese-Americans in the Relocation Centers*. Univ. of Arizona Press. 1969.
Stephan, John J. *Hawaii Under the Rising Sun, Japan's Plans for Conquest After Pearl Harbor*. Univ. of Hawaii Press. 1984.
Stimson, Henry L. *The Decision to Use the Atomic Bomb, An American Retrospective Writings from HARPER'S Magazine, 1950-1984*. Harper's Magazine Foundation. 1984.
Strong, Edward K., Jr. *Japanese in California*. Stanford University Press. 1934.
Tanabe, Eiji E. (Ed.) *Japanese in Southern California: A History of 70 Years*. Japanese Chamber of Commerce of Southern California. 1960.
Taylor, Vince. *Cabanataun—Japanese Death Camp*. Texian Press. 1985.
They Work For Victory. Japanese American Citizen League. Salt Lake City. n.d.
Thomas, Dorothy Swaine with Charles Kikuchi and James Sakoda. *The Salvage*. Univ. of California Press. 1952.
_____ and Richard S. Nishimoto. *The Spoilage*. Univ. of California Press. 1946.
Toland, John. *Infamy: Pearl Harbor and Its Aftermath*. Berkeley. 1982.
Turner, Stan. *The Years of Harvest: A History of the Tule Lake Basin*. 49th Avenue Press. Eugene, OR. 1987.
Uchida, Yoshiko. *Desert Exile: The Uprooting of a Japanese-American Family*. Univ. of Washington Press. 1982.
Ueno, Harry Y. *Manzanar Martyr: An Interview with Harry Y. Ueno*. The Oral History Program, California State University. 1986.
Walt, Gen. Lewis W. USMC(Ret.). *Eleventh Hour*. Caroline House. 1979.
Webber, Bert. *Retaliation: Japanese Attacks and Allied Countermeasures on the Pacific Coast in World War II*. Oregon State Univ. Press. 1975.
_____. *Silent Siege: Japanese Attacks Against North America in World War II*. YeGalleon. 1984.
_____. *Silent Siege-II: Japanese Attacks on North America in World War II*. Webb Research Gp. 1988.
Wilcox, Robert K. *Japan's Secret War*. Morrow. 1985.
Wilson, Robert A. and Bill Hosokawa. *East to America*. Morrow. 1980.
Winterbotham, F. W. *The Ultra Secret*. Dell. 1974.
Wohlstetter, Roberta. *Pearl Harbor: Warning and Decision*. Stanford Univ. Press. 1962.
Yoneda, Karl G. *Ganbatte: Sixty-Year Struggle of a Kibei Worker*. Univ. of Calif. Press [Asian-American Studies Center]. 1983.

MAGAZINES

Elisofon. "West Coast Japs Are Interned In Mountain Camp" in *Life*. April 6, 1942.
Mydans, Carl. "Tule Lake Segregation Center; At This Segregation Center Are 18,000 Japanese Considered Disloyal to U.S." in *Life*. March 20, 1944.
"Japan's Influence in America; Its clout in Washington; Its Role at U.S. Universities; Its Philanthropy and Image-Building" in *Business Week*. July 11, 1988.
"Japan and the United States; The Entire Contents For April 1944 Are Devoted To A Military Power We Must Defeat—A Pacific Problem We Must Solve" in *Fortune*. April 1944.

GOVERNMENT DOCUMENTS AND COMMISSIONS

Commission on Wartime Relocation and Internment of Civilians Act of July 1, 1980 (94 Stat. 964)
Executive Order No. 9066 February 19, 1942 (Franklin Delano Roosevelt)
Hearings before the Committee on the Judiciary, House of Representatives 98th Congress, 2nd Sess. on HR3387, HR4110, HR4322. Testimonies: Karl R. Bendetsen pp680-698; David Lowman pp430-549; Dr. Ken Matsugi pp568-599.
Hearings before the U.S. Judiciary, Subcommittee on Practice and Procedure, 96th Congress, 2nd Sess. on HR442, S1009, S1520 (1st Sess.). Testimonies: Frederic B. Wiener, Lillian Baker.
Hearings before the Subcommittee on Administrative Law and Governmental Relations of the Committee of the Judiciary, House of Representatives 98th Congress, 2nd Sess. on Japanese-American and Aleutian Relocation, HR3387, HR4110, HR4322. June 20, 21, 27, Sept. 12, 1984.
Hearing before the Subcommittee on Administrative Practice and Procedure of the Committee of the Judiciary, U.S. Senate, 98th Congress, 1st Sess. on S1520, The World War II Civil Liberties Violations Redress Act, and Reports of the Commission on Wartime Relocation and Internment of Civilians. July 27, 1983 (Printed for use of the Committee on the Judiciary).
The "Magic" Background of Pearl Harbor. Vol. 5 (of 8 volumes) U.S. Dept. of Defense. U.S. Gov. Print. Office. 1977-1978.
Personal Justice Denied. Commission on Wartime Relocation and Internment of Civilians [CWRIC] U.S. Gov. Print. Office. 1982.
_____ Addendum: *Recommendations*. 1983.
War Relocation Authority U.S. Dept. Interior (1942-1945) 11 Volumes. U.S. Gov. Print. Office. 1946. [Vol. 6: Reprint of 1943 Ed.; Vol. 8: 1939-1945 Refugees, Fort Ontario, N.Y.]

COURT CASES AND DOCUMENTS

Gordon Hirabayashi v. United States 320 U.S. 81 (1943)
Fred Toyosaburo Korematsu v. United States 323 U.S. 214-248 (1944)
Minoru Yasui v. United States 320 U.S. 115 (1943)
Ex parte Endo, 323 U.S. 283 (1944)

Ludecke v. Watkins 335 U.S. 160 (1948)
Johnson v. Eisentrager 339 U.S. 763 (1950)
Acheson v. Murakami 176F.2d953 (1948)
McGrath v. Abo 186F.2d776, 771; 342U.S. 832.
Alien Enemy Act of 1798 (U.S.)
Gentlemen's Agreement 1908 (Japan/U.S.)

UNPUBLISHED PAPERS AND MANUSCRIPTS

Ishida, Gladys. *The Japanese American Renunciants of Okyama Prefecture: Their Accommodation and Assimilation to Japanese Culture.* Univ. of Michigan. n.d.

Logan, Kay. *By Dawn's Early Light.* (included in Baker, *The Concentration Camp Conspiracy: A Second Pearl Harbor.*)

Sakoda, James M. *Minidoka: An Analysis of Changing Patterns of Social Interaction.* Ph.D. Dissertation, Univ. of California, Berkeley. 1949.

Yamashita, Shonin. *It Had To Be So.* (included in Baker, *The Concentration Camp Conspiracy: A Second Pearl Harbor.*)

ARCHIVAL RESOURCES

Archives of the Federal Bureau of Investigation
Archives of the Army Military Intelligence Division
Archives of the Army Signal Corps—Intelligence Section
Archives of the Naval Intelligence and Office of Naval Communications
Archives of the National Security Agency
Archives of the Univ. of the Pacific, Stuart Library.
The National Archives

Girls on prize-winning float at Tule Lake Relocation Center's Labor Day Parade, September 7, 1942. If these ladies were living on August 10, 1988, each is in line to receive $20,000 under P.L. 100-383 due to the obvious "human suffering" demonstrated in this picture by F. Stewart. (N.A. 210-GD-216)

Index

Matsugi, Ken 227
Matsui, (Rep.) Robert 101, 102, 207
Matsumoto, Fumi 47; Virginia 49
Matsunaga, (Sen.) Spark 25, 71, 72, 86-87, 95, 101, 200, 202
McCloy, John J. 9, 31, 59, 69, 200, *viii*
McCreight, Allen H. 16
McGavern, Wilhelmina *121*
McGrath v. *Abo* 227
McGrath, H. Read 17
Medal for Merit 222
Merritt, Ralph P. *116*, 165, 166
Mexican-Japanese 108
Mexico City Conference 206
Migita, Torao 35
military action 108; area 61, 64, 65, 101, 109, 216; Guards 54; Intelligence Service 61; necessity 111; Police 82
Miller, (Col.) Virgil R. 36
Mineta, (Rep.) Norman 101, 102
Minoru Yasui v. United States 227
Mitchell, Hugh B. 219
Miyake, Isomatsu 167
Miyake, Tatsuo *121*
Miyatake, Toyo 51, 62; *149*, *181*
Moeser, June D. 18
Moore, A. H. 203
Moppins, Curly 40
Morimitsu, Arthur T. 44
Moschetti, Frank 17; Maxine 17
mounted guards 94
Moxley, Elizabeth *162*
Mukai, Helen 47
Muraakmi, Yoshiteru 151
Murakami, Dickie 50; (Nurse) Helen 49
Murata, Kiyoaki 17; Ryuichi 195
Myer, Dillon S. *viii*, 9, 14, 29, 30, 31, 50, 52, 60, 68, 78, 200, 209, 210, 211, 222, 226

Nagao, Arthur 105; Charles 105-106
Nagasawa, T. 52
Nagashima, Albert *121*
Nagatomi, (Rev.) Shijo 169
Nail, Elizabeth *122*
Naito, (Rev.) Yukichi 169
Nakagawa, Mas *121*
Nakaji, Shig 172
Nakama, Christian 36
Nakamura, Nakaemon 195; Yaye *162*
Nakamura, Risshin 195
Nakano, Bert 77-79, 85-86; Chokichi 173; Ed 50; Lillian S. 86
Nakashima, Toy 203
Narita, Eiko 50
National Act of 1940 221
National American Ex-Prisoners of War 98-99
National Japanese American Student Relocation Coun-

cil 92; Program 103
National Student Council Relocation Program 31
Nicholas, Anita *120*
Nielsen, Aksel 172
Nielson, Melba 172
Nikkei 34
97-shiki O-bun In-ji-ki 221, 222
Nisei 33, 34, 38, 39, 41, 43, 45, 46, 50, 56, 61, 64, 101, 103, 199, 212, 214, 221; veterans 79
Nisen, Lucile 17
Nishi, Ruth 50
Nishikawa, Charles 38; Harry 38; Kiyoshi 40; Masato 38; Shigeo 38; (Rev.) Takeshi 169
Nishimura, George 118, 142
Noda, Pat 48
Noguchi, Isamu 34, 49
Nomura, Kichisaburo 100
Nunn, Ralph T. 18
nurses 47, 51

O'Keefe, Francis 111
O'Rourke, Joseph L. 88, 93
100th Infantry 107; Battalion 35, 36, 199
Obata, Professor 25
Oda, (Rev.) Hiromu 169
Office of Strategic Services (OSS) 43-44
Office of War Information (OWI) 43-44, 52
Ogi, Mamoru 118, 142
Okada, Robert 40
Okamoto, Kiyoshi 108
Okamura, Tom 38
Oki, Thomas 50
Oku, J. Momoto 48
Okubo, Mine 60, 63
Okura, Lili 48; Patrick 48; Susumu Babe 48
Okusu, Ben 38; Sandra Gail 38
Oltmans, Sarah *121*
Omi, (Rev.) Masahiro 169
Oriental Exclusion Order 40, 61, 106
Osato, Sono 34, 49
Oshima, Mike *122*
Oswego, (N.Y.) refugee camp 222
Otano, Harvey 83

Palm, Charles G. 17
Pedicord, Reece M. (MD) 210-211
Penn, (Judge) John G. 102
permanent resident aliens 106, 207
Personal Justice Denied 15, 20, 21, 23, 26, 33, 48, 57, 59, 70, 85, 94, 100, 102, 105, 197, 199, 207, 220
Peruvian Japanese 105, 108, 206-207
postal service, 32; *see also:* mail
Potts, Janet 220; Marion E. 118
Powell, John 25
Pringle Report 215
prison cells 200
prisoner of war camps 221

Members of pro-Japn *Hokoku Seimen Dan* club, with shaved heads, blow bugles and bow to the early morning Rising Sun in tribute to the Emperor of Imperial Japan then shout *banzai!* Many of these young men terrorized other evacuees often threatening bodily harm until many of the loyals renounced their American citizenship and joined the club. The goal was to go to Japan and fight against the United States. After being deported after the war, many of the former loyals headed for the United States authorities and petitioned for return of their citizenship claiming duress. Most were reinstated. But under Public Law 100-383, even the traitors who caused so much trouble then spent the rest of their working years in Japan, if alive today, are to be sought out in Japan then each paid $20,000 for "human suffering." See *Acheson v. Murakami* 176 F.2n 953. (N.A. 210-CLP-16, photograph by R. H. Ross)

NOTES